Debutante nation

Debutante nation
Feminism contests the 1890s

edited by
Susan Magarey
Sue Rowley
Susan Sheridan

ALLEN & UNWIN

© Copyright of individual pieces remains with the contributors.
© Copyright of this collection, Susan Magarey, Sue Rowley and Susan Sheridan, 1993

This book is copyright under the Berne Convention.
No reproduction without permission.

First published in 1993
Allen & Unwin Australia Pty Ltd
9 Atchison Street, St Leonards, NSW 2065 Australia

National Library of Australia
Cataloguing-in-Publication entry:

Debutante nation: feminism contests the 1890s.

　Bibliography.
　Includes index.
　ISBN 1 86373 296 9.

　1. Feminism—Australia—History. 2. Women—Australia—History.
　I. Magarey, Susan. II. Rowley, Sue. III. Sheridan, Susan.

305.420994

Set in 10/11 pt Times by Essay Composition, North Sydney

Printed by Chong Moh Offset Printing, Singapore

10   9   8   7   6   5   4   3   2   1

Contents

Illustrations   vii

Acknowledgments   ix

Contributors   x

Introduction   xiv

1 The politics of respectability: Identifying the masculinist context   1
   Marilyn Lake

2 The Feminist Legend: A new historicism?   16
   John Docker

3 A redivision of labour: Women and wage regulation in Victoria 1896–1903   27
   Jenny Lee

4 'Knocking out a living': Survival strategies and popular protest in the 1890s depression   38
   Bruce Scates

5 Reorganising the masculinist context: Conflicting masculinisms in the New South Wales Public Service Bill debates of 1895   50
   Desley Deacon

6	The sexual politics of selling and shopping *Gail Reekie*	59
7	Domestic dilemmas: Representations of servants and employers in the popular press *Paula Hamilton*	71
8	Sexual labour: Australia 1880–1910 *Susan Magarey*	91
9	The 'equals and comrades of men'?: *Tocsin* and 'the woman question' *Patricia Grimshaw*	100
10	The *Woman's Voice* on sexuality *Susan Sheridan*	114
11	Reproducing Empire: Exploring ideologies of gender and race on Australia's Pacific frontier *Claudia Knapman*	125
12	Sovereignty and sexual identity in political cartoons *Josie Castle and Helen Pringle*	136
13	'Woman' in federation poetry *Barbara Holloway*	150
14	The New Woman and the Coming Man: Gender and genre in the 'lost-race' romance *Robert Dixon*	163
15	Water, gold and honey: A discussion of *Kirkham's Find* *Dorothy Jones*	175
16	Things a bushwoman cannot do *Sue Rowley*	185
17	Henry Lawson, the drover's wife and the critics *Kay Schaffer*	199
Notes		211
Bibliography		246
Index		258

Illustrations

Fig. 1A Anne Zahalka, 'The Breakaway' 1985, 80×90 cm. xxv
Fig. 1B Anne Zahalka, 'The Immigrants' 1982, 70×90 cm, courtesy City Gallery, Melbourne. xxv
Fig. 1C Narelle Jubelin, 'Untitled Silhouette', 1989, metal framed petit point, 130×130 cms (Photographer: Shayne Higson) xxvi

7 Domestic dilemmas: Representations of servants and employers in the popular press

7.1 'A Domestic Matter', *Bulletin* 26 May 1883. 72

7.2 ' "Missus"—From Sarah Jane's point of view', *Bulletin* 23 June 1883, p. 12. 73

7.3 'She had been camped for years', *Bulletin* 19 August 1893, p. 12. 76

7.4 'History repeats itself', *Bulletin* 12 February 1887, p. 13. 78

7.5 'The sign-language', *Bulletin* 8 November 1890, p. 14. 79

7.6 'Biddyism', *Melbourne Punch* 29 November 1883, p. 218. 80

7.7 'Our "Servants" ', *Bulletin* 13 April 1889. 81

7.8 'He drew the line', *Bulletin* 30 January 1897, p. 11. 82

7.9 'A 'appy day', *Melbourne Punch* 22 November 1883, p. 204. 84

7.10 'Slightly different', *Bulletin* 24 April 1897, p. 10. 85

7.11 'It might have been', *Bulletin* 9 December 1899, p. 18.   86
7.12 'Kitty's Broom', *Bulletin* 10 December 1898, p. 15.   87
7.13 'What was said yesterday', *Bulletin* 22 August 1891, p. 11.   88
7.14 'Another case of temporary insanity', *Bulletin* 26 November 1898, p. 20.   89

12 Sovereignty and sexual identity in political cartoons
12.1 'The modern sphinx', *W.A. Bulletin* 14 September 1888.   137
12.2 'Innocent triflers', *Bulletin* 4 April 1885.   140
12.3 'The glorious twenty-sixth!' *Bulletin* 4 February 1899.   141
12.4 " 'There, take them; but you must wear a petticoat over them" ', *Bulletin* 24 November 1900.   143
12.5 'Anxious about his billet', *Bulletin* 25 August 1900.   144
12.6 'Arrival of the new baby', *Bulletin* 14 July 1990.   145
12.7 'Queensland has to give up slavery', *Bulletin* 1901.   146
12.8 'Prime Minister christens the baby', *Bulletin* 1902.   147
12.9 'The birth of the Commonwealth', *Melbourne Punch Annual*, 1901.   148

14 The New Woman and the Coming Man: Gender and genre in the 'lost-race' romance
14.1 'For a moment she stood still, her hands raised above her head ...', H. Rider Haggard, *She: A History of Adventure* (1887) Macdonald, London, 1963.   165
14.2 George Firth Scott, *The Last Lemurian: A Westralian Romance*, James Bowden, London, 1898.   167
14.3 *The Last Lemurian*.   169

16 Things a bushwoman cannot do
16.1 Leon (Sonny) Pole 'The Village Laundress', c. early 1890s, oil on canvas, 83 × 123.5 cm.   191

Acknowledgments

The Lauraine Diggins Fine Arts Collection, Caulfield, Victoria, for permission to reproduce 'The Village Laundress'.

Australian Historical Studies for permission to reproduce Marilyn Lake, 'The politics of respectability: Identifying the masculinist context', *Australian Historical Studies*, vol. 22, no. 86, 1986, pp. 116–131, and, in revised and shortened form, Jenny Lee, 'A redivision of labour: Victoria's wages boards in action, 1896–1903', *Australian Historical Studies*, vol. 22, no. 88, 1987, pp. 352–72.

The University of Adelaide, The Flinders University of South Australia and the University of Wollongong for financial assistance.

Contributors

Josie Castle teaches Australian history at the University of Wollongong. She has written on factory workers in Britain and nurses in Australia, and has just completed a history of the University of Wollongong.

Desley Deacon is Co-Director of the Clark Center for Australian Studies at the University of Texas at Austin, where she also teaches American Studies and Sociology. She is the author of *Managing Gender: The State, the New Middle Class and Women Workers 1830–1930*, and is currently writing a biography of American feminist sociologist and anthropologist Elsie Clews Parsons. During 1992 she had a visiting appointment in the Department of Sociology at the Australian National University, where she is teaching courses on gender and the social sciences.

Robert Dixon teaches in the English Department, James Cook University, and is currently writing on romance fiction in the period 1875–1914.

John Docker is the author of *The Nervous Nineties: Australian Cultural Life in the 1890s* (1991), *In a Critical Condition* (1984), and *Australian Cultural Elites* (1974). He is currently working on two books, one on modernism, postmodernism and popular culture, the other on ethnic and cultural identities.

Patricia Grimshaw is a Reader in the Department of History, University of Melbourne, where she teaches Women's Studies and History. She publishes in the area of Australian and Pacific women's history and is currently working on *A Short Feminist History of Australia* with Marilyn Lake, Marion Aveling and Ann McGrath.

Paula Hamilton lectures in Applied History and Cultural Studies at the University of Technology, Sydney. Her research interests include the history of domestic service, memory and popular culture, and museum studies.

Barbara Holloway is a Senior Tutor in English and Communications Studies at the University of New England. She is currently completing her doctoral thesis on race, place and gender in the construction of Euro-Australian identity in poetry from 1800–1938.

Dorothy Jones teaches in the English Department, University of Wollongong. Her writing focuses on women's writing in postcolonial contexts.

Narelle Jubelin is a Sydney-based artist who uses collected objects and images rendered in petit point to examine the circulation, reception and collection of cultural and aesthetic objects. Her work has been exhibited nationally and internationally in New York (1990), Aperto, La Biennale di Venezia (1990), Charleston, South Carolina (1991), and Chicago (1991). In 1991 she was resident in the Tokyo studio of the Visual Arts/Craft Board of the Australia Council. She is currently preparing work for an exhibition in Glasgow.

Claudia Knapman is a sociologist and historian who lectures in sociology at James Cook University of North Queensland. As well as writing on gender, race and colonialism, her teaching and research interests include the sociology of health and ageing.

Marilyn Lake is Director of Women's Studies at La Trobe University. Her books include *Double Time. Women in Victoria 150 Years*, co-edited with Farley Kelly (Penguin, 1985), *The Limits of Hope. Soldier Settlement in Victoria 1915–38* (OUP, 1987) and *Australians at Work. Commentaries and Sources*, co-edited with Charles Fox (McPhee-Gribble, 1990). Her articles include 'Women, gender and history', *Australian Feminist Studies*, 7/8, Summer 1988 and 'Female desires. The meaning of World War II, *Australian Historical Studies*, no. 95, October 1990. She is co-author of a forthcoming feminist history of Australia.

Jenny Lee has been editor of *Meanjin* since 1987. She co-edited *A People's History of Australia Since 1788* (4 vols, McPhee-Gribble/Penguin, 1988).

Susan Magarey is Director of the Research Centre for Women's Studies at Adelaide University and editor of the journal *Australian Feminist Studies*. She is the author of the prize-winning biography of Catherine Helen

Spence, *Unbridling the Tongues of Women* (Hale & Iremonger, 1985), and several articles on women's studies. She is currently working on a monograph about the women's movement and relations between the sexes in Australia around the turn of the century.

Helen Pringle teaches in the School of Political Science at the University of New South Wales, in the areas of political thought and sexual politics. She is writing a book on seventeenth-century political theory.

Gail Reekie is interested in the historical intersections between sex and consumer culture and is writing a book on the sexualisation of selling in Sydney's department stores to 1930. During 1991 she worked at Griffith University as Research Associate on a project funded by the Australian Research Council investigating the links between sexual cultures and demographic change.

Sue Rowley is Director of Visual Arts, School of Creative Arts, University of Wollongong, where she teaches arts theory and history. She writes and publishes on bush mythology, gender and national culture in 1890s painting and literature, and on craft theory, museum practice and feminism in the visual arts.

Bruce Scates lectures in History at the University of New South Wales. He has co-edited (with Rae Frances) a special issue of *Labour History* devoted to women's work and published extensively on unemployment and social protest. His current projects include an analysis of the construction of gender in Australia and Aotearoa/New Zealand and the conversion of his PhD thesis (on radicalism and the labour movement) into a book.

Kay Schaffer is an Associate Professor at Adelaide University where she teaches in the Women's Studies Department. She is the author of numerous articles on women's studies, feminist literary criticism and Australian cultural studies. Her book, *Woman and the Bush: Forces of Desire in the Australian Tradition*, was published in 1988 by Cambridge University Press. She is presently working on a study of Eliza Fraser.

Susan Sheridan teaches in the Women's Studies Unit at Flinders University. She is author of a prize-winning critical study, *Christina Stead* (Harvester/Wheatsheaf, 1988), editor of *Grafts: Feminist Cultural Criticism* (1988), and reviews editor of *Australian Feminist Studies*. Her current work includes a book on discourses of gender, nation and race in Australian women's writing and the direction of a research project on the *Australian Women's Weekly* in the postwar period.

Anne Zahalka is a Sydney-based artist working primarily with photography. Her large-scale photographic tableaux address and challenge dominant representations to do with place, identity, gender and culture. Through processes of photomontage, elaborate studio constructions or digital computer manipulation, she reconstructs icons of Australian and European culture in order to question and understand their influence, meaning and value. Ann Zahalka was artist-in-residence at the Künstlerhaus Betharien in Berlin in 1986–87. She has exhibited nationally and internationally, including the 1990 Sydney Biennale *The Readymade Boomerang* at the Art Gallery of New South Wales. In 1992 her work titled 'Landscape Represented' was included in a London exhibition on post-colonial representations of the Australian landscape.

Introduction

Perspectives

In societies that image time as linear progress, the last ten or so years of a century become at once a milestone and a fulcrum. Western time-frames depict revolution in France at the end of the eighteenth century both as a marker of the distance travelled on a road towards democracy and as an abrupt concentration of the previously gathering forces for change before they fanned out again, over the next century, in the successive revolutions that transformed the face of Europe. The *fin de siècle* of the nineteenth century figures in British historiography not only as a crisis of empire and the rule of property, but also as a turning point between a society in which the 'New Woman' provoked a frisson of desire and dread, and the society that succeeded it, a society that considered individual rights so differently that it could within decades grant women the right to vote.

We do not have to assent to the teleology of such histories in order to perceive similar imagery shaping projections for the 1990s, the period in which we write. The 1980s furnished more than enough material for such constructions. That decade saw political repression in the People's Republic of China, whole sections of the Berlin Wall knocked down, the continuing transformation of the political regimen of what was the Union of Soviet Socialist Republics and its ultimate demise. The 1990s began with horrific bloody conflict over the Persian Gulf between the United States of America and its allies and Iraq, whose likely allies had been rendered powerless. Such major events in international politics have brought new configurations in local oppositional politics throughout the West, and beyond. At the same time, some luminaries of theoretical and political analysis in the West, together with a host of lesser lights, announced crises in epistemology, the fragmentation of the rational subject, and the impossibility of grand narratives of emancipation.

In Australia, where fragments of Western societies cling to the seaboard of a vast continent a hemisphere away from such transformations, we are heirs to the same images of time. The final decade of the twentieth century was introduced for us by 1988, the bicentenary of white settlement in this country, marked—at least in official circles—by celebration and assertions of achieved national unity and identity—a unity and identity that were conceived almost exactly a century ago.

The bicentennial celebrations provoked renewed critical interrogation of such notions as national culture and identity. Aboriginal Australian activists, and their non-Aboriginal supporters, drew attention to Australia as a colonising power as well as a colony, and stressed the human costs of unified constructions of national identity. Official bicentennial histories might have devoted one volume, out of several, to Aboriginal Australian peoples. They might also, at least partly in response to protests raised by feminists during the 1970s, have endeavoured to include women, just as the celebratory claims of a unified national identity tried to integrate women into the national community. But both celebrations and histories demonstrated that simple incorporation is not possible. Assertions of national identity, unity and community are constructed by means of exclusions and repression.

Critical questions about those assertions and exclusions in 1988 led to renewed interrogation of the histories that depicted the twin births of Australian political nationalism and a distinctively Australian national culture, a century ago, in the 1890s, a decade that those histories have deemed 'legendary'. One of the goals of this collection is to show not only that such history-writing has been historicist and parochial, but also that it has perpetuated colonialist preoccupations for almost a century past the period of formal constitutional colonialism.

A second goal that we have shared in compiling this book is to show how very much more varied, and contested, were the social relations, the organisation of work practices, the negotiation of livelihoods, sexual behaviour, representations of masculinity and femininity, than narratives about 'the legend of the Nineties' would ever allow. The term 'contesting' in our sub-title, accordingly, refers to three kinds of contestation. One is between people, actions and behaviours, meanings and understandings during those so-called 'legendary' years. Another is between the historians who have created 'the legend of the Nineties' and our challenges to their reading of the past. The third is between individual challenges in this book—for no single 1990s perspective is presented here.

Just as we do not have to assent to the teleology of the histories we inherit, so we do not need to accord to either of these decades—the 1990s in which we write, or the 1890s about which we write—a historicist unity or *zeitgeist*. We have gestured towards the decade in which we are writing because these are the times from which we take our analytical bearings and points of departure. These are quite various enough, even within the covers of one book, to counteract any suggestion that we are constructing a singular analytical position, or writing of our own times as somehow unified and monolithic. Even the engagement with feminist frameworks of analysis, which runs throughout the book and constitutes its third goal, shows major differences in approach. Similarly, we have addressed the 1890s, the period upon which the articles in the book are focused, not because we see these years as constituting some kind of unity, but rather because we have wanted to contest the unity that has been assigned to them, a unity that has *depended* upon the exclusion of women and the repression of the feminine.

Feminist frameworks

Feminist historians and cultural critics have, of necessity, always defined their task in opposition to dominant narratives and analyses of the past. Initial observations about the absence of women in the received wisdoms of patriarchal historiography soon yielded place to a recognition that it would never be adequate simply to 'add women and stir'. Feminist historians who sought to rewrite social history in ways that included women found not only that they were embarking upon entirely new kinds of history, but also that their endeavour raised a host of new questions about the past. Such questions constituted new objects of enquiry. The various forms of 'first-wave' feminism, for instance, acquired a new and different focus. 'Gender' became more than a depoliticised euphemism for 'women'; it could be seen as a characteristic of mainstream political and constitutional events—inflecting visual representations of the new nation with ambiguity, and the language of nationalism with strident masculine separatism.

Feminist cultural critics who exhumed the works of women writers to counteract patriarchal representations of women were soon dissatisfied with a theory of women's exclusion from the making of Australian culture. It became clear that women's work formed a kind of female subculture, silenced in privileged discourses of national culture, but active in cultural production in such marginalised areas as romantic fiction and natural-history painting. The theoretical work that brought such perceptions in its train soon prompted further questions, about what was at stake in representing some genres of cultural expression as central and others as marginal, about the gendered characteristics of such spatio-political determinations, and about how they operated in constructing a national culture.

From such differing, though elbow-brushing, trajectories, various feminists working in art theory, literary and cultural criticism and history converged upon the legendary 1890s in Australia, and the assertions in which we had been schooled about the birth of a nation and a specifically Australian culture.

Milestones in the development of this critique had already appeared. Helen Grace's film *Serious Undertakings*, made in 1983, demonstrated the

INTRODUCTION

need for feminists to challenge directly patriarchal constructions of national identity, questioning their authority, exposing their silences. It deconstructs the intersections of gender, history, art and politics in the Australian cultural tradition, showing it to be a masculine one in which, as Kay Schaffer puts it in her essay in this volume, '*the feminine*, as distinct from the ways women have been defined by men and male culture, is wholly absent'. Marilyn Lake's article 'The politics of respectability', published in *Australian Historical Studies* in 1986, broke new ground by *naming* the politics that had constituted 'the Lone Hand', the free-wheeling bushman, untrammelled by domestic ties, as the symbol of Australian nationalism; she dubbed those politics 'masculinist'.

Lake's article, reproduced in this collection, provoked a heated debate in the pages of the journal of the Australian historical Establishment in which it had appeared. Chris McConville's 'response' argued that there was indeed, as Lake had contended, a battle for control of the national culture at the end of the last century, but that it was not between feminists and masculinists. Rather, he maintained, it was between middle-class reformers and the working classes, particularly the working-class young, an argument that echoes Bob Connell's and Terry Irving's in *Class Structure in Australian History* (1980). Judith Allen's 'reply' to McConville picked up one of the weakest points in his argument; he had endeavoured to dismiss Lake's depiction of 'masculinism' on the grounds that she had said nothing about the processes of socialisation by which masculinity was formed in the 1890s. Such an objection bore no relation to Lake's argument, contended Allen, for Lake's concern was with 'masculinism'—a political position in gender politics—rather than with masculinity, and formation of the masculine subject—the processes of inculcation, in a specific historical and cultural conjuncture, into sex-appropriate behaviours. Allen also contested McConville's insistence that the feminists of the 1890s had no claim to pre-eminence in campaigns based on 'respectability', since men occupied the leading positions in the middle-class reforming organisations of the period. This contention, Allen argued, simply ignored all the evidence of the mass mobilisation of women into the ranks of the Women's Christian Temperance Union during the 1890s, and of the importance of *feminist* agendas in the campaigns for sex-specific reforms such as changes to the age of consent and changes to divorce law.

The originality of Marilyn Lake's argument lies in three contentions. The first is that masculinity can be a subject of historical and cultural enquiry just as much as femininity, indeed that such enquiry is imperative since for so long it has been presented to us as gender-neutral, and simply 'human', and therefore universal. The second is that, as Allen points out, Lake identifies *masculinism* as a distinct political position, loosely analogous—though diametrically opposed—to the political positions represented by feminism. The third is that the decades around the turn of the nineteenth century can be seen as the era of a 'battle of the sexes' for control of the national culture.

The originality in Judith Allen's reply to McConville lies in her elaboration of Lake's references to 'a battle of the sexes' for control of the national culture. Space restrictions prevent us reproducing Allen's article here, but we can quote one important passage. 'Lake's article', she wrote:

> provides an occasion to consider the dichotomous and asymmetrical relationship between these two political positions—masculinism and feminism—at this moment in Australian history [the turn of the century]. For, whereas masculinism took to the hustings *in accord* with the masculine interests embedded in existing sexual relations, feminism tended to work *against* the prevailing or normative femininity implicated in both women's oppression and masculine interests. Masculinism supported the existing sexual status quo by intervening to make its libertarian and male supremacist dimensions more explicit and legitimate. As such, libertarian masculinism, on Lake's reading, emerges inescapably as a conservative position in the history of Australian sexual politics. Conversely, feminists challenged precisely libertarian masculinism in all its class complexions, especially the sexual economic transactions and acquiescences it demanded of women as a group ... Australian 'first wave' feminism emerges as a radical position in the sexual politics of the period.

This argument stands in direct contradiction to the depictions of 'first wave' feminism in mainstream histories as a limited concern of a small number of exclusively middle-class wowsers, bent on oppressing all men and working-class women as well. It signals that a major revision of turn-of-the-century feminism—of its nature, extent and political effectiveness as well as of its strong links with women's movements internationally—is under way.

That feminist revisionist history was the subject of Susan Magarey's 1988 article 'Jane and the feminist history group' in *Australian Feminist Studies*. Using the device of a medley of different voices, she explored the ways in which the political and intellectual inheritance of the women's liberation movement of the 1970s shaped the preoccupations of Australian feminist historiography, in particular its belated attention to 1890s feminism. This degree of reflexiveness about the conditions under which feminist frameworks are developed (also evident in the work of Ann Curthoys and others), as well as the innovative style of the essay, indicate the influence of poststructuralist challenges to the conventions of history-writing, and their underlying assumptions that the aim is to produce unified, single-voiced narratives of cause and effect.

Work by other scholars responsive to these challenges, cultural historians whose work also converged on the 1890s period and touched on questions of the gender order, included Sylvia Lawson's study of the *Bulletin*, *The Archibald Paradox* (1983), David Walker's work on nineteenth-century constructions of masculinity, published in *Labour History*, and John Docker's essays on popular culture drawing on Edward Said's

Orientalism and Bakhtin's notion of 'carnival' (some of which appear in his recent *The Nervous Nineties* (1991)).

More directly addressing feminist questions about representations of women is Sue Rowley's work on the paintings, poetry and fiction that were constructing the masculine Bush legend in the 1890s. Susan Sheridan's essays on women's writing attempted to show that its denigration was a necessary condition of the elevation of the Bush legend to the status of national myth, and that the women were themselves addressing questions of national identity, but from discursive positions different from those of male writers. Kay Schaffer's 1988 book, *Women and the Bush*, foregrounds the theoretical implications of a deconstructive method for reading 'the Australian cultural tradition' as a masculine construct.

Similarly, during the 1980s, feminist artists employed postmodern strategies of appropriation to examine the constricted representations of women in late nineteenth-century visual culture. Photographers Julie Brown-Rrap and Anne Zahalka have both reconstituted the famous paintings of Frederick McCubbin and Tom Roberts, to criticise both the displacement of women and the 'politically useful' circulation of the paintings as icons of national culture through the twentieth century. Narelle Jubelin's petit point appropriations in their elaborate, 'found' frames ironically debunked the heroic myths of nation formation. Some works by Anne Zahalka and Narelle Jubelin are reproduced in this volume.

Like these artists, feminist critics and historians writing about the 1890s became acutely conscious of how odd, how parochial, how redolent of the backwoods the early patriarchal depictions, from Vance Palmer's to Russel Ward's, appeared. What began to emerge was the extent to which their ostensible differentiations of Australia from an effete British culture were effectively coding nationalism as masculine. For it is masculinity that is celebrated in assertions of an Australian culture that is independent of ties to any skirts—whether those ruling the domestic hearth, or those preaching from church pulpits, or those of the mother country—an Australian culture expressed in the virility of young men assaulting the virgin bush, remote from the corrupting urban centres of imperial rule, drawing emotional warmth and support from a homosocial camaraderie that has undertones of misogynist and racist violence not far below the surface.

To set questions about women and gender at the centre of our analyses is not to propose that conflict between the sexes was 'the only show on the road' in the 1890s, but rather to demonstrate that the other shows—nationalism, colonialism, class struggle—look very different when this one is included. It is not our aim to insert gender as the single central interpretative device around which a coherence for the 1890s can be constructed: here is no claim that the turning of this key will unlock the past. There is no one window that we can press our noses against in order to see more clearly the streets and the interiors in which people once moved. Rather, our claim for this book is that it addresses as central questions about how the circumstances of women's lives and struggles were mutually constitutive of issues of culture, economics and politics, through which the 1890s have been conventionally understood.

Our title invokes a rite of passage specific to women across Anglo-Australian society, from Methodist church halls in country towns to the city mansions of the Establishment. We want it to suggest that most traditional depictions of nation-formation are not only gendered masculine but also distinctly solemn. Our image of the nation's début is intended to undercut this solemnity as well as to try out gendering the nation feminine: dancing rather than parliamentary processions; debutantes rather than bushranging desperadoes; a readiness to play with the gender of nationhood, like some cartoons from the period which play with gender ambiguity, even cross-dressing.

In this book

This book ranges widely, from pay rates to federation poetry, from bedrooms to parliamentary debates on the state. The materials under consideration vary from cartoons to the records of benevolent societies, from census statistics to feminist fiction. The reading and writing positions adopted by the contributors to this collection are similarly varied: indeed, the book contains several internal debates, notably between Bruce Scates and Jenny Lee, and between John Docker and Marilyn Lake. Nevertheless, the whole collection coheres around issues of gender in the 1890s, as read in the 1990s.

It is the fate of 'watershed' texts like 'The politics of respectability' to be subject to scrutiny and challenge, as well as elaboration, by their successors. We begin this collection by reprinting Marilyn Lake's 1986 essay to indicate the importance it has had in feminist revisions of the 1890s, and because reprinting it *in toto* makes it clear that, despite the representations of some critics, her argument proposes at least two models of masculinity current in the 1890s. We follow it with a challenge from cultural historian John Docker. In 'The feminist legend: A new historicism?', he suggests that the main effect of Lake's essay has been to usher in a new 'legend of the Nineties', a feminist version to replace the masculinist one. Docker sees a renewed contest over the definition of a national culture, where the new 'feminist legend' conceptualises 'masculinist' patriarchal power as monolithic and controlling. As he sees it, the feminist legend is a 'historicist' idea that the 1890s can be fully explained by the operation of power between the sexes: it has the same structure as previous legends, whether they focused on class struggle or on nationalism versus modernism (an influential literary account of the contest over the national culture).

If this were the case, feminists would have to ask themselves what had been gained by merely replacing one totalising narrative with another, only this time with 'women on top', so to speak. Readers of this book can judge for themselves the assumptions about power implicit in Lake's essay, and in the chapters which follow. But we might also accept the idea that legend-making *is* what's going on here, and see that process positively, not as one legend replacing another, or even as 'the truth' replacing all legends, but as the continuous process of making sense of the past in relation to present-day questions. 'The past' (which we have access to only through texts) is an object always being constructed by the discourses we use. What we construct are not necessarily legends that demand faith, but rather stories that serve particular purposes, alternative ways of telling. From the deconstructive position illustrated by our final chapter, Kay Schaffer's account of successive stories about 'the drover's wife', it could be deduced that it is only when legends fossilise into all-inclusive 'traditions' that the process of story-telling is blocked.

The fact that familiar historical materials can be read in new ways supports such a view of history-writing. Jenny Lee re-examines the records of the Victorian Wages Boards for evidence of the charge that women were taking men's jobs during the 1890s Depression (an accusation levelled at women also in the 1930s Depression, and at various intervals since). From a complex scenario involving young and adult workers of both sexes, reorganisations of the labour process, the agendas of both the labour movement and the state, she shows how the division of labour within the family has been constituted at one and the same time as a buffer against capitalist exploitation and a source of division and conservatism within the labour movement.

Bruce Scates considers the same industrial working-class scenario from the point of view of the women with unemployed or absent husbands, who resisted through their dealings with charity organisations and their participation in the mass demonstrations against unemployment. This focus allows him to emphasise other challenges made by working-class women to the gender order of the day, including masculinist assumptions about women that operated within the labour movement itself.

In contrast, an arena where women had no role to play at all, that of parliamentary debate, was an important scene of 'reorganising the masculinist context' through the 1895 New South Wales Public Service Bill, according to Desley Deacon. Her study of these records shows a division of opinion among these men over the question of married women's right to employment and a compromise solution, which was however swept away by administrative fiat. In this instance, the 1890s can be seen as providing a portent of the coming century's placing the principle of the family wage over the right of married women to proper employment conditions.

Two essays which consider less familiar kinds of historical material in order to open out gender conflicts around women's work are Gail Reekie's account of selling and shopping in the newly developing department stores, and Paula Hamilton's study of cartoon representations of domestic servants and employers. Using the David Jones company archive as a key source, Reekie composes a picture of male–female conflict that includes occasional alliances between women across class lines, most notably in the support of middle-class feminists for Early Closing and other improvements to the working conditions of 'shop girls', as well as the more predictable conflicts between female customers and male management, or between female and male employees. Domestic service, however, was still the major paid employment for women in this period; Paula Hamilton's work on cartoons about 'the servant problem' addresses several issues, including the way these cartoons coded general unease about class relations as well as changes in the position of women within middle-class marriage, the specific nature of class relations between women, and the use of cartoons as material for historical analysis.

All of these essays, stressing the centrality of conflicts in the gender order, offer important revisions of the 1890s as a key period in the development of an industrial society in Australia. Shifting the focus of attention from work to sex, the essays by Susan Magarey, Patricia Grimshaw and Susan Sheridan extend the analysis to an area that is usually considered separately from economic issues, under a rubric such as 'the history of sexuality'. Yet as Magarey indicates by her title, 'Sexual labour', such a separation can overlook the intimate connections, for women, between sex and work, and the role of changing conditions of marriage and child-bearing: her story of the 1890s construes one aspect of the well-documented family transition of the late nineteenth century as a 'strike against marriage' on the part of women.

Sexual discourses and practices underwent massive changes in this period, due to a combination of structural social changes and challenges from feminists and other advanced thinkers. That these particular changes were a source of distinct unease for the labour movement, occasioning significant disagreement among radical women and men, is demonstrated by Grimshaw's reading of the coverage of sexuality debates (as well as politics and work) in the Melbourne socialist journal *Tocsin*. In a comparable journal, the Sydney feminist *Woman's Voice*, many writers saw patriarchal sexual arrangements as the major source of present social ills, and Sheridan argues for a re-evaluation of the radicalism of their critiques, further undermining the masculinist dismissal of feminism as middle-class 'wowserism'.

Race relations, and the dominant discourses which constructed nationalist and democratic ideals as inseparable from a 'white Australia', constitute another area which is usually given only 'specialist' attention in historical narratives about the 1890s. Claudia Knapman's essay foregrounds these issues and their imbrication in gender ideologies. Knapman, in 'Reproducing Empire', looks at the upbringing of the white child as a focus for the race and gender ideologies that underpinned Australian expansion in the Pacific.

INTRODUCTION xxiii

In constructing what are virtually new objects of historical attention, this second group of essays employs comparative perspectives to highlight what might be distinctively Australian inflections of current debates on sexuality and race. Another feature, their work with new combinations of materials—popular representations in humorous and romantic journalism and fiction as well as archival documents—is further developed in the third group of essays.

The political cartoons analysed by Josie Castle and Helen Pringle reveal some intriguing 'hesitations at the heart of masculinity' in their use of cross-dressing to figure Australian national sovereignty and the coming Federation. Poetic constructions of the same phenomenon, argues Barbara Holloway, demonstrate a succession of feminine metaphors for 'Australia' which simultaneously represent the agents of desire for a collective identity as exclusively male.

Two familiar figures from 1890s radical discourse, the 'new woman' and the 'coming man', Robert Dixon argues, played major roles in the 'lost race' romance popularised by Rider Haggard, as it was elaborated by several Australian novelists. Women writers, whether poets of a different national identity, like Mary Gilmore or Dorothea Mackellar, or novelists like Mary Gaunt and her book *Kirkham's Find*, the subject of Dorothy Jones's essay, inevitably wrote from a different position. As she draws out the critical edge of the novel's representation of separate male and female spheres, Jones highlights its preoccupation with the question of women's work that was so crucial in the 1890s. In parallel, Sue Rowley attends to the spatial metaphor of separate spheres in her rereading of some key paintings in the male tradition representing women in the bush. Her title, 'Things a bushwoman cannot do', directly recalls the legendary short story by Henry Lawson, 'The Drover's Wife', which is the focus of the final essay in this collection. Here, Kay Schaffer traces the critical and creative uses to which the iconic figures of this bushwoman and her creator have been put since the 1890s, in a demonstration of the lasting vitality of this period in Australian imaginations.

Conclusion

The title of this book signals—in all its flurry and glamour—the emergence onto the stage of history of a new and uncertain figure of individuality. The sub-title expresses the contestations between people living in the 1890s, between cultural critics and historians who have represented this 'legendary' decade in the annals of Australia's past and present, and between the contributors to this book. At least the last form of contestation will undoubtedly continue. But capturing one of its moments, in the 1990s, within the covers of one book, is an achievement of collaboration, across disciplines as different as economic history and art theory, across the spatial distances that separate the contributors and the editors. For such collaboration, the editors thank the contributors for their cooperation and patience. As editors, we thank each other for inspiration and for fun. This book expresses a 1990s reconsideration of a relationship with feminists and their supporters a century ago. While we may still wish to debate their goals, their strategies and their rhetoric, nevertheless we share their conviction that 'the woman question' would need to be central to any struggle for a just and equitable society.

Susan Magarey
Sue Rowley
Susan Sheridan

Fig. 1A Anne Zahalka, 'The Breakaway'.

Fig. 1B Anne Zahalka, 'The Immigrants'.

Fig. 1C Narelle Jubelin, 'Untitled Silhouette'.

1 The politics of respectability: Identifying the masculinist context
Marilyn Lake

The history of womanhood has now been much studied, here and abroad, yet historians have been slow to recognise 'manhood', 'manliness' and 'masculinity' as social constructions requiring historical investigation and elucidation.[1] This is all the more remarkable in Australia as for men in this country their 'manhood' has so often seemed their chief source of pride and identity.

The men in most Australian history books are sex-less: they appear in most accounts as neutered and neutral historical agents. Men become universalised Man: White Man, Working Man, Nineteenth-Century Man, the Coming Man. Male historians have been blinded to the problematic nature of the sex of their subjects by their own sex-centredness. It is time that we started treating men, historically, as men, socialised into 'masculinity' (whose meanings have changed from one age to another, one society to another) and pursuing their 'masculinist' interests as men, as well as the interests of their class and race. In other words, it is time for historians interested in gender to move beyond 'women's history'— beyond the static conception of 'woman's role' which lies at the heart of 'contribution history'.[2] It is time that gender became a central category of all historical analysis. For just as women's history cannot be fruitfully written without reference to men, neither can men's history be properly written without reference to men's relations with women.

The gender factor has been obscured in Australian historical writing by a number of phenomena: by the dominance of a narrowly defined political history, by the sex-blind nature of much of what passes as class analysis and by the centrality in our historiography of organising concepts such as 'national character' and 'national tradition' and the dichotomy of 'respectability' and 'unrespectability'. I wish to suggest that the adoption of such conceptual frameworks has served to obscure one of the greatest political struggles in Australian history: the contest between men and women at the end of the nineteenth century for the control of the national culture. To cast the struggle in terms of respectability and unrespectability is to miss the sexual dynamic in history. An examination of this battle of the sexes suggests that its resolution involved the resolution of another, related, conflict: that between competing ideals of masculinity.

In his study of the national ethos in *The Australian Legend*, Russel Ward identified the pastoral workers as Australia's cultural heroes. The stockman and the shearer are represented as the supreme embodiments of the 'national character'. Although, like many analysts of the national character, he conflated a distinct set of male cultural practices with a 'national tradition', in identifying the emergence of a particular masculine ideal in Australia Ward has unwittingly made a significant contribution to our understanding of gender relations in Australia. In a review of Ward's thesis, Graeme Davison argued the importance of relating the Australian legend to 'the ideas and situation of those who created it'.[3] He pointed to the urban sources of the legend and demonstrated that it was an urban malaise which served as the springboard of the idealisation of the bush. But there is a further dimension to the 'ideas and situation' of the legendmakers which Davison only hints at. In a later study of 'national identity', Richard White stressed the 'masculine exclusiveness' of the bush ethos and pointed to the continuities between the culture of the bush workers and that of the men who, in the 1880s and 1890s, celebrated them in literature.[4] White cites the evidence of Arthur Jose who, in his memoir of 'the romantic nineties', had noted that 'the romance ... was singularly devoid of feminine interest ... It was not that kind of romance. There were a few girls among the Boy Authors, but they were tolerated there mainly because they made tea and organised refreshments'.[5] Richard White's analysis can be pushed further.

The Australian legend was a celebration of the 'one powerful and unique national type yet produced in the new land'—the Bushman.[6] It represented the promotion of a particular model of masculinity—the Lone Hand—by men with firm views about gender relations and who, whether married or not, enjoyed the pleasures of 'bachelordom'. Most importantly, the idealisation of the Lone Hand represented a rejection of the idealisation of Domestic Man which was integral to the cult of domesticity, imported to Australia in the cultural baggage of English immigrants. The cult of domesticity in England, Catherine Hall has pointed out, was vitally linked to the rise of Evangelicalism: 'Between 1780 and 1820, in the Evangelical struggle over anti-slavery and over the reform of manners and morals, a new view of the nation, of political power and of family life was forged. This view was to become a dominant one in the 1830s and 1840s.'[7] The Evangelicals were champions of married life and the joys of domesticity.

W. Cowper, the 'poet of domesticity', eulogised: 'Domestic happiness, thou only bliss of paradise that has survived the Fall.'[8]

For ideologues of domesticity in the colonies, the truly noble man was the one 'whose affections lure[d] him to the serene enjoyments of Domestic Life'. Men were promised that those prepared to find happiness at home could expect the status of 'Serene Highness'. The 'abandoned man' was defined as the one who had 'abandoned the joys of domestic life'.[9] The ideal of Domestic Man was actively fostered in Victoria by such evangelical groups as the Young Men's Christian Association (YMCA), founded in Melbourne in 1871 for the purpose of improving the moral, intellectual and social conditions of all within its reach. The object of the YMCA was a missionary one—to extend 'home influence' to all the boys in the colony.[10]

To the militants of the emergent men's press, 'home influence' was emasculating. The Sydney *Bulletin* liked to believe that in 'virile cultures' where 'home-life [had] not become so all absorbing',

> men live and struggle and fight out in the open most of the time. When they go to their homes they go to beat their wives. We live in the home. All our real life is home life. All our moral and mental life is the moral and mental life of men who are half women in their habits, men breathing always a domestic atmosphere...[11]

According to the *Bulletin*, home life trammelled a man's spirit and sapped his masculinity. And it robbed him of his independence. Randolph Bedford, prominent bohemian and *Bulletin* contributor, recalled how his father had encouraged him to 'go bush' with the words:

> You're me all over again, lad. There's only one thing that will tie you down, and that's responsibility. A wife and children will put the hobbles on you. You'll look over the fence at the horses who are going somewhere; but you'll have to stay in the paddock.[12]

The *Bulletin* was the most influential exponent of the separatist model of masculinity which lay at the heart of the eulogies to the Bushman. From its establishment in 1880 until 1902, this flamboyant magazine was edited by J.F. Archibald, described by Francis Adams as 'the most fascinating personality in Australia' and the 'one Australian journalist of genius'.[13] Archibald was an unhappily married, childless misogynist. His jaundiced views about the relations between men and women formed a major strand of the *Bulletin's* message.

J.F. Archibald was part of a self-styled Bohemia which flourished in Sydney and Melbourne in the late nineteenth century. In Sydney the bohemians gathered about the *Bulletin* and in Melbourne, for a brief time, around the *Bull-Ant*. They valued masculine camaraderie—the 'mateship' they projected on to the bush workers—and indulged in the pleasures of drinking, smoking, gambling. They ate together in city cafes or lodging houses and attended all-male Smoke Nights. As Sarah Stephen has observed, the values and economic necessities of marriage were the antithesis of the bohemian creed of 'wine, women and song' and 'art for art's sake'.[14] Many bohemians were in fact married, but their relationships with their families were often strained. Rudel O'Dowd, son of poet Bernard O'Dowd, wrote of the bitterness felt by his family at their father's desertion. He claimed that his mother's (necessary) devotion to the home had given rise to the unwarranted charge that she was unintelligent and uncultured.[15]

In Melbourne the thrice-married E.J. Brady and Louis Esson designed a community farm scheme where artists would have 'free sunsets, and none of the cruel distractions ordinary honest men have to face such as rent, firing, butcher's bills, complaining wives and squalling children'.[16] In Sydney, J.F. Archibald argued for the 'independence' of the journalist ('He should have no family ties or connections, because they are sure to sway him and prejudice his judgement') and berated marriage for bringing certain 'penury' to the unfortunate young men who embarked on it. The 'marriage contract [was] an entirely one-sided arrangement'; 'the men, in a word [had] all the worst of the bargain'.[17] In 1885 the *Bulletin* portrayed its man 'Above Suspicion'. He was free of family responsibilities (had no widowed mother), never attended church, had no connections with Sunday Schools, but did 'smoke, chew, drink, swear, and play cards'.[18] It was a portrait in which the Evangelical associations of Domestic Man were made plain. The anti-clericalism of the *Bulletin*'s Man Above Suspicion became a major component of the legendary Bushman's ethos.

Women were presented in the men's press as the spoilers of men's pleasures. The *Bull-Ant* carried a cartoon in 1891 entitled 'Too Much' which featured Randolph Bedford, thus:

> Randolph Bedford: 'Tell me, my angel, what to do to prove my love. Oh, that I might, like some knight of old, battle for you, suffer for you, die for you.'
> Sweet Girl: 'I wish you would give up smoking.'
> Randolph Bedford: 'Oh, come now, that's asking too much.'[19]

Women were portrayed in the *Bulletin* as vain, snobbish, conservative, parson-worshipping killjoys, and, as often as not, unprepossessing spinsters—Miss Evergreen—scheming to trap men into wedlock. Marriage was a state to be avoided or abandoned. The following 'joke' was typical in its message:

> Two married women and a dog were struck by lightning recently at Dubbo. Half the married men have been trying to get their wives to walk about the vicinity ever since. The dogs are kept tied up.[20]

In a more serious vein, the *Bulletin* campaigned consistently for reformed divorce legislation which would give men 'relief' from the 'holy chains of matrimony'.[21] When the 'nationalist' school of writers represented the pastoral workers as cultural heroes, they did so because in their apparent freedom from the ties of family and in their 'independence', these bushmen most closely approximated to their masculinist ideal. The pastoral industry provided the perfect subjects on which they could project their attitudes and values. They were Lone Hands and their much vaunted 'independence' was equated with mobility, the freedom to move. This 'nomad tribe' inhabited a world without families, though not without women. As Russel Ward points out, sexual relations between pastoral workers and Aboriginal women were common.[22] Indeed, from the bush worker's view, Aboriginal women were the perfect sexual partners, affording the men sexual pleasure without burdening them with family responsibility. As Henry Reynolds has noted, for 'most frontiersmen an encounter ended abruptly with ejaculation and withdrawal'.[23] The uses of white women were similarly episodic: many were abandoned in huts and homesteads. The bushman's heart, like the bohemian's, had learnt to 'love and roam'.[24]

In their sexual relations the bohemians seemed to prefer a 'plentiful sowing of wild oats', to use Archibald's phrase, to careful domestic nurture.[25] They courted ballet dancers, artist's models and prostitutes. They romanticised casual encounters with 'native' women. In *Those Were The Days* George Taylor commended the following poetic 'wonder piece', written by E.J. Brady:

> 'Twas down in Honolulu way off one night afar,
> The sea breeze comin' cooler across the coral bar,
> When Lulu's eyes were brighter than any girls I knew,
> When Lulu's teeth were whiter than any coral, too;
> Oh, Lulu, Lulu, Lulu, my warm Pacific pearl,
> My lovely, lively Lulu—My own Kanaka girl.[26]

The pleasures of the Pacific islands were also the theme of a cartoon in the *Bulletin* in April 1886, captioned 'An Innocent Absentee'. An 'innocent' husband, having been shipwrecked, was 'forced' to bide his time on an island in the company of an island woman.[27] Editor Archibald, commenting on the apparent fraternising of 'new Australia' men with South American women in Paraguay, suggested that men were moved by a timeless imperative: 'Men will drink and gamble, and prowl around to the back doors of dusky daughters of the land till the end of time...'[28] The bohemians regarded their sexual attitudes as libertarian, but failed to notice that women's experience of the (male) 'sex act' was often anything but pleasurable and frequently fraught with danger.

These were city men who promoted Bushmen as cultural heroes, but it is important to note that not all rural men qualified for heroic status. From the 1860s a new class of rural worker had moved across the colonies—the agriculturalists put on the land by the Selection Acts. The supporters of land reform had invoked the model of the yeoman: selectors were to be neither employers nor employees, but independent freeholders. In the event their lack of capital drove them into a network of dependencies. Unable to afford hired labour, most relied heavily on the unpaid work of their wives and children and unlike the roving men in the saddle, the selectors, as men bogged down in family life, could not be admitted to the pantheon of heroes. The 'smiling homesteads' envisaged by land reformers were replaced by images of 'sordid farms'. Indeed, 'by about 1890', according to Ward, 'the "cocky" had become, at least in the mythology of the migratory bushmen, a byword for meanness and stupidity'.[29] By 1900 the family men, Dad and Dave, had emerged as embodiments of everything unheroic, national objects of pity or mockery.

Henry Lawson, unhappily married, returned again and again in his verse to the pleasures of the 'careless, roaming life' and the nobility of the love between men encountered on the track, a love named mateship. In 'The Vagabond' he represented the family as a tyranny and the family man as a fool:

> Sacrifice all for the family's sake,
> Bow to their selfish rule.
> Slave till your big, soft heart, they break.
> The heart of the 'family fool'.[30]

The lone bushman was these writers' love object. In 1888 Francis Adams gushed:

> Yonder the band is playing
> and fine young people walk.
> They are envying each other and talking
> their pretty empty talk.
> There, in the shade on the outskirts,
> stretched on the grass, I see
> a man with a slouch hat, smoking.
> That is the man for me![31]

It is little wonder that the nationalist writers of the men's press greeted the advance of the 'new' trade unionism so warmly: for them it represented a great fraternity. The Labor movement was a men's movement. As Labor stalwart W.G. Spence later claimed, it 'had in it that feeling of mateship which [the bushman] understood already'. Or as William Lane so nicely put it, 'socialism ... is the desire to be mates, is the ideal of living together in harmony and brotherhood and loving kindness'.[32] One of the chief objects of the labour movement in Australia was the exclusion of 'cheap labour' in the form of the Chinese, children and women. Independence was considered the privilege of the white man. Unless women were to remain economically dependent, observed the *Bulletin*, the labour market would be ruined for white men no less than by Asian competition.[33]

By the late nineteenth century the gulf between the experience of manhood and womanhood, even allowing for class differences, was large. The separation of work from home, which occurred with industrialisation, gained an added dimension in Australia from the dominance of the pastoral industry in the Australian economy. The Drover's Wife and her kind were left alone with the children because their husbands were away at work, droving, shearing or boundary riding. In the towns and cities this sexual apartheid was reinforced by the casual nature of much employment, the consequent mobility of labour and the acute segregation of the labour market. When women joined the paid workforce, they usually worked in different jobs than men, and when in the same occupations, such as teaching, they worked at different levels of the hierarchy. After work, the separation often continued, with men seeking a haven away from their home in the public house or their private club.

Although men and women inhabited different worlds, they were bound together by economics. Denied access to a living wage on the assumption that they were supported by men, women were thus forced into relations of dependence. The prescription became self-fulfilling. Locked into economic dependency, women's material (and often emotional) fate thus depended on men's circumstances and predilections. In this situation, men's cultural practices could have profound implications for women and children; and there were particularly injurious consequences of the style of masculinity propagated by the champions of the Bushman.

Given the demographic imbalances of nineteenth-century Australia— with men outnumbering women—the promotion of the Lone Hand as the ideal Australian was in some ways making a virtue out of necessity. Large numbers of men were compelled to be bachelors for life whether they liked it or not. By the 1880s, however, the excess of males was declining and the proportion of men marrying in Australia beginning to increase. Significantly, large numbers of men were of quite an advanced age, with habits already set, when they embarked on marriage.[34]

Just as the independent, free-wheeling Bushman was being enshrined as Australia's cultural hero, the balancing of the sexes was resulting in more men entering wedlock. But while these men were willing to try the anticipated comforts of a marriage, many, like Randolph Bedford, were not so willing to forgo the traditional pleasures of Australian masculinity. And within a family context, masculinist cultural practices could take on dramatically new meanings. If men chose to spend a large proportion of their earnings on drinking, tobacco and gambling, the result well might be a deprived diet for their family and barefooted children. Drinking bouts could exacerbate domestic tensions and precipitate wife-beating and child abuse. Men exercising their presumed right of access to women's bodies could produce unwanted children and spread venereal disease. Encouraged to roam the country in search of work and freedom, men's departures could render their families destitute. As Kay Daniels has noted, 'women often paid for the "mobility" of the nomad tribe'; the prevalence of desertion as a factor in pauperism is documented in government records and in legislation.[35]

Research has also established that drinking and tobacco consumption were widespread in nineteenth-century Australia. Tony Dingle has shown that beer drinking reached unprecedented levels in late nineteenth-century Australia, although the absolute amounts drunk annually never challenged the higher per capita levels consumed in Britain. More significant, however, in its implications for social relationships was the peculiar pattern of drinking in the colonies: 'the short bouts of excessive drinking' and the exclusion of women from drinking rituals. 'Much drunkenness,' Dingle wrote, 'resulted from long spells of continuous drinking, but it did not result in high levels of annual drink consumption because such binges only took place infrequently.'[36] When Australian men drank, they were likely to get drunk. This was true of the city as well as the bush. In towns and suburbs, husbands frequented corner pubs. In her study of Richmond at the turn of the century, Janet McCalman found that many wives and daughters '*believed*' their menfolk drank to excess, even if their excesses were only occasional'. 'Of course,' McCalman added, 'living on an inadequate income—and all working-class incomes were inadequate—there was never really enough money to spend on alcohol and cigarettes'.[37]

It is clear that drinking and smoking in the convict period were common among both men and women of the 'lower orders', but increasingly, as women were locked into family life, these pastimes came to be regarded as a masculine prerogative. It became unacceptable for women to drink in public, as their exclusion from hotels symbolised. Kay Saunders' study of domestic violence in Queensland in the late nineteenth century has shown that men frequently justified beating their wives by pointing out that the women had been drinking. A husband, she stated, 'would assault his wife if she drank alcohol, particularly in a hotel. It was considered that drinking alcohol, whether in moderation or to excess, as was the common practice in colonial Queensland, was a male preserve and totally forbidden to women.'[38]

Contemporary witnesses and historical research both suggest that wife-beating was so routine in colonial Australia as to be taken for granted. Michael Power, a farmer in the Hawkesbury Valley in the late 1830s, said of his marriage: 'we were always very comfortable; scolding is nothing between man and wife; I have often struck her, but that is nothing between man and wife'.[39] François-Maurice Lepailleur, camped at Parramatta in 1841, noted: 'We hear more women crying in the night here than birds singing in the woods during the day.'[40] Further south, Penelope Selby wrote from the Port Phillip District in 1849: 'Another peculiarity of this country is that men, gentle and simple, are rather fond of beating their wives—a gentleman residing in Belfast killed his the other day. He had not been married six months.'[41] In studies of Western Australia and Queensland later in the century, Margaret Grellier and Kay Saunders both concluded that male domestic violence was widespread and commonly considered to be a 'natural' event or a 'necessary' corrective to female wilfulness. Both showed that these attitudes informed the operation of the law; police were reluctant to prosecute, judges and magistrates frequently condoned a man's violence towards his wife on the grounds that the woman had not fulfilled her wifely obligations or adopted a properly submissive demeanour. Janet McCalman suggests that such attitudes still prevailed in twentieth-century Richmond. One resident recalled:

It was quite common for men to bash up their wives and the strange thing was, if you were to kick a dog another man would kick you. But if you were having an argument with your wife nobody would interfere.[42]

Richmond residents often associated domestic brawls with particular local pubs.

In June 1886, the *Bulletin* made reference to the number of wife-beating cases currently before the courts: 'it would seem that there is...a desire on the part of the wallopers to prove the necessity for the passing of the new Divorce Act'.[43] Like most nineteenth-century observers, the *Bulletin* associated domestic violence with excessive drinking. The alleged relationship between the axe and the bottle was made explicit in cartoons and verse concocted in support of legislation to liberalise divorce laws—legislation necessary, in the *Bulletin*'s view, to free men from matrimonial bonds. From her study of Queensland court records, Kay Saunders concluded that 'most of the divorce petitions and protection order injunctions submitted by women include evidence of excessive alcohol consumption on the part of husbands'.[44] Whether or not alcohol 'caused' domestic violence is beside the point: women *believed* there was a connection and this belief became the springboard of their political mobilisation.

Women's vulnerability to assault lay in their dependence and their dependence was increased by large numbers of children. By the 1870s in Australia the average completed family included eight children. Women's adult lives drained away in a series of pregnancies, miscarriages, births and periods of lactation. Earning an independent income in these circumstances was never easy. Mothers sought work compatible with child-minding such as taking in lodgers or people's washing, doing piecework for the clothing industry or freelance prostitution. Genteel women with some education ran post offices or schools from home. Increasing numbers of women found themselves juggling work and child care, in some cases because they left home and in others because their husbands abandoned them.

In the men's press of late nineteenth-century Australia, the carefree roaming life was elevated to an heroic status. Families 'put the hobbles' on men. Clearly, many husbands and fathers had no choice but to travel in search of work, but equally clearly, there were powerful cultural endorsements of these men's rejection of domesticity. The extent of family desertion, as Susan Tiffin has demonstrated, emerged as an issue of nationwide debate in the 1880s.[45] A major cause of concern to policymakers was the increasing cost of this practice to the State, a concern evident in Justice Windeyer's pronouncement in 1885:

> Whilst the Court will make every allowance for men who by adverse circumstances are really compelled to leave their wives in search of honest employment, it will give no countenance to a class of men, already too large, who, preferring to spend their time in dissipated idleness, seek no settled employment, leave their wives to the mercy of strangers [and] fill our charitable institutions with their deserted children...[46]

Again, evidence from early twentieth-century Richmond suggests the persistence of the roving disposition among some men and their insouciant attitude to family responsibilities. One woman's father worked in a sawmill up the bush, returning home every fortnight with 'about 35 shillings ... and a couple of bottles of wine. And that would be all we'd see of him. Off he'd go—it didn't worry him. It was my mother who had all the trouble.'[47]

Women coped with the consequences of men's actions, but they also engaged in many individual acts of rebellion. The domestic consequences of the bohemian/bushman lifestyle form the theme of Henry Lawson's 'Mitchell' stories. Mitchell and his mate were shearers. At the end of the season when they were preparing to return home, Mitchell tells his mate, with feeling, that men should be more considerate towards their wives:

> Think of the trouble she takes to get you a good dinner, and how she keeps it hot between two plates in the oven, and waits hour after hour till the dinner gets dried up, and all the morning's work is wasted. Think how it hurts her, and how anxious she'll be (especially if you're inclined to booze) for fear that something has happened to you ... But about the dinner waiting. Try and put yourself in her place. Wouldn't you get mad under the same circumstances? I know I would.[48]

Mitchell's wife, we are informed towards the end of 'Mitchell on Matrimony', has left him. Mitchell's creator was writing from the heart. Bertha Lawson recounted in her 'memories' how she was continually persuaded by a remorseful Henry 'how grateful he always was, how firmly determined never to fail [her] again'; but in the end 'Bohemia with its trials and temptations claimed him again'.[49]

Many women deserted by their husbands went to court in an effort to compel payments of maintenance, while others instituted proceedings for divorce or judicial separation. Women who found themselves pregnant with unwanted children sought out abortionists or attempted to effect their own terminations. After childbirth, many committed infanticide or placed their infants with 'baby farmers', often to enable them to take paid work. Other women railed against their husbands' selfishness in spending money on tobacco and alcohol that was needed for children, and pleaded for them to change their ways. Women tried to persuade their husbands to take the pledge against alcohol and to give up smoking. The home was a battleground and the issue was masculinist culture—or in Wardian terms, the 'national character'. Cartoons depicted the struggle over drinking and smoking:

> 'Why *Do* you smoke so much, Augustus?'
> 'Why you see it strengthens the teeth, my Dear.'
> 'Oh Does it? I thought it only strengthened the Breath.'[50]

Verse in the *Bull-Ant* elaborated the same theme:

> Oh, it's tough on a man when he wants a smoke,
> And his wife is a kicker, by gob,

> And she croons out her cruel and endless croak
> From her throne by the opposite hob;
> And reminds him her curtains are clean and white,
> And her dinner's distressed by the smell—
> Such a man is a martyr from moon till night,
> He'd be happier smoking in H--l.[51]

A *Bulletin* cartoon in 1888 depicted a barman feeding a man his drink. The caption explained: 'Mr Smile often promised his wife he would never raise a drop of liquor to his lips again, but, though he has not broken the promise, the whisky gets there just the same.'[52]

From the 1880s, individual protests merged into collective mobilisation as private battles became public campaigns. One outcome of the balancing of the sexes in the colonies which resulted in more men marrying was a marked decline in the proportion of women marrying. By 1881, in Melbourne, marriageable females far outnumbered marriageable males.[53] Unmarried women of the middle class could more easily find the time and energy to devote to political causes. At the same time, many of those who did marry began to effectively limit their families. Many of the leaders of the late nineteenth-century women's movement were single, or if married, had few children or none at all.

Historical accounts of the women's movement both in Australia and overseas, imbued with idealist assumptions about the determining role of ideology (whether the 'rationalism' of William Leach's account or the power of 'purity' and 'pollution' beliefs as in the work of Phillida Bunkle), have for the most part ignored, or played down, the material context of women's response to nineteenth-century feminism.[54] The temperance movement achieved a mass following. The material basis of women's receptivity to the feminist message was their role in reproduction; *their* workplace was their home.

The response to the women's movement in Australia, both friendly and hostile, can only be understood, I suggest, in its relationship to the ascendancy of the masculinist culture outlined earlier. The women's movement aimed at dethroning the style of masculinity championed by the men's press—a style of masculinity that had deleterious consequences for the lives of women. 'Whisky, Seduction, Gambling and Cruelty'—these were the targets of the Women's Sphere.[55] To depict women's concerns with temperance and social purity in terms of 'respectability' is to ignore the sexual politics; to describe the campaigners as Wowsers is to stigmatise them in the language of their masculinist enemies. The women's movements in Britain and the United States shared similar concerns but in Australia, where masculinist values had been elevated to the status of national traditions, feminist activism acquired a particularly subversive, counter-cultural dimension. These women's aims were limited but they were no less threatening for that. They sought to curtail masculine privilege and those practices most injurious to women and children—notably drinking, smoking, gambling and male sexual indulgence. They did not seek a total independence for women, but to make their dependence a happier and more secure state. They sought to change mankind—to make men more considerate and responsible fathers, more companionable husbands. Recognising their lack of power to effect radical change, all campaigns converged in the demand for female suffrage.

The women's temperance campaigns were of course part of a wider crusade initiated by the Protestant churches against social evil, but as J.D. Bollen has commented, on the Drink issue, 'churchmen were joined as never before in public life by women'.[56] Not surprisingly, the masculinist press responded venomously to what they perceived, rightly, to be a female project of cultural reconstruction. Feminists were mocked, abused and insulted. They were 'officious busybodies' and 'leathery social interferists'. When a woman became interested in political rights she became 'hoarse and hysterical'.

> She neglects her hair, and allows her stockings to fall into holes; she wears her hat with a sort of reckless abandon, and takes no more pride in complexion pastes and remedies for wrinkles, warts and outstanding freckles; she becomes an ache and an aggravation, and a thorn planted in the side of man ...[57]

The response of the men's press, threatened and abusive as it was, shows more insight into the significance and meaning of the women's movement than many historians have recognised. A whole way of life was at risk. When women temperance advocates argued that railway workers should not drink on the job, the *Bull-Ant* commented:

> Last week a deputation of 'lovely women' which realises that the staple article of food for men in these parts, is drink with a bite in it and who are fully alive to the fact that man, as aforesaid, possesses a good appetite and is on deck every time the liquor is to be had, waited on the Minister ... Things in general are pretty bad now, but what life would be like with this class in the ascendant, it isn't good for the mind of men to dwell upon ...[58]

The *Bulletin*, too, feared for men's privilege. Reporting an international feminist meeting in the United States in 1888, the editor commented:

> A permanent and international organisation has been the outcome of the Washington meeting of this globe's conference of the plain women thereof, and man may now take his pipe and his blankets and make tracks for the wilderness ... Besides equality with man, the temperance movement is the broadest plank of the woman's platform, and she has a whole timber-stack of smaller planks ranging from the abolition of opium to the abolition of war.

'Indeed,' concluded the *Bulletin*, 'abolition of everything is the advanced woman's *raison d'être*, but there is nothing she yearns for the abolition of more than that of her natural rival—man.'[59]

Clearly, if life could not be lived on men's terms, then it did not seem worth living. In the *Bulletin*'s view, one of men's basic rights was the right of sexual access to women and it reserved some of its most vindictive comment for the feminist call for an end to sexual double standards and the espousal of the ideal of chastity or 'purity'. One of the leading exponents of temperance and purity in the colonies was Bessie Harrison Lee and in both the *Bulletin* and the *Bull-Ant* she became a prime target of attack and the subject of derisory front-page cartoons. Bessie Harrison Lee had come to the conclusion that a large part of women's physical and economic suffering was due to men's sexual indulgence. In *Marriage and Heredity* she wrote:

> The sufferings and patient endurance of numbers of women first forced the matter upon me. One in particular was the case of a woman I attended in a critical illness. Her constitution was utterly undermined with the burden and care of a large small family. By the united skill of doctors and nurses she was brought back from the very brink of the grave; but the doctor warned her husband that her life would pay the forfeit of any indiscretion on his part. Three months later our bitter tears fell on the grave of the gentle woman, who had been as surely murdered as any other victim of man's passion.[60]

Bessie Harrison Lee argued that as women were the victims of men's sexual selfishness and often suffered as a consequence the burden of continuous childbearing, men should be inculcated in the virtues of sexual restraint. In a contribution to the 'marriage debate' in the *Herald* in 1888, she advocated birth control ('My advice to those who cannot afford a family is not to have one') and propagated a view of marriage not as prostitution, but as a 'sweet companionship'.[61]

The *Bulletin* pounced, advising readers that 'that well-known champion of "Women's Rights" ', Mrs Harrison-Lee (with a hyphen), had solemnly painted 'a frigid picture of polar moonbeam happiness by marriage according to the tenets of the Abelites'. The letter was such a funny one, according to the *Bulletin*, that it deserved immortality—'as an early specimen of unconscious humour in an Australian woman'. After quoting passages of Lee's letter to the *Herald* which referred to her conception of marriage as a 'union of souls, a sweet companionship, a mutual help and sympathy' this most strident of the masculinist magazines commented:

> After reading this letter over one would naturally ask: 'Why marry at all?' Or, why should not women marry each other, the old maid joined in icy wedlock to the other old maid?
> ...We are told that in Heaven there is neither marriage nor giving in marriage. The cynical man will admit that that would be Heaven indeed.[62]

In subsequent issues, the *Bulletin* made its own contribution to the 'marriage debate'. It linked the rise of feminism with the twin evils of the decline in the birthrate, or 'racial suicide', and the propagation of the doctrine of 'companionate marriage': 'Marriage plays too important a part in the life of the modern civilised man. He is cramped and coffined in on every hand ... He is forced to look to the home, to conventional marriage, for all his character-culture, his higher excitements as an intellectual being, and he finds it bitterly inadequate.' The only marriage worth contemplating, from the *Bulletin*'s point of view, was the libertarian Bohemian marriage of persons 'who do not want too much from each other'. That these marriages allowed freedom to men at the expense of women's utter confinement was not considered. The *Bulletin* concluded that 'the same causes which operate to drive a man into his home, to narrow down his social life, operate also to limit population'.[63] A rise in the birthrate might divert the energies of interfering women and stave off emasculation.

The outcome of this struggle for cultural control between masculinists and feminists involved a complicated set of compromises. Shortage of space permits only the briefest sketch. The first point is that the feminist demands for men's reform coincided with the increasing need of an urbanised, industrialising society for a disciplined, sober and efficient workforce. Women's objectives and those of employers and the state were differently motivated, but they converged and triumphed. A classic instance of this was the introduction of six o'clock closing of hotels in 1916. 'Honest, sober and industrious' became the standard terms of recommendation for the post-war working man.[64]

Secondly, the emergent labour movement, welcomed so effusively by the *Bulletin*, was in fact a bearer of mixed messages for men. While placing great emphasis on mateship, some in the movement argued that women could be mates too—albeit in their different spheres. William Lane, perhaps the most charismatic labour leader of the late 1880s, promoted a style of masculinity the exact opposite of that idealised by the *Bulletin*. For Lane the 'manly' man was straight, temperate and monogamistic. Whereas the *Bulletin* depicted the nomadic bushman in heroic terms, Lane described a pathetic figure deprived of family: 'aged too soon, wifeless and childless, racked with rheumatism'. The New Australia Cooperative Settlement Association promised to 'secure the most complete homelife to its members'. Significantly, one of the major issues to cause disaffection in Paraguay was the refusal of some colonists to abide by Lane's injunctions to temperance, a fact which gave rise to much malicious mirth in the *Bulletin* office. Although Lane left Australia in 1893, his vision of a new society whose economic arrangements would permit men to be sober and responsible breadwinners and women, the 'weary sex', relieved of the necessity to support a family, could be free to care for home and family, was shared by many in the Labor movement.[65]

By the 1920s misogynists were in retreat; the culture had been, to a degree, 'feminised'. Whereas the 1880s and 1890s had been the great years of the men's press in Australia, by the 1920s *Woman's World*, *Everylady's Journal* and *The Woman* were in the ascendant. Masculinity was defined in terms of responsible breadwinning. When Justice Higgins decreed in the Harvester Judgement of 1907 that a man should be paid sufficient to keep a wife and three children in 'frugal comfort', he was locking men into breadwinning just as surely as he was confirming women in dependency. By 1918 Judge Heydon, president of the Board of Trade, was sure that 'A boy knows from birth he will be a breadwinner; that is his lot in life.' Two years later the Royal Commission into the Basic Wage could stigmatise some men's distaste for the national obligations of husbandhood and fatherhood as 'unmanly'. 'Single life' was to be discouraged.[66] A decade later a woman's contempt for a husband who had beaten and humiliated her found expression in the charge that he was not 'man enough to support his wife and little ones'.[67]

In the light of the challenge to men's autonomy and independence which these various developments posed, it is tempting to see the celebration of Australian masculinity under the banner of Anzac as a mythic reparation to 'hobbled' men.

2 The Feminist Legend: A new historicism?
John Docker

> 17. It's not glorious and grand and free to be on the track. Try it.
> 18. A shearing-shed is not what city people picture it to be—if they imagine it at all; it is perhaps the most degrading hell on the face of this earth. Ask any better-class shearer.
> 19. An Australian lake is not a lake; it is either a sheet of brackish water or a patch of dry sand.
> 20. Least said about shanties the better.
> 21. The poetical bushman does not exist; the majority of the men out-back now are from the cities. The real native out-back bushman is narrow-minded, densely ignorant, invulnerably thick-headed. How could he be otherwise?
> —Henry Lawson, 'Some popular Australian mistakes', *Bulletin*, 18 November 1893.

In my *In a Critical Condition* (1984) I tried to highlight a conflict in Australian literary historiography between radical nationalists and New Critics/Leavisites over the character of the 1890s. In the 1950s the radical nationalists, writers, critics and historians like Nettie Palmer, Vance Palmer, A.A. Phillips, Russel Ward, Clem Christesen and Stephen Murray-Smith saw in the ballads, stories and poems of the Nineties, often published in the *Bulletin*, a spirit of social optimism, of egalitarianism and democracy, sharing and collectivity, irreverence and anti-authoritarianism. The New Critics/Leavisites, Vincent Buckley, G.A. Wilkes, Leonie Kramer, H.P. Heseltine, saw in the writing of the Nineties a different spirit, a spirit we recognise from modernism, with its view of history as decline, devolution, crisis, nausea, and its focus on qualities like alienation, disillusion and failure, in relationships, in friendship, in relations with the natural world. Though they were so sharply opposed, I still felt that the radical nationalists and the New Critics/Leavisites shared an underlying philosophy of history. They were equally historicist, and they were both in search of essences and unities, the assumption of a common centre to a culture.[1]

Feminist historians and critics are the latest to put in a bid for an interpretative framework that will encompass the Nineties. The essence of the Nineties, they find, is not modernist gloom and despair, uncertainty, pessimism, ambivalence, but an aggressive and self-confident masculinism. The Nineties then becomes an 'expressive unity', everywhere revealing and expressing this essence. The radical nationalists of the 1950s, whom the New Critics/Leavisites of the 1960s and 1970s were opposing, are resurrected and (like Hegel) turned on their heads by the feminists of the 1980s.

In her essay 'The politics of respectability: Identifying the masculinist context',[2] Marilyn Lake, chief proponent of what I will refer to as the Feminist Legend of the Nineties, offers a striking reworking of Russel Ward's account of the Australian national ethos. In a famous passage at the beginning of *The Australian Legend* (1958), Ward specifies the qualities of the 'typical Australian'. He is rough and ready in his manners and quick to decry affectation. He is a great improviser. He doesn't usually feel any desire to work very hard, except in an emergency. He swears a lot, gambles often, and drinks deeply, at least on occasion. He has a dry laconic leg-pulling humour, though he is usually taciturn rather than talkative. He is stoical. Sceptical. A believer in equality. A knocker of the eminent, except sporting heroes. Fiercely independent, he hates officiousness and authority, as in military officers and the police. Yet he is very hospitable and will stick to his mates. He is a rolling stone, nomadic, by implication untrammelled by family, by women and children.[3]

For Russel Ward and the radical nationalists, such legendary values derived from the lives and consciousness of the outback workers themselves, the upcountry bullockies, drovers, shearers and boundary riders of the 1890s, who became ideal types for the rest of Australians. In this century of suburbanism and consumerism and predominant city existence, their legendary values, forged in a close relationship to Australia's distinctive natural environment, perhaps live on only unconsciously. But such values are always there to be tapped into, so that Australia again could become an ideal totality, a community sharing and unified around the same admirable values.

Marilyn Lake follows Graeme Davison's urban reorientation of the sources of this legend, Davison arguing that it was city writers, particularly those living in alienation and loneliness in boarding houses in Sydney, who looked to the pastoral interior for alternative visions.[4] But Lake has little time or sympathy for romantic and modernist visions of lonely poets and short story writers in shirt-sleeves, leaning out of windows at dusk in narrow streets, longing for wide vistas and outback freedom. To the contrary, Lake believes that such Sydney writers and journalists were confidently engaged in an ongoing city-based gender campaign in the 1890s, inspired by 'masculinism', a militant ideology of dominance.

In these terms, Ward's legendary values were largely the creation of the city bohemian writers and journalists of the Nineties period clustered in Sydney around the *Bulletin*, which was indeed the 'most strident of the masculinist magazines' of the time. These male, male-centred, and male-loving bohemians intensely disliked the Christian and feminist temperance activists of the day, with their idealisation of Domestic Man. The bohemian boys by contrast enjoyed and wanted to hang onto—however much it injured women and children, including their occasional own—their particular masculine ideal, of bachelordom, male camaraderie, smoking, gambling, drinking, and casual predatory sexual encounters idealised to themselves as sexual libertarianism.

These values of their city life they projected onto the Bush, translating male camaraderie as mateship, and a bachelor lifestyle as the bushman's nomadic freedom from family ties. The journalists of the *Bulletin* and writers like Lawson, in thus promoting the bushmen as cultural heroes, were really creating them in their own self-admiring image.

The *Bulletin*'s 'masculinist ideal', says Lake, became 'typical'. It enjoyed 'ascendancy' in the Nineties, deriding and excluding women and feminists as well as the temperance movement in general, though they resisted and fought hard against impossible odds. However, not long after, in the new century, this libertarian masculinism of the male press and male writers suddenly historically lost out. A new vigorous women's journalism grew and spread; temperance had, thankfully, a major victory with the introduction in 1916 of six o'clock closing; and all this coincided with the taming and disciplining of the workforce required by capitalism, with all men apparently becoming sober, responsible, and industrious. How the *Bulletin*'s masculinist ethos, which had stood up so well in the Nineties, could so quickly go limp is, I think, a bit of a puzzle, unless whatever capitalism wants, it gets. But by the 1920s Australian culture had, Lake concludes, been successfully 'feminised'.

To consider Lake's account of the Nineties we need to centre-stage and spotlight the question of historicism. In the last decade debate has raged over New Historicism, a movement that challenged the text-centred formalism pursued in American criticism from the New Critics to the Deconstructionists. Influenced by poststructuralism and especially by Foucault, the New Historicism wishes to see in literary periods (so far they've dwelt largely in Renaissance studies) a play of discourses, discourses that may be discontinuous and fragmented.

But the New Historicists have also been accused, by the American literary theorist Frank Lentricchia, of following another part of Foucault's legacy (as in *Discipline and Punish*), an historicist stress, in a 'totalitarian narrative', on Power as everywhere dominating and controlling.[5] The American feminist historian Judith Lowder Newton argues that in male

New Historicist narratives, Power is conceived as being constituted by 'elite male values' which are presented as typical of the way a culture is constructed as a whole.[6] Yet what Newton accuses male New Historicists of doing is exactly, I think, what Marilyn Lake and the Feminist Legend do.

The Feminist Legend is following the historicist side of Foucault, perceiving the domination everywhere in its chosen historical period of a single Power, masculinism. The elite male values of this Power, produced by those associated with the Sydney *Bulletin*, are then presented as typical of the way culture in the Nineties is constructed as a whole.

I would rather stress, in terms of a postmodernist philosophy of discordant patterns, the presence of heterogeneity as well as unifying forces, the centrifugal as well as the centripetal, discontinuity as well as continuity, disorder as well as order. Attitudes and values in the Nineties, including the constitution of subjectivity and cultural identity, could be multiple, inconsistent, conflicting, uncertain, contradictory.

It's questions, enigmas, puzzles time

In cultural studies, historicism is frequently allied with structuralism, the reduction of a society or culture or text to a single structure, or single opposition. For Lake the 'legendary Bushman's ethos' is the '*Bulletin*'s message', its single meaning.

If any suspicion of contradiction strays into the sights of the Feminist Legend, it is minimised or dismissed. Lake notes, for example, that William Lane, journalist, writer, utopian socialist, was perhaps the most charismatic labour leader of the late 1880s, and that he promoted a style of masculinity, emphasising temperance, man's need of wife and children, and monogamy, that was the exact opposite of that idealised by the *Bulletin*. But, Lake suggests, Lane's alternative vision and the labour movement for which he spoke was only an 'emergent' force in the Nineties, apparently only flowering in the 1920s, when Australian society had a new centre, an 'ascendant' female-influenced culture.

This seems very odd. Lane and the labour movement only 'emergent' in the Nineties? Surely he and it were major forces in the period. Lane's pro-feminist *The Workingman's Paradise* was published in 1892. He was a prominent journalist into the early 1890s, including writing a column in the Brisbane *Worker* under the pseudonym of Lucinda Sharpe, campaigning for the rights of women. He was prominent in the arguments and debates that raged in labour and socialist circles and publications. He helped form The New Australia Cooperative Settlement Association, many of whose members sailed off, with Lane, in 1893 to Paraguay to establish a utopian socialist colony, a decisive step which helped focus the attention of Australian society on millennarial desires, and was keenly debated, for and against, throughout the decade, particularly after reports of splits, difficulties and disillusionment came filtering back. William Lane not in the very thick of Nineties arguments and clashes of ideas, values, visions? Surely such a peculiar claim is forced on Lake by her historicist search for the one single dominant force in a period.

Curiously, the Feminist Legend ignores the body of interpretation and commentary on the Nineties by the New Critics and Leavisites, who were institutionally powerful in the 1960s and 1970s, and who suggested, like Manning Clark in his *In Search of Henry Lawson,* that the Bushman in the 1890s was *not* an idealised figure, was not eulogised, not celebrated, not heroised.[7]

In their modernist way the New Critics/Leavisites were easily able to point to Nineties writing that suggested that for the Bushman, as well as for Bushwomen, outback life was frequently a site of harshness, misery, loneliness, solitude, violence, terror; of lack of mateship, of uncaring and betrayal. My complaint against the New Critics/Leavisites in *In a Critical Condition* was not that such attitudes in Nineties writing didn't amply exist, but that they wished to say they were the only attitudes worth considering: they were being essentialist, historicist, just like the radical nationalists, just like the Feminist Legend.

Clearly, it is now necessary to restate the New Critical point that in much Nineties writing the Bushman was simply not heroised. Nineties masculinism, says Lake, offered 'eulogies to the Bushman'. Is Barcroft Boake's 'Where the Dead Men Lie' a eulogy to the Bush and women-spurning Bushmen?

> East and backward pale faces turning—
> That's how the dead men lie!
> Gaunt arms stretched with a voiceless yearning—
> That's how the dead men lie!
> Oft in the fragrant hush of nooning
> Hearing again their mothers' crooning,
> Wrapt for aye in a dreamful swooning—
> That's how the dead men lie!

Published in the *Bulletin* in 1891, the poem associates bush life with the bleak and despairing. Boake himself suicided in the following year.

The Nineties nationalist school of writers, says Lake, 'represented the pastoral workers as cultural heroes'. This can hardly be said of famous Henry Lawson fiction like 'Hungerford' (1893), a sketch of a desolate outback town on the New South Wales–Queensland border: 'The country looks as though a great ash-heap had been spread out there, and mulga scrub and firewood planted—and neglected. The country looks just as bad for a hundred miles round Hungerford, and beyond that it gets worse—a blasted, barren wilderness that doesn't even howl. If it howled it would be a relief.' The narrator and his mate are a new object of interest in the town; a trooper comes over to see if they represent a disturbance. 'Then he left us, and later on we saw him sitting with the rest of the population on a bench under the hotel verandah. Next morning we rolled up our swags and left Hungerford to the North-West.'

In Lawson's 'The Union Buries its Dead' (1893) a young man dies while swimming some horses across the Darling. It turns out, from his swag, that he belongs to the General Labourers' Union, and that he's a Catholic.

> ...The departed was a 'Roman', and the majority of the town were otherwise—but unionism is stronger than creed. Drink, however, is stronger than unionism; and, when the hearse presently arrived, more than two-thirds of the funeral were unable to follow. They were too drunk.

All are strangers to the corpse, who turns out to have been using an assumed name. A drover drops into line for a while, but drops out when he sees a friend on a pub verandah. Various drunks perform a grotesque pantomime of attempted respect. All is heat and dust. The priest is perfunctory and a publican, a pillar of the local church, turns the event into farce by holding the priest's straw hat throughout some two inches above his head.

In 'The Union Buries its Dead' the narrator refers ironically to idealised portraits of bush funerals:

> I have left out the wattle—because it wasn't there. I have also neglected to mention the heart-broken old mate, with his grizzled head bowed and great pearly drops streaming down his rugged cheeks. He was absent—he was probably 'Out Back'. For similar reasons I have omitted reference to the suspicious moisture in the eyes of a bearded bush ruffian named Bill. Bill failed to turn up, and the only moisture was that which was induced by the heat. I have left out the 'sad Australian sunset' because the sun was not going down at the time. The burial took place exactly at mid-day.

During the early 1890s Lawson was engaged in what became known as The *Bulletin* Debate, with A.B. Paterson, precisely over the issue of idealising the Australian Bush.[8] In 'Up the Country', Lawson's first shot, the narrator says he's glad he's back in town, drinking beer and lemon squashes, for in the outback, instead of the 'pleasant scenes of which our poets boast', you find a land where, while their drover husbands are away, gaunt and haggard women live alone and work like men, and the ever-maddening flies are fiercer than the plagues of Egypt.

The debate may have been staged at first but it became increasingly sharp, as we can see from our epigraph, Lawson's 'Some Popular Australian Mistakes', a numbered critique of the Banjo's eulogies to the Bush, which concludes with the narrator's plea: 'We wish to Heaven that Australian writers would leave off trying to make a paradise out of the Out Back Hell; if only out of consideration for the poor, hopeless, half-starved wretches who carry swags through it and look in vain for work—and ask in vain for tucker very often.' As if anticipating Marilyn Lake's (and Graeme Davison's) later view, in Lawson's 'The City Bushman' the creation of the bush as arcadia, as idealised heroic male life, is perceived as the work precisely of the romanticising urban poet, object of derision, signpost of contempt.

Given these Lawson writings and his conflict with Paterson, we can now suggest that what Lake identifies as the nationalist 'school' of writers was not at all a school, was not in the least unified. Paterson's eulogising ballads, when they came out in book form in 1895 as *The Man from Snowy River and Other Verses*, sold phenomenally well. But Lawson's books of verse and short stories were also very popular. This suggests that the Nineties was a field of difference, of debate, of continuous argument.

That journal

We don't have to doubt that there was lots of interest in Nineties writing in the rural, the pastoral, the outback, the Never-Never, of various kinds and in various genres, from naturalism and realism to fantasy modes. We can think here of the (itself highly varied) writing of Lawson, the ballads of Paterson, Barbara Baynton's tales of Gothic terror, or the romance-melodrama novels of lost continents in central Australia (the 'Lemurian' literature) that interested Rosa Praed and to which she contributed. The Nineties is a period of great, and often surprising, diversity.

The *Bulletin* and its literary Red Page, while resenting the claims to superiority of what it saw as a parochial English literary establishment centred in London, was interested in a wide range of literatures, French, German, American. A.G. Stephens, Red Page editor, was a lifelong Francophile. He was also fond of the poetry of the Celtic Twilight, as we can see in his review of Roderic Quinn's *The Hidden Tide* (1899), Quinn being one of Lake's despised Sydney Bohemians. Stephens likens Quinn's verse not to the attitudes of a tough Bushman but to the bubbles a child blows, bubbles 'blown by the breath of the Muse into a profound and secret sky whither only inner eye and ear may follow them, and as they rise shining, and singing, singing, singing as they shine'.[9] This is hardly the voice of Bush masculinism. The poetry of the Celtic Twilight was concerned not with the Australian bush but with a hidden realm of the spirit, a realm of Dream attended by sadness and regret because so elusive, so rarely glimpsed, so ever deferred.

The Nineties was notable also for its interest in the urban, in city experience and its values and meanings, and beyond the urban, in things international and cosmopolitan, and even Oriental and exotic. Victor Daley, a key figure in the boy Bohemians' Dawn and Dusk Club, wrote poems like 'The Call of the City' and 'After Sunset' addressing the rival attractions of city and country, coming down on the side of the city as the inescapable Sorceress, as Oriental, mysterious, magical.

J.F. Archibald looms large in Marilyn Lake's gallery of masculinist villains; she excoriates the *Bulletin*'s long-term editor as an 'unhappily married, childless misogynist'. Yet the biographical evidence concerning Archibald is perhaps more intriguing and puzzling than Lake suggests. Archibald's father was an Irish-born policeman, and the son was baptised

John Feltham. But sometime in the 1870s, Archibald, the young journalist, adopted the given names Jules François. He then went about publicly claiming that he was of French and Jewish descent. This claim was believed, associates and writers like A.G. Stephens and A.B. Paterson indeed regarding Archibald as Jewish and therefore to be viewed in their mind as Oriental.[10]

Archibald was, like Stephens, a Francophile, at a time when 'French' signified the cosmopolitan, 'Paris', worldliness, sophistication, urbanity, poetry, the literary life at its most intense and full. But what did Archibald hope being 'Jewish' might signify? If late nineteenth-century colonial society was not free of anti-semitism, and indeed Archibald's own *Bulletin*, in jokes and cartoons, was a contributor to it, why did Archibald publicly seek to be recognised as Semitic? Why wasn't he satisfied with his inherited Irish–Australian identity? Was he trying to suggest that his identity was confused, problematic, contradictory, multifaceted, that in part he was indeed Irish–Australian, in part he was a cultural and even ethnic 'outsider' to Australian society, both French and also a Semite, an Oriental, an alien, not the 'one', but an 'other' or others?

Archibald's interests in the cosmopolitan, the international and the exotic (as in his encouraging Louis Becke to publish in the *Bulletin* stories of the Pacific, stories which quickly became very popular)[11] don't of course mean that his attitudes and influence weren't sexist or masculinist. What such interests do suggest, however, is that Jules François Archibald, Archibald of the *Bulletin*, was very far from being as Marilyn Lake represents him, simple architect of an inturned bush legend.

The *Bulletin*, the *Bulletin*, the *Bulletin*—in according it such centrality, Lake and the Feminist Legend are accepting a 1950s radical nationalist myth that the journal 'equals' the Nineties.[12] But did the *Bulletin* then actually talk about the Bush that much? When I turned over its pages for my own research into the period, I found that its writers and cartoonists really did not devote much time to discussing or glancing at the Bushman. That legendary gentleman simply wasn't a preoccupying interest.

In *The Archibald Paradox* Sylvia Lawson argues that we should recognise the *Bulletin* of the Nineties as an 'open text', as multifaceted and multi-stranded, and as frequently uncertain, trying out attitudes and arguments; Archibald was not the only editor, and the various editors, cartoonists, contributors, presented a carnival clamour of discordant voices about important issues of the period, including gender. It is a little curious that Sylvia Lawson's work has not yet influenced feminist debate on the *Bulletin* as much as it might.

I very much agree with the poststructuralist, anti-historicist approach of *The Archibald Paradox*. The *Bulletin*'s interests were many, varied and contradictory. There was the abundant racism, and there was also dislike of Britain's imperial bullying around the globe and its brutal dispossession of indigenous peoples.[13] There was contempt for the Fat Man, but suspicion of any all-embracing socialist or utopian alternative, *Bulletin* writers being scornful, for example, of William Lane's New Australia colony in Paraguay, as puritanic, authoritarian, and forcing the local people off their land.[14]

Archibald and other writers also took more than a passing interest in a phenomenon that originated far from either littoral or inland Australia, the European Enlightenment. They frequently hoped that its values, of equality, freedom, social justice, rationality, might prevail in New World Australia. But they often felt moved to notice, with irony, sarcasm, scorn, that Britain's legacy of Old World values and structures persisted in colonial society, in entrenched inequalities of class, huge disparities of wealth, and grovelling towards authority and titles, a reverence they did their best to reverse.

Persisting as well was the harshness of inherited British law, which had shown its bloody hand in its treatment of the convicts and continued to show it in the frequent hangings that, in the view of *Bulletin* writers and Archibald in particular, marred Australian history and society. No issue and passion marks *Bulletin* writing more than hatred of hanging, hanging judges, and the death penalty in Australia. Rationality should urgently be introduced into the law, from reducing the despotic power of judges, to providing legal training for JPs.

In terms of the Enlightenment, *Bulletin* writers applied sardonic humour to those forces they felt were hindering men in Australia from being free, equal, and rational, in particular, superstition of any kind, in religion, missionaries, spiritualists, spooks, faddists, and—women. For women, ruled by emotion, instinct, intuition, illogic, were a major enemy of reason and a rational society. Furthermore, in so often accusing men of rape (always unfairly, in the opinion of *Bulletin* writers), women were murderous, because they knew the penalty for rape was hanging. If *Bulletin* writers and cartoonists were so often misogynist, it was because they so often perceived women as antithetical to Enlightenment rationalism.

Enlightenment rationalism was not the single overriding discourse of the *Bulletin*, which could also be interested in the influence on society of differences of climate, or country and city, or race and ethnicity. Even attitudes to women and gender were, as Sylvia Lawson suggests, ambivalent. *Bulletin* writers admired prominent feminists like Louisa Lawson and Catherine Helen Spence, and were attracted and intrigued as well as scornful and ridiculing towards wearers of the new Rational Dress.

> 'Rational Dress' showed up at Melb. Princess's Theatre one night last week in the form of shapely-limbed damsels clad in cycling garb and riding 'bikes' astride. The effect was distinctly pleasing... But the free length of stocking displayed accentuates one fact. The universal knicker will only be a favourite with the possessors of good calves. The owners of pipe-stem extremities below the knee had better stick to the enshrouding skirt, which leaves all to the imagination.[15]

Bulletin writers, cartoonists and contributors were undoubtedly fascinated by such unconventional behaviour. They shouted at and caricatured the New Woman, patronised and corrected her, even sometimes cautiously approved; but they didn't, really, quite know what to think. Sometimes they simply reported or included photos of the extraordinary new doings of women (entering an attorney's office as articled clerk, typing, running the lift in a block of flats, becoming a house-surgeon at the Melbourne Women's Hospital). They kept worrying at what was happening to gender relations. They kept mixing misogyny with ambivalence and uncertainty.[16]

Finally

Doesn't the Feminist Legend involve a slighting of 'first wave' feminism of the Nineties? Women were very much on the move in the 1890s. The era was marked by their growing participation in the workforce and in a wider range of occupations; increased entry into education at all levels, from elementary to university; and by a falling birthrate and low marriage rates.[17] The era also was witness to the smoking, bicycling, Rational Dress and trousers-wearing New Woman, that spectacular cultural figure admired by Miles Franklin.[18]

According to Lake, feminism, which had been so negligible and peripheral in the Nineties, crushed beneath the *Bulletin*'s Bush masculinism, rose from the ashes and triumphed in the new century. Yet feminism flourished in the Nineties, in an explosion of writing by women, in many different forms and genres, from Gothic and romance-melodrama to children's literature; in argument and debate; in the vigour of the suffrage movement, and the achievement of the vote in colony after colony and then in the new Federation. The movement was so robust that it encompassed many differences and orientations, from the suffrage-centred to the socialist-feminist. Contrary to Lake, then, it might rather be the case that feminism, with its rapid political organisation, its respected public figures, its witty journalism as in Louisa Lawson's *The Dawn*, was important and influential in the Nineties' period itself, and that the *Bulletin*'s frequent anti-feminism was a defensive, confused position.

What of cultural representations of women outside of the *Bulletin*, for example, on the popular stage, in music hall, vaudeville, theatre? In her *The Victorian Popular Ballad* J.S. Bratton writes that women in late nineteenth-century British music hall songs and performance presented themselves as active rather than passive participants in events of every kind, as having opinions and powers of their own, and as equal partners in sexual matters.[19] Could it be that women in colonial music hall and vaudeville, drawing on long cultural traditions of World Upside Down, of inversion and reversal, presented themselves in a similarly independent way, or even more robustly?[20] The New Woman, too, might be seen in these terms, as an inversionary figure, extending the cultural tradition (in Natalie

Davis's terms) of 'women on top', woman as signifying the unruly and disorderly.[21]

As I argue in detail elsewhere, when Rolf Boldrewood's *Robbery Under Arms* (1882–1923) was adapted for the popular stage by Dampier and Walch, a key change involved the character of Aileen Marston, who in Boldrewood's novel was but a quiet, timid, fearful, tearful and marginal presence; she despises bushranging, believes her brothers Dick and Jim should work steadily and industriously in life, and in the end consigns herself to a convent. In *Robbery Under Arms* the exuberant melodrama (first performed in 1890), Aileen is transformed. After initially saying she disapproves of bushranging, she quickly reveals herself to be spunky, gutsy, independent, forthright, mischievous, irrepressible. A dashing horse-rider, it's not long before she in effect becomes a member of Starlight's bushranger gang. Indeed, Aileen Marston pretty well steals the show. Her character builds on the vigorous colonial theatre tradition of the currency lass, as well as the stage presence and mythology of Kate Kelly. Aileen is also admired in the play as a Maid Marian figure, not the pale demure Maid of polite culture, but the robust carnivalesque 'woman on top' of popular festive tradition. *Robbery Under Arms* was one of the most successful Australian plays of the Nineties, delighting its urban mass audiences.[22]

One last thing I'd like to stress. Recent historiography has urged that historians be aware of contemporary literary theory. Cultural phenomena like journals and newspapers have to be explored in a textually sensitive way. As Dominick LaCapra argues, drawing on Derrida, we only know history through and as texts and (always, already) the meanings of those texts are multiple, ambiguous, and finally undecidable.[23] In the light of such historiography and theory, Lake's notion and language of a text possessing a single 'message' seems crude and reductive.

3 A redivision of labour: Women and wage regulation in Victoria 1896–1903
Jenny Lee

The decade of the 1890s saw significant changes in the gender and age compositions of the manufacturing labour force. In 1890 males comprised almost three-quarters of the workforce in Victorian registered factories. In 1895 this had slipped to 67 per cent, and by 1900 to 64 per cent. Adult men constituted about 51.9 per cent of the workforce in 1890, 49.5 per cent in 1895 and 47.2 per cent in 1900. Significantly, too, the gain in female employment was entirely among adult women; the female manufacturing workforce was beginning to acquire an air of permanence.[1]

Even before 1890, the subdivision of labour processes and mechanisation of manufacturing had undermined the technical basis for the crafts' skill monopoly, dislodging craftsmen from the pivotal position they had played in manufacturing. The depression of the 1890s exacerbated structural trends that had profound consequences for the organisation of labour. These trends implied persistent unemployment and under-employment among established craftsmen. If the cry after the gold rushes was 'what shall we do with our boys?', that after the collapse of the land boom was 'what shall we do with our men?'[2]

The problem was often blamed on the presence of women in the factories. In 1897 *Tocsin* (18 November) invoked labour's First Commandment—'Thou shalt not scab'—against working women and commented that:

> women are...the most dangerous and the most numerous class of 'free labourers'. And every advance in machinery rendering it possible to do without the acquired experience of trained artisans makes the day come nearer when the men of the community shall be absolutely idle, and their places taken by low-paid and poorly-fed women.

Similarly, at an 1898 boot trade meeting the anarchist 'Chummy' Fleming complained that 'in the "paradise for the working man"...the people who were doing the work were women, girls and helpless children'.[3]

The shifting composition of the manufacturing labour market, coupled with the continuing stagnation of the construction industry, which had been the main alternative avenue of manual employment for men in the cities, had profound implications for the division of labour within the family. Adult male unemployment had reached close to 30 per cent in the early 1890s, and a substantial proportion of those still employed had been working less than a full week; even in the late 1890s adult male unemployment persisted at around ten per cent. There had also been an exodus of men from Melbourne, many leaving their families to fend for themselves.[4]

It became imperative for other family members to find work, even at low wages. Over the decade, the workforce participation rates of boys under twenty increased marginally, and of adult women substantially. But the range of jobs in which women were employed remained narrow. In 1891, almost 82 per cent of the women working in registered factories in Victoria were in the apparel and textile trades, and the figure was still 75 per cent in 1901.[5] The rush of new workers into a very restricted range of jobs, many of them in industries where subcontracting and outwork were endemic, accentuated the downward spiral of wages. By the middle of the decade, female and juvenile wages had fallen to such low levels that three or four other family members had to work to compensate for the loss of an unskilled man's income.[6] There was rising concern that low juvenile wages were acting as the thin end of the wedge for a general lowering of men's wage standards that would erode the family wage and in turn force more married women onto the labour market.

The growth of population and the rise of factory production during the 1880s had placed the craft system under strain, but the following decade saw its wholesale dismemberment in many trades. The crises of the early 1890s had profound repercussions in the manufacturing industry as the demand for capital goods plummeted. The market for consumer goods also slumped; unemployment and under-employment rose, wages were cut and the inflow of immigrants turned into an exodus.[7] Many manufacturing firms closed, and those that survived did so only by implementing substantial reductions in their labour costs. Several of the craft unions fought hard to resist, but they could not hold their membership in a labour market where 'able-bodied men were offering to work for little more than their food'.[8] In any event, they seldom had the support of women, juveniles or machinists, who were increasingly forming the core of the factory workforce.

The 1890s marked a crisis period for craft unionism, with wide ramifications for the industrial working class as a whole. The exclusivism of the craft unions had confirmed the subordinate status of juveniles, women and the unskilled within the labour market, helping to constitute them as a reservoir of cheap labour that could be brought in to dislodge craftsmen wherever the technical basis of the crafts' skill monopoly was undermined by subdivision and mechanisation. Though employment became steadier and earnings less erratic in the later 1890s, prices also rose and the barriers to the re-employment of craftsmen remained high.[9]

With the 1896 Factories and Shops Act, the Victorian legislature took a pioneering step towards wage regulation in manufacturing industry. The new Act established six Wages Boards to cover furniture-making, baking, bootmaking and three branches of the clothing trades. Each Board was to comprise equal numbers of employer and employee representatives under a 'neutral' chairman with a casting vote, and each was equipped with power to specify mandatory minimum wage levels and the proportions of learners to be employed in its trade.

From about 1897 there were signs of a revival of interest in trade unionism.[10] An alliance of Trades Hall and Anti-Sweating League activists mounted a series of campaigns for new Wages Boards. The Wages Board system soon became the centre of a political tug-of-war. On the one hand labour produced a barrage of requests for state intervention in new industries; on the other, employer opposition mounted. Pressure from labour produced legislation to allow Wages Boards to be established on a resolution of either House. The consequent expansion of the Boards from 1900 to mid 1901 was curtailed by stiffening employer opposition from 1901 to 1902. By 1903 the powerful conservative backlash against the Wages Boards led to a substantial reduction in their powers, and the establishment of an Industrial Appeals Court with power to review the Boards' decisions. Little remained of the original vision but a 'tame cat' wage regulation system that Victorian employers could counterpose to the emerging federal arbitration courts.

Yet if men's earnings are taken as an index of labour's gains from the Wages Board system before 1903, it is difficult to explain the vehemence of the employer reaction.[11] A mere handful of highly skilled workers and supervisory hands gained the pre-depression skilled wage standard of 60 shillings a week. Most tradesmen's wage levels ranged between 45s and 50s, with the bootmakers going as low as 36s.[12] Quite commonly the minimum wages set were substantially below the ruling market rates for experienced hands.[13] The primary significance of the early Wages Board determinations, and the roots of the employer backlash, lay not so much in the increases that the Boards prescribed for adult men as in the Boards' attempts to influence the division of labour within the factories.

The agenda labour brought to the Boards represented an attempt to reinstitute some control over entry to the trades by restricting outwork, insisting on direct employment rather than subcontracting as a norm and penalising employers who did not make provision for training their juvenile hands, and to reassert the primacy of men's claims to receive a family wage. How far labour was able to put its agenda into effect was to depend very largely on whether it succeeded in gaining support across class lines, either from dissident employers or from the chairmen of the Boards. The processes of the early Wages Boards therefore shed a considerable amount of light, not only on the internal structure and politics of the working class, but also on the basis of the strategic alliance with sections of the bourgeoisie which was so much a feature of the organised labour movement during this period.

A common thread of many of the Boards' determinations was their tendency to stabilise the division of labour, reclaim jobs for men and put a brake on the helter-skelter mechanisation which, in the boot trade at least, had become so rapid that new machines were being superseded in a matter of a year or two.[14] As the jam manufacturers complained in their protests against the Tinsmiths' Board's decisions, the Board had deliberately set out to

> curtail the use of labour-saving machinery and stamp out female operatives, although as we need not point out, all progress in mechanical arts has had for its incentive the cheapening of production by the substitution of labour-saving machinery, calling for less skill and attention on the part of the operatives.[15]

This was an overstatement. The intention was seldom to prevent labour-saving machinery being used, but rather to exact for workingmen a share in the resultant productivity gains.

The crux of labour's demands was the belief that men should have sufficient wages to allow them to support a family, and sufficient leisure time to permit them (if they so desired) to maintain their presence in the household. The Royal Commission that inquired into the Act in 1900–1 heard many complaints about the effects of long working hours on men's domestic life; one cook, for example, claimed that he had gone for seven consecutive days without seeing his children awake.[16] To secure a family wage and shorter working hours, the unions looked to various mechanisms of labour market closure. The Wages Boards' powers to specify wage levels, limit working hours and restrict the proportions of learners offered almost infinite possibilities in this regard.

Equal pay for women was suggested by labour representatives on at least six Boards before 1903, with varying degrees of success. In each case the circumstances were broadly similar: an operation that had previously been an integral part of a skilled, masculine job had been hived off and mechanised for large-volume production, and women had been brought into direct competition with craftsmen. Though the labour representatives invariably couched their arguments in terms of equity, their clear intention was to exclude women. This strategy gained considerable support from the smaller employers, and resulted in some of the most controversial of the early Wages Board determinations.

The Pastrycooks' Union did not get employer support for its equal pay campaign.[17] The Tinsmiths' Board, on the other hand, was marked by an unusual degree of unanimity: the specialist master tinsmiths, alarmed at the tendency for the jam and biscuit factories to make their own tins with machinery on the premises, supported the institution of a minimum rate of 46s 6d for all hands employed on soldering machines. As this implied that the women and juveniles working the machines should be paid only 1s 6d per week less than experienced tradesmen, it aroused an outraged protest from the jam manufacturers.[18] Likewise, the largest employer in the cigar trade, Jacobs, Hart and Co., had brought in American machinery to allow them to employ women in stripping and booking the leaf. The Cigar Makers' Society and the other employers in the trade combined to set the minimum wage for this work at 40s a week irrespective of gender.[19] A similar coalition on the Brushmakers' Board carried through a determination based entirely on equal pay, fully realising that this would not meet with the approval of the two employers who had recently begun to employ women.[20] Finally, the Clothing Board, which had long been marked by friction between the master tailors and the manufacturers of stock clothing, included in its 1901 determination a provision for equal pay for male and female seam pressers.[21]

The principle of equal or near-equal pay was not only applied to adult women. Although it was a long-standing custom to pay boys rather more than girls,[22] equal pay for male and female learners was prescribed by the Cigar, Confectionery, Jam and Woollen Boards, and in many other trades the rates set for male and female learners were identical for the first three or four years of their employment.[23]

But of far greater significance was the application of equal pay rates in all-male trades. In fact, equal pay was the default position on all the Boards: unless a Board specifically prescribed pay differentials based on gender and age, minimum wages were set for all persons performing a designated function. While in the longer term this may have acted as a barrier to women's employment, its immediate intention was to redefine the boundaries between men's and boys' work.

These moves gained active support from sections of manufacturing capital. The scenario varied from trade to trade. In some cases, as in printing, clothing and furniture, the nucleus of support came initially from established union employers who wished to boost their share of the market. This alliance, broadly along the lines of that envisaged by the Act's liberal proponents, nevertheless proved short-lived; as is clear from the case of the furniture trade, these employers were not prepared to tolerate the use of the Boards to effect significant wage improvements in their own factories, and virtually none actively supported the Boards by 1902–03. A less predictable but more enduring source of support for the employees on the Boards came from small employers at the 'quality' end of their trades who were still using craft methods and feared that they were being left behind by their competitors. Most also catered primarily for a local market, and had long recognised the relationship between high wages and strong domestic demand. Their motivation, however, was not entirely economic: as their evidence to the 1901 Royal Commission attested, many had a strong sense of themselves as initiates to the crafts and shared with the unions a powerful craft culture, whose linchpins were a view of the craft as a lifetime vocation or 'calling', a belief in the moral necessity of workmen receiving a living wage, a devotion to high standards of workmanship and an attachment to an order of workplace relationships in which boys knew their place and women, if they were admitted at all, were segregated into clearly defined, subordinate roles.[24]

Labour's other potential allies on the Boards were the chairmen, several of whom married a belief in the social importance of men receiving living wages with an abiding suspicion of the moral and physical effects of factory employment on women and children.[25] Harrison Ord, the Chief Inspector of Factories, shared many of these values. Ord exerted a considerable influence over the progress of wage regulation, especially in controversial cases. To take two determinations with practically identical effects—those of the Tinsmiths' and Brushmakers' Boards—in the former case Ord opposed the determination on the grounds that it would prejudice intercolonial trade, and the determination was never put into effect; in the latter case, the determination was enforced with Ord's support, the Chief Inspector arguing for women's exclusion on the grounds that 'it would be no great hardship if these girls did have to leave the trade whereas if the men are driven out they and their families will be in the position of highly skilled workmen whose skill has suddenly become useless'.[26]

Such support was clearly sectional: it was support for the claims of working men in the name of support for the working class. Here we have a situation that broadly accords with Heidi Hartmann's argument for the centrality of the family wage in the reconciliation of capitalism and patriarchy.[27] The family wage, backed by 'protective' legislation and, in this case, a thoroughgoing intervention in the division of labour within the factories, represented a bargain struck between male workers and *certain* capitalists (though not, it must be noted, the capitalist class as a whole), with the support of the 'liberal' professional stratum.

Juveniles and women had no such allies, in spite of the histrionics of the anti-sweaters. Nor were there strong unions to monitor the enforcement of Wages Board determinations in the predominantly female trades. The situation was further complicated by the fact that, when women did venture to express an opinion, they were often divided among themselves. In a number of cases where female workers' jobs were threatened, they did protest to the Board in question or to the Chief Inspector. These protests, however, were often instigated by the employers, and little heed was paid to them. On the other hand, there were many women who supported the enforcement of the family wage. In the hat-making trade, for example, the women employed as trimmers and binders joined with the men to oppose the use of juvenile labour. There was an element of altruism in some women's attitudes towards wage regulation. Thus 'Mrs A.', one of the anonymous witnesses to the 1901 Commission, supported the Clothing Board's determination for the sake of the wage increases it gave to other members of her family, even though it is clear from the tenor of her evidence that it had actually reduced her own earnings.[28]

The Wages Boards gave permanency to the segregation of women within the trades and their exclusion from the elite branches.[29] The minimum wages set, though often higher than the rates ruling earlier, were sufficient only for a working woman to support herself, and any hope of women strengthening their industrial bargaining position was neutralised by the generous allowances made for the employment of learners. The plea that large numbers of learners were needed to replace women who left work on marriage, though increasingly at odds with women's actual behaviour, was enough to ensure that more learners were permitted than in male trades.

It was in the clothing trades that the contrast between the impact of state regulation on men's and women's work was most apparent. To begin with, the lowest-paid, all-female dressmaking and millinery trades were only brought under Wages Boards after 1905. Of the sections of the trade that were regulated earlier, underclothing and shirt-making were also preponderantly female. The Boards for both set wage minima at a mere 16s a week for adult women and allowed employers to start young girls at 2s 6d a week. While the Shirt Board did at least restrict the proportions of learners to one for each three adults, the Underclothing Board allowed two learners for each adult hand.

The Underclothing and Shirt Boards also provided for piece-payment. However, the first Underclothing Board reached complete deadlock on the piece-rate scale. When a new Board finally brought down a determination in 1899, it effectively allowed manufacturers to set their own piece-rates. Though the scale adopted was supposed to allow an average hand to earn the 16s minimum wage, the fact that in 1900 the average earnings of adult piece-workers were only 14s 11d suggests that the manufacturers were being less than scrupulous in assessing 'average' production.[30] Furthermore, the fact that the workers were not organised made it easy for manufacturers to breach the Boards' provisions.

By contrast, in the manufacture of men's and boys' clothing, where men still had a strong presence, the main initial thrust of the Wages Board was to centralise production in factories. Here, the large employers and master craftsmen joined with the labour representatives to reduce competition by putting a stop to the multiplication of outworkers. The piece-rates in the clothing trade were raised substantially. Even after one of the master tailors voted with the labour representatives for a 20s rate for women working indoors, manufacturers found it a paying proposition to shift the bulk of their production into factories.[31]

The principal beneficiaries of the Clothing Board's determinations were the craftsmen, both masters and employees. Both stood to gain from the elimination of undercutting by middlemen supplying work to outdoor hands. The master tailors, who already paid their highly skilled hands better than the minimum, faced no higher wage bills, while the male employees consolidated their hold over the best-paid work, secured a limitation on learners and improved their own prospects of earning a steady income.

The gains for the women in the trade are, to say the least, problematic. The outworkers, who alone had no representatives on the Board, were the biggest losers: though nominal rates were increased, the centralisation of production in factories meant that women whose family commitments made it impossible for them to shift to indoor work lost the meagre livelihood they had previously earned. Some retreated to the poorly paid underclothing, shirt and dressmaking trades.[32] Wages for the indoor female hands did rise considerably. The same broad tendency was evident in printing and bootmaking, the two major trades outside textiles in which women were entrenched.

Food processing was the other major area of female employment covered by Wages Boards. Here again, the coverage was only partial: the jam and confectionery trades had Boards, but not the manufacture of grocers' sundries and biscuits.

The food processing trades represented the new face of Victorian industrial capitalism. Their very expansion marked a significant extension of capitalist production into an area in which domestic, non-market production had previously been dominant. Capital in these trades was highly concentrated, and production was strongly export-oriented. The factories were far larger than the Victorian average of about 13 hands per establishment: in 1901, the mean number of employees in confectionery factories was 38, in jam more than 63, in grocers' sundries 22 and in biscuits a high 181.[33]

All these industries had taken subdivision to an extreme, and their methods of production closely resembled modern assembly-line techniques. All employed numerous women and juveniles; the proportion of adult men in the factory workforce in 1901 was 30 per cent in the jam trade, 29 per cent in biscuits and grocers' sundries and 19 per cent in confectionery. Within the factories there was a rigid division of labour along gender lines. Women were very poorly paid: for adult women, average wages ranged from 11s 11d in confectionery to 15s 3d in biscuit-making and grocers' sundries, while the range for adult men was from 32s 10d in jam-making to 36s 7d in biscuit-making.[34]

Though nominally all had unions, there were formidable obstacles to the improvement of wages in these industries. The rigid factory discipline, ruthless victimisation of malcontents, and the lack of any continuity of trade union tradition among the women and juvenile workers prevented the unions from gaining more than a toehold.

Furthermore, a State regulatory apparatus based on trade coverage could only approach these large, diversified companies in a piecemeal manner. And the factory proprietors had organising traditions of their own. In biscuit-making, for example, the leading manufacturers had long maintained a price cartel,[35] and among the manufacturers' ranks were several stalwarts of the increasingly aggressive Victorian Employers' Federation.

The impact of wage regulation on these industries was consequently small. The manufacturers conceded slight pay increases as a result of the Pastrycooks' and Confectioners' determinations, but the Tinsmiths' Board determination was not applied to the jam and biscuit factories. And on the Jam Board, alone of all the Wages Boards, an employee representative defected to vote for a determination which set the minimum for men at 30s and for women at a mere 14s. It was later alleged that the defector was the only employee representative who still had a job after the determination was passed.[36] The Jam and Confectioners' Board determinations were also conspicuous for the complete absence of any restrictions on the employment of juveniles at general work and for the wide differentials they entrenched between male and female rates of pay. In confectionery, for instance, the male labourers' wage of 40s was far ahead of the rate paid adult women for 'best work', which stood at only 17s.

In some industries, higher wage levels and the supersession of piecerates by regular weekly wages spurred employers to experiment with a variety of measures to increase the 'density' of the working day. One of the most common devices was the institution of 'task' work, where the workers were required to meet high production targets before they would be paid the minimum wage. This system was widespread in boot, clothing and furniture factories by the turn of the century.[37] Mechanisation and subdivision also continued apace, one notable feature being the increasing use of electricity as a source of power. As Mary Wyse, a Wages Board representative, described the consequences in the clothing factories, the workwoman 'is not supposed to leave her seat until she leaves off'.[38]

The centralisation of production in factories, and the increasingly rigid work discipline applied, militated against the wider employment of married women. As outworkers, women had at least been able to combine child-rearing and household management with paid labour. To combine household labour with a 48-hour week of factory work, by contrast, imposed an insupportable burden which women with children would undertake only *in extremis*. The dissociation of paid labour from the home not only disadvantaged women who were sole breadwinners, but also reduced the scope for women whose husbands were poorly paid to supplement the family's income by taking work in. In turn, the enforced transience of women in the workforce provided added justification for their continuing segregation into the worst-paid jobs, giving greater permanency to the lines of demarcation that had been codified by the Wages Boards.

The advent of state regulation also had important consequences for the labour movement. It is inconceivable that the trade unions could have managed by industrial action alone to re-establish the boundaries between men's, women's and boys' work as swiftly and decisively as they did with the assistance of the state. The unions' weakness on the ground was highlighted in 1901–03 by their complete inability to mount any resistance to employer victimisation; delegates on at least five of the Boards were sacked by their employers and apparently black-listed, but the unions appear to have been incapable of taking action to have them reinstated.[39]

With their early successes in reclaiming the key sections of the labour process for men and establishing a structure which broadly expressed men's prior claims to a breadwinner's wage, the unions were able to consolidate themselves as vehicles for the expression of workingmen's industrial concerns while retaining much of the exclusivist character of their craft origins. There were other important ramifications for the complexion of the labour movement.

First, the reclaiming of de-skilled industrial work for men rested on a fundamentally arbitrary system of classification and demarcation, which not only entrenched divisions within the workplace but also had to be constantly renegotiated as the reorganisation of the labour process continued, involving the trade unions in constant struggles among themselves and reinforcing their dependence on the state to effect labour market closure.

Secondly, the industrial labour movement's agenda continued to be dominated by the problem of securing a 'fair day's work for a fair day's pay', where the concept of 'fairness' applied was in both cases predicated upon a social division of labour in which men's primary responsibility to their families was expressed, not within the home, but in the capitalist labour market. Within this framework, the labour movement could offer no fundamental challenge to the construction of wage labour as an intensive, exclusive activity that was quite incompatible with the assumption of day-to-day responsibility for the affairs of a household.

At times the division of labour along age and gender lines within the workplace appears to conform so precisely to, and so neatly reinforce, the patterns of authority within the household that it is tempting to take it as preordained, an integral feature of capitalist social relations. To do so, however, is to neglect the active role played by the industrial labour movement and its allies in shaping that division of labour. The developments described here represent only a moment in the continuing process of challenge and reconstruction through which the division of labour within the family has been constituted simultaneously as a buffer against the most obvious forms of capitalist exploitation, a fundamental source of cleavage within the working class and a powerful constraint on oppositional tendencies within the labour movement.

4 'Knocking out a living': Survival strategies and popular protest in the 1890s depression
Bruce Scates

I

Our memory of the 1890s depression is fragmentary. With a few outstanding exceptions, women's plight and protest has eluded the historical narrative; much has been written on the decline of trade unionism and the rise of a labour party; little on a woman's more immediate struggle to clothe and feed a family. Such a history has been largely institutional in its focus; the public rather than the private sphere has been central to its discourse. It is also a history which, as Marilyn Lake has noted, is 'gender blind' in much of its analysis.[1]

This chapter examines the way a family functioned in the absence of a man's wage, evaluating the economic contribution of women and children and exploring the household economy as a whole. Charity was often all that stood between survival and starvation. Women kept this vital lifeline open, negotiating the thin line which divided 'deserving' from 'undeserving' poor. Finally, this chapter will assess the part women played in unemployed resistance. What contribution did women make to the mass mobilisations of the 1890s? Did their involvement challenge or enforce the gender order of the day?

The failure of the male breadwinner has been examined at length elsewhere.[2] Unable to feed their families, many men left them altogether. Men quit the city 'on mere speculation', convinced something would 'turn up' if they walked long enough or far enough. Others were ordered out by charity or government. Assistance was withheld from the families of able-bodied men unwilling to try their luck in the country while relief projects by location and intention forced men onto the land and their dependents onto charity.[3] Daily the benevolent asylums, hospitals and ration depots were besieged by desperate women, 'destitute, homeless, almost demented'.[4]

The help men would send such families varied with every situation. Often they'd left home 'in a mysterious manner', angered by their failure as breadwinners and providers but still unsure of their intentions. In March 1895, Mrs Laird 'and her 4 little children' sought the grudging shelter of Sydney's Benevolent Asylum protesting all the while that her husband 'did not intend to desert her'. Perhaps he didn't. Mobility was a feature of unskilled labour and short-term separation from one's family not at all uncommon. But having left the district it was all too easy to move on, time and distance numbing a man's conscience.[5] In cases like these the search for work was also a flight from responsibility: unemployed men began new lives and new families as far afield as South Africa, New Zealand and Western Australia. For the families they left behind there were no such fresh beginnings. Women waited for months, sometimes years, 'daily expecting a [letter or] remittance'. And at the end of all the waiting lay a bitter resolution. Mrs Meehan's husband 'went away to join some boat', leaving his wife to care for three young children. After months of poverty and charity, she '[gave] up all hope of hearing from her husband'.[6]

Separation, voluntary or otherwise, did not always end in desertion. Charity records of the period are littered with instances of restored breadwinners recalling their families from poverty. But for every success there were many more failures. Men returned 'with nothing but sore feet from the country', complaining the work they found was scarcely enough to sustain them. And men coming home were not always welcome. Between June 1896 and May 1897 Mrs Lindsay's husband left her on no fewer than three occasions. Employed for the most part on government relief schemes, he sent home barely enough to pay the rent, let alone clothe and feed his family. With each return, Mrs Lindsay's assistance was reviewed and reduced accordingly, even though her husband had little hope of finding employment. Men like Lindsay usually stayed to sire another dependent, adding yet another mouth to a mother's misery.[7]

II

The loss of male breadwinners made the family increasingly reliant on the labour of women and children. Throughout the 1880s they had occupied the periphery of the paid economy, working long hours at 'unskilled' jobs for very little pay. Even so, their contribution was crucial to the family's survival. In this 'regime of economic insecurity', meagre earnings 'tipped the balance against destitution for a day, a week, sometimes a year'.[8] The onset of the depression made that balance more precarious still. Many families which turned to charity or pleaded for the remittance of their school fees existed solely on the labour of wife and child. Women took in washing and sewing, struggling to 'knock out a living' with mangle or pin.[9]

Those with space to spare would sometimes take in boarders, others 'went out' as charwomen, offering their services for payment in cash and kind.[10] The streets, like the home, provided income of a sort. Women, 'pitiable' in their appearance, accosted visitors to the city 'till well into the night': many carried 'babies in their arms', pleading with passersby to purchase flowers, matches or soap. Street trade like this was usually 'a disguised form of begging'. Often it was a front for prostitution as well. The most successful flower-seller was usually the prettiest: she made far more by selling her body as well.[11]

Whether her labour was respectable or otherwise a number of factors limited a woman's ability to provide. Women's work, as Jane Lewis has noted, is 'structured' by her family; paid labour has always to be balanced with the unpaid labour of caring for children and home.[12] This was as true of work attempted within the home as of that taken outside. Mrs Somerville, a character from *The Workingman's Paradise,* endured the thankless, 'ceaseless' toil of every outworker. On a 'busy' day she might put in 18 hours at her machine; but her labour was broken and distracted by children and by chores. Mrs Somerville was a seamstress but she was also a mother. All day long a child clung to her breast.[13] What to do with the children was an even greater problem for those who worked 'away'. Lucy Edwards, 'an honest hardworking woman', averaged a pound a week in 1893, just enough to keep a family of five alive. To earn it she left two children in the care of an 'adopted' nine-year-old 'sister' and hurried the others off to school. That same year her youngest son was found 'wandering' the streets of Sydney. He was sent to the 'Vernon', the converted hulk which served as home and prison for 'uncontrollable' boys.[14] Others took their children with them. Charwomen carried babies in their baskets, 'female beggars' kept their families by their side.[15] But the separation of work and home was never easy to assail. Domestic servants were usually employed on the condition they were unencumbered; ironically the 'encumbrance' was sometimes a master's child.[16]

Domestic responsibilities were but one of the many handicaps a female breadwinner faced. Women's work, then as today, was the least 'skilled' and the poorest paid.[17] Most of it was an extension of her (unpaid) labour in the home; male employers did not pay well for washing, cleaning and sewing; such services were extracted without payment from daughters, mothers and wives. Moreover women workers were dispersed and disorganised. Denied the benefits of trade unionism, they were unable to achieve a fair or even a uniform rate of pay.[18] Charring is a typical example. At one pound a week Mrs Edwards was doing well. Mary Graham, a woman of five years experience, averaged six shillings, hardly 'enough' to get by.[19] Indeed most of women's occupations offered at best 'a poor living'. Mrs Kelly, a washerwoman in inner-city Sydney, 'work[ed] all day yet her earnings were barely sufficient to clothe her family and pay the rent'. Mrs Elliot, widow and mother to three dependent children, was cheated by her employers and did not get paid at all.[20] Even when women took on the role of surrogate wives or parents their efforts were poorly rewarded. Mrs Wilcox's boarder brought in 8s; each week she fell short of the 14s rent.[21] Prostitution was probably the only work which paid—but it had its costs as well. Women were exposed to the dangers of male violence, pregnancy and disease: many became addicted to alcohol, some to laudanum and opium as well. Once discovered, these women were outcast from society, labelled 'deviant' by the authorities and denied access to charitable aid. Ironically the one line of work which could provide for their families often meant their families were taken away. James Cronan was sent to the 'Vernon' on 9 February 1891. He had been 'found' by the police a few days earlier, 'play[ing] in the same room' where women 'immorally conducted themselves' with men. His mother protested frantically as Cronan was led away, 'crying he was her baby and should be given back'. Mrs Cronan, too, was forcibly removed from the court.[22]

Prostitution differed from other women's industries in more ways than one: even in the depressed 1890s a prostitute's services were always in demand. In other trades, unemployment and under-employment crippled a woman's capacity to earn. Washerwomen complained of a 'bad run' of work, charwomen that there was not enough cleaning to be found.[23] Their employment prospects were limited by the financial austerity of the times. Domestic help was often cut as once comfortable families struggled to economise. Moreover, more competed for work than ever before. The streets were filled with hawkers of every kind, 'old and young, tainted and untainted', offering goods no one wanted to buy.[24] Washerwomen competed not just with one another but also with the commercial laundries set up by charitable concerns. Perhaps the cruellest irony of the depression is that those who preached the benefits of industry to the poor, now took their means of living away.[25] Newcomers to the trade and young or single parents found the going hardest of all. When Mrs Robert's husband 'went away' she bought herself a mangle, hoping to earn enough to keep herself and her son alive. Every week she struggled to make up the 2s 6d instalments, let alone find the money for rent, clothes and food. The mangle which had promised economic independence proved nothing but a burden: charity alone saved it from being repossessed.[26]

Women's employment prospects were better in the factory than they were in the home. While men were turned away in their hundreds, female vacancies remained. This 'gradual substitution of female for male factory labour' proved profoundly disturbing to contemporaries. 'Factory labour' was thought work unsuited to a woman, it jeopardised their reproductive functions and caused them to 'neglect' their families as well. Even more alarming was the thought that women might 'usurp' men's place as breadwinners and providers; not that men had provided so very well before. Feminist historians have assessed these developments differently. In a recent and influential article, Jenny Lee has argued that the 1890s saw the 'displacement' of men by women and machines.[27] Employers mechanised as a cost-cutting measure, destroying the 'skills' invariably monopolised by men and creating opportunities for women's work in their place. This process was accelerated by protective legislation. Rae Frances' recent study of the boot, clothing and printing trades has suggested, by contrast, that while women's unemployment rate *was* significantly lower than men's, this had much to do with the industries in which they were employed. Boot, clothing and food processing were essential industries and not as hard hit by the depression as engineering or consumer-durable concerns. Growth in these industries had levelled out in the 1880s; come the depression, they had less far to fall. The aggregate number of women workers did increase, but this had more to do with the redefinition of 'factory' by the wages boards (from establishments employing four rather than six workers) than a major shift in the gender division of labour.[28]

Those women who did find work had little chance of usurping the male wage. In the first place their wages were lower, averaging around half that of a man. And while women may not have been turned away from their factories, they frequently worked at half or even quarter time. John Wing, (male) secretary of the (female) Tailoresses Union, estimated that his members earned 12s a week in 1893. Under-employment on this scale was a cost-cutting measure on the part of the employers but it also suggests women's 'hidden' labour in the home. Many agreed to their part-time hours, for supporting a family necessitated other work as well.[29]

Raising revenue was one way of coping with the depression, another was making do with less. In the case of the pawnshop, these two strategies went hand in hand. Regular visits could defer the day that creditor and landlord settled their accounts; a shilling here and there bought both time and the means to make ends meet. Indeed, the pawnshop was essential to the domestic economy of the unemployed: its grudging and careful use gives many insights into the priorities of the poor. First went 'jewellery', crockery and furniture; poverty left no room for sentiment or comfort. Women sold wedding rings to buy boots for their children, homes were 'stripped of everything' simply 'to get bread'. Last to be sold was the mangle or the sewing machine. Some saw in them the promise of future self-reliance, all prized them as a symbol of a family's self-respect.[30] Even the Charity Organisation Society, a society not known for its sympathy for the poor, was moved by the self-denial of many unemployed. Case no. 6248 consisted of a married couple and five children, 'starving in one of the suburbs'.

The officer found them 'late in the evening ... the woman and children lying on the floor with a few old sacks to cover them, no food, and children existing on what they could beg'. Families like this one had sold all they could and huddled together for security and warmth. Often such visitors followed 'their' family to the pawnshop, redeeming the overcoats, blankets and baby clothes the cold, sick and hungry could no longer spare.[31]

Making do with less involved a 'domestic economy' crucial to the survival of the unemployed. Though their work in the home was often devalued, women's skills alone 'meant the difference between subsistence and ... starvation'.[32] Families were sent to scavenge at markets and 'dust tips' or scratched out vegetable gardens in vacant lots and backyards. Women bartered goods with neighbours and begged the charity of relatives and friends. And everything that came into a home was made to go further than ever before. Clothing was patched and repatched, shoes sewn together, even tea leaves dried, strained and dried again.[33] In each case women assumed management of the household economy, negotiating patterns of survival in the absence of a male wage. And in each case they became mistresses of the arithmetic of poverty. Sago was bought in preference to flour: it cost less, was less nutritious but seemed to fill a belly more. Creditors were carefully evaluated, landlord, baker and grocer stretched to the limit of patience or goodwill.[34] Well before these meagre resources were exhausted women went without. Female applicants to the Benevolent Society were often described as 'malnourished' while visitors to the homes of the poor found women 'wasting away'. Women such as these gave what little they had to their children, 'starving themselves in order to feed their [own]'.[35]

Hunger and illness often went together. The homes of the unemployed, one schoolmaster noted, were places of 'much sickness'. Young and old alike caught cold through want of clothing; a poor diet and little of it lowered resistance to disease. The Bingham family in Redfern, Sydney was typical of many. The father, a butcher by trade, 'earned very little', the mother, 'by washing' brought in a little more. On a combined income of around 10s a week they struggled to support a family of six children. One child died of inflammation of the lungs, a complication of influenza. Another contracted pleurisy and 'friends in the country took him away'. A third child was hospitalised with an unspecified complaint; given rates of infant recovery he was unlikely to return.[36]

Shelter, like sustenance, was a daily struggle. Families crowded into cellars, slums and tenements, as many as 30 people sharing a few rooms in Fitzroy.[37] Others camped on the fringes of the inner city, mending torn sheets with canvas and bags.[38] Finally there were those whose only shelter was the street. In March 1893 Annie Lewis and child were admitted to the Benevolent Asylum. Her husband having gone 'up the country', they were easily evicted. Homeless and destitute, they found nowhere else to sleep but the Domain.[39]

Keeping a family together was often as difficult as keeping it alive. The best option was leaving one's children with friends or relatives. Here, as in the American experience, family and kinship networks provided emotional reassurance and physical support. The wider and closer a community or family, the less 'the margin of insecurity' for the poor.[40] But family structures in Australia were not as strong or extensive as they were in the

United States. The fortunate had a mother or aunt or cousin they might call on. Many had none at all.[41] For these the Benevolent Asylum was the next best option. Usually mother and child were admitted together, discharging themselves to the husband as soon as he found work. But other arrangements were not uncommon. With men unable to find work, wives 'took a situation' as servants, surrendering their children to the Asylum. Widowed husbands 'unemployed and unable to provide shelter' traded their paternity for irregular payments to the State Children's Department.[42] Actions such as these were far from individual choices: they were demanded by a labour market in which production and reproduction, earning a living and caring for children were set rigidly apart.

Other alternatives were scarcely choices at all. Infants were found abandoned in doorways, parks and graveyards. Most were wrapped securely, some with a note proclaiming their name. Clearly their discovery was intended: the mothers of such children simply could not afford another mouth to feed.[43] And many mouths were silenced altogether. Throughout the depression the rate of infanticide continued to rise. Parents dropped, knocked, or smothered their bundles, deaths easily excused as accidents in a Coroner's Court.[44] Baby farming was a less painful option, though the end result was often the same. At its best, baby farming offered an extended form of child-care. Children could be boarded out in hard times and reunited with their family when things 'came good'. But such reunions were uncommon. The life cycle of a working-class family meant that many months would pass before a mother could afford to reclaim her infant. By that time it had often perished. Infant mortality rates were alarmingly high in the nineteenth century, and separation from a nursing and watchful mother narrowed the chances of survival even more.[45]

III

For all women the options were few. A small proportion belonged to trade unions but unlike many male societies these made no provision for the relief of unemployed members. And unlike men women could not expect relief work. Clearing scrub and digging ditches were masculine vocations; few suggested that the government find work for women as well. The reasons were ideological as well as economic. In an era of financial austerity, when the state cut back relief projects for failed (male) breadwinners, it was hardly likely to provide work for 'dependents' in their place. So instead of generating employment the state voted funds to charity: it was an appalling mismanagement of relief.[46]

Charity, for its part, constructed an elaborate system of surveillance. Staffed mainly by middle-class women, its principal purpose was to distinguish between the deserving and undeserving poor. Some of these women acted in a spirit of Christian self-sacrifice: others used charity as a means to affirm their social status. All were denied any other outlet for their time, talent and energy.[47] The sexual inequalities of colonial society were faithfully replicated by its charities. While lady volunteers visited the poor, men (for the most part) confined themselves to the tasks of management and patronage. This gender division of labour is best illustrated by the relationship between the Melbourne Ladies Benevolent Society (MLBS) and the Charity Organisation Society (COS). The last was a male-dominated body; its meetings (often presided over by the Governor) given to discussing papers on the condition of the poor. The Ladies, by contrast, were burdened with the task of finding them. Weekly, sometimes daily, their visits took them through the poorest houses and districts, confronting the human debris of the depression. Even then their efforts were undone by male intervention. The COS took it upon itself to investigate 'doubtful' cases: creatures of sentiment, women could not always distinguish between the deserving and undeserving poor.[48]

Charity's primary endeavour was not so much to assist the poor as to remodel patterns of behaviour. Women were required to conform to a stereotype of femininity fashioned in the late nineteenth century: they were to be clean and caring, honest and homely, sober and spiritual. Expectations such as these overrode even the most elementary considerations of a family's survival. In May 1890, Mrs Rumison (unemployed and deserted) was reprimanded for allowing her daughter to work in a factory: relief would be discontinued if she would not find her 'a proper place in service'. That same year Jane Norton was warned 'of the impropriety of allowing a man to reside in her house'. Ironically, taking in a lodger was probably Mrs Norton's last hope of a respectable wage.[49]

Eventually even the most deserving were deserted. As the depression deepened neither the state nor the voluntary agencies it subsidised made adequate provision for the growing number of workless. Ironically, the first casualties in what one historian has called a 'charity crisis' were the principles on which philanthropy was founded.[50] For all the talk of the sanctity of family life, homes were broken up the moment they become economically unviable. Men were sent off to find work, women 'removed to the country' and children surrendered to the asylum.[51] The economies practised by charity were equally drastic. In September 1892, the MLBS resolved that bread alone be given to the workless. A fortnight later, with funds and volunteers exhausted, the society refused to take on any new cases.[52] Sydney's Benevolent Society reached a similar resolution. Relief to the unemployed was cut and cut again; even the sugar ration was reduced. Finally, when the depression was at its deepest the society repudiated all responsibility for the 'unemployed'. Workless men and women were turned away with their families, only to come back again as broken and malnourished men, deserted wives and abandoned children. Only then could their poverty compel assistance.[53]

Compelling assistance was the major concern of unemployed resistance in this period. For all the literature surrounding the 1890s, agitation by the unemployed has received very little attention. And what has been written is overwhelmingly male in its focus. It is men who march on parliamentary buildings, men who form the deputations and men who receive them. Moreover, the men of the Nineties have become what Marilyn Lake has called 'neutered historical constructs': we examine their class, their politics, never their gender.[54] And yet the rhetoric of manhood dominates the discourse of this period, transcending political boundaries. Disappointed by the failure of mass demonstrations, agitators claimed the unemployed had 'lost their manhood': a man would fight for the right to work, a weakling beg bread from charity. Conservatives used much the same language to draw a different conclusion. The distinguishing feature of 'A MAN', one explained, was his steady self-reliance, 'A MAN' did not expect the state to provide for him, let alone his wife and children. Both conceptions of masculinity had one thing in common: the assumption that men alone were breadwinners and providers.[55] 'Leaving wife and little ones with an empty cupboard' was hard enough; harder still was the thought that they were made to manage without them.[56]

The lament of failed breadwinners was the refrain of almost every demonstration. Indeed, some of the most powerful symbols of protest were the symbols of defeated manhood. Men marched with shovels through the streets of Melbourne, declaring not just their willingness to work but also the masculine prerogative to toil. The demonstrations themselves were an attempt to recover the camaraderie of the workplace. A man's waking hours were mostly spent in the company of men: work meant more than wages, it provided a sense of identity, a source of social orientation. In this light the decision to march the streets 'in military formation' was more than a gesture to threaten the authorities. Banded together, men hoped to retrieve a sense of purpose and order.[57]

The pattern of women's protest is very different. Charity was the principal site of their struggle. While men gathered in the streets to demand work from the government, women argued over rations in an equally unrelenting battle to feed their families. Many complained at the size and quality of their orders, demanding oatmeal, tinned milk and other such 'luxuries' for sick and malnourished children. Others cheated charity, refusing to declare what little work they had found and (in one remarkable instance) wheeling 'a double perambulator...full of groceries and meat' from one rations depot to another.[58] Countless were reprimanded for 'discourtesy' or refused to 'have their things inquired into'. The price of such 'insolence' was the cold, hunger and sickness that attended suspension of an order.[59] On occasions such as these women defied the deference and dependency on which philanthropy was founded. Mary Kelly applied for assistance 'under the influence of drink', flouting her improvidence. Another woman tore up her inquiry card and announced that she 'would not be treated like a pauper'.[60]

Outbursts such as these were punished by contemporaries—but are usually ignored altogether by historians. Usually women's activity is seen as incidental to that of their menfolk, an unimportant exception to their political passivity. Contemporaries thought otherwise. In September 1892, Melbourne's police noted the effect three female orators had upon a crowd gathered outside St Paul's Cathedral. Each 'portrayed cases of poverty', indicting the failure of church, state and charity to provide for the needy. Their audience numbered 600 people: at least 50 of these were women. Mass demonstrations attracted even greater gatherings. In May 1892, a procession of Melbourne's wives and mothers marched on the city's parliamentary buildings. Many carried babes in arms, the public and private spheres blurring in their protest. All pleaded for work for their 'husbands and sons', the men on whom these women were ultimately dependent.[61]

Demonstrations like this one recall a rich tradition of women's protest. As early as the eighteenth century mothers had marched their families through the streets, their protest 'a sort of militant extension of women's duties'. This radicalisation of domestic duties was equally apparent in Australia. Women sewed banners and embroidered slogans, turning their domestic skills to the purposes of radical iconography. And then they carried them through the streets, marching alongside men in torchlit procession.[62] Behaviour such as this also echoes what E.P. Thompson has called the 'moral economy' of plebeian demonstration. In pre-industrial societies moral economy was manifest in the bread riot: violence often broke out when the price of bread rose above an affordable level and women (traditionally the arbiters of the domestic economy) played an important role in such protest. A similar moral economy motivated the women of colonial society. All believed their menfolk had a right to work, all knew that when that right was refused they would be the ones to care for broken husbands and hungry children. Protest was a product of their domestic responsibilities.[63] But women's protest was much more than a simple assertion of traditional duties. Domesticity, as Jane Rendell has noted, 'could both limit and broaden horizons', enforcing women's traditional place in the home but challenging accepted notions of passivity and ignorance as well.[64]

Nor is there a simple continuity from one generation of protest to another. The women of nineteenth-century Melbourne demanded work not bread. More importantly, they demanded work for themselves as well as their husbands. In June 1892 a 'female assemblage' numbering more than 400 streamed along Russell Street, 'tapping rather heavily with their umbrellas at the glass windows and doors...of (Melbourne's) Chinese laundries'. Every Chinese person they passed en route was 'loudly groaned at', for their establishments competed with a traditionally female industry.[65] Here we see what Ann Curthoys has called 'the intersection of class, race and gender', each an overlapping determinant of women's oppression. Still more importantly, the incident emphasises the value women placed upon their paid as well as their unpaid labour. It is often assumed that industrialisation brought about a division of home and work, confining women to the care of men and children. Clearly this was not the case, particularly when economic depression eroded the viability of a male breadwinner's earnings. When women protested, then, they did so not just as wives and mothers but also as workers: paid workers on whom their families depended. Their 'economic citizenship' (as John Bohstedt calls it) was crucial to their radicalism. Finally, these women benefited from what Judith Smart has called 'a culture of unionisation'.[66] The bread riot was a spontaneous rebellion; though its participants followed a certain protocol of protest, their ideology was vague and their objectives limited. The same could not be said of the women of nineteenth-century Melbourne. Literate and articulate, many joined the ranks of radical societies. Others loaned their support to an autonomous women's movement. Launching the Brazilian League from the banks of the Yarra, Mrs Brazil claimed it 'would do more [for women] than any [other] society'.[67]

Indeed, as the 1890s progressed it is possible to speak of a feminisation of protest, women's involvement in the unemployed agitation influencing both its pattern and purpose. At first demonstrators marched the well-trodden route from the Yarra Bank to Treasury or Trades Hall to Parliament. But as the movement gained momentum, processions became less predictable. Marchers made 'detours' through depressed inner-city suburbs, partly to confuse police but also to augment their numbers. Tramping from house to house, neighbourhood to neighbourhood, they brought protest home to the community. Women left chores and children to take their place in processions or marched with their young ones beside them.[68] Women also widened the objectives of protest. While men demanded relief work of the government, women took the lead in creating their own employment. Cooperative laundries were established in Sydney and Melbourne. Nurtured by community networks, they rendered aid to hundreds of the workless.[69] The same community ties are evident in the struggle against evictions. In the depressed inner city, entire streets turned out to do battle with the bailiffs. Women played a prominent part in such disturbances, often prompting the crowd to action.[70] And while men asked for work to provide for their families, women devised ways to survive without male breadwinners. In 1894 the Active Service Brigade formed the first of its 'foster families' in Sydney. Part creche, part refuge, the Brigade's barracks offered cheap and collective care for the children of the workless.[71] In every case women's demands were eminently practical in nature: the unemployed agitation was about survival as well as protest.

But perhaps the most important feature of women's protest in this period is the challenge it presents to the focus of contemporary feminist analysis. Elsewhere, I have disputed the view that the labour movement was pre-eminently a defence of male privilege.[72] The point that I want to make here is that women's extraordinary contribution to working-class family survival and political mobilisation, the strength and versatility of their protest, marks the labour movement as an arena in which women also contested stereotypes of femininity in this period, just as they did in other arenas that feminist historians have examined more closely.

5 Reorganising the masculinist context: Conflicting masculinisms in the New South Wales Public Service Bill debates of 1895

Desley Deacon

I

The battle of the sexes is never straightforward. Cross-cutting effects, particularly of class, race and state, cause alliances to shift and concepts of equality, advantage and disadvantage to change and conflict.[1] The perennial problem of getting the battle lines into focus is exacerbated in a transitional period such as the 1890s, when old and new forces came into confrontations that were resolved, often in unforeseen ways, in the following two decades. The 1890s was a period, then, of multiple and contradictory voices, of unresolved arguments and of false leads, a period of masculinist and feminist reorganisation which encompasses Marilyn Lake's misogynist bohemians, Chris McConville's beer-drinking, sexually active city women and Judith Allen's wife-beaters and pack rapists.[2]

The confused character of the 1890s is nowhere more evident than in the controversies over women's work. The debate over the New South Wales Public Service Bill of 1895 is particularly instructive.[3] Clearly intended to further male interests, the Bill was masculinist in a different way from the libertarian misogyny of the *Bulletin* of the 1880s. Although it presaged, and established the machinery for, the technocratic paternalism of the family wage concept two decades later, that concept was foreign to most of the men who debated the Bill, and was far more simplistic than the originators of the Bill ever intended. In examining this debate, therefore, we are able to see a confluence of different concepts of masculinity and femininity and witness the emergence of those concepts that were to prevail in the early twentieth century and the machinery that facilitated their victory over competing voices.

The New South Wales Public Service Act of 1895 was the culmination of many decades of pressure from public servants for uniform and predictable conditions of employment and objective recruitment, promotion and retirement criteria. It came at the end of a period in which political control of the public service was an important part of a patronage system of government. This period was also marked by a system of equality by default whereby women in country and suburban post and telegraph offices enjoyed the same terms and conditions of employment as men, and women were beginning to infiltrate city head offices in a wider range of departments.[4]

The Act was a paradoxical document. On the one hand it was a charter for the merit principle and the abolition of privilege. On the other hand it set formal limits on women's public service employment for the first time in New South Wales. It gave male public servants a high degree of autonomy from political control and allowed them considerable control over their own labour market conditions. At the same time it imposed new controls over women's labour market participation, and established a secure basis for the machinery of state intervention which enabled those controls to be extended to the female population as a whole.

The Bill as it was presented to Parliament contained two clauses concerning women. The first banned *married* women from public service employment. The second gave a proposed Public Service Board wide discretion to facilitate and make regulations for the employment of *single* women. Neither clause accurately reflected the concerns of parliamentarians expressed in the debate on the Bill. The Bill was presented by Premier Reid as a charter for the extension of women's employment opportunities, and this principle was so widely approved for single women that little attention was paid to the actual wording of the clause dealing with that question. Only Tom Bavister, the independent Labor member for Ashfield, noticed that the Board was being granted large and indefinite powers, and urged unsuccessfully that parliament's intentions concerning equal pay for female employees should be clearly specified. The proposed ban on the employment of married women, on the other hand, provoked extensive and heated opposition. The controversy over this ban revealed strong support for a *laissez-faire* attitude to women's work, providing little hint of the tenacity with which the family wage concept and its associated paternalistic ideology were to take hold within a decade.[5]

The right of married women to work was one of the major questions of principle discussed during the Bill's Second Reading debate. Most parliamentarians were shocked by the prohibition against married women. They saw it as a 'barbarous restriction' of women's rights which was out of tune with the meritocratic spirit of the Bill, as well as with custom and progress. E.W. O'Sullivan, the Protectionist member for Queanbeyan and one of the leading supporters of public service reform, put this view clearly:

> Why should we penalise a woman for fulfilling her natural functions? A woman may be a competent postmistress or teacher, but the moment she takes to herself a partner for life she must leave the service. I am surprised that those who stand

up for fair play for women should give their approval to a provision of that character. A woman should not be compelled to leave the service because she gets married any more than a man should be compelled to do so.

O'Sullivan was supported by A.B. Piddington, Free Trade member for Tamworth, and William Lyne, the Protectionist member for Hume. Piddington argued that the prohibition against married women was out of step with the two objects the Bill was designed to achieve—the highest possible efficiency for the civil service and the greatest justice to civil servants and to members of the community who wanted to get into the service. It was also in conflict with the Premier's stated aim of promoting the employment of women through the Bill. 'If the service is in future to be open to women', he asked, 'why should married women be picked out, as if they were some inferior caste of females, to be thrust out of the public service?' What is more, he argued, the requirement that women civil servants give up their positions on marriage was a 'peculiar and almost shocking injustice' which could result in women being tied to bad marriages because of lack of access to the means of economic independence. The important point was not the women's married status but 'that the state shall be faithfully and well served,' and 'of all the instances where the state is, perhaps, more economically, and more thoroughly and happily served, it is precisely the instance where married women are teachers with their husbands'. Lyne joined Piddington in condemning the prohibition as 'an absurdity, a hardship, and a cruelty to women who are willing to provide for their children'. In fact, he argued, 'the married women are those who should be first considered'.

Free Trade members for city electorates, such as Frank Cotton, William McMillan and David Storey, based their arguments against the offending clause on the principles of liberalism. Cotton put the case clearly when he declared that:

> ...to the fullest extent...a woman should have all the rights of citizenship, and I have no sympathy whatever with our barbaric methods of legislation which simply consider a woman as the property of her husband, and, in the legal jargon of our statutes, classify married women with idiots, and lunatics...

The voices in favour of the prohibition against married women were divided as to their reasons. Only Samuel Whiddon and Jacob Garrard, Free Trade members for Sydney–Cook and Sherbrooke, argued at length that women's place was in the home and associated masculinity and femininity with breadwinning and dependence respectively. Garrard, the Minister of Public Instruction, articulated the craft unions' attitude to appropriate sex roles clearly when he expressed contempt for 'so-called men' who live on their wives' salaries and stated flatly that 'when a woman marries she ought to be dependent on her husband'. In a revealing passage he described with repugnance the egalitarian practices in some schools which allowed women to combine work and motherhood:

It is positively indecent sometimes for big boys and girls in our schools to be taught by married women. For months there are on certain occasions exhibitions that ought not to be put before them...We have instances where mothers who are teaching in schools, not only go home during the day and attend to their infants, and thus interrupt their ordinary work, but also have their infants brought to the schools.

Most of the support for the clause was couched in terms of opposition to patronage. This was obviously the main concern of Premier Reid, who seemed to have considered the prohibition on married women seriously for the first time during the debate. Although he was apparently sympathetic to the view that women's place was in the home, he showed no consistent stand on the question beyond some vague commitment to equal opportunity and for the elimination of what he called 'perfect family monopolies'. The question of gender was not central to the argument over patronage, but it could readily be used for political advantage. John McElhone, the Free Trade member for Fitzroy, pushed this advantage further than anyone else in the debate by citing the cases of Sydney Maxted, head of Charitable Institutions, and his wife, Sophia, matron of the State Children's Relief, who, he claimed, together earned about £1000 a year, and Lizzie Ferris and Ellen Cross, post and telegraph mistresses at Waverley and Leichhardt, whose husbands held senior positions in the public service. 'It is an outrage upon public decency that such a thing should be allowed', he argued. 'The sooner these married women are all put out of the service to allow deserving, honest men to take their places the better.'

These lone voices, supported only by a few brief interjections, were quickly silenced. Frank Cotton and William Hughes, the young Labor member for Sydney–Lang, poured scorn on Garrard's 'prurient minded prudery'. Presenting an alternative view of masculinity and femininity, Cotton lauded the gifted, well-trained married woman who attended to her professional duties 'while at the same time wearing the crown of a mother, and occupying what I regard as the highest position of a woman'. As for masculinity, 'if that woman, with all her gifts, were to be thrust out of a school and had to work in a garret...that would be regarded as an outrage on decency and morality, and revolting to one's manhood'.

II

This debate over the employment of married women suggests that there was little parliamentary support for the position articulated in the Bill. The main concerns of most of the Bill's supporters were the abolition of patronage and the provision of equality of opportunity. There was consensus that family favouritism should be eliminated; but at the same time there was agreement that the Bill should provide women with 'fair play in connection with public employment'. 'Fair play' for the dominant voices in this debate meant the recognition that women needed jobs to support themselves and their families, either wholly or partially, and that they had the right to earn their own living, whether married or single, in the same way as men.

The absence in this debate of the shrill libertarian masculinism of the *Bulletin* bohemians is striking. In fact, when we identify the origin of the dominant voice of the debate we find an alternative rural male voice to that of the urban construct, the Lone Hand.[6] William Lyne and E.W. O'Sullivan, two of the most outspoken advocates for 'fair play' for women, were long-term members for country districts, Lyne for Hume and O'Sullivan for Queanbeyan. They were spokesmen for those country men the *Bulletin* writers pictured as misogynist and libertarian, and they drew upon the same set of experiences from which these bush heroes were derived: the breakup of rural families due to the failure of selections, the decline of the rural economy, and government retrenchment of public works.[7]

The countryman's voice expressed in the opinions of Lyne and O'Sullivan showed an infinitely more complex and sympathetic understanding of women's situation in this period of economic and social dislocation than the simplistic masculinism of the *Bulletin*. This understanding was based on several sets of experiences they brought to the debate. First of all they were used to seeing women contributing visibly to the family economy on farms, in schools, in family businesses and in the sort of public service work that was available in every country town, the post office. In the decentralised public service of the period prior to self-government, family patronage had placed the post offices of the 'halfway metropolises' West Maitland, Moreton and Parramatta in the hands of relatively young widows. By 1869 Eliza Daly at West Maitland controlled the largest amount of post office business in New South Wales and earned the highest salary of any official postmaster or postmistress. Relatively untouched by the centralising tendencies of some other departments after self-government, the Post Office continued its system of local and family patronage and its favourable treatment of women until the early 1890s and incorporated those practices into the new Telegraph Department established in the 1860s. Women in post and telegraph positions were paid the same as men, had no formal bar to their career progress, and could continue to work when they married. Mrs Cross and Mrs Ferris, two of McElhone's targets in the Public Service Bill debates, had joined the Post Office as young women in the mid 1870s, had married early in their careers, and were in their forties when they were threatened with dismissal by the Bill.[8]

Lyne and O'Sullivan were aware of the demands of country women such as these for the right to work. They also understood the experience of numerous women in struggling farming families who fled to the city, part of a female 'Push from the Bush' which formed a distinctive strand of the feminist movement in the 1890s. Louisa Lawson was typical of such women. Born near Mudgee in 1848, she married young and her first son,

Henry, was born in a tent on the goldfields in 1867. After some years of nomadic goldfields life Louisa and her husband took up a 40-acre selection in 1873. The farm was, in Henry Lawson's words, 'a miserable little hell'. Unable to support the family on the farm, Lawson's father was away from home on contracting jobs for long periods of time, a common experience in selectors' families, and Louisa ran the farm, supplementing her income by dressmaking and running the local post office. In 1883 she gave up the land and her husband. She took her family to Sydney where she supported herself and the children by running a boarding house and then by journalism, first with the short-lived *Republican* and then with the feminist journal *The Dawn*, which dispensed the sensible advice of the independent country woman for over a decade.[9]

Lyne and O'Sullivan also brought into the public service debates their awareness of the need to extend employment opportunities for young unmarried women, a concern they shared with the urban new middle class. The tradition of family enterprise on farms and small businesses in country towns created expectations that each member of the family should contribute to the family economy. As the population of the country towns grew at the expense of the farming community the number of managers, government employees and journalists without family businesses in which to employ their children increased. Their children and those of the petty bourgeoisie who could not be accommodated in family businesses had to seek work in the paid labour force. To their numbers were added the children of selectors who were failing in large numbers by the 1880s. Lyne's awareness of the problems of his constituency is indicated by his encouragement of the Post and Telegraph Offices to extend employment opportunities for women in the 1880s, and his government's attempt between 1899 to 1901 to implement the provisions of the Public Service Act to facilitate the employment of single women in line with the intentions of the Public Service Bill.[10]

III

If this debate can be taken as an indication, the actual bushman did not share the form of masculinism attributed to him by the *Bulletin* writers. Where then did the masculinism of the Bill come from? After all, it did propose a blanket restriction on the right of married women to hold public service jobs, a right that few parliamentarians, particularly those from country districts, were willing to abrogate. The proposed restriction did not come from the press either. Indeed, the *Sydney Morning Herald* denounced the prohibition against women as 'unjust and absurd'. It did not come from the Royal Commission on the Civil Service, which said nothing about the employment of women in its 1895 report. It appeared not to come from Reid, who showed no commitment to retaining it, except in the watered-down version that was finally passed.

There is considerable evidence that the hidden voice behind the Public Service Bill was that of T.A. Coghlan, Government Statistician, 'éminence grise' of the Reid government, and frequent *Bulletin* contributor. Coghlan later claimed the Public Service Act as his own creation. Certainly its provisions were consistent with his ideas on political economy, and he and his former Public Works colleague Joseph Barling were appointed to the new Public Service Board to oversee its administration.[11]

Coghlan brought a new and particularly effective form of masculinism into the debates on women's place, couched in the rationalism of the professional expert. Representing a powerful new group of public service professionals, many with working-class connections or sympathies, he attempted to work out a 'rational' gender order which protected male jobs without discriminating unduly against single women who 'had' to work. His policies on women's work derived from a carefully articulated set of economic theories which elevated to the status of 'laws' the basic tenets of the craft unionism with which he had grown up in the railway suburb of Redfern. These included the desirability of intervention in the labour market to ensure an adequate wage to the male worker, and the exclusion of groups such as Chinese and partially dependent women from the workforce for that purpose. Where male workers expected and demanded high wages sufficient to keep a family, he argued, the standard of living of the whole community was highest. Competition of married women or partially supported single women for jobs endangered the prosperity of all. Repudiating the concept of a family economy in which every member contributed to the economic welfare of the whole—a concept central to the rural economy of Lyne, O'Sullivan and Louisa Lawson—he advocated instead the family-wage system of the respectable urban working class.

Coghlan's technocratic masculinism derived from his membership of a rising new middle class with a strong stake in the future of the public service that had provided generous opportunities for upward mobility for ambitious working-class boys like himself. In the period of political and economic instability prior to the introduction of the Public Service Bill, the public service had been under considerable attack, and its security was in jeopardy. Applying his labour market theories to the public service, Coghlan drafted a strong Bill which moved control of the public service from politicians to public service leaders. His reforms gave the public service a high degree of stability and protection; they provided conditions of entry favourable to the men of his own class and their allies, the petty bourgeoisie and the working class; and they established the public service as the logical ally of the working class in carrying out economic and social reforms. Coghlan's attempts to regulate women's employment in line with his ideas of a prosperous labour market and proper gender relations were an integral part of this overall plan, and his ability to mobilise the coercive machinery of the state behind his ideas made these attempts particularly effective.

Coghlan's ideas on women's employment differed from the craft union formula in one important way. Craft unionism had no solution to the problem of 'the superfluous women' who did not have, or did not wish for, a husband, father or brother to support them. The failure of many small selectors on the land, the growth of the educated, salaried middle class, and the unaccustomed rate of unemployment and under-employment of the late 1880s and early 1890s had given increased urgency to demands for employment opportunities for such women. The women in question were often the sisters, mothers, widows and daughters of the public servants, journalists, professionals and academics who made up the male half of the expanding urban educated classes of which Coghlan was a leading member. He had, therefore, to find a formula which allowed 'superfluous women' to earn a living without endangering what he saw as the basis of the nation's prosperity, the family wage paid to the male worker.

The Public Service Bill devised by Coghlan attempted to solve this dilemma by barring married women but encouraging the employment of single women. It is apparent from the policies of the Public Service Board while Coghlan was a member from 1896 to 1900 that he intended that single women be employed on equal terms with men, in order to avoid the danger of undercutting men's wages. These policies gave a feminist cast to Coghlan's activities, and Rose Scott regarded Coghlan as an ally, thanking him in 1902 for 'all your kindness ... and sympathy with regard to women'.[12] However, the Act merely recast misogyny in a paternalist mould. Rather than conferring equal treatment on women as a right, it allowed the careful monitoring of female employment by the Board and gave the Board extraordinary powers to treat women as a separate group in ways that were at the Board's discretion to decide. Although Coghlan apparently meant the Act to guarantee single women equal treatment (albeit in the ultimate interests of men), its paternalistic approach actually provided the opportunity for new restrictions to be imposed under the different circumstances of the early twentieth century.[13]

IV

The New South Wales Public Service Act stands at a pivotal point in the history of masculinism, feminism and women's work in Australia, providing echoes and portents of ideas and practices about to be abandoned or to become dominant. The voices of the independent country woman and the country man who championed her rights in the masculine forum of the parliamentary debate were already eclipsed in 1895. Despite the dominance of their point of view in the debate over married women's right to work the clause that was finally passed was a compromise. A married woman could be barred from public employment, but only if her husband was already employed, and then only in a department other than Public Instruction.[14] This partial victory for the country voice proved illusory, however. Ignoring the debate and the revised clause entirely the Public Service Board, of which Coghlan was a member, immediately dismissed married women and terminated their further appointment to clerical and professional positions. This arbitrary administrative act seemed to go unchallenged, even by women's groups whose supporters' jobs were directly involved, and the issue of the rights of married women disappeared completely from public debate.[15]

Elements of Coghlan's voice proved more enduring. His experiment with the equal treatment of single women was swiftly dispensed with as labour and capital set the terms of the debate over work in the new class wars of the early twentieth century.[16] His legacy was instead the ideology of the family wage and a secure public service capable of providing the machinery to institutionalise that ideology. Roughly formulated in 1905 as a wage enabling a male worker 'to lead a human life, *to marry and bring up a family* and maintain them and himself with, at any rate, some small degree of comfort',[17] this masculinist conception of a just wage had developed by 1930 into a set of prescriptive labour market principles and practices that associated breadwinning with masculinity and made dependence the 'natural' status of women. Embodied in the family-wage decisions of the state Industrial Court and in the regulations and practices of the state personnel system, and disseminated through state resources such as the infant welfare program and reports of the census, this prescription for women's dependence was coercive as well as ideological—in short, the ideological and coercive resources of the state were deployed to construct and uphold this particular view of men's and women's place in the family and the labour market.[18]

V

The Public Service Bill debate of 1895 provides a glimpse into the process of masculinist reorganisation during the 1890s that led to the hegemony of rationalist paternalistic masculinism. During those years the generous understanding of the actual country man was obscured and replaced by the misogynist urban reinterpretation that Lake describes.[19] But at the same time the noisy libertarian vision of the Lone Hand was quietly being transformed into the 'hobbled' male of craft union respectability with the help of the rationality of the professional 'expert' and the state machinery the expert controlled. The debate and its aftermath demonstrate the profound importance of gender as a central category of historical analysis: even when objectivity, rationality and merit are being discussed, the concepts themselves and their practice are inevitably gendered. But the debate also demonstrates that gender is deeply classed. Men have a history as a sex, that is clear; but their interests, and the weapons, resources, strategies and alliances they bring to the advocacy of those interests are transformed, like women's, by their material circumstances.

6 The sexual politics of selling and shopping
Gail Reekie

In October 1891, the London office of David Jones and Company offered Santa Maria Baker, a first hand milliner working with an Old Bond Street establishment, a free passage to work in its Sydney drapery house. Baker was engaged for a period of one year at an annual salary of £156 on condition that she agree, among other things, to 'readily and cheerfully obey all the lawful orders, commands, directions and instructions of the Employers'. By August of the following year, Miss Baker was patently failing to cheerfully obey orders. On her initial inspection of the millinery showroom, Baker told them that she 'felt a little uncomfortable at the prices'. Given the opportunity to manage the showroom during busy periods, Baker, according to partner John Pomeroy, was 'an uncertain quantity' who lacked managerial abilities. Baker's discontent increased with the appointment shortly afterwards of Miss Caroline Suttle as manageress of the millinery department at a salary of £200 a year. Baker, disappointed and angry at not being given the position of manageress of the millinery showroom, failed to execute Suttle's designs on the grounds that she considered Suttle's taste 'vile'. She proudly reported to one of the partners that she had not made a single hat since her arrival in the millinery department five months earlier. The partners decided that Baker had to go. Agreeing to resign only on condition that she be paid two months salary, the milliner calmly informed her bemused employers that she was an accomplished artist and intended to continue her career in the colony by giving painting lessons. William Newman remarked ruefully to Edward Lloyd Jones that the Sydney partners 'feel inclined to think that in some way this young lady has imposed upon us ... We feel quite in a dilemma about the case but have no doubt about the prudence of letting her go'.[1]

Santa Maria Baker's use of David Jones as a stepping stone towards an independent career in the colonies and her refusal to submit to the paternalism characteristic of nineteenth-century retail employment provides a good example of the tensions and negotiations worked out between men and women in the 1890s drapery store. The large Australian drapery houses of this period (also known as emporia or universal providers and, by the 1920s, department stores) were cultural institutions and social spaces populated largely by women but controlled exclusively by men.[2] Clothing manufacture, shopping and selling were characteristically female activities. Eugenie McNeil recollected:

> We always visited the Civil Service [Stores] in Pitt Street, walked under Farmer's arcades and crossed from Waters' on the corner of King Street to look at the windows of David Jones' only store further down in George Street. Stores were of course open on Friday nights and there was always a pleasant air of festivity about shopping then. Salesgirls were deferential and a shopwalker in frock coat and striped trousers would hurry forward with chairs, to see we were receiving every courtesy and to reprimand the girl if her attention happened to wander for a moment.[3]

The big city stores generally increased women's opportunities for respectable paid work and improved the conditions under which they conducted the unpaid labour of shopping. In pursuing the pleasures and possibilities of the culture of consumption, however, women encountered opposition from men anxious to preserve what they considered to be masculine territory. The stores became significant sites of contestation and negotiation between women and men.

This analysis of retailing in the 1890s focuses on the opposing interests of women and men and their struggle for control over the emergent culture of consumption. Susan Porter Benson has shown how the American department store accommodated the distinct and frequently opposed cultures of saleswomen, customers and managers, each attempting to protect their interests and defend their rights and privileges.[4] These occupation-based categories, while usefully illuminating class divisions within the category 'women', tend to obscure a broader division by sex which sometimes cut across class lines. The drapery store, I argue, brought together women of different classes (shop assistants, tailoresses, customers and feminists) and men of different classes (male employees, proprietors and store managers) in projects specific to their sex.

Using Sydney as a case study, this chapter examines the sexual politics of selling and shopping by detailing patterns of conflict and negotiation between women and men as distinctly sexed categories. Marilyn Lake has argued that this period was remarkable for its sexual antagonism. Men's traditional misogyny took a new form as egalitarianist socialist leaders and bohemian writers articulated and promoted a masculinist ideology and lifestyle based on an emphatic rejection of values associated with conjugality, domesticity, femininity and feminism.[5] This masculinism was not restricted to those men who extolled the virtues of the working man, as Judith Allen suggests in her contribution to the debate. Members of parliament also resisted feminists' attempts to place legislative constraints on forms of masculine behaviour that were damaging to women and children.[6] The work of these feminist historians suggests that the ideas and practices of late-nineteenth-century masculinism bonded men of all classes in promoting the rights of men and denying, if not vehemently opposing, those of women. Working women and feminists responded by moving to protect their interests either individually or collectively. Such sexual conflicts and negotiations took place over the counters and in the showrooms and workrooms of the big stores, in the political and legislative arena, in public meetings and early-closing campaigns, and in the women's press of the 1890s.

Sydney's retail industry was transformed between 1880 and 1900 by the rise of the big city stores. Stores such as Anthony Hordern and Sons, David Jones and Farmers began their commercial lives between 1820 and 1880 as specialty drapery establishments selling staple drapery goods such as dresses (that is, dress materials such as tweed, calico, silk and serge); trimmings and haberdashery; manchester; millinery; ready-made mantles (cloaks and outer garments), costumes (skirts and jackets) and men's clothing; women's underwear and corsets; men's mercery (shirts, collars, ties, underwear); boots and ladies' shoes; hosiery, gloves and parasols; and high-class dressmaking and tailoring. These establishments gradually expanded between 1880 and 1900 from small shops into 'universal providers' or 'emporia' selling fancy goods, china and kitchenware, grocery, ironmongery and hardware, leather goods, furniture and furnishings, pharmaceutical products and toys in addition to the staple drapery lines. A second generation of drapery proprietors—Grace Brothers, Mark Foy and Marcus Clark among them—entered the Sydney retail trade as fully fledged universal providers in the 1880s and 1890s.

Store proprietors had, by the 1890s, begun to realise the benefits of rationalising their businesses and adopting more efficient methods of selling to a mass market. Proprietors began to adopt 'scientific' methods of advertising and display utilising the services of 'expert adsmiths', including the extensive use of glass display cases and decorative shop fronts, scenic effects and *'tableaux vivants'*.[7] Increasing attention was paid to the organisation of retail space. As stores expanded, retail firms such as David Jones placed their goods into discrete departments arranged to keep women's goods and men's goods (and hence female and male customers) separate.[8] The cash boy was replaced from the late 1880s by automatic cash delivery systems in which hollow balls or tubes containing money and cash slips were propelled to a central cash desk staffed by women.[9]

Although the depression of the 1890s worried retailers, the larger stores appear to have had the resources and clientele with which to survive its worst effects. Letters sent to the head of David Jones in Sydney from the company's London office suggest that store owners were disturbed by the worsening economic conditions and labour unrest in 1891.[10] Retailers dismissed staff, reduced salaries, and postponed employee welfare provisions such as David Jones' proposed pension schemes.[11] The *Australian Storekeepers' Journal* reported in 1896 that there were several thousand more drapery employees out of employment than there had been in 1891.[12] If employees bore the heaviest burden of the depression, customers benefited from stores selling off stock at 'ridiculously low prices'.[13] Proprietors' anxiety about trade depression was alleviated by the frequent observation that business continued to be brisk and the stores were full of customers.[14] As the *Draper and Warehouseman* observed in 1892, 'Things will have to be very bad indeed...before Australians cease to clothe themselves well and comfortably.'[15]

Most of the major drapery stores were also engaged in the manufacture of clothing: mainly tailoring, dressmaking, millinery, shirts and underclothing. The introduction of steam-powered sewing machines and other technological developments in the late nineteenth century encouraged retail firms to expand their manufacturing activities. Anthony Hordern and Sons' clothing factory, completed in 1898, was reported to be the largest in the colonies, and by 1901 retailers manufactured at least 30 per cent of all the garments they sold.[16] Handmade methods of clothing production in the retail sector, however, continued to share an important role with machine production until the early years of the twentieth century. Tailors, milliners and dressmakers were key personnel in the large drapery stores, commanding status and salaries equal to or higher than those of heads of department or buyers.[17]

These sales and manufacturing workers were increasingly female. Census data and arbitration court records suggest that drapery employment became feminised in the two decades following 1890: women constituted 17 per cent of all Australian drapery employees (that is, sales, manufacturing and clerical workers) in 1891, and had increased their share to over 50 per cent by 1911.[18] The feminisation of retailing was partly attributable to the expansion of the women's departments, especially in the ready-made clothing sections, as a result of the trend towards the mass production of drapery commodities.

As the case of the recalcitrant Santa Maria Baker suggests, this increase in the employment of women caused some tension between male managers and their female employees. David Jones engaged its heads of showrooms, workroom managers, tailors, dressmakers and milliners through its London office. Correspondence with members of the firm in Sydney suggests that the male partners frequently encountered problems with women who appeared to be conscious of their value in a situation of high demand for skilled labour. Several women requested higher salaries, interview expenses, longer engagements, payment for the period of the sea voyage from London to Sydney, and protested salary reductions on the grounds that this contravened the terms of their agreement with the company.[19] It was, according to John Woodward in London, almost impossible to find a dressmaker who combined a 'skilful hand' with 'a pretty face and figure'.[20] Others were reported to be restless, too exacting, hot-tempered, over-confident, offhand, common, talkative, showy, unpunctual, unable to give accurate quotes 'leading to apologies and explanations', and subject to 'misconduct, insubordination or manifest incapacity'.[21]

Friction between male managers and skilled women employees was particularly evident in correspondence concerning problems identified in the millinery department in 1891–92. The millinery department was crucial to the success of the drapery store as 'its productions are perhaps more talked about by ladies than any other goods and we do not like to see it under a cloud'.[22] In July 1891 the head of the showroom was reported to be distracted as a result of her impending marriage and irritated with the head milliner who, she stated, had lost control of the women in her charge, allowing them to produce shoddy work. A number of women (including Santa Maria Baker) were subsequently engaged to run the workroom but proved to be unsuitable. Satisfied finally with Caroline Suttle in the workroom and Miss Crothy in the showroom (who, moreover, worked harmoniously with each other), the firm reluctantly agreed with them that Mr Wilcox, a member of the firm's London office, was sending unsuitable and 'second rate' models to Sydney. Mr Wilcox's colleagues attributed his problems to men's general incapacity to understand women's tastes in hats:

...the Millinery productions of recent seasons are almost outside the comprehension of the masculine mind—they are fantastic vagaries, grotesque and highly fanciful elegancies, with no standard of fashion, style or construction—it is only the feminine mind which can rise to such lofty heights of beauty and nothingness.[23]

The only solution was to appoint a 'lady buyer' to the millinery department in the hope she would be better attuned to customers' needs and tastes.[24]

The problems encountered in David Jones' millinery department suggest the importance that the men of the retail trade attached to understanding a woman's mind in order to retain her custom. Men, according to the *Draper and Warehouseman*, found it difficult to understand women's 'highly strung nervous temperaments' and 'absolute craving for change'.[25] Women customers who never knew what they wanted—'Tabbies'—and 'cranky' shoppers were continual problems for retailers.[26] Retailers were fully conscious of the need to make their goods, services and displays attractive to women, and to ensure that their assistants treated women with gentleness and 'manly civility'.[27] The curtness and incivility displayed by some draper's assistants (the term 'draper's assistant' implies a male employee) to women customers was 'like throwing a stone into the water; for women will talk'.[28] Even the gentlemen of David Jones had 'occasionally to bear the gentle insinuation from a customer that she has not been able to obtain what they [sic] wanted'.[29] Conflict between retailers and customers was perhaps most intense when women refused to pay for goods by leaving accounts unpaid, presenting dishonoured cheques, or shoplifting.[30] As Benson suggests, the managers of the big stores did not get it all their own way. They had to constantly negotiate with and cater to the needs of women.

Less skilled, working-class women workers were as likely to encounter resentment from their male co-workers as they were from management. When male tailors employed by David Jones went on strike in 1891, the company allocated half of its workroom to machine work for trouser making and engaged women to work the sewing machines. The tailors opposed the employment of cheaper female labour, predicting (wrongly) that as soon as the strike was over the women would be dismissed.[31] Women's work, argued Peter Strong of the Tailoresses Union at the 1891 Royal Commission on Strikes, was not as good as the men's because 'they have not the same judgement in building—that is, putting the stuff in the proper places for strength'. Strong implied that women entered the retail tailoring trade out of a misplaced sense of social status: they 'have the idea that putting dresses on and going to a shop is a great deal higher than being in domestic service'.[32]

This tension between male and female tailors resurfaced when women employed by Anthony Hordern and Sons went on strike over the principle of union membership in 1901. The male-dominated Sydney Labour Council refused to support the women's action and recommended a return to work.[33] A similar attempt to exclude women was initiated shortly afterwards by male sales assistants opposed to what they saw as the dangerous feminisation of 'their' industry. This hostility to the incursion of cheap female labour into retailing and, more specifically, to women working in 'men's' departments such as mercery, dresses and hardware emerged into public discourse when the first Shop Assistants' Union was established in 1902.[34]

The wages, hours and working conditions of saleswomen were matters of considerable concern to a number of female reformers in the 1890s. The first female inspectors appointed under the New South Wales Factories and Shops Act of 1896 demonstrated their concern and commitment to ending the exploitation of female shop assistants.[35] In openly criticising male employers on women's behalf, women like Annie Duncan placed themselves explicitly in feminist opposition to the masculinist work culture of the department store. Duncan identified several recurring problems in shop employment. First, she had to insist in a number of shops that separate lavatories be provided for women. She argued that the lack of adequate sanitary conveniences for women had severe consequences for their health, citing the findings of a medical practitioner who attributed a case of anaemia with ovarian congestion to habitual constipation due to the lack of toilets in the workplace.[36] Duncan similarly criticised retailers' refusal to allow shop assistants to make use of the seating provided for them under the Act on the grounds that standing all day long resulted in complaints such as phthisis, pulmonalis and womb troubles, the curtailment of life and vitality, and women's reduced strength in childbirth.[37]

Duncan had a keen eye for male intimidation of women in the workplace. Female shop assistants were too frightened of being dismissed to sit down, and 'many a tired woman would think more than twice before she sat down in the awful presence of the "shop walker" '.[38] She tried to conduct her inspections unaccompanied by the proprietor because she knew how difficult it was for women and youths to speak freely 'with the eye of the employer upon a woman or lad who anticipated dismissal if she or he were suspected of giving evidence against the employer'.[39]

Duncan was critical above all of the extended hours that many women were forced to work. She noted the adverse effects of

> The long hours, the fatigue of always being on their feet, the oppressive atmosphere of gas-lighted, crowded shops, the necessity for constant alertness and civility under great provocation, the shortening of meal hours, the tidying up of stock long after customers have gone, followed by the weary tramp home towards midnight.[40]

The Act left the hours of women over 18 unregulated, and allowed some shopkeepers to use long meal breaks to keep assistants at work from 8 a.m. to 10 p.m.[41] In identifying problems associated with the length of the working day for women shop workers, Annie Duncan was in sympathy with Rose Scott, Eliza Pottie, members of the newly founded New South Wales National Council of Women and other women supporters of the Early Closing Movement.[42] As the Senior Showroom Employees of Grace Brothers impatiently informed Rose Scott in 1897, the provisions of the Factories and Shops Act were a 'farce' and what was needed was an act 'compelling shops to close at six, not an act passed working a certain number of hours weekly'.[43]

Shop employment was frequently likened to a form of 'white slavery', a phrase strategically used by a variety of concerned individuals and organisations to denote the seriousness of the female shop assistant's situation.[44] The 'white slavery' rhetoric had been used by English feminists and feminist supporters since at least the 1820s to describe the general sexual subjugation of women to men and, after 1885 when W.T. Stead published the 'Maiden Tribute of Modern Babylon', the traffic in young girls abducted and coerced into prostitution in particular. The term was adopted by a number of Australian groups (not always feminist) involved in campaigns to eradicate or control prostitution and was still current in the 1890s.[45] Its adoption by the advocates of early closing suggests that they identified women shop assistants' exploitation as sexual as well as economic. Like the innocent girls who were bought and sold in the white slave trade, women employed in shops were assumed to be in moral danger. Some reformers explicitly suggested that late working hours and poor wages tempted shop girls into prostitution. An article by British reformer Margaret Irwin, quoted in the *Woman's Voice* in 1895, concluded:

> We cannot wonder that some of the weaker [shop girls], girls whose whole life is one long despairing struggle with weariness and poverty, should be tempted by the galling spectacle of their sisters attired in silk, bedecked with jewellery, and faring sumptuously, to make a fatal plunge into the social maelstrom.[46]

A Sydney general merchant was probably not alone in believing that shorter hours 'gives young girls less excuse for being out at night'. Feminists, for rather different reasons, fought for workplace legislation that kept young women away from public places at night.[47]

Scott, like Duncan, drew her listeners' attention to the physical effects of long hours on women's health. She reported in a paper read to the National Council of Women in 1898 that female shop assistants suffered from anaemia, dyspepsia and neuroses that could be transmitted to their children.[48] However, Scott was also moved by the effects of poor working conditions on the

> minds, bodies and souls of young girls. I felt, what a farce it was for People to talk the claptrap nonsense of Home being a Woman's Sphere when here, before me, were young women, representing 100s of other young women, whose tired souls could only see life as a treadmill, with sometimes insulting and brutal men as task Masters.[49]

In expressing her concern that shop girls had little time or inclination to think about marriage or home, Scott conformed to the nineteenth-century feminist stress on the social elevation of marriage, domesticity and woman's sphere. More unusual was her recognition that shop assistants were frequently employed for their sexual appeal—'Good Looks, merely to add to the other shop decorations'—in an argument that anticipates twentieth-century feminist critiques of the sexual objectification of women.[50]

Scott's speech also reinforces Annie Duncan's and Eugenie McNeill's criticisms of the 'awful presence of the shop walker'. The shopwalker was a figure of considerable authority in the large stores, responsible for hiring and dismissing staff, directing their work and enforcing discipline in the department. One shop girl referred to the shopwalker as a 'savage monarch' who bullied, abused and insulted sales assistants.[51] Scott revealed that these men used their proprietorial and patriarchal power in 'insulting and brutal' forms. The shopwalker's masculine authority over younger, female subordinates sexualised the power relations between the store management and female shop assistants. The language used by Scott and her contemporaries hints at the possibility that shopwalkers used their power to harass and extract sexual pleasure from their interactions with the saleswomen in their charge.

Although it was common for women shoppers to be blamed for the situation of the female shop assistant, some feminists disagreed. By reportedly demanding that shopkeepers remain open late into the evening, 'thoughtless or ignorant' women were seen by retailers, government officials and members of the Early Closing Movement as responsible for the sweating of the woman shop assistant. Some feminists, however, refused to accept the accusation that women were the principal oppressors of their poor sisters across the counter. In proposing that 'those who got the eight-hour day for themselves should do their shopping in reasonable time', Rose Scott pointed the finger of blame specifically at working-class men.[52] Miss McKenny argued that the lady in search of a bargain after 6 p.m. was 'a creation of fancy not fact', as ladies preferred to shop in daylight. She pointed out that working-class wives had no option but to wait until the children were in bed before doing their shopping, usually late on a Saturday after her husband had been paid.[53]

The comments of Scott and her sister reformers suggest that feminism made a distinctive contribution to the philosophy of the early closing movement of the 1890s. Feminists identified the negative effects on women's bodies and on their ability to enjoy the rewards of womanhood, whether they be cultural, domestic or maternal, of long hours standing behind the counter. In drawing on the imagery of shop work as a form of 'white slavery', feminists effectively suggested that store proprietors created the conditions under which young women might be sexually exploited. They implied, moreover, that retailers and shopwalkers were capable of using their power as men, a power embedded in sexual meanings, to intimidate vulnerable women into submission. Men and masculinist forms of behaviour, rather than the class of 'employers', appear to have been the principal targets of the feminist campaign to defend the female shop assistant. Their action, and particularly the contribution of Rose Scott, was instrumental in the passing of the New South Wales Early Closing Act of 1899.

Rose Scott and the 'new women' of the 1890s were active in another form of critical engagement with the male entrepreneurs of the culture of consumption. Conventional wisdom, shared by retailers, held that women were unable to resist the appeal of fashion and followed it slavishly. The *Australian Storekeepers' Journal*, for example, argued that women considered it their mission to wear beautiful and fashionable clothes, hence the drapery trade's prosperity was largely due to woman's 'innate taste for adorning herself'.[54] Women active in the women's movement and those who contributed to the growing number of women's journals in the 1890s made it clear, however, that they had a distinctively female rationale for buying beautiful clothes and furnishings for the home. It was important, argued *Happy Homes*, for women to demonstrate neatness, order and pride in their dress at home in order to maintain self-respect and fulfil their duty to 'beautify, to ornament the world'.[55] The *Woman's Voice* urged young women to study seriously, preferably at school, the rules of colour and ornament and the art of being well dressed.[56]

Dress was seen by some women as an explicitly political form of female resistance to the sexual order. Defending the love of fashion as one of women's prerogatives, the *Woman* argued that women could utilise fashion as 'one of their most potent weapons to their improvement'.[57] Rose Scott agreed that dress not only served as an important means of defining a woman's character, but asserted that being well dressed gave her 'more influence and power which she can use for good if she so pleases'.[58] The *Woman's Voice* paid some attention to Rational Dress in 1894 and the following year conducted a debate about the 'ethics of dress'. Lady Jephson argued, for example, that the quality of garments was more important than their quantity. Women should 'band together with determination and tenacity of purpose to resist this ever-increasing evil of frightful extravagance in dress'.[59] A second contributor concurred that new women should make a stand against the tyranny of ornament and embellishment, advocating instead an emphasis on good cut and good material.[60]

Louisa Lawson, writing in the *Dawn*, was similarly unimpressed with the excesses of female fashion. She believed that too much female clothing was extravagant, restrictive, and over-embellished with frills and tucks. Critical of 'the masses of lace, feathers, frippery, and even part of deceased fowls, that partly cover, or are skewered to the many female heads' sporting fashionable millinery, Lawson advocated good quality, plain and untrimmed bonnets. Rather than buy a new hat each season, Lawson advised her readers to refurbish last year's old straw hat by trimming it with new wired bows.[61] A clever woman could use remnants, fresh flowers and her own dressmaking skills to make a pretty dress.[62]

While these statements may have indicated a preference for bourgeois standards of respectability in dress, what was more importantly at stake in this feminist journal was the new woman's struggle to win credibility and political effectiveness while maintaining the pleasures of womanhood. Although feminists condemned the frivolous excesses of fashion, rational dressers and 'blue stockings' were also gently criticised for neglecting the 'aesthetics of dress' in their search for a practical, convenient and ethical wardrobe. Cleverness was seen to be no excuse to be 'unkempt, untidy or unbecoming'.[63]

Other new women explicitly charged men with reaping the profits from women's desire for fashionable clothing:

> ...we wear cashmere or serge, or we are puffed up or flattened as it suits the maker of fabrics and Worth to decide. Isn't it comical? Hundreds of women getting into this, or that, or the other extraordinary rig, in order that men may grow rich by trading on their love of novelty.[64]

Rose Scott asked: 'How many animals and birds have died to make our clothes, how many human beings have toiled over the production of them?'[65] The anti-plumage movement, which aimed to stop the killing and torturing of birds and animals whose feathers and skins were used in women's fashionable clothing, had its female supporters in the women's press of the 1890s. Frances Levy of the Society for the Prevention of Cruelty to Animals Women's Branch pleaded with readers of *Woman's Voice* to 'refuse to buy these bloodstained fashions'.[66] Mrs Molyneux Parkes of the National Council of Women pointed out, however, that it was not women who were to blame for the abuse of birds and animals, but 'the men who set the fashions [and] displayed the tempting feathers in shops'. Rose Scott agreed that 'Men controlled the fashions, and owned the shops where they were set'.[67]

Scott was unusually direct in unambiguously naming men as the major beneficiaries and controllers of the fashion industry, of retailing, and of the culture of consumption in the 1890s. To protect both their pecuniary interests and masculine prerogatives, proprietors and managers attempted to ensure that saleswomen were attractive, efficient and accommodating, and that they remained on their feet long into the night. They were anxious, for similar reasons, to encourage women customers to buy as many items of fashionable clothing as their purses would stand. Where the owner's interests lay ultimately in establishing a retail empire as a lasting monument to his business acumen, wealth and prestige, his manager (the great majority of departmental managers and all executive officers were male) needed to exploit women in order to enhance his own career and social position.

The interests of the working-class man associated with the retail trade, on the other hand, centred on the imperative to safeguard his job and hence his masculine status as a breadwinner. What these men of different classes held in common were their efforts to control and regulate women's behaviour in order to maintain a sexual order which enhanced their personal and social power by privileging a masculine vision of the world. Whether they owned, managed or worked in the big stores, men strenuously defended their right to occupy retail spaces and control retailing activities.

However, as this chapter has shown, women demonstrated a range of non-compliant responses to the masculinism of retailing. These responses were positioned along a continuum ranging from individual forms of resistance and negotiation at one end to feminist forms of political activism at the other. Women contested men's control of the retail industry with a range of strategies: by articulating an oppositional ethics of dress that emphasised quality over quantity; by bargaining with their employers; by striking in defiance of a male-dominated Trades and Labour Council; by investigating and publicising the oppressive conditions under which shop assistants worked; and by placing political pressure on employers and members of parliament to improve working conditions and enforce early closing. Women involved in the campaign to improve working conditions for shop assistants, moreover, drew on a range of arguments which had identifiably feminist aims and antecedents.

The conflict between feminists and masculinists which Lake has identified in the male literary establishment and socialist movements of the 1890s clearly had its counterparts in other institutions. In the world of retailing, this sexual politics was not so much a struggle for control over the national culture, as Lake suggests, as a contest between women and men over the effects and implications of an international culture of consumption. Although men and women in Sydney probably gave meanings to their actions largely within a local context, both groups must have been aware of the wider context in which their negotiations were taking place. Working men were part of a worldwide socialist movement, retailers routinely looked to Britain, Europe and especially the United States for knowledge and guidance, and feminists such as Rose Scott were fully conscious of belonging to an international movement dedicated to the advancement of women's rights. It would not be surprising, then, if further feminist research revealed that the contest between masculinism and feminism that Lake located primarily in the 1890s was restricted neither to that period nor to Australia. The interpretive frameworks of 'nation' and national culture increasingly appear to be unequal to the important task of giving women their past.

7 Domestic dilemmas: Representations of servants and employers in the popular press
Paula Hamilton

> We don't so much write *the* meaning of a period as a history of some possible meanings; we study what was able to emerge within, and against, what seems at first glance at least, to be a dominant field of social perception.
> —Dana Polan, *Power and Paranoia*[1]

Opposite the sports page of an 1880s *Bulletin*, there is a cartoon spread across the columns that leaves little space for any text. Titled 'A Domestic Matter', the cartoon consists of a series of vignettes arranged around the large figure of a servant crushing a male and female employer with her foot. Arms crossed, the servant takes up an aggressive stance. She wears a Gaelic cross around her neck. Five smaller scenes depict various domestic episodes in which the servant tyrannises her employers. The way in which this cartoon and its central figure dominate the page make it powerful reading, even to a 1990s reader (figure 7.1).

A few weeks later the cartoonist, Livingston Hopkins, reiterated the cartoon in reverse: this time the central focus was two figures, with the mistress towering in control over the maid and the five vignettes surrounding it depicting instances of employer cruelty. The representation of domestic employment is significantly altered. First, the male employer included in the first cartoon as the object of servant tyranny is absent from the second as the tyrant. Second, the visual impact of the latter drawing is not as striking, because of both the split focus and the smaller stature of the central figures. Third, the less overt racism against the Irish makes it less shocking to a late-twentieth-century viewer (figure 7.2).

These cartoons portray two opposing sides in a domestic struggle; they also delineate the conventions of a discourse about domestic relations and domestic service. They form part of a masculinist representation of the

Fig. 7.1 'A Domestic Matter'.

domestic sphere that emerged in the late nineteenth century in such popular magazines as the *Melbourne Punch* and the *Bulletin*. As such, they constitute a set of dominant images and narratives which in turn helped to shape aspects of domestic experience. Male cartoonists working for the press carried on an imaginary dialogue with readers about the nature of home life, and used relations between servant and employer as the principal vehicle for representing the social unease evident in the domestic sphere.[2]

Traditionally, humour is one of the ways that a society works through problematic areas in the culture. In this case study humour gives social

DOMESTIC DILEMMAS 73

Fig. 7.2 '"Missus"—From Sarah Jane's point of view'.

expression to domestic problems which would not normally surface in public discourse. Referring to Jürgen Habermas's theory, Bommes and Wright note that 'the public sphere recuperates and domesticates social problems, taking up their content and granting them public status, but organising them nevertheless, according to the logic of dominance'.[3] This can also be applied to humour. As a mode of entertainment, humour took several different forms in the late nineteenth-century popular press, including jokes, limericks, stories and humorous poems. Cartoons were a relatively new addition to the repertoire and they tended to be used at first by magazines specialising in satire.[4] During this period the predominant form of the cartoon was the visually illustrated verbal joke. (The illustration on its own or the combination of written text and image was less frequently the source of humour.) As a representational strategy available at the time, cartoons probably had some relationship to contemporary oral culture: they replicated the stories men told each other or women; and they replicated the stories journalists picked up and retold in the papers in ballad form and in short pithy item sections such as 'Pepper and Salt' in the *Bulletin*.

The newspaper cartoon was one of the more recently available discursive forms that men used to satirise aspects of domestic life, along with the political and social events of their day. It was not generally available to women at this time, even in the all-female-produced *Dawn* newspaper. Very few other newspapers or magazines during this period used this form of visual depiction as comprehensively as the *Bulletin* and none commented as extensively on the domestic sphere. There were no cartoons, for example, in the *Sydney Morning Herald* or the *Daily Telegraph* and other papers which did use them, such as the *Lone Hand*, rarely commented on domestic life.

The press at the time carried many articles on servant–mistress relations by employers who were relying on their own experience. This was also the case with many of the cartoonists.[5] Men and women may not have attached the same meanings to these stories, which might have originated within the home but found their way into the press. Penny Russell observes that the diary of a male householder recorded amusement at his wife's fear of servant power, but female employers themselves did not see the joke.[6] It appears that at least some men refused to acknowledge the dimensions of the servant 'problem', though we know from women's writing that middle-class wives constantly defined it as the bane of their lives and the major thorn in the side of a serene domestic life.

However, the persistent images of servant–employer relations within popular media from the period 1880 to 1900 point to the significance of domestic service as a social and cultural institution within colonial society. The publication of cartoons in journals and magazines which attracted readerships that cut across class and gender lines suggest that interest in these issues was not restricted to women and employers. Indeed, it is possible for the *Bulletin*, at least, that cartoonists had different audiences in mind for this humour, or different attitudes to them. An initial reading of the cartoons suggests considerable unresolved tension between servants and their employers. Read metaphorically, these cartoons suggest the lack of ease that characterised the 1890s in class relations, on the one hand, and gender relations, on the other.

Historians have tended to conceive of class relations and conflict as operating in the public sphere. Neither in contemporaneous cultural expression nor in subsequent historical and literary writing have the myth-making possibilities of domestic representation been explored. To many in the 1990s, the prevalence of domestic service is itself a matter of surprise. The focus on the public arena has served to distract attention from the enactment of class relations in domestic life. For many women, children and, indeed, men, the inter-class relations that domestic service set up were the most profound and intimate experiences of class difference. Underlying this lack of attention to class relations in domestic contexts is a failure to theorise adequately about class relations between women. The home was an arena where the mobilisation of class power and interest was played out principally between the servant and her female employer. Yet it is frequently assumed that class conflict, and even class relations generally, lay outside the experience of most women. Kingston does address this issue directly in her recent work, but she argues that class conflict was redefined as deference relations between men and women and concludes that the experience of class conflict was very much muted. 'Deference,' she says, 'was subsumed into the traditional duties and responsibilities of women towards men, seen not for what it was, but as a natural attribute of femininity.'[7]

However, while such representations of domestic servants can be interpreted as expressions of class unease, their meanings are not limited to this question. Such an interpretation tends to privilege class but marginalise issues of gender and lose sight of specifically female working-class subjects: the servants themselves. Therefore, this chapter pursues three avenues of interpretation. It examines the representations of domestic service in terms of the 'servant problem', as it was widely known by the employers. Secondly, it treats the representations as metaphorical expressions of both generalised class unease and the inter-class relations of women in the private sphere. Finally, it suggests ways in which we might explore the use of images of domestic service as metaphors for more generalised gender relations, which were in flux.

'The servant problem'

There is remarkable consistency in the narratives written by nineteenth-century Australian bourgeois women (and less often men) about servants, in both time (for the better part of the century) and place: their stories were similar to others written, for example, in Canada, the United States and South Africa. For most of that period employers defined their relations as a 'problem'. 'The servant problem' was the constant theme of writings in the press, letters, diaries and pamphlets of middle-class women and men, though it was more sharply evident in the period 1880 to 1900, when employers' language suggested very clearly the perceived limits to their power in the domestic sphere.[8] The recurring adjectives in jokes and stories characterise servants as ignorant and incompetent as well as impertinent, insolent and disobedient. In such rhetoric, employers always assumed that servants' unfamiliarity with or ignorance of domestic practices indicated incapability and stupidity. They were also, according to one employer, 'indolent, extravagant and indifferent to employer interests'. The desired characteristics were, conversely, youth, tractability, diligence, respectability and a respectful demeanour.[9]

SHE HAD BEEN CAMPED FOR YEARS.

MISTRESS (*watching new domestic from the back-blocks making the bed and punching it in the middle*): "Why are you digging your fist in like that, Eliza?"

ELIZA: "Making a hole for the hip-bone, mum."

Fig. 7.3 'She had been camped for years'.

Ignorance was, consequently, a recurring theme of cartoons about servants (and one which often characterises unequal power relations between two social groups—see similar cartoons of Aboriginal people in the twentieth century, and contemporary 'ethnic' jokes). Figure 7.3 is set rather unusually in the employer's bedroom, where the servant is making the bed. The viewer's 'complicity' with the employer is implied: the viewer is positioned 'behind' the employer, watching with her as the servant digs her fist into the bed. The caption reads: 'She Had Been Camped for Years'. The cartoon satirises the servant's lack of experience with the urbane domestic practices of her employer. The servant is identified as both a country woman and Irish.

On the same theme, Livingston Hopkins' cartoon (figure 7.4) seems particularly vicious. An Irish servant (revealed by the accent in the caption) is blown up trying to cut corners in her domestic tasks. This cartoon differs slightly in form from the previous one, being more dependent on the visual image rather than the accompanying text. In these representations, stupidity and ignorance are registered on the servants themselves. The considerable number of jokes specifically related to Irishwomen's incompetence with lighting fires may have had some basis in fact: it is possible that since peat was the main source of fuel in Ireland, they lacked experience with wood or coal.[10] Class and ethnic cultural differences between employers and servants were interpreted by employers as clear evidence of servant stupidity. The following limerick complements the cartoon imagery of Irish servant ignorance:

> Our Servant we call Mary Ann
> She came from County Cavan
> But to lessen her toil
> Lit the fire with the oil
> Now we miss her and also the can.
> (*Bulletin*, 26 September 1887)

Absent from this characterisation was any appreciation of employer responsibility for the 'problem'. Later in the century, some counter-narratives, tiny but insistent voices in letters to editors by servants, accused employers of cruelty and harshness, and of assuming total control over time and lives. These voices marked the death of any relationship based on deference (which was being slowly eroded over a long period of time). But the reassessment by social liberals of the nature of the 'problem' was brought about by the growing number of working-class women voting with their feet away from domestic service jobs. Yet liberal reassessment was itself often fundamentally misogynistic: responsibility for the 'problem' was shifted to the 'tyrannising' mistress, with the male household head as mediator. Like Livingston Hopkins' cartoon reversals in figures 1 and 2, men figured in representations as the object of servant tyranny but were never represented as oppressors.

There were a number of reasons for the rejection of domestic service. First, in the large cities at least, considerable residential expansion and suburban building during the 1880s increased demand for servants to service the expanding middle class. At the same time, opportunities for working-class women to take up other kinds of employment were increasing, and more working men became sufficiently prosperous to keep their unmarried daughters at home after leaving school. The decline of assisted migration programs by the end of the century in most states contributed to

Fig. 7.4 'History repeats itself'.

the acute shortage of domestic servants at this time. Thus, while just over half the female work force was employed in some form of domestic service, the actual proportion of women in this occupation had fallen by the end of the century.[11]

Obviously the absence of servants had important ramifications for a number of aspects of home life, particularly the work and responsibilities of bourgeois women (as well as its impact on the lives of working-class women). However, as Faye Dudden notes of the United States, historians

DOMESTIC DILEMMAS 79

have hitherto had little to say about the cultural and social effects of the decline in domestic service.[12] In Australia, the process of reconstituting the 'servantless' bourgeois household had only just begun and was not completed until the 1940s. The cause of the 'problem' continued to be located in the servant, or at most, in the relations between servant and employer. What finds expression in these cartoons is, in fact, employer exasperation

THE SIGN-LANGUAGE.

EUROPEAN LADY (to newly-engaged housemaid): "WHEN I WAVE MY HAND YOU HAVE TO COME."

COLONIAL GIRL: "YES, MUM, AND WHEN I SHAKE MY HEAD, THEN I WON'T COME."

Fig. 7.5 'The sign-language'.

Fig. 7.6 'Biddyism'.

about lack of control over the labour market: demand outstripped supply, notably of young girls. The numbers of unemployed older women registered with government labour bureaus testified to the narrow definition by the bourgeoisie of 'suitable' employees.[13]

Consequently, those women who did remain in service were able to exert marginally greater control over conditions of their employment. The numerous cartoons which had as their theme servant 'insolence' and 'truculence' can be read alternatively in terms of servant negotiation over the conditions of her employment. Almost invariably, these cartoons represented the servant in a symbolically aggressive stance, with arms akimbo, hands on her hips. Sometimes the *Bulletin*'s depiction of this conflict called upon the discourse of egalitarianism to cut across easy reader identification with the mistress. Thus in 'The Sign-Language' (figure 7.5) the 'colonial girl' refuses to defer to her newcomer mistress's imperious manner. The ambiguous nature of the cartoon is signified by the representation of the two figures. Mistress and servant are almost the same height and the servant is the more lightly shaded and attractive. Significantly, the viewer is positioned to take up the servant's 'point of view', gazing with her at the mistress.

From the 1880s, the cartoons played on a fear that domestic servants would follow industrial workers in combining to form unions. The idea of a

DOMESTIC DILEMMAS

OUR "SERVANTS."

LORD OF THE MANOR *(knocking timidly at the door)*: "Oh! **Miss Bridget, please,** here is your coffee. I've lit the fire and laid the table. If you wouldn't mind getting up presently and cooking the breakfast—I'm afraid it's after nine o'clock."

Fig. 7.7 'Our "Servants"'.

servants' union was contemplated with anxious derision. A number of the cartoons, in the *Melbourne Punch* especially, took up the theme of servant negotiation over wages and conditions. Greater servant power was viewed by employers—and the *Melbourne Punch* assumed its cartoon readers *were* employers—as another instance of aggression by unskilled labour. Characteristic of the captions to these cartoons is a reference by the servant to the collective body of domestic workers. Hers, she implies, is not an individual case. Domestic service is mockingly referred to by the *Melbourne Punch* as 'the profession'. In these cartoons, it is usual for the servant to adopt a stance that attempts to exert power over her seated mistress. (See figure 7.6.)

Calls for a servants' union were countered in public debates with the

HE DREW THE LINE.
MRS. POTTS POINT *(to servant)*: "*Mary, I really cannot have that young man of yours about here. People will think he comes after my daughter.*"
MARY: "*You needn't be afraid, mum. My young gentleman is very partickler indeed.*"

Fig. 7.8 'He drew the line'.

threat of a 'mistress union.'[14] Much of the rhetoric of employers was characterised by a strong sense of grievance and moral righteousness, as though the natural order of things had been cruelly reversed. Cartoons depicting the inversion of servant–master relations can be interpreted as responses to this 'disruption' to the natural order. Though inversion or role reversal play was not commonly used by popular press cartoonists in Australia, the device has a long history as a conventional mode of representation for shifts in power relations. Parody, satire and mockery in popular written and visual texts of all kinds used inversion of servant–master relationships particularly at times of threatening social and economic change when bourgeois authority was threatened. Natalie Zemon Davis argues that this form is significant not only as a 'safety valve for conflicts within the system...but it is also part of the conflict over efforts to change the basic distribution of power within society'.[15] The particular cartoon used in this case, however, is unusual. Here the servant is completely absent (behind closed doors) and only the male 'Lord of the Manor' appears (figure 7.7). The cartoon suggests a perception by the cartoonist (also the author of figures 1 and 2) that suffering domestic tyranny by servants was not confined to women, but cut across gender lines. In tyrannising a man, the loss of power and status indicated by the inversion was all the more pointed.

Informing this was an important shift in the nature of the relationship between servants and employers. A wage–labour nexus was replacing the earlier power relations which operated, at least partly, on the basis of deference. (This feudal arrangement, however, was negotiated with difficulty in Australia.) This made the existence of domestic service within the private sphere even more problematic.

The servant's refusal of deference was a refusal of the traditional basis of the relationship in which the mistress operated *in loco parentis*, exercising control over the servant's time and life. This helps to explain one particular motif which was repeated often in representations of domestic life: mistresses' intervention in servants' courting. These cartoons usually depicted a youthful servant, drawn often (but not always) as diminutive in size. The exchange takes place in the employers drawing or lounge room—in 'mistress' space—as though the servant has been summoned. However, many of the captions reflect a deeper fear that the distance separating the two groups can no longer be maintained. In figure 7.8, the cartoonist uses the courting theme to define servant resistance sympathetically.

Class and gender relations in the domestic sphere

By the 1890s, male cartoonists focused on representations that attributed to the mistress two specific anxieties about loss of authority and control within the domestic sphere. On the one hand, servants were perceived to be members of a potentially threatening and inferior class. On the other hand, servants were seen to present sexual competition.

Central to bourgeois perceptions of the working-class servant was the notion of an 'unruly class' that was uncivilised and unrestrained. The live-in employer–employee relationship intensified the experience of difference between class-specific cultural practices, differences which were a source of great tension. Figure 7.9 reproduces an 1880s *Melbourne Punch* cartoon in which the caption makes a joke very much at the servant's expense, revealing her to be 'lacking' in culture. The servant's loyalty to her own community implies disloyalty to the employer: she is 'the viper in the nest'.

A 'APPY DAY.
Mistress.—" WELL, MARY, HOW DID YOU ENJOY YOUR HOLIDAY?"
Mary.—" OH, SPLENDIFEROUS, 'M; I HAD ELEVEN RIDES ON THE MERRY-GO-ROUND, TEN BOTTLES OF GINGER BEER, AND FAINTED TWICE."

Fig. 7.9 'A 'appy day'.

The *Bulletin*, however, sometimes used this tension to expose the hypocrisy of the bourgeois family, and mock the social rituals that involved keeping up appearances.[16]

The visual depiction of the servant was, in general, unflattering. Quite often these cartoons portrayed the servant as unfeminine, ugly, with a large, thick peasant build. She is usually Irish, or at least from a rural background. Irish stereotypes inform the representation of the servant as aggressive, drunken, slovenly and apelike in her degeneracy. Sometimes obvious differences in dress were employed, with the servant either wearing a cap and apron or overdressed and ridiculous in a parody of bourgeois femininity. The mistress's clothing was by contrast more tasteful and more richly detailed, and she was likely to be taller, older, thinner, more finely drawn and darkly shaded than her servant. The space occupied by the servant within the bourgeois household was 'contaminated' by her class-based traits (figure 7.10).

DOMESTIC DILEMMAS

The 'look' of a servant was a central element in the construction of her femininity, and this issue was deeply implicated in the intimate relations in a household. Cartoonists exploited the many ambiguities relating to servant

SLIGHTLY DIFFERENT.

Mrs. Smith *(who has been makin' private enquiries)*: "*I thought you told me you left your last place on account of your religion, Bridget!*"

Bridget: "*I did, mum. I tould them they were miserable prodistants for atin' mate on Fridays!*"

Fig. 7.10 'Slightly different'.

sexuality. The most desirable qualities in a servant—ornamental beauty and hardy youth—were perceived also to constitute a dangerous element in the home. The most frequently sought-after servant was a young single woman, whose youthful, compliant femininity was seen to preserve deferent relations. These were also, however, the women most attractive to the men living in the household, with whom they were forced into a paradoxically intimate but simultaneously distant relationship. In spite of the long tradition of assumed sexual availability of servants for the master of the house or his son, class relations prevented marriage between them. In Australia, the discourse of egalitarianism cuts across traditional class practices, making marriage a possibility for socially ambitious maids. The cartoonists represented this as a dilemma for bourgeois women forced into sexual competition with their servants. For men, however, a servant who

Fig. 7.11 'It might have been'.

was 'too good for her position' could be 'worthy' of his attentions. For example, a satirical poem and illustrative drawing by the cartoonist Binns chides the servant who loses her opportunity through stupidity. (figure 7.11).

Further, there were significant differences in the cartoon portrayal of servants when the theme involved sexuality or marriage. The servants who rivalled their mistresses for the attention of the master were represented as pretty or beautiful, emphasising not their difference from the mistress but

DOMESTIC DILEMMAS 87

Fig. 7.12 'Kitty's Broom'.

their similarity to her. The servant is reclaimed for the (bourgeois) feminine. Such a servant is always young and often idealised as the object of male desire. In 'Kittys Broom', for example, the work of the servant is associated with her capacity to render the world more beautiful because she is herself beautiful (figure 7.12).

When the subject of the cartoon was gender relations, the servant herself was frequently absent, the cartoon depicting an exchange between husband and wife, mother and daughter, or bourgeois woman and friend. The caption reveals the male employers attraction to or liaison with the servant. In figure 7.13, for instance, the guileless young daughter informs her surprised mother that Father has been kissing the new nursemaid. Both husband and maid are implicated in the disloyalty. The point of these cartoons is that the betrayal is visited on the mistress and she is the constant element in the representation. It was rare that the husband and maid were caught out by the wife, although in one such instance, the elderly employer is found by his wife courting the servant (figure 7.14). The man is drawn on his knees pleading with a slightly bemused maid and the caption—'Another Case of Temporary Insanity'—identifies the male employer as the subject of ridicule, which is unusual even for the *Bulletin*.

Other scholars have documented the possible explanations for the acute tension in bourgeois domestic life which emerges during the 1890s.[17]

WHAT WAS SAID YESTERDAY.

MAMMA (to her little daughter): "There, now, I'm busy, run away and play with the old cat."
DAUGHTER: "Why, Mamma, that's just what the new nursemaid said to Pa yesterday when he kissed her."

Fig. 7.13 'What was said yesterday'.

Though the rhetoric of 'separate spheres' was sustained, the basis on which it organised women's domestic experience shifted. The central area of change was the redefining of a bourgeois woman's role from manager to dependent wife and mother—a complex process taking place over several years which involved changes in relationships between children and par-

DOMESTIC DILEMMAS

Fig. 7.14 'Another case of temporary insanity'.

ents as well as in intimate relations between husband and wife. At the same time, there was an easing of the rigidity of the boundaries of each domain. The terms under which men entered the domestic sphere, for example, were being renegotiated and, for bourgeois women, broader educational opportunities and employment meant marginally greater representation in the public sphere.

Although the *Bulletin* cartoonists during the 1880s and 1890s experimented with cartoon conventions in some ways, they rigidly conformed to them in others which limited their representational possibilities on issues of topical interest. This study of the servant 'problem' reveals initially a great deal of dissatisfaction with power relations in the domestic sphere between employers (both male and female) and their servant employees. Metaphorically, these cartoons reinforce the view of other scholars in this collection that there was a deep unease in class relations, and that domestic service was an institution which involved daily and intimate negotiation of those tensions. Beyond this, the cartoons also suggest a specifically masculine concern about the limits and nature of women's power in the domestic sphere, both in terms of domestic responsibilities and in terms of male and female sexual relations.

To return to the first two cartoons: masculine representation of the domestic spheré in the popular press at this time revealed some perception of the tensions there which would have been shared by many, if not most employers, who identified themselves with the class threatened by aggressive servants (figure 7.1). However, the absence of the man from the position of domestic tyranniser in figure 2, leaving only the woman as tyrant, reveals that other representations related to a specifically male viewpoint—men were rarely able to turn the joke on themselves.

8 Sexual labour: Australia 1880–1910
Susan Magarey

The title suggests that my subject is prostitution (sex work) or, perhaps, the gendering of the labour market. It is both. But the principal focus of this chapter is the marriage bed as a site of struggle.

The period I am considering, 1880–1910, has long been a legend in the historiography of colonial Australia. During these years the separate outposts of Britain's empire in Australia welded themselves into a single nation-state. Accelerating, if interrupted, industrialisation and urbanisation brought sharper polarisation of the interests of capital and labour, and the formation of new political parties to contest those interests. At the same time, or so the legend runs—contradictorily—this period saw the birth of a unifying spirit of nationalism, and a sense of national identity focused upon images of wild hop scrub, stringy-bark, and bushmen—droving, shearing, drinking, whoring, writing to their mates with thumbnails dipped in tar.

The legend has, of course, been challenged and revised by successive generations of historians and cultural critics. Most recently, feminist analyses by Marilyn Lake and Judith Allen have pointed out that it has been a particularly masculinist story, one which not only gives centre stage to a select and exclusively masculine drama, but also, by failing to recognise its own sex-specificity, falsely assumes that it is sex-neutral, and universal.[1]

From their perspective (which is shared by several feminist cultural critics),[2] it is possible to depict these three decades as a period of major structural and cultural changes in the relations between women and men. From this perspective, we see an industrial revolution opening up a wider range of opportunities in the labour market for women as well as men, even, for a brief time in the 1890s, giving women some dubious labour market advantages over men.[3] From this perspective, we see, too, a second revolution—the changes that demographers have called 'the Australian fertility transition'—during which the fertility rate of married women dropped by 8 per cent in the 1880s, and then plunged a further 18 per cent in the 1890s, never to return to its former exhausting level.[4]

From this perspective we also see the entire period engaged in contests between feminism and masculinism—over definitions of work, sexual practices, political rights, behaviours deemed feminine and masculine. At their sharpest, such contests show first-wave feminists in public political campaigns—for the vote, for women's access to divorce, for increase in the age of consent, for protection of women and children in industrial workplaces. They also show masculinists marshalling forces against female suffrage, against any change in the double standard of sexual morality, against women's participation in the non-domestic labour market. Such contests were seldom a neat polarisation of women and men: members of both sexes can be found on each side of this political division. Nor did such contests occur often as head-on clashes, or even direct encounters. Rather, march and counter-march, gesture and effacement, assertion and contradiction, crisscross the period.

This feminist lens brings into sharp focus a surprising set of statistics. For the first century of Australia's colonial history (1788–1888), men had outnumbered women in the colonising population; even in 1891 there was an excess of fifteen men for every 100 women. But that figure represents a levelling-out in the disproportion between the sexes that had begun by the 1880s. Accordingly, it could have been expected that a growing proportion of men would marry and form families, making the period one of transition from a frontier society to a largely domestic society. However, while the proportion of men who married did increase in those years, it did not increase nearly as much as could have been expected. And the proportion of women who married plummeted. Between 1891 and 1901 the proportion of women aged between 25 and 29 who did not marry almost doubled, rising to more than 10 per cent in all colonies except Tasmania. In Victoria, in 1901, the proportion of women in this age group who had not married was as high as 51 per cent.[5]

These statistics require more attention and explanation than has so far been accorded them. Explanations for similar phenomena in Britain and the United States have emphasised demographic and economic forces: the so-called 'superfluous women' in Britain, unable to marry because they outnumbered the men available; the combined effects of economic depression and heightened expectations about living standards leading men to postpone marriage in both Britain and North America.[6] In Australia, there were 'superfluous' *men,* not women, but contemporary explanations for women not marrying were still given entirely in terms of 'the great commercial crisis of 1893' and the burden for men of 'supplying the increased requirements of living' and therefore postponing marriage.[7] Demographers have simply echoed these views ever since. One demographer, to be sure, did observe that 'some kind of breakdown of the existing facilities for courtship and marriage' might better explain men's postponement of marriage in the period. He noted, as well, that of the 51 per cent of Victorian women who did not marry in the 1890s, 21 per cent were still unmarried in 1921, when they were between 45 and 49 years old.[8] But he, like his predecessors, was still attributing choice over marriage exclusively to men. And the most recent and authoritative pronouncement on these statistics states unequivocally: 'women played a generally passive role in changing marriage patterns in the last quarter of the nineteenth century'.[9] In the context provided by feminist revisions of the period, such a judgment appears highly questionable.

Further, the similarity in the marital statistics in the very different demographic and economic conditions of Australia, Britain and the United States would suggest, I think, that there were other factors at work as well as economic and demographic forces. If it is possible to concede that women themselves might have exercised some choice in relation to marriage, then those factors must include the considerations that women weighed up in deciding for or against marriage. These were both positive and negative.

Marriage as a trade

> For want of bread to eat and clothes to wear—
> Because work failed and streets were deep in snow,
> And this meant food and fire—she fell so low,
> Sinning for dear life's sake, in sheer despair.
> Or, because life was else so bald and bare
> The natural woman in her craved to know
> The warmth of passion as pale buds do blow
> And feel the noonday sun and fertile air.
>
> And who condemns? She who for vulgar gain
> And in cold blood, and not for love or need,
> Has sold her body to more vile disgrace—
> The prosperous matron with her comely face—
> Wife by the law, but prostitute in deed,
> In whose gross wedlock womanhood is slain.

This sonnet was included in Ada Cambridge's *Unspoken Thoughts*, published in 1887.[10] The view of marriage that the poem expresses—that a wife's sexual contract with her husband was analogous to that of a (female) prostitute with her (male) client—was a view expressed by a number of influential feminists throughout the English-speaking world at this time.

'[A] woman who sold herself, even for a ring and a new name, need hold her skirt aside for no creature in the street,' declared the heroine of Olive Schreiner's *Story of an African Farm*. 'They both earn their bread in the one way.'[11] Of course, Cambridge and Schreiner—who was to become an influential feminist theorist in England—were condemning marriages made for financial gain or respectability rather than love. Rose Scott, leader of the campaign for female suffrage in New South Wales, apostrophised the mothers of Australia in the same vein: 'Wd I cd persuade you that one ought to show your girls that marriage without love is a degradation as great for them as for the poor women in the Streets.'[12]

But there were others in Australia who considered *all* marriages to be economic transactions. They did not highlight the parallel between wives and prostitutes trading possession of their bodies for a livelihood, as did, for instance, North American feminist theorist Charlotte Perkins Gilman, Russian-born Emma Goldman, and English feminist Cicely Hamilton.[13] But they did, nevertheless, make it clear that they considered marriage for women to have been, fundamentally, a means to a livelihood. South Australian feminist Catherine Spence, observing the 'widespread movement which is going on all over the world for the admission of women to new fields of labour', commented as early as 1878 that economic independence for women would eliminate the double standard of sexual morality, and enable the woman of the future to *choose* 'not between destitution and marriage but between the modest competence she can earn and the modest competence her lover offers'.[14] Thirty-one years later, Annie Golding, president of the Women's Progressive Association in New South Wales, told the Third Australian Catholic Congress that 'The comparative economic independence of women has removed the incentive to marry merely for a home, and will eventually place marriage on a higher plane'.[15] In claiming, optimistically, that changes in the labour market were modifying the economic imperative to marry, by allowing women a choice between economic independence and marriage, Spence and Golding were both right and wrong at the same time. Alternatives to marriage *were* opening up for women between 1880 and 1900, but not as extensively or as permanently as they hoped.

The principal form of paid employment for working-class women continued throughout the period to be domestic service, but the proportion of women working as domestic servants declined as other forms of employment became available in the new industries and rapidly growing cities. This occurred most dramatically during the 1890s. A state-aided victory for employers over a militant labour movement, followed by the economic depression and drought, left the predominantly male trade unions impoverished and demoralised. Capitalists took advantage of these conditions to introduce new machinery without having to negotiate with unions over definitions of jobs and rates of pay. New machines made possible new divisions in work processes, new classifications of work performed, and employment of a different kind of worker. Traditional craftsmen were replaced by cheaper semi-skilled and unskilled machinists, most of them young, many of them women.[16]

Developments in white-collar work followed a comparable pattern. Industrialisation and urbanisation were accompanied by an expansion in state-provided, and state-regulated infrastructure. This opened up new forms of employment in state instrumentalities. Women moved into those jobs, usually the kinds of work deemed to require the least skill: they found jobs as pupil teachers in state elementary schools, as postal workers and telegraphists, and as clerical workers in colonial bureaucracies.[17]

The two decades during which extra-domestic employment opportunities opened up most extensively for women were the same decades during which the proportion of women marrying tumbled dramatically. This suggests strongly that, given a choice, a significant proportion of women preferred economic independence to marriage. If a feminist perspective will allow us to recast the nationalist, masculinist 'legend of the Nineties' as a time of 'war between the sexes', as Marilyn Lake has suggested, then perhaps the marital statistics for this period can be dubbed women's 'strike against marriage'. For, while the most powerful discourses of the period assumed, as 'common sense', that all women desired marriage, one of the considerations that women would have weighed in deciding whether or nor to marry was an emergent counter-discourse concerning marriage, a discourse which articulated—connected—three distinct, though related, sets of concerns. These were with love; with a belief that women put up with sex, rather than enjoying it, and then only because of their desire for children; and with the earning of livings. This was a feminist discourse concerning sexual labour.

Sexual labour

There was, first, the shock of discovering that marriage meant *sexual* labour. 'Can anything be more revolting to a pure-minded girl', wrote feminist Bessie Harrison Lee to the Melbourne *Herald* in 1888:

> [than] to find after the words of Christ Himself have joined her to the man she loves and reveres that he at once claims sole right over her body, whether she wills it or no.[18]

Another of Cambridge's poems, called 'A Wife's Protest', exclaims against the 'smouldering shame' and 'inward torment of reproach' induced by each night's enforced suffering: 'No dumb brute from his brother brutes/ Endures such wanton wrong'.[19] A character in Cambridge's novel, *Sisters,* published in 1904, reflecting on her new condition of widowhood, tells her sister that she is happy now because 'I'm clean now—I never thought to be again—to know anything so exquisitely sweet, either in earth or heaven—I'm clean, body and soul, day and night, inside and outside, at last.' Her sister, once she realised 'what this meant'—the novelist's words—exclaimed, 'Oh, *poor* girl!'[20]

Second, there was the danger of involuntary infection. It was not only feminists who saw this as a risk for married women. A police officer implementing Tasmania's Contagious Diseases legislation in Launceston drew official attention in 1886 to 'cases of married women infected through the misconduct of their husbands'.[21] A doctor commenting on the inadequacy of the Contagious Diseases legislation in Queensland made the same observation in 1911.[22] 'Disease is rampant,' declared Rose Scott, lecturing on 'the social problem', 'and even enters the homes of the innocent and affects the guilty and the guiltless alike—not only for one but sometimes for many generations!'[23]

Third, there was the seeming inevitability of conception, pregnancy and childbirth, over and over again. Constant maternity was bad for women, as everyone purchasing items from Brettena Smyth's array of 'Ladies Abdominal Belts', 'Obstetric Binders' and 'Womb Supports' knew only too well.[24] Constant maternity was grindingly hard work. 'Every child that a woman bears,' wrote Clara Weekes to the *Woman's Sphere* in 1903,

> entails on the majority of them nine months of misery, more or less acute, with a culminating period of agony at the end. When this is repeated from ten to sixteen, or even twenty times...is it to be wondered at that many mothers die quite young from sheer exhaustion.[25]

Constant maternity could kill women. Bessie Harrison Lee recounted in 1893 the tragic end of a young mother whose husband had been warned by the doctor that 'her life would pay the forfeit of any indiscretion on his part'. The woman died, said Lee, 'as surely murdered as any other victim of man's passion'.[26] Maternal mortality in childbirth increased in New South Wales between 1890 and 1902 by no less than 50 per cent on the rate for 1881–1900.[27]

Fourth, there was the risk of being widowed or deserted, left with children to provide for but nowhere to turn for provision. In Western Australia in 1901, the census discovered no fewer than 28 per cent of men living apart from their wives, and that figure did not include women who had been widowed or divorced.[28]

Finally, there was the belief held strongly at least in the medical profession that, as Alexander Paterson, M.D., maintained, 'Women do not feel the same intoxicating pleasure in the sexual act which their husbands do'. He, like the many other doctors performing ovariotomies on women, considered sexual desire in women to be dangerous:

> When...sexual passion has been awakened in her it sometimes becomes so dominating as to constitute a disease—erotomania—and run riot, seeking both natural and unnatural vent.[29]

Of course, feminists sought to change all of the horrors associated with sexual labour. They argued for girls to be taught about sex before they encountered the marriage bed.[30] They campaigned against men's vice, 'the animal in man' as Rose Scott called it, and sought to 'rescue' the prostitutes who were its consequence.[31] They urged limitation of the size of families, and promoted notions of 'purer' relationships, marriages 'on a higher plane' in Annie Golding's words, to encourage restraint in men.[32] Abstinence within marriage heightened the spiritual nature of the partners' union, maintained Bessie Harrison Lee.[33] 'Man's love is too physical' lamented Rose Scott in a narrative in which she imagined three unsuccessful attempts to persuade ardent admirers of her waving hair, blue eyes and pink cheeks of the superiority of an exclusively 'Spiritual love'.[34] Some feminists, like Scott, simply by living them, demonstrated the possibility of active and fulfilled lives without benefit of marriage or the pollutions of sexual labour.[35] Some feminists advocated contraception. Others preached voluntary motherhood.[36] They were a tiny minority, but a publicly visible and vocal one. Their efforts to render sexual labour less dangerous and arduous for women contributed importantly to the dissemination and circulation of an understanding of sexual labour that could make economic independence, however meagre, a preferable option to marriage. And that understanding marked a major transformation in relationships between women and men.

Conclusion

The strike against marriage was short-lived. The increased opportunities for women to earn an independent living beyond the domestic sphere were sharply contracted. As the union movement recovered from industrial defeat and economic depression towards the end of the 1890s, it took action not only against the employers but also against the women who had moved into the new semi-skilled and unskilled labour market.[37] These women, argued the working men and their union representatives, were out of their proper sphere.[38] Similarly, a new generation of professional government officials holding the view that the only proper sphere, at least for married women, was the home, began introducing government regulations to prohibit employment of married women, and to restrict that of single women in white-collar jobs.[39] The determinations that these men brought into effect, often cooperating together, and with employers, across class divisions, segmented the Australian labour market into primary and secondary sections, the demarcation between the two being determined by sex.[40]

However, the strike against marriage may have had far greater ramifications than appears at first sight. One appears in demographer Peter McDonald's observation that a significant proportion of the women not marrying in the 1890s remained permanently single.[41] A second appears in the widespread move towards voluntary, rather than compulsory, motherhood. An option available to an industrial workforce that cannot afford to remain on strike indefinitely is to bargain for wages and conditions. If the reduction in extra-domestic labour-market opportunities closed off the possibility of choosing economic independence, then women, once again trading possession of their bodies in marriage for a livelihood, could at least seek greater control over the conditions of their sexual labour. The fall in women's fertility rates occurred over a longer period than 'the strike against marriage'. But, from the feminist perspective that I outlined at the beginning of this chapter, the considerations implicated in the strike would appear to have been a significant contributing factor in the demographic revolution, 'the Australian fertility transition'.

In 1903 the New South Wales government succumbed to panic, ostensibly about the need to populate the vast expanses of Australia with white Anglo-Celtic protestants, and established a royal commission to enquire into the decline in the birthrate. The commissioners' report presented in 1904 gave vent to an array of class-based, eugenicist and racist prejudices. But the principal object of their masculinist condemnation, one which transformed their language from forceful to hysterical, was what they dubbed women's 'selfishness' in seeking to control their fertility.[42] Judith Allen has already pointed out that this commission 'might usefully be understood in the spirit of an industrial inquiry'.[43] I would argue that it was certainly that, and that the commissioners' hysterical pronouncements against women's 'selfishness' expressed a masculinist protest against the same understanding of sexual labour as was being put into circulation by feminists.

The understanding that marriage meant a wife's subjection to her husband was by no means new. The predominantly Anglo-Celtic population of Australia had brought with it a history of at least two centuries during which, as feminist political theorist Carole Pateman has shown, despite the change from status to contract as the principle around which relationships between men were organised, relationships between husbands and wives had remained essentially feudal, relationships in which men owned their wives—as masters had once owned their serfs—body and soul. It was not only feminists who had protested against what William Thompson, in 1825, dubbed the 'white slave code' of marriage, and John Stuart Mill rejected in 1851, shortly before he married Harriet Taylor, observing that under the existing marriage law a wife is 'the actual bond-servant of her husband: no less so, as far as legal obligation goes, than slaves commonly so called'.[44] What *was* new in the 1890s in Australia was the understanding of sexual labour, in marriage, *as labour*. And that understanding brought into the marriage bed the possibility of negotiation, of differing—indeed competing—rights and responsibilities, of the possibility of marriage becoming a contractual relationship, even if still—as in contracts between masters and men, employers and workers—a contract between unequal parties, instead of a merging of women in their husbands' legal and sexual beings as a God-given order of nature. The 'strike against marriage', and the discursive construction of marital sex *as* work, occurred in the same period as legal changes enabling women to retain control of their own property after marriage, conceding to women some—if still profoundly unequal—access to divorce, and, finally, yielding to suffragists' concerted

SEXUAL LABOUR 99

campaign, women's right to vote.[45] It is difficult to avoid the conclusion that all of these changes were, very largely, achievements of the discursive understandings that were fed by, and fuelled, first-wave feminism.

Masculinist rhetoric throughout this period sought to confirm both imagined and real divisions between the separate spheres of women and men. In the terms established by such rhetoric, the only women who worked outside the domestic sphere for their livings were sex-workers, prostitutes, 'fallen women'. Over and over again, women working in industry, or in shops, or in offices, were deemed 'immoral'—either already in, or soon to join, the ranks of those who earned their livings by selling sex. 'Fallen women', in such rhetorical terms, were differentiated sharply from women in their proper sphere, exercising the 'sacred' domestic functions of wife and mother. The discursive construction of marital sex, for women, *as work* cut across this divide, and hence across the imputed separateness of the separate spheres.

9 The 'equals and comrades of men'?: *Tocsin* and 'the woman question'
Patricia Grimshaw

As Marilyn Lake has persuasively argued, the 'gender factor' has been obscured in Australian historical writing by 'the dominance of a narrowly defined political history', and 'the sex-blind nature of much of what passes as class analysis'.[1] The radical labour men who owned cooperatively and wrote for the Victorian socialist paper, the *Tocsin*, from its establishment in 1897, undoubtedly contributed to a lively debate in the later 1890s on the nature of the class-based relations of employer and worker, couched in male terms. The journal can also be read, however, as significant not only for representations of class relations, or 'the social question', but for 'the woman question', that other vital problem which agitated the minds of late-nineteenth-century colonial Australians, along with political theorists and social activists in the industrialising societies of the North. And clearly, as Lake has demonstrated of *Bulletin* writers, the chief *Tocsin* columnists—Bernard O'Dowd, John Buckley Castien and Tom Tunnecliffe among them[2] —reveal the extent to which a gendered sense of their identity as men, their masculinity, informed and shaped not only their responses to women's involvement in current social transformations, but their own supposedly gender-blind analysis of the relationship between capital and labour.[3]

The *Tocsin* co-editors, columnists and correspondents did not, however, assume a unified or coherent masculinist labour stance on women's issues. Certainly, the dominant voice represented a strategy to contextualise key problematised aspects of women's life experiences within a class perspective. A central narrative asserted that working-class women were, like working-class men, oppressed by capitalists, who frustrated the choices of those whose undervalued labour underpinned the privileged lifestyle of the selfish rich. As well as 'fat men' there were 'fat women', capitalists' wives and daughters, who benefited from the system, and utilised sex-specific means to oppress both working-class men and women alike. But a class-based critique of the particularities of women's lives entailed an awkward confrontation between theoretical and experiential considerations.

In the first place, the principal writers drew on a range of theory which was itself highly disputed: Marxism, utopian socialism and Christian socialism all found their adherents in the journal, with their varying visions of a just society, and their contrasting notions of how to achieve one. In the second place, advocates of socialist feminism raised their voices, albeit in fragmented ways. Despite the best efforts of August Bebel in *Women and Socialism* and Friedrich Engels' *The Origin of the Family, Private Property and the State*, published in 1878 and 1884 respectively, Marxists had by no means solved the theoretical challenge of marrying Marxism and feminism. The promising insights of earlier non-Marxist socialists, as the historian Barbara Taylor has demonstrated for Britain, had been gradually silenced.[4] Edward Bellamy's utopian vision of an equitable gendered society in *Looking Backwards*, published in 1888, had its admirers in the *Tocsin*, although his American optimism coexisted uneasily with European pessimism. Dispersed insights from these several traditions surfaced constantly in the paper, while offering no coherent program or policy for incorporating women's emancipation within a materialist framework. While the subject positions of writers could not always be discerned with confidence, since some men occasionally used female names to put 'the woman's point of view', experiential discussion from labour women themselves also found a modest but important place in the *Tocsin's* pages, especially after a commentator using the byline 'Ruth' was allotted regular space and women letter-writers began to appear in correspondence columns. Hence theory and practice were thrown into fruitful juxtaposition for those interested in the intersection of class and gender in the labour movement.

There were three areas relating to women's lives that preoccupied writers in the *Tocsin* in the late 1890s. First, there were issues of women's civil liberties and the women's movement; second, the problem of freeing working-class women, both paid workers and housewives, from a poverty which they shared with men but to which women had a gender-specific relationship; and third, the need to free women from a specifically female oppression related to the contexts of sexuality and reproduction. What was noticeable about the principal male writers' representations of the problematised woman was that sympathy appeared strongest the further the distance from issues of male, as against bourgeois, oppression of women. Civil liberties issues elicited warm democratic and egalitarian solidarity. The suffering of the female worker exploited by employers in the waged labour force played on chivalrous instincts, as did the plight of the poor widowed mother or the anxious impoverished wife, victims of uncaring capitalists. Yet even within such political and economic critiques, a certain caution was evident over labour women's predilection for pro-women rather than pro-labour orientations, and discussion of the conditions and rewards of women's waged and unwaged work disturbed labour men's complacency. Nevertheless, explicit concern for women on these various fronts might enhance *Tocsin* men's sense of masculinity as protectors of and protagonists for women as well as affirming their generalised attachment to social justice. This was not the case, however, with women's problems of sexuality and reproduction, which confused and threatened many male writers. And as the focus of debate shifted from civic and industrial concerns towards sexual politics, so too did the contestation between dominant socialist and alternative socialist feminist voices become more pronounced and more heated.

The *Tocsin* writers uniformly gave impressive support to a wide range of legal and political reforms for women, testimony to the impetus for women's civil emancipation which came from the Left in the colonies, a significant factor in the eventual achievement of these reforms. Space was found in the paper for advocacy of such varied issues as married women's property and child custody rights, women's right to enter higher educational institutions, including professional courses, women's right to serve on juries and plead as individuals in courts, and the legitimate presence of women as equals in all democratic forums, from school committees to town halls and colonial parliaments. How could the University of Melbourne Senate reject the admission of women, a columnist on one occasion demanded: 'the male graduates of the colony have had the unmanliness, the intellectual and moral cowardice, to refuse to women who have passed the same examinations as themselves...the voting rights in University legislation which they themselves enjoy'.[5] *Tocsin* writers weighed in forcefully against opponents of women's suffrage, accusing them of explicit or veiled contempt for women's abilities, and blinkered hostility towards women's right to democratic citizenship. When a deputation of 300 Victorian women met with the Legislative Council to lobby for the franchise, and were received with derision, the *Tocsin* replied indignantly with the headline: 'The "Upper" House: Shameful Treatment of Decent Women'. Many councillors had been drinking, the writer asserted, and came to 'oggle' and 'giggle'. 'The weighty, business-like, and earnest speeches of good women voicing the aspirations and heart-wishes of hundreds of thousands were interrupted by low jests and idiotic exclamations, such as "Who'll mind the babies?", "New Woman", and others not fit to print.' Furthermore, one councillor went so far as to accost two of the younger delegates with the remark, 'You girls, you don't want votes. You want—something else.' Replied the *Tocsin*: 'His leering pause deserved six months without option...Such are the types of the bulk of those who denied woman the right to have a voice in the laws she has to obey, and in the expenditure for which she has to provide.'[6]

Just as the *Tocsin* maintained consistent support for women's civil rights, so too it praised, by and large, the feminists in the non-party women's associations. It was seldom that a *Bulletin*-style vendetta surfaced, although one writer, 'Scout', described a Woman's Christian Temperance Union deputation as 'masculine women—hard-faced, aggressive, and fierce-looking', quite simply 'the ugliest collection of females it has ever been my misfortune to encounter at one time, and I have had some experience of gaols and lunatic asylums'. (He feared they were campaigning to have the age of consent raised to 17½ years.[7]) But most *Tocsin* writers applauded the Woman's Christian Temperance Union and the various suffrage groups for their outspoken campaigns, describing them as progressive movements.

Certainly, the *Tocsin* sought to encourage the organised women's movement towards a generous recognition of the real meaning of equality, and to embrace all women, including working-class women, in their goals. The leaders of the suffrage campaign were urged to print simply written polemical literature, so that the movement could become a mass movement, and hence a strong force for genuine democracy.[8] If the *Tocsin* needed evidence of the progressive nature of the campaign as it existed, however, writers found it in the actions of those collecting signatures to anti-suffrage petitions, who enticed signatories with the promise that they would thereby be helping to keep down the working classes.[9] When factory managers at Swallow and Ariel's in Port Melbourne had the audacity to pressure their own female employees to sign it,[10] under false pretences, the *Tocsin* could display publicly the anti-suffrage movement's duplicity and naked power. The *Tocsin* stood fair and square on the egalitarian ground of sexual equality; or so writers prided themselves.

Yet the dominant voice of the *Tocsin* was neither detached from current definitions of femininity as clearly bounded from masculinity, nor did it always eschew the concerns of class-based politics. On the one hand writers called upon women to be 'comrades' of men, and scorned the arch gallantry at the basis of the *Age's* advocacy position on emancipation. 'One can only hope that TOCSIN democrats are guiltless of that greatest of stains on the honour of comradeship, skilfully veiled contemptuous patronage,' wrote one.[11] His hopes were not borne out. The *Tocsin* wanted a community of 'full-blooded, full-minded, morally-balanced men and women',[12] but despite the gender-blind adjectives, their vision of the relationship of the two sexes to the activism of the labour cause, the very tasks for which political emancipation was demanded, had a decidedly sex-specific ring, as the following exchanges illustrate.

The first concerned the proper attitude of wives of labour activists to their husbands' personal emotional and material needs. Under the headline 'The Worker: A Candid Criticism', a columnist named 'A Woman' (undoubtedly a man), weighed in against the male worker she refused any longer to tolerate: the 'slave' who accepted his servile status. This worker deserved his wrongs if he accepted them 'in tame and cowardly submission'. 'I have coddled the slave; called him a man when I knew there was no manhood in him. I will do so no longer.'[13] But when a manly worker did embrace the workers' cause, and toiled not only in the workplace by day but in trade meetings and political rallies by night, what then should similarly politically sensitised women be doing? According to one writer (co-editor Tom Tunnecliffe using the pseudonym 'Camille'), such men deserved feminine compassion.

> You women in the forefront of the fight: you cannot speak, you will not write, can you not create a hundred little havens where world-weary and battle-stained travellers may find a rest, and re-equip them for the fight, a hundred hearths round which they might gather in their isolation and loneliness, a hundred hands they might clasp...This is peculiarly your work—work which only women can do—to cheer, to inspire, to stimulate, shed around the men who are away at the front the aroma of your love...[14]

An alternative version of the male activist's domestic relationships, however, appeared in a piece, 'An Agitator's Wife'. The same old story, the labour wife in the piece complained of her husband, 'working for freedom and keeping your own wife a prisoner inside the four walls of the house'. She underlined the irony of her situation thus:

> My husband, my intelligent husband, 'our gifted and energetic comrade', spends his days at work, and his nights at committee or other meetings, and his Sundays on the top of a four-legged stool ranting like a Hallelujah lassie, and I am left stuck up here to look after his squalling children, and cook his meals, and wash his clothes, and then he will mount the platform and tell the crowd that 'the Socialistic party are the only party who, in seeking the emancipation of women, are actuated by principle, and not by expediency'.

This hypocrite, like other socialists, she continued, preached the new society to come, based on the right perception of love and duty, but neglected his own wife and children, so that his baby scarcely recognised him. So much for this 'revolutionist, the man who talks of "planting the flag of the future upon the barricades", but turns white with fear if I ask him to hold the baby whilst I run a message'.[15]

A second interchange took place between the 'We Women' columnist, 'Ruth', and a male writer who used the nom-de-plume 'Ajax'. Expressing outrage at the continuing practice of sweating, 'Ruth' called for the emergence of a female leader who might have the compelling power to awaken her fellow women from apathy, a woman who could inspire a community to swift action on behalf of deeply exploited women and children.[16] 'Ajax' responded, as he thought, sympathetically, to 'our comrade Ruth's passionate appeal for some Christ-embodied Spirit of Womanhood to rise and wake humanity to justice with a compelling vision of its Wrong'. With Ruskinian romanticism, 'Ajax' waxed eloquent on the inspirational potential of women's moral qualities. It was in woman's capacity to ennoble and elevate man's nature that her worth lay. 'It is in this that she becomes, in the sublime, the Comrade of Man.'[17]

'Ruth' herself was by no means distanced from convictions of women's special qualities. To be womanly was to be motherly, although motherly to all children, and to any cause, not just their own particular children's or circle's: 'The ideal which the wife and mother makes for herself, the manner in which she understands duty and life, contain the fate of the community', she believed.[18] 'Ruth's' stance was nevertheless at odds with 'Ajax's' male relational representation of womanhood, and her reply was terse; 'Ajax' had quite missed her meaning.

> What was called for was no 'spirit', Christ-embodied, mystical, or divine, but just a real live practical woman, large-hearted and true, with heart and soul afire with enthusiasm and zeal in the workers' cause, her fellow-women's cause. You men must look to your own higher self to influence you. We women have been your toys and divinities, just as you choose to use us, for some ages past, and we are tired, very, very tired. Now we intend to assert ourselves, and be neither dolls nor goddesses, 'Ajax', but real flesh and blood women, equals and comrades.[19]

Women would demonstrate comradeship best by looking outwards from their homes to the work which men, however willing, could not do, while joining with men equally where it counted.

A third exchange centred on the orientation of a new labour women's organisation established in 1898, the Women's Political and Social Crusade. When a group of labour women first sought a women-only forum, the *Tocsin* was enthusiastic, but keen to ensure that its focus would be left-wing policy formation on issues affecting the working class, particularly working-class women and children. The Woman's Political and Social Crusade, the *Tocsin* announced approvingly, was not to be a body working for the benefit of women only, 'but a body of women working for the general political and social welfare of the community…'[20] The Crusade became subject to pressure, however, when cross-class, gender-specific feminist concerns seemed to predominate.

The women wrote down a preamble and set of aims, of which the first was stated unequivocally: 'To secure to women political equality, economic justice, judicial equity, and the removal of all abuses that retard and prevent women attaining their full rights of citizenship, for taxation without citizenship is tyranny.' This had a decidedly feminist flavour, as did the rest of the document. By the time Mrs Ada Turnbull presided at the first general meeting, objections had already been raised that the written statement created the impression that 'the Crusade was merely for the benefit of women', whereas its intentions were surely, more rightly, for 'general social and political work'. The report in the *Tocsin* related succinctly that 'the preamble and rules were practically re-cast, and framed in the direction indicated'.[21] The Trades Hall Council was impressed, and allowed the Crusade to rent a room for meetings. The *Tocsin* smiled at the women again when Crusade members lobbied against a women's suffrage bill which did not include a clause eliminating plural voting: 'most Women Franchise bodies are apathetic on this issue'.[22] The Crusade could now be described as a 'plucky, useful, and vigilantly democratic society of women'.[23] Labour women getting together apparently needed careful surveillance initially to make sure they were not seduced from the correct, Left, path.

Women leaving the four walls of home for socialist discussion and policy formation with their left-wing sisters may have been applauded. Women leaving home for waged work was a different matter. Some labour women attempted to promote positive images of women as waged workers. 'Ruth', for example, replied to a woman correspondent in these terms: 'Every girl, even if an only child or only girl in the family, should learn some trade or profession by which she can support herself, or she runs the risk of having no object in life but one, to get married...'[24] She urged acceptance of girls' and women's capacities to attain a sturdy independence, and economic viability through employment. Women were underpaid, certainly, grievously so. There were many young women keeping themselves and paying railway fares out of a weekly wage of less than ten shillings—some even keeping a child as well.[25] And admittedly, the female workforce was divided into those who were self-supporting (usually single women) and those daughters or married women whose earnings merely contributed to a family wage, whose presence tended to lower the female wage for women without a male provider. The answer was clear—a minimum wage for women workers sufficient for an independent female livelihood.[26] And as for the gender division of waged labour, a passage from a New York journalist was cited approvingly: 'People had once referred to masculine work and feminine work as though these categories were a law of nature, but recent experience showed plainly that it was nothing of the kind. It was simply plain work—human work, with no sex at all.'[27]

This was a markedly different reading of gender in industrialising societies from the one presented by the dominant *Tocsin* voice. Underlying the *Tocsin's* analysis of the working class and its discontents was a longing for the best of all possible worlds, where a man could keep his family in decent comfort, and no woman would need to subject herself to the burdens of the public workplace.

> The TOCSIN does not believe that woman should be compelled to take part in what may be called the outside struggle for existence, and does not think that she would do so of her own motion if the fruits of man's outside toil were fairly and equitably allotted to him.[28]

And again, on another occasion:

> Given the power to maintain and educate a family decently, men will so perform their natural duties to women that very few women will need to come

into the outside world of competition at all. And the TOCSIN believes very strongly that that's how it should be.[29]

Overall, thought the main writers of the *Tocsin*, there was only a sort of purgatory awaiting women in the workforce, where their labour was exploited, their blood poisoned, their ears deafened, their bodies crippled. Whereas women's instincts urged them towards wifehood and motherhood, foul and dangerous workplaces withered these hopes, through their 'sunless monotony, insufficient nourishment and *ennui* of the very soul'.[30] The columnist 'Tocsynic' went so far as to describe female waged workers as 'spayed women', such was the destructive quality of the environment for these potential bearers of children.[31] (A 'lady critic' was quick to object to this comparison of women with animals, though did not succeed in eliciting an apology.)[32] As true democrats, the *Tocsin* knew that socialist men should accept women's right to enter any sphere of work she chose, but 'whether it is in the best interests of the race that she should have to assert her undoubted right is a somewhat arguable question'.[33] Moreover, waged work for women, while robbing working-class women of their capacity for motherhood, sustained wealthy women as a 'loafing class' freed for leisure, luxury and refinement.

The *Tocsin* recorded appalling details illustrating the unquestionable miseries of many working women's lives. Regarding domestic service, it was not so much the work itself as the condition of 'domestic slavery', the constraints of power and status surrounding the mistress–maid relationship, which most offended them: 'The fact of social inferiority is expressed in many petty ways, by the use of the Christian name, by the requirement of livery when not on duty, by a servile manner, and, more than all, by social isolation.'[34] But the sheer horror of the work itself came to the fore when factory work was under consideration. So many items which labour-movement people themselves ate, wore or used were stained with women's agony or disgrace in their very manufacture. Melbourne itself had its equivalents of the English matchworkers' 'phossy jaw': the crippled and mutilated young of the city's workers' suburbs, epitomised by the North Melbourne girl encountered by a Crusade member. A lemon cutter at Hoadley's jam factory, her hands were gradually being eaten away. 'Jam appears to be an innocent looking enough sort of thing, yet even it is spiced with human agony.'[35]

The conditions of waged work threatened the health and reproductive capacities of girls and women, thereby serving as justification for a long-term goal of a womanless workplace. The resulting alternative of women allotted wageless domestic exclusion would, hopefully, be self-chosen, as befitted a democratic society. When a factory worker, a single mother, was forced by law to exclude all her children from school for six weeks because one child contracted measles, the *Tocsin* was sympathetic, but pointed out the real moral of the story: that it was 'utterly anomalous in a rich community that any mother of young children should have to leave home to earn their crusts of bread in a factory'.[36] When Trades Hall investigators interviewed young women in a cartridge factory who worked from 7.30 a.m. to 5.30 p.m. for a meagre seven to nine shillings a week, exposed to constant danger from explosives without safety precautions, the *Tocsin* acknowledged that many were the main support of widowed mothers, or assisting their families financially while their fathers sought work. This pragmatic need itself did not preoccupy the *Tocsin*, however, which focused on the employer's capacity to control the girls, kept 'docile and dumb to their sufferings ... in meek subjection to a condition that was a blot upon civilisation'.[37] What concerned the Tocsin was not the young women's need for an income, but solely their health and happiness.

The *Tocsin*'s chivalrous stance on oppressive conditions for female factory workers could be considered less than altruistic, however, when set beside the paper's key focus on women's work: the threat of women's lower wages to men's work opportunities and conditions. The concern of labour men to get women out of the workplace and into the home was more than tangentially underwritten by their opaque desire to exclude a major threat to men, simply as men, as well as in their capacity as family breadwinners. The danger that lower-waged women would replace men in work which either sex could perform had surfaced in the painful economic downturn of the decade. Women were every day becoming more skilled, more competent at all manner of trades.[38] Hence it was not to be wondered at that it was common

> for married women machinists, fitters, etc., to take employment in the boot factories from which their husbands have been turned away owing to the depression. They are taken on because they will work for less than their husbands will work for.[39]

This made no economic sense for the working-class family. It made no sense, either, for working-class masculine identity.

If women were to be in the workforce for the foreseeable future, and if the gender of a factory operative was becoming decreasingly relevant in machine-based tasks, some alternative strategy of despatching women back to the private household had to be contemplated. Since the rate of wages was affected just as much 'by woman's accepting lower than the current male rate as it would be by the influx of meagrely-living foreigners' the answer would have to be encouraging unionism among women.

> It cannot, therefore, be too strongly urged on all interested in the maintenance of a wage sufficient to keep a family in reasonable comfort—and this is, perhaps, the real aim of all our social agitations—that they should do all they can do to stimulate women's trade unions into existence, to infuse something of a workers' *esprit de corps* into these 'free labourers', to resist any attempt to fix different rates of wages for man's and woman's work involving equal skill, and thereby jointly benefit in the long run both man and woman.[40]

The difficulty was that men's interests and women's interests now clashed so often in departments of factory work over women's willingness to accept lower wages that many men were reluctant to assist women to organise. But there was danger for trade unionism itself in the existence of 'such a large body of unorganised but regular female workers in the various factories at the mercy of an owner's whim, and capable of competing with their fathers and brothers at sweating rates when it suits their owner's interests'.[41] Bringing women within the 'moral education' which unionism provided would teach them that they had duties as well as rights, and provide a 'mental education' which would show women 'the economic folly of cutting the throat of one's husband, lover, father or brother'.

The socialist feminist response to women's need for unions stressed, by contrast, the empowering potential of such organisations for women workers themselves. How extraordinary that that great building, the Trades Hall, was almost entirely devoted to 'the male element', 'Ruth' wrote:

> Why did not dressmakers, type-writers, shop assistants, box-makers, paperbag makers, boot machinists, women clerks, domestic servants, nurses, waitresses, tobacco operatives, bookbinders, stationery employe[e]s organise? And join their fellow men proudly marching in the labour movement processions, bringing their own energy to improve the lot of workers.[42]

Socialist feminists sought that democratic comradeship of equals which labour men in other contexts acknowledged, not a prioritisation of the interests of male workers over women's by means of a spurious settlement.

What of the experiences of the wife and mother within the home, so much vaunted as the site of appropriate female labour? There was occasional recognition that in fact wives and daughters on farms often performed very heavy work. In an article entitled 'Unsexing Women,' a columnist described as misplaced philanthropy a recent outcry over heavy physical work required from reformatory girls. Selectors' wives and daughters all over the colony habitually performed such onerous farm labour as wood-jamming and tank-sinking.

> We must be simply oozing with hypocrisy when we can at one moment thrill with indignant anger at the thought of a few girls being dehumanised by work unfit for women, and at the next accept with sickening complacency the fact that tens of thousands of the mothers and future mothers of the Victorian people are daily, and have been for years past, compelled...to bullock their way through life in similar fashion. Such work will, no doubt, develop masculine muscles in these women, but it will also, and assuredly, unsex them. And we have no right—we in the towns—to be parasites on an unsexed country womanhood.[43]

The labour of farming women drew sympathetic attention in this way because it was patently physical work performed in full view out of doors. Notably, this particular columnist focused, once again, on the propriety of the tasks, not on the significance of this labour for the women, their families, or the colonial economy. There were few comparable references to the housework of urban working-class wives as also 'real' work, comparable to rural labour or to public waged work. Certainly it was admitted that some housewives performed their duties in appalling environments, in rented slum houses with ruthless exploitative landlords; certainly it was admitted that some housewives became pinched and worn with the wearisome struggle to stretch a husband's inadequate wage to cover the household's needs; certainly some housewives were known to be suddenly left without resources when husbands were injured, became ill or died leaving no provision for their widows. The material value of housework, however, or the burden of it in ordinary as in extraordinary circumstances was rarely addressed. What was more, where the tensions of housework were noted, the source of trouble was some agent outside of the marital relationship: landlords, employers or politicians, with their icy indifference to the housewife's struggle for a dignified existence, abounded.

Again, however, other voices contested this dominant representation. In the first place, some pointed out that while technology was lightening men's burdens of heavy physical toil, few were applying technology to the home to lighten women's: housewives were still labouring in the dark ages. 'Ruth', in particular, had clearly been reading the American radical Charlotte Perkins Gilman's *Women and Economics* when she advocated that 'The kitchen should be abolished from the home, laundry work should be done by machinery and male labour, a gigantic system of kindergartens should take care of the youth and instruct them better than they are today ... '[44] This was a novel alternative to calls for the preservation of the working-class family.

Furthermore, columnists could enter the thornier grounds of the intimate oppression by men of women. When a writer described the colony of Victoria as 'this land of deserted wives',[45] this implied a deliberate choice by husbands to impoverish wives and children. When some writers excused men for excessive drinking, since the desire for stimulants came from long hours of labour, others pointed out that husbands thereby consumed their wives' and children's livelihoods, and staggered home to beat them physically into the bargain. These issues bought into the painful arena of sexual politics being waged within the working-class home, the counterpart to the contested site of male and female workers in the factory. Yet within the home, not only the ideology of the decent working-class family but the ideology of the sentimental and affective bonds of marriage was interrogated. More broadly, these debates questioned the social context of sexual and reproductive practices, whether contained within the conjugal family or outside it.

There was considerable sympathy in the *Tocsin* for individual women whose entrapment in unhappy sexualised situations was publicly revealed in moments of crisis, through suicides, seductions, legal battles, imprisonments. The usual explanation told how such women were abused by individual aberrant men, as they found themselves with impaired health from abortions or prostitution, with illegitimate children to brand them for life, or abandoned to destitution when lovers or de facto husbands deserted them. The usual poverty of the women provided the context for their vulnerability, an oppression deepened by the hypocrisy of a bourgeois world which could exploit female wage-earners and starve working-class wives, only to condemn them for transgressing the moral code. When a young woman who had recently undergone an abortion was found drowned in the Yarra, the *Tocsin* proclaimed: 'The abortionist is not to blame. The crime lies with society. The false basis on which our social system is built is responsible for this and every other outrage...'[46] In particular, the very debauched plutocrats whose greed and speculation in the 1880s plunged the colony into eventual depression had impoverished women, and hence caused the 'smell of aborting drugs that so loads the Australian atmosphere at present'.[47]

Others pointed, however, to 'the Criminal Court where the everlasting case of Man v. Woman continually crops up', as in the trial by jury of a man accused of seducing and impregnating a fifteen-year-old girl. But the 'sexual bias in the minds of those twelve men was too strong for justice', a writer angrily asserted, when the court found for the accused.[48] Of another trial of a woman, 'Ruth' wrote:

> It is a merciless injustice to have only men on the jury, men to judge, men to plead, and men to give evidence in the case of a mother accused of the murder of her infant, where the sentence of death depends upon the mental and physical state of a woman within a few weeks of the birth of a child, a state which no human being but a mother can ever know anything about.[49]

If male courts defaulted, and if the fathers, husbands and brothers of Victoria woefully failed to take pre-emptive action to prevent assaults on and sexual exploitation of women and girls, then women themselves had best take action: 'Ruth' thought the suffrage would help and had a strategy: 'That all the women of Victoria go out on strike, refusing to live with or do any sort of work for the lords of creation, until the vote is given them. Why, friend, even an attempt to organise such a strike, and our franchise is won.'[50]

The dominant voice in the *Tocsin* asserted legal monogamous marriage, and childbearing contained legitimately within it, as the rightful path to sexuality and reproduction for decent socialists. As the decrease in the marriage rate, the rising age of marriage, the numbers of couples in 'concubinage' and the rising rate of illegitimacy all became strongly evident in published official statistics, many were appalled.[51] Socialism was not synonymous with free love, they hastened to stress, whatever the capitalist's libel. More than the rest, it was the declining numbers of births, evidence of deliberate steps to prevent conception within marriage, which was most shocking, since it struck at the core of their social vision. In the first place, there was no problem of too many children, merely a problem of unequal distribution of wealth: Bebel among others had demonstrated the poverty of Malthusian doctrines.[52] 'Population should not be regulated and unnaturally restricted to comply with the cruel conditions of civilization, but Modern Civilization and the Science of political economy must be expanded in order to meet abundantly the needs of a naturally and lawfully expanding population,' an editorial declared. 'This is the Spirit of Socialism...' The *Tocsin* held to this belief, 'not because it cares a jot for the opinions of Popes, Priests or Parsons, but because it has a veneration for Nature and all her holy laws'. Contraception struck 'a foul blow at the sublime instincts of motherhood and paternity: it would transform marriage literally into sanctified prostitution, and undermine and destroy the sacred institution of the Family for ever'.[53] The use of 'preventive checks' was equated with every other obvious form of capitalist decadence: evil-smelling gutters, diseased meat and vegetables, adulteration of milk, goods tainted with the human misery involved in their manufacture, the 'lunatic system' of distribution provided by private enterprise.[54] To call legitimately conceived babies 'the crumpled rose-leaves of the bed of marriage', as did the *Age,* was morally degrading.[55]

But others saw sexuality and childbearing from different positions. One young woman, living with a man without benefit of clergy, justified 'free love' as a more moral basis for a heterosexual relationship. Would it be preferable if, having married, the man lost his love for her, yet she might compel him to live with her and support her, or that she similarly might be compelled to stay with him?[56] When the Full Court decided in a divorce case that a wife could be said to have deserted her husband when, even while living under the same roof, she refused to sleep with him, one writer swiftly perceived that this put women in a position 'little higher than a chattel-slave'. A wife would be left without any option to further pregnancies except at the risk of divorce and losing custody of the children she already possessed.[57] When a Board of Works Commissioner of Irish origin boasted at a public meeting of having thirteen children, a writer took him to task. Such self-indulgence was frequently enjoyed by a man at the expense of a 'terrible sacrifice on the part of woman...Has the rearing of thirteen children been conducive to the enjoyment of health and of freedom on the part of the mother?'[58]

'Ruth' in her 'We Women' column summed up thus the response of women she knew. It was all very well, she said, for men such as the Church of England Archbishop Carr to speak of the duty of wives to bear children:

> but the fact remains, and a sad fact, too, that the conditions of life for the average wife are so hard that the 'duty' has become a burden, the joy of motherhood has turned to bitterness, and she is putting aside the 'duty', laying down the burden, reluctantly for the most part, not because the love for motherhood is less, but the struggle has become so great 'she just can't bear it'.[59]

By the 1890s, then, the Victorian labour movement paper the *Tocsin* was showing consistent support for the enfranchisement of women and other civil-rights issues. Women were told that they should anticipate harnessing their new freedoms to the labour cause, to the improvement of the living and working conditions of the labouring class and of the working-class family. Yet women's lives constituted a challenge for male labour analysts.

Women's problems were too complex, too diverse to be accommodated in neat categorisations. It was hard to discern where the good socialist should stand on women's sexuality, on prostitution, on reproduction, or to decide how women's experiences of domestic abuse related to class issues, to capitalism. Nor could the male labour movement decide successfully how to encourage wives, whom they wanted dependent, to become independent activists in support of male claims, or to persuade waged girls and women, whom they regarded with suspicion, to renounce competition with male workers. And a few women and men in the journal, socialist feminists, complicated these matters with their own oppositional opinions.

The path to the 'family wage' registered eventually in the 1907 Harvester judgement had been part of a bewildered search for a reform agenda for working-class women, whose untidy lives defied coherent, unitary solutions. Perhaps the contestation over key gendered issues in the *Tocsin* points to one possibility. As socialists looked to the state to solve 'the social problem' of conflicting interests of capital and labour, socialist feminists looked in turn to the state to solve 'the woman problem' of conflicting interests of men and women within the working class. But the resolutions set in train in the early century were partial and hence transitory.

10 The *Woman's Voice* on sexuality
Susan Sheridan

'The question which underlies the declaration of the rights of woman'—
(Maybanke Wolstoneholme, 1895)

Sexuality, male and female, was a central issue in the 1890s crisis in gender relations. Women took part in the public debate which constructed as its subjects the 'social evils' of prostitution and venereal disease, and in some instances made of this debate a vehicle for the expression of sexual desires and dissatisfactions which were rarely articulated in the fiction and personal writing of the period.[1] The radical press, such as the socialist *Worker*, offered women writers some opportunity to discuss prostitution and venereal disease as social problems caused by capitalist greed; but Louisa Lawson, advocating marriage reform in the *Dawn*, did not hesitate to single out male sexual behaviour as the main problem.[2] The *Woman's Voice*, published in Sydney from 1894 to 1895, shared her distinctively feminist perspective on the widely recognised problem area of sex, marriage and motherhood, but took it further, making sexual reform central to its vision of social transformation.

This journal is one of the few extant examples of Australian feminists participating in the outspoken critique of masculine sexual habits and expectations which some of their North American and British colleagues were developing, and which has been the focus of recent feminist reconsiderations of the suffrage period.[3] My concern here is not so much with evidence of that conflict in the marriage bed which is the subject of Susan Magarey's contribution to this volume (chapter 8), but with the ways in which feminist radicals conceptualised sexuality and its central place in the transformation of contemporary culture.

Maybanke Wolstoneholme, when she became editor and proprietor of the *Woman's Voice*, was a prominent suffragist in her late forties. Since her husband deserted them ten years earlier, she had supported herself and her children by running a school, Maybanke College, at her home in the Sydney suburb of Dulwich Hill, and she had recently obtained a divorce under the reformed Act. In these respects alone, she was an advanced woman, and evidently she did not shrink from naming herself as one, part of a minority within the minority of women activists of the period. She made the *Woman's Voice* a vehicle for the most progressive ideas, not only on sexuality and women's civil rights, but on such issues as the abolition of prisons and anti-militarism. *Woman's Voice* featured articles on the full range of subjects with which feminists concerned themselves, domestic and public. As president at the time of the Womanhood Suffrage League of NSW, Wolstoneholme provided good coverage of the activities of the League and related associations such as the Women's Christian Temperance Union.

Here I have confined discussion to the journal's treatment of sexual issues, not just because it is unusually frank in this respect, but also because of Wolstoneholme's belief that sexuality is the root of the problem—she even uses this metaphor in the epigraph to 'A Vital Question', the *Voice's* major article on compulsory motherhood, by quoting from Luke 3, 9: 'And now also the axe is laid unto the root of the trees.' For her, 'the underlying question' of women's rights was women's desire for sexual autonomy within marriage, the meaning of which included their right to say no to unwanted sexual intercourse, freedom from 'compulsory motherhood', freedom from physical abuse and what modern feminists would call marital rape. The meanings varied, but feminists who held this view insisted on the link between women's sexual autonomy and the moral and physical health of society, and advocated continence rather than contraception as the means of ensuring the end of the double standard and 'compulsory motherhood', and the elevation of marriage above the level of a form of trade or prostitution.[4]

In this chapter I argue that the concepts of sexuality represented in the *Woman's Voice* drew on the most radical of available discourses and constituted, as its editor claimed, a vanguard position within Australian feminist thinking of the period. It is still necessary to challenge the folktale that women wowsers sought to emasculate freedom-loving men, and to understand how these feminist radicals came to see the social control of male sexuality (both by legislation and by a regimen of self-control) as the solution to the fundamental problem of women's individual powerlessness and its concomitant social effects—prostitution, disease and crime.[5] What they effectively did was to focus on male rather than female sexuality as problematic, as the object of public scrutiny and reform. They successfully used the new 'scientific' discourse on sexuality (in particular, eugenics) against men instead of women ('the Sex').

Wolstoneholme saw herself as belonging to the vanguard. In her final editorial she concluded that the journal was 'born ten years in advance of the times' but that should be no cause for regret, for:

> the thoughts I have sent out ... are the expression of living Truth, will do the work Truth always does. They may be shunned as disagreeable, or flouted as vulgar, but they will live when fashion and foolishness are forgotten. And though my feeble woman's voice may cease, I shall know that I have done a little of the rough work of the pioneer, and have made the path a trifle clearer for the women, a crowd of which no man can number, who, in a few years will follow. [5a]

It is clear from the first issue that she is passionately interested in ideas, in 'the subjects that interest thinking women' and in the free expression of opinion, including opinions which 'differ from our own, because our object is to encourage thought, the great lever of humanity'.[6] As a journal of ideas it is a veritable compendium of 'advanced thought' in the period. Yet for women, speaking out was itself considered 'licentious' and an 'effrontery'. Such accusations are anticipated by the *Woman's Voice* motto: 'Democratic but not revolutionary, Womanly but not weak, Fearless without effrontery, Liberal without license'. Wolstoneholme did meet with opposition in her attempt to open up for discussion such issues as the reform of marriage, the Contagious Diseases Acts, sex education for children and, most controversial of all, compulsory motherhood or 'prostitution inside and outside the marriage bed'. In dealing with these subjects 'usually avoided by the wise, shrouded by the prurient, and cheapened by the vulgar', wrote an admirer in 1919, 'she was not afraid' though she was 'insulted in letters to her own and other journals, and was cut by the members of a prominent women's association in Sydney'.[7] While building solidarity among women was a primary concern for Wolstoneholme, as it was for her sister-editor Louisa Lawson, she was willing, if necessary, to jeopardise the progress of that project in favour of opening up unpopular and 'disreputable' subjects for public discussion.

Yet the published responses of *Woman's Voice* readers, both male and female, on sex questions were on the whole positive. It appears that the editor had tapped into a small but articulate and well-read group of Australians engaged in feminist critiques of the patriarchal sexual order. For it was not only women of advanced views who located the root of the social problem in relations between the sexes. There are several regular male correspondents to the *Voice*, and articles and speeches by men like H.H. Champion are reprinted approvingly.[8] The 'new man' of the period was often vociferous in his support for women's criticisms of masculinist behaviour and beliefs as undermining the moral and social health of the nation.[9]

Wolstoneholme opens the *Voice*'s attack on marriage abuse by reprinting an article on the subject of marriage, sex and perfectionism by the notorious American sex reformer Tennessee Claflin (September 8, 1894).

She follows this up with an editorial on November 17 which invokes the heroine of Olive Schreiner's key feminist novel, *Story of an African Farm*, refusing to sacrifice her independence in marriage. As was her habit, she addresses her theme in the form of a dialogue between two characters: 'a high-spirited, thoughtful girl' and her 'experienced mother'. To the girl's view that legal marriage should not be necessary where there is real love, the mother advances reasons for caution; but the editorial voice returns to point out that for the many women now moving, from choice or necessity, into the world of work, marriage is no longer seen as 'an easy method of earning a living', and lists the 'dozen disabilities (which) perplex the married woman which the single girl avoids'. 'The alteration of our marriage customs' has already begun, as evidenced by present divorce laws, and she directs readers to a story reprinted from the *Sketch* later in the issue on this very question of free unions—a story which attributes the failure of such a union entirely to the man's faithlessness (*Voice* p. 98).

It is hardly surprising that some read her as advocating free unions.[10] In the next issue (December 1, 1894) she reports the furore that followed this editorial, including a libellous attack by a country newspaper, wrongly crediting her with 'advocacy of libertinism'. Nothing could be further from the case, she claims, and goes on to defend herself by listing the abuses to which heterosexual relations are subject—prostitution, illegitimacy, baby-farming, abortion, adultery, not to mention marriage agencies, divorces, the 'marketing' of marriageable daughters, and the harm done by romantic 'paper-covered serials'. These abuses, the object of ten years worth of books 'from Olive Schreiner to Ella Dixon' setting forth the revolt of women against them, are, she claims,

> the things which are undermining the sacredness and the beauty and the usefulness of the permanent marriage tie, and which are destroying the possibility of the lasting union, made in the Heaven of man's higher nature, which all pure men and women desire to establish... (*Voice* p. 110)

The appeal to 'pure' men and women, of course, had not protected Thomas Hardy from scandal either, when he subtitled *Tess of the D'Urbervilles* (1891) 'a pure woman'; nevertheless here it functions as a potent signifier of engagement in the international 'social purity' movement, with its attack on the double standard and its defence of women's right to bodily integrity. By the turn of the century the ideal of marital mutuality and the woman's right to say no had been absorbed into American middle-class consciousness, according to Gordon and DuBois, and there is evidence that this was also the case in Australasia.[11]

Wolstoneholme concludes her self-defence by reiterating the important role of the Voice in combating popular representations:

> the newspapers which hide these things, and instead publish columns of glamour about Brussels lace, and orange blossom, decorated churches, and wedding breakfasts, are doing more to degrade marriage than is the quiet voice

which calls attention to the corruption which these things hide, and which they neither cure nor palliate. (*Voice* p. 110)

(The 'quiet voice of the home' was a favourite epithet for the journal.)

Supportive letters on the subject appeared in this and the next few issues.[12] She must have been enormously heartened by the letter of support from that old campaigner Henrietta Dugdale,[13] who praised the *Voice* as that of 'the thoroughly upright, courageous, truly pure woman' and urged her to forge ahead, despite insults, for 'those (men) who misinterpret our efforts for a purer life are either corrupt or unjust; from such we neither demand nor expect anything advantageous' (*Voice* p. 142).

Yet others wrote anxious enquiries about what could be done, advocating education for both sexes on the subject. It emerges clearly that their concern is not with the abolition of marriage but with its reform, and in particular with the right of wives to say no to their husbands' exercise of what law and custom had established as their conjugal rights. This was the central and least mentionable sexual issue for feminists, who often, it has been argued, displaced their knowledge of marital abuse and rape onto their concern with the plight of prostitutes;[14] and it also seems likely that much of the melodramatic but euphemistic language employed about venereal disease performs a similar function.

In her letter to the *Voice*, Henrietta Dugdale named this horror of 'enforced maternity' as one of several 'vile facts' which men have cowed women into remaining silent about. Women's silence gives men 'the desired immunity, with the natural result of "speckled toads", (see "Heavenly Twins") physically and mentally speckled' (*Voice* p. 142). An examination of the meaning of this curious phrase from Sarah Grand's best-selling novel of 1894,[15] mentioned several times in the *Voice*, can give us an insight into the place and significance of this whole issue for many feminists. The 'speckled toad' in the novel is the child of a syphilitic man, deformed in some unspecified way, whose mother goes mad and dies soon after its birth, having also contracted the dread disease (*The Heavenly Twins* vol. 1, p. 301). This incident is the melodramatic exemplum of the novel's thesis that women must be saved by education from the culpable ignorance of the ways of the world which leads them to marry impure men. The novel's heroine, Evadne, marries such a man but refuses to consummate the union when she discovers the truth about his past, rejecting her mother's conventional womanly wisdom that it is her duty to redeem him; but ultimately she succumbs to an hysterical condition caused by the 'unnatural' life she has had to lead. In this text, then, the single standard of sexual chastity before marriage is shown to be necessary for the mental and physical health of women and children; but, beyond the problem of disease, Evadne's near-tragic fate suggests that a woman like her cannot survive well without sex-love (which is carefully distinguished from mere passion) and its corollary, motherhood—unless she finds some intellectual outlet for her energies (a course she has promised her husband not to take).

In the text of the *Woman's Voice* a similar model of female and male sexuality is implied. It is a model both more sophisticated than the 'wowser' view would have it, and more optimistic about the possibility of reforming 'the animal in man' than some recent feminist interpretations of first-wave feminism would allow.

'Prostitution within the marriage bond', or compulsory conjugal relations, was a central issue in the *Woman's Voice* debates on sexuality. As early as 1869 Elizabeth Cady Stanton had referred to 'legalised prostitution within marriage' and it was discussed in the 1888 Report of the International Council of Women.[16] In Britain Elizabeth Wolstenholme Elmy had drawn the attention of the Dialectical Society to the issue of marital rape in connection with the proposed Criminal Code Bill, in 1880, which would exclude wives from the definition of rape; and she pursued this theme vigorously over the following decades in the context of more generalised feminist critiques of the marriage institution.[17] In the *Woman's Voice* it was introduced as an issue of voluntary *motherhood*, and tied closely to appeals for the improvement of the race and society.

The issue was raised first by *Woman's Voice* correspondents, rather than by the editor herself. In response to an article recommending that mothers teach their sons sexual self-control, Lucy Taylor protests in the strongest terms against the implication that such control need only be exercised *until* marriage. Quoting Bellamy's *Looking Backwards* in support of her theme of the awesome social responsibility of motherhood, she warns that:

> Love that will give a wife her freedom is a love worthy of the keeping, and it should be the sacred right of woman to determine when and under what circumstances she shall take upon herself the sacred office of maternity. (*Voice* p. 80)

It is clear that this determination is not to be effected by contraception but by continence when, in a later letter, she asks rhetorically: 'Are we to suppose that the instinct of propagation is God-directed when we see the weary, patient, submissive look on many women's faces today?' (*Voice* pp. 104–5). Abstinence was the only form of birth control acceptable to the majority of nineteenth-century feminists: it 'helped women strengthen their ability to say no to their husbands' sexual demands, for example, while contraception and abortion would have weakened it'.[18]

'Enforced motherhood is the bane of hundreds of women's lives today,' writes another correspondent, 'Veritas', asking whether a union where 'the body is used for the gratification of animal passions' can possibly 'beget desirable progeny'. 'The crux of social reform', she concludes, 'is the establishment of equal marriages and the individual responsibility of parents' (*Voice* p. 131). Furthermore the reform of marriage, writes M. Sanger Evans, cannot be guaranteed by love, for 'love (so-called) is often but sensuality, veiled by a thin covering of sentimental emotionalism and a conventional appearance of delicacy' (*Voice* p. 167).

This construction of sensuality itself as undesirable, if not evil (and not confined to the male) is elaborated in the quotation from theosophist Annie Besant[19] which the editor prints in her 'Shafts of Thought' column:

> Men and women ... have to hold this instinct in complete control, to transmute it from passion into tender, self-denying affection, to develope [sic] the intellectual at the expense of the animal, and thus to raise the whole man to the human stage, in which every intellectual and physical capacity shall subserve the purposes of the soul. (*Voice* p. 174)

Remarkable here are the slippages between 'man' and 'human', and the hierarchical imagery of transformation, a reference to the evolutionary process that would raise men and women from the 'childhood of the race' ('an age of impulse, passion and appetite') into a 'higher grade of conscious existence' characterised by a 'regard and care for others, instead of the self'.[20]

In her editorial of June 29, 1895, Wolstoneholme refers to voluntary motherhood as 'the question that underlies the declaration of the rights of woman', for the personal independence of woman is more crucial than her economic or political independence, and it is an issue that affects women of all social classes. Without love, sex in marriage is prostitution: this theme is reiterated by her contributors and correspondents. But it is not just an issue of personal autonomy, important though that is. By the mid 1890s, eugenic concerns with quality control of the population are appealed to in the same breath as the long patriarchal tradition of conjugal rights is attacked. 'The mother's right to choose'—which is God's law, observable in the animal world—is also 'a subject which involves the highest interests of the race' because 'children born to unwilling mothers—the offspring of sensual gratification—can never become a noble people'. The danger was as much moral as physical because of the current theory of prenatal influence (which still figured prominently in Wolstoneholme's 1919 guidebook on child-rearing, *Mother Lore*[21]). As DuBois and Gordon put it, 'the crucial role of women in reshaping the race became the basis of a demand for important shifts in power relations between men and women'.[22] The potential contradiction between the feminists' need to defend the sanctity of motherhood and their concern with women being reduced to mere 'breeding machines'[23] is resolved by proving the social necessity of sexual abstinence on the part of men.

Eugenics as well as theosophical doctrine were embraced by the general reform movement, which provided a valuable support for such feminist protests as that against compulsory motherhood. It is significant that Wolstoneholme quotes several articles on this subject from the Boston social-reform journal *Arena*. She reprints most of a long article entitled 'Prostitution within the Marriage Bond' by its editor, B.O. Flower,[24] under the title 'A Vital Question' over three issues of the *Voice* in late 1895, just before it closed down. This constituted the most sustained discussion of sexual issues in the journal's brief history.

'The church and society,' Flower wrote, 'have tacitly sanctioned prostitution when veiled by the respectability accorded by the marriage ceremony.' Here he is principally concerned with the consequences for the wife and potential offspring of the man whose sexual indulgences have diseased his mind and body, that is, with the way such men bring prostitution into marriage ('the sacrifice of virginity and the rights of the unborn'). He attacks in the name of morality and 'the race'. However when he develops his case by quoting the words of several (unnamed) American feminists, the object of criticism becomes more general—not the syphilitic man but the horrible moral consequences of compulsory conjugal relations. The 'wife who is nightly the victim of the unholy passion of her master' is robbed of that 'absolute ownership of her own body' which is her right, indeed her sacred obligation to motherhood. As a consequence she is liable to produce 'children of lust' who will 'inherit the violent and ungovernable passions of their fathers' and themselves be incapable of resisting their own or others' lust. Thus the individual suffering of women produces a social problem of vast dimensions.

Flower goes on to attack 'pulpit, platform and press' for their silence on this issue; he considers the reasons a woman might have for staying on in such an abusive situation, and proposes as the only solution women's financial and legal autonomy, together with general education and ultimately a moral reformation led by 'awakened womanhood'.

The prolific response from *Woman's Voice* readers, particularly the men, to the publication of 'A Vital Question' provides a good illustration of Foucault's thesis about the incitement to discourse on sexuality.[25] 'E.C.T.' (a regular correspondent) wonders whether Flower's implication that 'men are sexually much too strong for women' might not encourage bigamy, and speculates that if men 'actually became less incontinent, their force would recuperate so much that the shock of contact would prove less endurable still to such supposed delicate female organism'; still, he goes on, some women are 'stronger in this respect than their husbands', and if women generally were healthier and more knowledgeable about physiology, 'the matter' (of mismatched sexual drives) would be solved (*Voice* p. 376). This faith in the efficacy of physiological knowledge is often expressed in the pages of the *Voice*, part of the Enlightenment tradition of scientific social reform, and E.C.T. himself in a later letter refers to the value of the theosophists emphasising the compatibility of reason and religion. A further linking of God's and Nature's laws is made in response to his letter by another man, who is eager to point out that the 'shock' referred to 'is not the shock imparted by pure God-designed manhood, however robust, but the shock of a morally-diseased animalism', and that 'no MAN in his innermost soul feels ashamed of being all that the word implies', though he ought be deeply ashamed of 'break(ing) the normal bounds of Nature's ideal' (*Voice* p. 391). However, the appeal to Nature is given a different, less benign slant by the correspondent who argues that 'when her holy of holies has been despised and trampled upon' Nature punishes the children born of loveless marriages with a 'defective instinct for downward trend, before conscious existence even begins' (*Voice* p. 410).

Another, signing himself 'A New Man', pooh-poohs E.C.T.'s view that 'chastity ... gives greater power in sexual matters'; instead, he says, 'the reserve force goes to the brain'. He has harsh words to say about immoral men ('male prostitutes') and repeats the widely quoted 'scientific fact' that '80 per cent of women's diseases are due to the previous or present immorality of the husbands' (*Voice* p. 411). A woman correspondent blames 'excessive indulgence, principally the husband's fault' for the rapid consumption suffered by a young woman within two years of her marriage (*Voice* p. 411). For all these writers with a scientific bent, the answer lies in education for self-control, and in 'pure knowledge' of physiology and maternity; physiological instruction is seen as the only remedy necessary, because sex is a natural process, good in itself if not abused. It was this aspect of the matter which Wolstoneholme was to take up in her campaign for sex education.

In this secular and scientific discourse on sexuality, there is nothing inevitable about male abuse of women, and there are suggestions (however discreet) that women too experience sexual desire. In its construction of the problem of what feminists would now call marital rape, the issue is not women's supposed passionlessness,[26] but men's corruption, 'sensualism'. Blame is placed on individual men, but also on the legal and customary expectation that marriages should produce children, regardless of the woman's desire. In the claim that a woman should only bear a child to a man she loves, it is implied that female desire is indistinguishably sexual and maternal. It's interesting that one of the few passages from Flower's article which Wolstoneholme does not reprint is concerned with female desire: he quotes a male correspondent's view that 'the majority of girls' feel no passion because they 'lack the saving grace of the feeling of love' and so they submit to men's passion, inside or outside marriage, because 'it is bred into their every fibre that they are given their sexuality as a means of making a living'.[27] The idea that passion is redeemed by love is a commonplace of the period, though not so common as the view that it is redeemed by procreation.

Another variation from the straight reproduction of Flower's article is that Wolstoneholme extracts some especially inspirational paragraphs on female autonomy to quote anonymously in her regular column, 'Shafts of Thought'. They urge the need to educate children in exalted ideals and also 'thorough knowledge of the functions of nature' and emphasise that woman's 'sacred obligations' in this respect are owed 'to herself, to society, and to the unborn'—not, it is implied, to her husband:

> The truth is, woman at her best and noblest must be monarch of the marriage-bed. We must begin in the creatory if we are to benefit the race, and woman must rescue and take care of herself and consciously assume all responsibilities

of maternity on behalf of her children. No woman has any right to part with the absolute ownership of her own body; but she has the right to be protected against all forms of brute force. No woman has any business to marry anything less than a man. No woman has any right to marry any man who will sow the seeds of hereditary disease in her darlings; no, not for all the money in the world! No woman has any right, according to the highest law, to bear a child to a man she does not love.[28]

The inspirational mode of address here verges on the hortatory, yet the emphasis on women's capacity to assume these responsibilities is empowering. Its vehemence might suggest the urgency with which the debasement of motherhood was viewed—though how much this was seen as a racial issue is hard to determine in this context.[29] Yet it is a straight and narrow path that is laid out: no question of the woman who wants a child more than she wants a love marriage; nor of sexual love, far less passion, without the desire to bear children.

A succinct summary of the feminist construction of sex, motherhood and social change presented in *Woman's Voice* is provided by a regular correspondent, 'Alexa', as she critically reviews the notorious Dr Balls-Headley's treatise on *The Evolution of the Diseases of Women*.[30] She takes him to task for characterising women as breeding machines: 'Everything we had thought to be of importance, the higher nature of man or woman, the sacredness of individuality are all seen to be as nothing in comparison with a rabbit-like fecundity on the part of woman and unrestrained indulgence for the superior sex'. She ridicules his blaming women's woes on 'a single life, mental culture and tight-lacing' while omitting the real causes—ill-health, 'the effect of pre-natal conditions on the unborn woman' and 'in married life, perhaps the commonest cause of all, what I may style being too much married' (*Voice* p. 246). The 'prostitution in marriage' issue is again central. What Alexa calls for is 'the due restraint (not the suppression) of the sexual instinct in a wholesome, hygienic, social and economic environment' (*Voice* p. 255).

The *Voice's* representations of sexuality, women's autonomy and social order belong to the late nineteenth rather than the twentieth century, but are constructed within the most radical discourses of that period. However it is far from easy to determine what was 'progressive' and what 'conservative' in this discourse on sexuality; nor is it possible to identify a single feminist position and its opposite.[31] The range of feminist positions represented in the *Woman's Voice* suggests that distinctions between health reformers and social-purity campaigners were far from clear-cut at this time.[32] Indeed, their goals were not so different—that is, social transformation via the moral regeneration of individuals—but their means were opposed: education versus conversion. Both were engaged in public campaigns aimed at private transformation, using related discourses (one secular, the other religious) of social regulation by means of sexual self-regulation. The language of scientific enlightenment used by *Women's Voice* contributors is shot through with religious metaphor. And there were feminists in both camps.

What was distinctively feminist was the demand for women's sexual autonomy, their bodily integrity, within a discourse on sexuality which constructed male desire as aggressive and anarchic, female desire as recessive or exclusively maternal. Consequently it was a matter of gaining freedom *from* male sexual demands, and the positive development of psychic love, spiritual or companionate marriage, to replace the sordid realities of marriage as a trade or exchange requiring female dependence and subordination. In the 1890s an alternative begins to emerge, prefiguring the psychological theories of female sexuality which prevailed in the 1920s: the possibility of an active desire in women which is neither mad nor bad, and which does not conflict with her right to autonomy in marriage.

In reconsidering conflict between the sexes in Australia in the 1890s a reading of the *Woman's Voice* on sexuality can show how feminist discourse, neither peripheral to nor completely independent of other social discourses, continuously helps to shape what can be thought, and therefore what can be changed.

11 Reproducing Empire: Exploring ideologies of gender and race on Australia's Pacific frontier
Claudia Knapman

Over past decades, studies of Afro-Americans in the United States of America have drawn attention to the salience of gender in any analysis of contemporary 'race' relations. Elsewhere academics have examined the ways in which gender and race intersect and cannot be conflated into single, uniform variables. Novelists have movingly depicted the complexity of male–female relationships in which race is an unavoidable element.[1] However, '[m]ost commentaries on Australian racism assume that men and women are affected equally by racist behaviour',[2] and that the formulation of racial ideologies is gender neutral.

Modern Australia has been built around explicit racial and cultural exclusions, with boundaries constructed against both Aboriginal people at home and foreign 'others' from overseas.[3] This process of exclusion is inseparable from the conceptualisation of white women as producers and guardians of a white nation. As Marie de Lepervanche has demonstrated, arguments for 'social cohesion' and the 'national interest' in the present immigration debates are rooted in and sustained by the interwoven racism and sexism which have been part of Australian life for over 200 years.[4]

While ideologies are not immutable, racist and sexist patterns of thought and behaviour are so deeply engrained in our culture that they are characterised by their dominance and resilience rather than by significant shifts in content and boundaries. Their taken-for-granted status is not limited to everyday interactions and popular beliefs, for these assumptions also permeate scholarly interpretation and analysis. Twentieth-century accounts of the past unwittingly incorporate and reinforce these ideologies. Thus, early efforts at rewriting encounters between white settlers and indigenous Australians to include women added women to existing interpretations.

Such contribution history 'asserts that women were there too. [But there] is no effort to rethink the definition of the historically significant'.[5]

In reconsidering the isolation of Australian history, Donald Denoon suggested 'that the essence and the implications of many Australian ideas became manifest *only* in those extreme situations which Australians encountered abroad'.[6] With regard to the 'nature and dynamic of Australian race relations' and 'distinctively female experience, as opposed to male anxiety and fantasy',[7] the Pacific frontier provides such a location for detailed analysis of Australian ideas. It also provides an excellent opportunity for examining the dominant explanatory frameworks which need to be dismantled in a rewriting of colonial history.

During the 1860s and early 1870s Fiji was the 'next' frontier: prospective settlers and adventurers from Australia and New Zealand were attracted by the dream of a plantation society, in which it was believed to be the destiny of the white man to build a self-sustaining white community.[8] This dream was shaken but not shattered by the collapse in the price of cotton. Fiji became a British Crown Colony in 1874; this, with the possibility of a profitable sugar industry, restored settler confidence. Most Fijians chose not to work as contract labour, and the first male and female Indian indentured labourers arrived in 1879 to meet the new colony's labour requirements. The Colonial Sugar Refining Company of Australia (CSR) established its first mill at Nausori in 1882, expanding its operations to four mills by 1903. By the turn of the century the European population had reached 2459 of whom 982 were female; Fijians numbered 94 397 and Indians 17 105.[9] While Fiji has never been a European settler society, many among the small white population hoped that it might follow the Australian or New Zealand pattern and become 'a white man's country'; others aspired to a lifestyle they had experienced (or imagined) in India, the West Indies or Ceylon. White minority control of political and economic life, the establishment of a separate Fijian administration, and Indian status being determined by servitude, ensured that the divisions in the population were institutionalised on racial lines.

The rationale for this structural division of the population was a racial ideology which, although expressed in a variety of ways and incorporating a range of often conflicting opinions, justified white elitism and control. This ideology was inextricably linked to meanings associated with differences of sex. This intersection of two kinds of colonisation will be discussed in the next section. A third colonisation—that of the white colonial child—will be explored also.

A detailed examination of the characteristics and sources of white racism and sexism in colonial Fiji can be found elsewhere.[10] While it is not possible to explore the ideology of race and the associated constructions of black males and females in this chapter, it is important to recognise that these are integrally related to white gender constructions. Much work needs to be done in examining the European stereotypes of Fijian and

Indian men and women, the gender ideologies within those cultures, and the relationships of both to the circumstances of real men and women. What is clear is the complex interaction between race and gender ideologies and associated practices. Here I want to emphasise four ways in which white racism and white sexism were inseparable, and how this entanglement is clarified (in line with Denoon's argument) by referring to the lives of white women in Fiji.

First, in nineteenth-century gender ideology women were the moral guardians of the home and, by extension, of the nation. Kerreen Reiger points out that the definition of the home in terms of sanctity and a domestic retreat was 'not peculiar to Australia but was part of a widespread bourgeois ideology of the family. Its strength in Australia was doubtless increased by the ideology and actual patterns of home ownership'.[11] It was this desire for a place of their own and future prosperity—the pursuit of the Australian dream—that attracted settlers to try their luck in Fiji. The additional element of risk heightened the need for demonstrable evidence of success. Installation of a white wife and children could be interpreted as a sign of actual or impending achievement of their goal, thus further increasing the emphasis on the home as a private retreat and the woman as its sacred guardian. European men in Fiji expressed the view, shared by those in societies of British origin, that the woman was 'the Angel in the House',[12] but this took on special significance in the context of the white mistress training and presiding over 'black' servants, some of whom were recently 'savages'. The image of white womanhood also incorporated aspects derived from Australian experience. Specifically, Anne Summers' conceptualisation of Australian wives and mothers, entrusted with the moral guardianship of society, as 'God's Police' is relevant.[13] This, too, had enhanced importance in a social context where maintaining the separation of the races was thought to be critical to family survival.

It followed from the moral imperative of their role in the home that the fate of the nation depended on women acting as sources and protectors of virtue and values. This has been demonstrated for Britain[14] and Australia: 'Women were therefore the lynchpin of hearth and home and on their nest-building efforts would depend the future of the nation.'[15] Again, this was much more vital in a small, vulnerable social group where the maintenance of minority power and status was seen to depend on racial purity. Kerreen Reiger points out that in Australia it was not women's work in the household which was of concern here, but their supportive and refining influence upon husbands and children.[16] These spiritual attributes of white womanhood were heightened in Fiji in the colonial racial–gender mythology which incorporated the expectation that white women did not need to work even in the home. So the invisible racial component of the moral emphasis on women as guardians of the home and nation becomes explicit in Australia's frontier colonialism in the Pacific, where the *white* woman was unquestionably the protector of the white home and the hoped-for future *white* nation.

Second, women were construed as dependants. Analyses of the nineteenth-century British woman emphasise the relationship between her restricted action in what was regarded as the real world—the world of public, paid work—and the rise of the middle classes, committed to the goal of self-advancement through hard work. Her gracious living, removed from the competitiveness of industry and commerce, was interpreted as a visible sign of male success. Desley Deacon has shown how this criterion of material success was transferred to the level of the nation in Australia by reference to the New South Wales government statistician. His 'beliefs about the economic basis of national prosperity led...to a wholesale attack on the family economy and the employment of married women and partially dependent daughters'.[17] The Fiji statistician held similar views and the census figures did not accurately reflect women's participation in the economic life of the colony. They did reflect a strong belief that European women were best categorised by the Domestic Duties classification as dependants: a belief reinforced by the experience of emigration in search of a better life than Australia itself could offer. A lifestyle which emphasised the importance of women as consumers rather than producers required the demonstration of their unlimited leisure, their use of the services of others and their high standard of living, again testifying to the success of their husband or father as a provider and to his achievement of a better life, as noted above. In addition, this emphasis on women's dependence was strengthened by the fact that this new and better life rested on European control of Fijian and Indian labour; hence, a racial dimension was integral to the notion that women (of the 'superior race') need not and should not work.

This leads into the third aspect, the way in which white racism and white sexism intersected in class relations. In reality, of course, women did work and not only in the home. What is surprising in a society with such a clearly institutionalised racial hierarchy is just how much and how varied was the paid and unpaid work they did. For while women's work was under-enumerated and unrecognised in Australia, women of European origin were not generally excluded from occupations on the basis of their race; in predominantly white societies women did work as charwomen, housemaids, fruit-pickers and factory workers. In Fiji, white women who were responsible for the economic support of their families were restricted not just by a gender-differentiated labour market, but by a racial division which impinged further on those gender proscriptions. No white woman of any class could be a paid household domestic or a paid field labourer, for example, because labourers were black; white women were not supposed to need nor want to work anyway, and if what were thought of as 'exceptional' circumstances (such as widowhood) necessitated it, white women did not do manual work, by definition. This ideology of white female dependence, together with the associated limitations on women's work deriving from racial constructs, meant that many women showed enormous initiative in finding 'suitable' ways of earning an income. It meant also that white women were automatically regarded as 'upper' or 'middle' class. Although white society was characterised by quite marked internal class divisions, and white women's real circumstances and class origins might have been common knowledge, no white woman was other than 'a lady': consciousness of race overshadowed distinctions of class.

This denial of the working-class status of any white women was reinforced by their assigned moral status. The overlap is most clearly demonstrated by the fact that no white woman could work as a prostitute. Elsewhere I have argued that the categorisation of women into 'good' and 'bad' in Victorian England[18] and in Australia[19] took a distinctly racial form in Fiji.[20] While the sources of this identity lie deep in British thought, they are not so obvious in an overwhelmingly white society. However, the circumstances of colonisation and frontier life in Australia reveal how Aboriginal female identity assigned by Europeans, and ensuing social relations, conform to the general pattern characterising race–gender constructions in Fiji. In Australia, the 'extreme dehumanization' of Aboriginal women was the concrete expression of a 'conflation of sexist and racist ideology'. Sexist attitudes to women received unbridled expression, and racist attitudes to Aborigines denied Aboriginal women even the limited protection, idealisation or courtesy afforded to white women.[21] In Fiji, the white woman was always 'respectable', whereas at the most general level black women, whether Fijian or Indian, were not. From the days of earliest contact, the liaison of foreign men and Fijian women was interpreted in terms of the moral laxity of 'native' women and their sexual availability. Indian indentured women, at the very bottom of the hierarchy of status and power, were regarded as 'loose' for having migrated[22] and Indian living quarters were referred to as brothels.[23] In terms of economic class, all Indian women were categorised as manual labourers, either as field workers or as domestic servants. While the aristocratic background and authority of some Fijian women demanded that they be shown deference, overall the white woman's 'superior' morality and class position were exalted by the devaluation of non-white women.

A fourth dimension of the race–gender conjuncture is the depiction of women as reproducers of the nation and race. Reference has been made already to the importance attached to women's guiding influence in the home for both family and nation. A powerful ideology of motherhood converged with this in a concern for healthy children and racial strength. The state of the nation and the race permeated discussions of motherhood and reproduction in turn-of-the-century Britain, with the home being seen as the cradle of the imperial race and mothers being held responsible for the

Empire's manpower.[24] Awareness of a growing British emphasis on a healthy and expanding population as a source of national strength, and widespread disquiet about high infant mortality rates and a decline in the birthrate, prompted particular attention to motherhood in Australia from the mid 1890s. Statistical studies and a Royal Commission in 1903–04, fuelled discussion of child-bearing and rearing as a duty to the state.[25] While environmental public health initiatives were critical to improvement in child health, a direct solution adopted to address the problem of infant mortality was the 'scientific' education of women to raise the quality of maternal care. Home visits by health workers were justified in the context of improving the health of the population.[26] In other words, women were held responsible for the future of the Australian nation.

Adequate statistics are not available for Fiji, but we do know that families were large, that Fijians often expressed surprise at the frequency with which European women bore children, that contraception was not as readily available as it was in Australia and that infant deaths occurred in most families. Reproduction assumed even greater importance given the political and economic circumstances and the cultural climate of a white minority situation. Missionary commitment placed special emphasis on the Victorian family as a model of 'civilised' Christian behaviour, and the residence in Fiji of white women in general presupposed the reproduction necessary for permanent white settlement. Settlers who believed that Fiji was destined to become a white man's country were attempting to pass on the fruits of their success to the next generation. Even if women in private favoured having fewer children, the pressures of men who saw this as 'characteristic of a decadent state of society'[27] are likely to have been stronger in the colonising and civilising atmosphere of European society in Fiji.

Moreover, the health of the race could not be separated from its purity in the Fijian context. Once more we are confronted by the inseparability of gender- and race-based issues. White women were in a critical position for the realisation of the colonial aspirations of white males. Because of this, it was essential that their reproductive power be controlled. White women's moral status, economic dependence and superior class position were necessary components of an ideology which held them to be not just the guardians, but the producers and reproducers of the social (and necessarily racial) order.

While many white women shared these assumptions—and *worked* hard to achieve the desired lifestyle—undoubtedly the 'civilising mission' was regarded as a male enterprise. While ostensibly gender neutral, the very terms 'settler' and 'frontier society' carried connotations of adventure, hardship and bravery that were at odds with nineteenth-century images of white womanhood. White women were thought to be biologically unsuited to a tropical climate, physical hardship was regarded as dangerous to such weakly constituted people, and their emotional sensibilities required protection from the rough-and-ready manners of ungentlemanly whites and the nudity and curiosity of 'savages'. The presence of white women was therefore an indication of the serious intentions of white male settlers to establish a white community; a community in which such women were depicted as useless in a practical and economically productive sense, but in which they were valued for the physical, social and emotional comforts they could provide for the real (male) colonisers. Their life experiences, their economic contributions to white survival, their positive relationships with Fijians and Indians, and their interests were trivialised or ignored.[28] In the final analysis, it was their power to reproduce the colonial elite that was most highly valued and which was the essential focus of the prescriptions and prohibitions of white femininity.

From this it follows that the children of empire-builders assume a hitherto unacknowledged importance in the reproduction of colonial society. Despite the existence of class differences and sectional interests, Europeans in Fiji formed a ruling caste in which all whites benefited from the birth-ascribed quality of whiteness. While varied life experiences ensured there was no single European colonial childhood, there was a common emphasis on rearing the child *as a European*, able to fit into an appropriate place in white society. From a European viewpoint this place presupposed whites' general superiority to blacks, and a specific superiority to all Indians and most Fijians. It guaranteed access to status, rewards and opportunities denied to all but a few members of the non-white groups, and largely determined who could be one's schoolmate, friend, colleague, spouse, neighbour, master or servant.

Whether first, second or third generation, children born in the dependencies of metropolitan countries have much to tell us about the processes and effects of colonisation and migration, and about the maintenance of superior and subordinate groups in colonial societies. As the British novelist William Boyd, himself an expatriate child in Africa, wrote: 'I have an intuition that if you want to understand the mood and character of a nation or race, a very effective short-cut is to study the way they educate their young.'[29] Historians of the family have reached similar conclusions on a more general level about the way in which child-rearing behaviour and attitudes act as a cultural index to a particular society.[30] To date there has been little scholarly interest in this aspect of colonialism. What is needed is more than another contribution history, this time adding the details of childhood to the existing historical record. An examination of colonial childhoods must explore the ways in which ideologies of gender and race intersected in, and shaped, the life experiences of real children. If we agree with Denoon's suggestion that a crystallisation of ideas takes place in extreme situations overseas, then studying white Fijian childhoods would elucidate 'the essence and the implications of many Australian ideas'[31] about childhood and social and cultural reproduction.

From an examination of child-rearing practices among white families in late nineteenth and early twentieth-century Fiji two broad models can be identified. The first was predicated on the inherent corruptibility of the child and emphasised early training and little autonomy; the second implied a conception of childhood primarily as a time of play, with some mandatory household tasks but in which formal training for adulthood began in the second decade of life. Real childhoods approximated these models to varying degrees. It is possible to discern a general pattern in which missionary and upper-class families favoured the former model and firmly controlled the activities of their children (for different reasons). The second model can be found at all socioeconomic levels, but more commonly among middle and lower-class families, who favoured a less formal approach and allowed their children a greater degree of freedom.

The motivation in the case of missionary families was twofold. In the earlier years and in more remote areas, it was to protect their children from demoralising contact with un-Christian and uncivilised people, and enforced a separation from all 'contaminating' influences. By the end of the century, the use of the child as a Christian model for and teacher of Fijian children was more common. While this involved contact with rather than separation from Fijians, it was built upon a firm grounding in Methodist theology. So the child was inspired, in the words of one thirteen-year-old-girl, 'to lead a better life both in the home and out, in all I do, say, or think'.[32] In the upper-class family—typical of the well-to-do planter— children had all their physical needs supplied by a (black) servant, frequently had a (white) nursery governess to supervise daily activities, and between the ages of five and seven were sent away to boarding school in Australia or New Zealand. Strict gender differentiation was maintained before this and during the annual holidays, with sons being encouraged to accompany their fathers when supervising the labour and to engage in physical, outdoor activities, whereas girls remained at home. In the alternative model children also had the services of a (black) nurse, although not necessarily exclusively for their own needs. Regardless of sex, they could join in games and local adventures as soon as they could keep up with other children. Town children, in particular, lived a neighbourhood life, attended the local school and roamed at will, sometimes in the company of Fijian servants' children. For girls, this freedom was curtailed at about age ten, when their lives became more closely tied to the home; but for both boys and girls, adolescence brought an end to this easy-going freedom, whether in Fiji or overseas. Many more children were sent overseas for schooling at eleven or twelve years of age. As with those who were sent away earlier, this reflected their parents' desire to secure an Australian or New Zealand education for their children, and to prevent association with Fijians, Indians and lower-status Europeans.

The most significant features of these child-rearing patterns are first, the early familiar contact with Fijian and Indian servants, and second, the reclaiming of the white child by white society at adolescence if not before. The infant-nurse relationship established a positive attitude to Fijians or Indians and, since children spoke the language of their servants, Fijian or Hindustani was often their first language. For children who were not sent away at a very young age, this early warmth developed into an awareness of people of other races as individuals through play with household servants, participation in their work and common deference to the mistress and master of the household. Often, this understanding was furthered by play with Fijian children through the early school years. In such ways the interaction between black and white was mediated by the European child.[33]

It needs to be borne in mind, however, that the child's experiences took place against a background of institutionalised differentiation and discrimination. The racial hierarchy of superiority and inferiority permeated public and private life through residential location, architecture, lifestyle, various official and unofficial segregationist practices and mistress/master–servant relationships. Even the intimate, positive contact of infancy and early childhood demonstrated that the white child was the property of a white master and mistress, and the focus of special treatment. All of this reinforced the general lapse during adolescence of the white child's earlier easy familiarity with Fijians and Indians. New educational or occupational circumstances effectively enforced the racial separation required for appropriate adult behaviour. For those sent overseas, the institutional hothouse setting of the boarding school, without the everyday experience of Australian domestic life, provided yet another lesson in their difference from 'others'. The British origins of the colonial boarding schools should not be forgotten in this context. The British public school 'lay somewhere near the heart of the imperial ethic'[34] and its products showed a 'curious mixture of sheltered innocence and self-confidence...They believed in fair play, in supporting the under-dog and in hard and fast prefectorial attitudes that allowed no room for lies or deceit or disloyalty. They remained seniors in charge of juniors, paternalists at heart'.[35]

The adult imperialist's paternalism was crystallised in the imagery of the family, describing the relationship between colonised and colonisers in terms of the 'native' child under the tutelage of the white father.[36] This placed the 'native' and the white child in the same relationship to the authority figure, but it was a subordination which the child outgrew whereas the 'native' did not. Nevertheless, it is likely that the child's early personal contact with the servant and the servant's culture was strengthened by this shared symbolic identity and actual status as a minor. Perhaps were children in colonial Fiji. Interview data indicates that uncertainty about the significance of colour and ascribed status was quite common, although rarely acknowledged. Ann McGrath's research implies that a similar phenomenon may exist among white adults who were reared with Aboriginal servants in Australia. She notes that the white children learnt Aboriginal languages and developed an understanding of law and thought patterns. Even if as adults they rejected the black women who had nursed them, the experience left a deep impression.[37] Despite the separating mechanisms white society used to control its young, and the adult dismissal of early experiences, these children had to some extent lived in two discontinuous worlds. The need to belong as an adult to the dominant, white world did not obliterate their former relationship to the 'other'.

To summarise, with some exceptions, white children were seen as adjuncts to the adult world and as not having any part in it until they reached adolescence. On the one hand they were excluded from adult society and their 'corruptibility' was protected by segregation, particularly in boarding establishments. On the other, they were regarded as incomplete beings, whose early experiences were insubstantial and could be replaced by appropriate training later. In both cases, the child's ability to construct his or her own world and the impact of early socialisation were discounted. The child, like the woman and the non-white, was not regarded as a full person.

The racial and gender ideologies and their ambiguities found a single focus in the person of the white child. The child belonged in the domestic sphere of the white woman, but he or she shared the minor status and, initially, the company and language of the non-white adult. On *both* counts the child was less than a complete person from the dominant white perspective. Becoming an adult entailed the search common to those of British origin for an identity distinct from that of their parents. For females this ideally involved substitution of one household for another through marriage, whereas for males—the real actors in colonial society—it presupposed separation from the (female) home. That white adult identity involved dissociation from non-white cultures and people has been demonstrated, and it is a logical necessity in a colonial social order in which the elite was defined in racial terms. Given the particular conceptions of childhood and the associated child-rearing strategies that were employed, this separation was assumed to be possible. It was the child's *future* position and status as a white adult that was the central issue of childhood for white colonialism, not the child's experiences in the present. The young child was a non-entity in an indeterminate position, aligned with both white and black. The older child was a young master or mistress expected to conform to the dominant race and gender ideologies and assume the correct structural position in colonial society. The contradictions of the colonial situation are personified in the white child. If the first colonisation in Fiji was that of race, the second was that of gender and the third, that of the child.

The unravelling of ideologies, of their relationships to each other and to actual behaviour has barely begun in the colonial context. This chapter has looked at a few of the ways white ideologies intersect. Because stereotypes are simplifications and rationalisations of power relationships, such constructions are beset by contradictions and lack coherence. White females were construed as the antithesis of black males and yet both were regarded as white male property; they were opposites but both were in subordinate positions. Their separation was essential to maintain racial purity and racially based authority, but because men were regarded as intellectually superior to women, male labourers were often assigned as domestic servants. Control of the black man's labour and land and the white woman's fertility were critical to white colonial rule and white male identity and status. The ideological devaluation of the 'other' race and the 'other' sex were necessary to justify both of these appropriations.

The nineteenth-century meanings attached to particular physical characteristics permeated social organisation and are the antecedents of contemporary attitudes, values, laws and behaviour. These devaluations extended to the historical record and have been incorporated into our methods of analysis and our explanations of the colonial past. The child, a minor on two grounds, does not appear at all. Women and non-whites had no voices of their own in our histories, but were portrayed in terms of the racial and gender ideologies. Perhaps this colonisation of historical explanation is the most significant of all the ways in which race and gender intersect. It is particularly obvious in the way in which a stereotype of the dependent and peripheral white woman has been brought into the action of the male colonising endeavour to 'explain' white racism and racial conflict. This can be demonstrated not just for Fiji, but for a whole range of mixed-race colonial situations.[38] The white woman's moral purity, emotional and physical fragility, concern for social niceties and preoccupation with defending her home and children have been used to account for racial tensions rooted in far more fundamental economic and political conflicts of interests. Twentieth-century academic interpretation has built upon nineteenth-century ideologies. Those ideologies intersect and, although unable to withstand detailed scrutiny as representations of reality, they are reified by continual usage. Revisiting Australia's Pacific frontier in colonial Fiji from a feminist viewpoint involves more than reorienting history-writing with gender at the centre. It demands that the interrelationships of gender, class and race be examined and that the life experiences of all social actors be addressed. This necessitates a decolonisation of the historical record and of explanatory frameworks, in order that 'other' questions can be asked and 'other' voices can be heard.

12 Sovereignty and sexual identity in political cartoons
Josie Castle and Helen Pringle

The aim of this chapter is to explore a pictorial mythology unfolding in cartoons of turn-of-the-century Australia. The cartoons we consider present an array of female figures. The problem that these cartoons pose for us has to do with the dilemmas of civic and political identity in a society for which self-government was an urgent practical question. For us, these cartoons constitute a record of the way in which this society took that question and tried to resolve it in the order of thought.

The cartoons we consider can be clustered into two main groups. The first comprises images of clearly identifiable women, whether as allegories of daily life or as allegories of statehood. The depiction of such female figures as markers of civic identity is thoroughly conventional, finding its place in a long tradition of the use of women to bear the symbolic burdens of virtues like justice, temperance, courage or wisdom.[1] More surprising is the second group of cartoons, which comprises images of men (usually prominent politicians) in travesty. Although their 'true sex' is apparently not in doubt, these cartoon men masquerade as nurses, midwives and washerwomen. The most striking of this second group is a cartoon of Edmund Barton, the first Prime Minister, nursing the new infant Australia. Such images trade on associations of women with maternity and cleanliness, but in doing so they figure forth ambiguity and uncertainty about the questions of self-government and independence.[2]

In order to understand both groups of cartoons more fully, we have chosen to isolate a seemingly anomalous cartoon printed in the *W.A. Bulletin* of April 1888 entitled 'The Modern Sphinx', a cartoon which recalls the story of Oedipus and the Sphinx. The modern sphinx provides a key link between the two main groups of cartoons. Lying between the feminine allegories of civic identity and Nurse Barton, the modern sphinx enables us to identify these images as displaying a vacillating commitment to autonomy, experienced not only as a political dilemma but as a hesitation at the heart of masculinity itself.

Fig. 12.1 'The Modern Sphinx'. In olden days unwary knights were enticed into the clutches of the sphinx, who granted them their liberty if they could guess correctly, in three tries, the conundrum given them. If not they were swallowed up.—*Ancient legend. Modern Sphinx (to fettered W.A.): Can you govern yourself?*

The background to our exploration is the posing of the problem of self-government in the 1890s. A long period of unprecedented growth in the colonies ended in 1890–91 with a steep fall in national income. Economic depression, drought, civil unrest and the challenge of socialism dominated the 1890s. Political federation of the colonies assumed the status of 'sovereign remedy' for all these problems of economic security. The remedy for other problems was less settled. Male politicians were beset by continued demands for women's suffrage, unsettled by the presence of women in the universities, and disturbed by female claims to enter the male professions of medicine and law. The sharp decline in the birth rate already apparent in 1891, and confirmed in the 1901 census, provoked in male authority figures like Timothy Coghlan and Octavius Beale[3] an unease as to an implied rejection of motherhood. The cartoons we consider comment on the social conflict generated by this decade of recession and a demographic transition which threatened the traditional role of women and the gender order.

The achievement of nationhood was shadowed by the stain of the convict past and the strains of continuing subordination to the Imperial mother with her hostility to the emerging White Australia policy. The argument of this chapter is that, given continuing ambivalence over the Imperial connection, the achievement of nationhood was difficult for cartoonists to image: the pictures they drew reflect unease and ambivalence over political compromise. The turmoil and uncertainty about political and social forms are reflected in the cartoonists' search for an appropriate icon for the new nation. Importantly, political fears expressed in *content* are echoed by representational anxieties of *form*: the unsteadiness of classical figures in expressing nationhood is related to the mutability of a derivative society. No definitive icon of an Australian identity emerged to parallel, say, the development of Marianne in revolutionary France.

Conflict in the gender order of the 1890s is inscribed in the allegorical use of the female figure in cartoons. The use of males in drag, in its inversion and suspension of normality, emerges at a time of dislocation in the relations between men and women. This political crisis is expressed through motifs that also suggest fears about virility, loss of manhood, enslavement, and the stability of sexual difference. Cross-dressing in cartoons testifies to the incongruity and novelty of a situation where the legitimate figures of power have cleared the way for a new political order. Cross-dressing here functions as a way to test out anxieties about virility and legitimacy. Masculine identity is costumed in frocks not to provoke laughter in the Benny Hill mode, but to provoke reflection on an insufficient or flawed masculinity.

Riddles of the sphinx

Let us turn first to the anomaly among our cartoons, the cartoon of 'The Modern Sphinx', drawn by Herbert C. Gibbs (figure 12.1). It depicts a desert landscape, with pyramids. Out of the desert looms a stern-faced sphinx, emblazoned 'Imperial Government'. A maiden in classical dress stands with her face turned to the sphinx, her hands tied behind her back. In the place of the questioner/hero figure of Oedipus, the cartoon shows a woman in fetters, a depiction which departs in its physical appearance, dress and posture from canonical norms.

Gibbs' cartoon is technically unremarkable, but it carries the symbolic burden of the story of Oedipus and the sphinx.[4] It takes up the story at the point where Oedipus, having unwittingly murdered his father, confronts the sphinx (whose name means 'throttler'). By answering the sphinx's riddle, Oedipus claims both the sovereignty of Thebes and the bed of the rightful titular queen Jocasta (not knowing she is his mother). By begetting children from Jocasta, Oedipus becomes at once his own father and his own child, three generations rolled up in one: the signs of legitimate and ordered succession to the power of manhood and of the city have gone haywire. The tale of Oedipus not only concerns the stormy relations of one particularly troubled Greek family, but is at once a cautionary tale of how rightfully to transmit power and how legitimately to accede to rule, woven about a search for personal and political identity. Oedipus the questioner is in fact the pretender to rule, the fraudulent substitute for the genuine article.

But at the centre of Gibbs' allusions, there is seemingly a mistake: by putting a woman in the place of Oedipus, Gibbs has pushed off-balance the classical motifs of the story. No iconographic warrant can be found in classical or modern sources, whether literary or pictorial, of the sphinx story, for a maiden to take the role of questioner, nor for the detail of her fetters.[5] The masculinity of the figure of the interlocutor/hero had been maintained right through the iconographical adventures which otherwise befell sphinx stories in their estrangement from the classical repertoire of imagery.[6] In European art of the late nineteenth century, for example, the sphinx's demeanour had been feminised to an extreme not foreshadowed in the classical sources, to sustain associations with men's anxiety and with enigma: the sphinx's voracity posed an ominous yet ill-defined threat to manhood more terrible than the Medusa.[7] Oedipus' sex-change in Gibbs' cartoon is even more odd given the general trend in the late nineteenth century towards the masculinisation of civic, political and even scientific imagery.[8]

Gibbs' cartoon re-enacts the story of Oedipus, but with, in the place of the hero figure, a hesitation which takes the form of gender inversion, in dress and character. Both figures in the cartoon are in fact feminine: in the one case, the excessive power of Imperial Government, and in the other, the flawed and deficient power of the questioner. Between these two figures, the lethal riddling of the sphinx acts as a bar to a properly constituted and orderly transmission of power, and a successfully accomplished manhood. Mother rather than father holds the key to inheritance of the patrimony of power and hence accession to legitimate sonhood. The symbolic Oedipal freight of blighted succession and of an interrupted legitimacy is carried in Gibbs' cartoon in the anxiety of being misbegotten, of being an illegitimate pretender to rule, of being weak and womanish.

In Gibbs' cartoon, political authority takes the form of a question rather than of a settled representation. The cartoon presents inversion in the order of gender as a sign of a political crisis. The question of authority being as yet unanswered, all is out of place, and manhood can only find a furtive place in the figure of the fettered woman. What Neil Hertz has called 'semiotic restlessness' prevails.[9] In colonial conditions, cartoonists roamed over the semiotic field in search of a just and true representation of a properly constituted manhood capable of assuming civic identity.

Fig. 12.2 'Innocent triflers'. Or, the joys of his first and her second childhood.

The trouble with goddesses

The semiotic field of nineteenth-century Australian cartooning in its presentation of the dilemmas of civic identity was underpopulated with indigenous figures. One of the most important icons used to stand for incipient national life in the 1890s was 'The Little Boy at Manly', his innocence related to the sexlessness of his pre-adolescent status (see figure 12.2). This figure was the creation of Livingston Hopkins ('Hop'), an American expatriate who was the *Bulletin*'s chief cartoonist from 1883 until 1913. In his autobiography, Hopkins explained the difficulties of acclimatising the classical female figures of virtue and civic identity in Australia:

> I dont know whether I ought to let you into a secret...
> Every nation, as you are aware, has some mythical figure, usually of the gentler sex, to personify the national spirit; e.g., in Great Britain, Britannia; in Germany, Germania; in the United States, Columbia, etc., and all more or less dressed up to the ancient Greek ideal of Minerva.
> These ladies are very useful to the graphic artist, and figure frequently in political cartoons, especially those of a prim allegorical character; but when it comes to depicting the more rugged phases of national life, it is found that the masculine myths such as John Bull and Brother Jonathon of that ilk, will stand more knocking about than the lady deities.
> In my early days on the *Bulletin*, whenever we had occasion for a goddess, or other personification of Australia, we had to import one at great expense to the establishment, and somehow or other we always found Minerva difficult to acclimatize. There was, therefore, a vacancy at the *Bulletin* office for a myth that was willing to make itself generally useful.

Fig. 12.3 'The glorious twenty-sixth!' *Premier Turner:* My friend, you'll have to get off your pedestal presently, to oblige a lady.

Later, among the donations made by a generous public to the Soudan Contingent, was one from 'A Little Boy at Manly'. Hopkins continued,

> What he gave, whether it was a fiddle, a warming pan, or a bottle of 'Pain-killer' is of no moment now. A journalistic whim of the moment turned the phrase 'Little Boy at Manly' to satirical account as typifying the well-meant impetuousity of a young colony in espousing a cause that was well able to take care of itself—in the opinion of one journal at least. Our artist, in the course of dealing with the Contingent episode, had occasion to drag in the 'Little Boy at Manly' from time to time, and, to make a long story short, 'The Little Boy at Manly' got promoted to the position of office myth, which he seemed to grow into naturally, and so filled a long-felt want.[10]

The little boy from Manly occupies a place midway between man and woman; his invention did not put an end to semiotic wanderlust.

Cartoonists like Hop seemed to have no difficulty in finding female subjects for allegories of daily life—to depict uppity servanthood, frivolous and spendthrift gentlewomen, moral rectitude ('God's Police'), or snobbery (in the characters of 'Push Society'). But when it came to illustrating civic dilemmas for the occasion solemn, both conservative and radical cartoonists faced a vacancy in civic representation. Various other allegorical figures applied for the vacancy. Nicholas Chevalier of the *Melbourne*

Punch, for example, cast Mr Kangaroo Bull, a progeny of John Bull, in the vacant role in 1857, but this aspirant seems not to have been capable of an extension from the small grazier against inefficient land legislation to a substitute Minerva embodying an emerging Australian identity.

Throughout the late nineteenth century, cartoonists tried to displace the convict from the field of the political representation of Australia. In 1864, Edward Jukes Greig in a cartoon for *Punch* pictured Australia as a toga-ed and tiara-ed figure standing on the globe of New South Wales, surrounded with panels of justice, charity, agriculture and trade. The cartoon's legend protested, 'AUSTRALIA HAS OTHER SYMPATHIES THAN THOSE WITH CRIME: Dedicated, without permission, to her traducers'. In a 1885 cartoon in *Australian Tit-Bits*, New South Wales is portrayed as a beautiful but wanton maid who rests her head on a convict with chains (labelled 'Recidivism' and 'Convict') on his legs and neck. The convict shields his eyes from the shining dawn of Australia in the distance. The woman's broken lyre 'Patriotism' is cast aside and the caption ascribes the secret of New South Wales' opposition to nationalism as: she cannot bear to break with *old associations*!'. In a cartoon by Vincent in the *Bulletin* of 4 February 1899, 'THE GLORIOUS TWENTY-SIXTH!', the Victorian Premier Turner pokes the convict off the pedestal of 'Australian Nationalism', while pointing to a belaurelled maiden, 'Federation', who hitches up her skirts in order to ascend to the convict's place (see figure 12.3).

The vacancy in representation noted by Hop was not definitively filled: no one symbol with invariable features came to stand for the emerging nation. The figure of woman was promiscuously used: in the cartoons we have considered, there seems little consistency in the portrayal of women as virtues of one sort or another (or as vices), nor are they any more consistently thought of as nature, for example, than as culture. Our cartoon women appear as comely girls, as old crones, whores, damsels in distress, lion tamers, servants, even as Miss or Mrs Victoria.[11]

After the referendum approving federation, Australia increasingly came to be presented in the guise of a maiden, classically frocked like Gibbs' questioner. For example, 'AN OMINOUS START' by Fred Leist in the *Bulletin* of November 1899 shows Australia covering her face in grief as her troops depart to the Boer War: 'And so my first national act is to back up a wanton deed of blood and rapine!' Australia's classical regalia (and Roman hairstyle) has grace as well as bulk in 'THE LADY AND THE TIGER' in *Melbourne Punch* (1898), in which she tames the tiger Reid with her whip labelled 'Elections'.

Citizenship in drag

We have seen Gibbs' cartoon as part of an exercise in symbolic power and its manipulation, interpreting the sex-change of the questioner in terms of the enigma of ordered and orderly succession. A crisis in political legit-

Fig. 12.4 ' "There, take them; but you must wear a petticoat over them." '

imacy is signalled in the cartoon as sexual ambiguity, such that the questioner (and the figure who is questioned) comes across as a woman. We want to relate this cartoon, in which a womanly figure appears in a place which we might expect (given classical antecedents) should be occupied by a man, to a series in which often quite specific social facts dictate our expectations. In this context, the cartoons of men in frocks figure uncertainty and ambiguity.

But why should uncertainty be shown in this way? The representations of women in cartoons did not *mirror* changes in society in any simple way. In 1888, the date of Gibbs' cartoon, women were without the vote, and were debarred from other means of political action.[12] Granting women the vote meant surrendering a domain of masculine authority, and the prelude to the act was fraught with bitterness and unease. Thus Hop in a cartoon in the *Bulletin* of 24 November 1900 shows NSW Premier Lyne (who proposed to grant women the vote but without the right to sit in parliament) with a rather ugly and bespectacled suffragist peering out from behind a screen. Lyne offers her a pair of checked breeches, the civic privilege of the vote, but with the caveat: 'There, take them; but you must wear a petticoat over them' (see figure 12.4).

Far from simply reflecting the social relations and thought of the community, our cartoons seem to bring it into question. Cross-dressed men in cartoons present a political problem, of the proper relations between generations of men, in terms of fears about virility, loss of manhood, enslavement—and the representational stability of sexual difference itself. They challenge any fixed or *just* idea of emblematic forms. They seem to point to the threat of losing the control or security of one's self-representations.

The crisis of political representation came to a head at the time of Federation: what sort of figure could stand for Australia, in order to portray

Fig. 12.5 'Anxious about his billet'.
Bulletin office myth: I was a thinkin', Sir, as you wouldn't want me no longer. You'll want a bigger boy'n me to be the myth of federated Australiar?
Chief engineer of the cartoon machine: H'm! Think we'll keep you on a while to help look after the new baby, and to make yourself generally useful. P'raps you'll grow. In the meantime, wash your face, and run out and look up a suitable site for the capital.

its new status? A cartoon of Hop from the *Bulletin* of August 1900 draws together these strands of specific issues of self-government and of security

Fig. 12.6 'Arrival of the new baby'. *Nurse Barton*: He ain't much to look at now. But wait till he grows!

of representation (see figure 12.5). The little boy from Manly approaches Hop, anxious about his symbolic future in a federated Australia. Alas, the little boy did not grow to a cartoon manhood, but was edged out as an indicator of national political life by figures of political leaders in drag.

A handful of cartoons that heralded federation portray Edmund Barton in frocks, and it is these we would like to link to the Gibbs cartoon, as effecting a similar feminisation in their reflection on the dilemmas of citizenship. The image in the Barton cartoons is usually of a mature female, either washerwoman or nurse-midwife. Barton as midwife signals the low-life origins of this stereotype by carrying an umbrella (or gamp), the badge of Sarah Gamp, the drunken and disreputable nurse in *Martin Chuzzlewit*, who summed up the lowly status of nursing in the late nineteenth century.

The first of the Barton group is a cartoon by Hop from the *Bulletin* of 14 July 1900, which shows a rather portly and prissily dressed 'Nurse Barton' with bag and umbrella in one hand, and a baby whose ribbon says 'Commonwealth' in the other (see figure 12.6). Hopkins was rather fond of the motif of political men as nurses. One of his earliest cartoons on the question of federation, in the *Bulletin* of 1891, shows Nurse Parkes (Parkes was chairman of the first Federation Convention in 1891) holding the infant Federation, feeding it from a bottle labelled Public Approval. When the leadership of the Federation movement passed to Barton, Hop turned to portraying Barton in the Nursie role. After the Queensland referendum on federation, he drew 'THE LAST ADDITION TO THE FAMILY' (1899), in which black baby Queensland, resting on the lap of Nurse Barton, sucks its thumb while the other colonial children crowd around.[13]

The second Barton cartoon by Hop, from the *Bulletin* of 1901, shows the prime minister with a masculine face and hairstyle but wearing a frock and slippers with an apron marked 'Commonwealth'. He brandishes a sponge marked 'A White Australia' over a figure crawling with black stick-

Fig. 12.7 'Queensland has to give up slavery'. *Barton* (loq.): You dirty boy!

figures, 'Black Queensland'. Barton admonishes, 'You dirty boy!' (see figure 12.7). (This cartoon recalls the cover cartoon of the *Bulletin* of 3 April 1897, showing a middle-aged woman scrubbing down, with 'Anti Slavery Soap', a loin-clothed black. The caption reads, 'Queensland offers to join the Convention.—An Unpleasant Preliminary.')

SOVEREIGNTY AND SEXUAL IDENTITY IN POLITICAL CARTOONS 147

Fig. 12.8 'Prime Minister christens the baby'.

A third cartoon which belongs in an equivocal way to the series of feminised Bartons is from the *Bulletin* of 1902. It shows Barton in a priest's frock christening the howling baby 'Commonwealth', whose date of birth, 1 January 1901, is noted on its christening robe. Barton draws the 'Blud of State Contingents' from the font, while a forlorn woman, classically attired, stands to one side (see figure 12.8).

No full-blown masculine image had emerged by Federation to represent the spirit or identity of the new nation. Instead the masculine image is 'disguised' in women's clothing. The questions broached in these cartoons are not only concerned with the form of independence. They also bring into play sexual anxiety, and fears regarding the fitness for autonomy or self-sufficiency of Australian manhood. The cartoon figures of Barton, like Gibbs' questioner, are fraught with ambiguity: what animates them are questions of identity. They relate to Oedipus' quest for his identity. Can

Fig. 12.9 'The birth of the Commonwealth'.

*The fair new nation
    cometh, drawn
By six proud states so fair
    and tall.
She was their child;
    now, strange to tell,
She is the mother of them all!*

Australia's manhood answer the question of who are you?, can it be master of its own representations?

Semiotic restlessness is seen, in Gibbs' cartoon, in the unsteadiness of the classical figure, its amenability to mutation by alignment with a new set of conditions, and in the Barton cartoons in the equivocality of the masculine image. The anxieties seen here are fears of being misbegotten, of not being able to place oneself in an orderly and legitimate succession of power, of not being able to lay claim to a proper name but of having the name of Australia reflect one's own uncertain filiation.

More than this, finally, the uncertainty of representation is linked to the mystery of birth. The merriest of all the Federation cartoons we considered is 'THE BIRTH OF THE COMMONWEALTH', by Dauncey, in the 1901 *Punch Annual*. Here the six states are gambolling nymphs who with silken cords draw into the twentieth century the shell chariot of Venus, in which rides a resplendent 'Commonwealth' (see figure 12.9). The image evoked by the cartoon's legend, in which the child becomes the mother of her parent, echoes the strangeness of Oedipus' own scrambled identity, in which orderly succession has been subverted.

The cartoons considered here are 'dress rehearsals': they 'try on' autonomy, to see how it fits. They call into play women's clothing and manners to testify to the novelty of the situation, where the legitimate masters of power and descent have cleared the way for a new political order. Our real subject, then, is not representations of women, but rather constructions of feminine figures symbolically outfitted in the masculine dilemmas of autonomy and independence. Our topic in the end turns out to be an iconography less of woman than of masculinity in a moment of equivocation, one which signals a moment of change, a crisis of identity and of name. The questions raised by the sphinx concern legitimacy. The crisis of gender in turn-of-the-century Australia is not an economic one so much as one of identity, of knowing who 'we' are.

13 'Woman' in federation poetry
Barbara Holloway

> The federation poet is a fearful scourge just now, he is as lively as an electric eel in a hot oil can, and runs off line after line of verse with a flippancy that is appalling.
>
> —*Clipper* 1898[1]

In the tangled political and cultural events during, before and after Federation, writers attempted to generate a political cohesion through inscription of a common political vision. In poetry of the period the use of allegorical representations of Woman as State and Nature in the cultural production of 'federation' and 'Australia' is endemic. However, political, literary and social histories of the 1890s have largely ignored such imaging, written though it was in direct response to federalism and to the acquisition of a formal Australian political identity. The poetry that has been anthologised and analysed has been the work which endorses the 'bush ethos' and 'the legend of the Nineties'. This chapter examines other verse to identify ways in which images of Woman were used to create 'Australia.' The image of Woman was used to find definitions when there were none, to attribute value, to give body to geographical and political abstractions, and to articulate desire. It was in poetry that a desired power relationship with both place and polis could be enacted on the model of patriarchal gender relations.

It seems that such representations cannot be discussed in isolation from representations of men as agents of desire, either singly as possessors of the land or communally as chivalrous citizens grouped as brothers, legions or 'mates', ready to have their blood shed in expiation of the Australian past and in affirmation of their new political identity. In addition to creating meaning for 'Australia', these images of both Woman and Citizen served to obliterate historical, economic, class and cultural differences among men. While poets set themselves the task of naming an 'Australia' that could be shared and admired by all who were endorsed as suitable citizens to live within 'her' definitions, their naming also served as part of the ideology defining women's subjectivity. Perhaps for this reason, few women wrote poems drawing on the allegorical Woman as an image of civic collectivity and those poems I've traced by women appear to image Australia as a self-determining being, not to be defined by the poet or the polis.

In 'the legend of the Nineties' generated in the 1950s, the poetry of political fervour has been distinguished from poetry that had bush life as its immediate subject. The former has been dismissed as conservative, and interesting only as symptomatic of efforts to reach a collective nationalism through conventional rhetorical expressions of patriotism and public virtues. The latter is generally categorised as radical, anti-establishment, peculiarly Australian and truly symptomatic of the native ethos of the Nineties. The two are read as antithetical to each other, but they are in fact inseparably connected, as is made clear by their use of the images of Woman. There is a common expression of fear of women, or of Woman, as a seductive predator likely to draw men outside safe bounds, margins, or brotherhood. Both heroise an ideal Woman as a focal point for collective male service. The difference is in the relationship of the male to other males, rather than the relationship of male to female. The female figure provides a consistent *lingua franca* within which to define male relations of power, political ideals, poetic vision and interaction with the environment.

Federation poetry thus drew on two overlapping conventions of ascriptions of femaleness, two sets of gender relations. The conservative is more accurately called the utopian. It was largely political in intent, and drew on the conventions of classical and neo-classical poetry in which Liberty, the State, Democracy and so on are represented as the heroic Woman, and in visual arts as the ideal female form. These poems often set out to define the political state, Australia, and sometimes included the urban social condition. A strong adherence to the poetic rhetoric of the Enlightenment was embedded in many Australian poetic practices from the early century. This, adapted to late nineteenth-century cultural and poetic changes, provided a system for utopian discourse.

The second may be called paradisal, and it was the convention within which nature is female, and the land is a woman. These are the Bush poems, in which the poet sets out to elaborate the relationship of men to the particularly Australian extra-urban physical environment. The paradisal was very often defined by its oppposite, the hellish. This is Australia as the hag, the drought-stricken land in which men died because of the treacherous female *genius loci*. 'Her' rise coincides with the economic push to appropriate inappropriate land for agriculture and pastoralism, but also with the rise of feminism.

The paradisal, however, was also reliant on the representation of nature in romantic poetic conventions, with an infusion of popular ballads. Representation of women and desire was imaged more often in narrative form, such as that found in *The Bulletin Reciter*, or George Essex Evans' long poems of noble bushmen and heroically loyal or perfidiously unfaithful bush fiancées.

The cloud before dawn

In colonial circumstances, the conventional metaphors in traditional poetic discourse had to be re-oriented, to arrive at an intelligible and powerful representation of the immediate. A progression of metaphors can be traced from the latter half of the nineteenth century in which Australia is first 'phantasmagoria', 'impenetrable' or 'undecipherable'. It was at this stage imaged as a mist, cloud or darkness, as the space between moon and sun, inchoate intellectual matter. Progression to another image was then needed to provide metaphors of access, a mediation between 'phantasmagoria' and meaning. These were the metaphors of night-before-dawn, followed by a dawn which 'firms' into variations of allegorical Woman. The Bride, the Mother and the Daughter focus desire in political production, supplemented by allegorical female representations of Prosperity, Corruption, and Democracy, among others.

The centrality of woman in the task of geopolitical imaging is admirably demonstrated in Marcus Clarke's preface to Adam Lindsay Gordon's *Sea Spray and Smoke Drift*:

> Australia has rightly been named the Land of the Dawning. Wrapped in the mist of early morning, her history looms vague and gigantic. The lonely horseman riding between the moonlight and the day sees vast shadows creeping across the shelterless and silent plains...
>
> There is a poem in every form of tree or flower, but the poetry which lives in the trees and flowers of Australia differs from those of other countries. Europe is the home of knightly songs, of bright deeds and clear morning thought. Asia sinks beneath the weighty recollections of her past magnificence, as the Suttee sinks, jewel-burdened, upon the corpse of dead grandeur, destructive even in its death. America swiftly hurries on her way, rapid, glittering, insatiable even as one of her own giant waterfalls. From the jungles of Africa, and the creeper-tangled groves of the islands of the South, arise, from the glowing hearts of a thousand flowers, heavy and intoxicating odours—the Upas-poison which dwells in barbaric sensuality. In Australia alone is to be found the Grotesque, the Weird, the strange scribblings of nature learning how to write.[2]

Clarke presents in outline almost all the images that create the discourse of federation poetry. Firstly, there is a concept of 'Australia' as 'phantasmagoria', associated with mists, shadows and undefined shapes. Simultaneously, 'Australia' is very specifically gendered: female, a woman, and a geopolitical concept like the other continents and the 'islands of the south'. This is in contrast to Europe, which is identified with masculinity, then poetry, heroism and 'thought'—that is, with the Word. The European horseman in Australia is 'lonely', and is in process between night and day, between obscurity and self-knowledge. 'He' is mobile, individual and specific, 'she' is static and multiplicitous. 'He' is sensitive to a femaleness expressed as 'subtle charm'—but it is the charm of a 'fantastic land of monstrosities'.

The negative definitions of femaleness associated with other places in the passage define women in terms of the sexually dangerous and predatory. For the nervous masculinity of Clarke's knight-horseman, Australia promises to be disturbing, being later identified with 'the Grotesque, and the Weird'. Where could this place her as female partner to the 'lonely horseman', owner of 'knightly songs, of bright deeds and clear morning thought'? There was a deep ambivalence in the simultaneous desire and distrust of Woman projected in images of Australian male subjectivity. Her very morality, and thus her status, are deeply suspect. This metaphorical expression reflects an uncertain power relationship to place.

The national Woman's arrival

The summoning-up of such concepts in conventional poetic discourse presented problems that had their own conventional solutions. The classical convention of the femaleness of the state provided much-used access to philosophical notions of form and substance. According to the Aristotelian tradition, there is a contrast between passive matter, the female stuff of origin, and the active masculine form, which is stamped on matter. Thus the source of the state stands in metaphorical relation to its male originators both as mother—possessing the *original* material from which they will make form—and as bride or daughter to the male agents, poets, politicians who shape the designated quality from inchoate matter. It is easy to see how the female-gendered representations of concepts of state, liberty, and so on, were almost inevitably placed in a sexual or maternal relationship to the male activists: 'she' first provides matter in which the new state will be embodied. Because the male activist seeks to inscribe a certain form of state, he is imaged as *choosing* a second woman who will be the origin of the ideal daughter or bride. That process of choice is most easily imaged within the conventions of sexual desire, which automatically leads to the imaging of ideals of female behaviour in order to designate precisely the qualities the state-creator desires.

Within poetry of the period we find Australia defined through male relations to Woman. The imaging of inchoate origins gives us the impenetrable mists, clouds and darkness from which a woman mysteriously emerges in Clarke's essay as in many poems. In the imagined sequence of events that characterises these poems, the original undefined condition becomes accessible as night or cloud to the senses of the special men who watch. From this, a star, or the light of dawn, is seen and a woman then emerges. She either gives birth to the new polis, or she is the polis, as decreed by men with shared vision who promise a paradisal home for other men worthy of sharing the vision. The poem concludes with utopian hope for the future, the consummation.

The inchoate origins of the named condition, Australia, are represented as having no previous existence, no history, no condition prior to night or space; as O'Dowd's much-anthologised sonnet has it:

> Last sea-thing dredged by sailor Time from Space,
> Are you a drift Sargasso...?

('Australia' 1903[3])

In this poem, far from a boundless existence outside history, the condition, Australia, is defined by its relation to Time, and Time is the ubiquitious imperial explorer/sailor: 'Captain Cook, I presume'. In a walking definition of phantasmagoria, the concept 'Australia' is, in rapid succession, a drifting island land mass, the home of a chosen race, a wise virgin and a flickering treacherous light. In the conflicting mixture of 'auguries and omens', closure is reached only with a proper relationship to Woman inscribed as the one solid given feature of Australia: 'A virgin helpmate Ocean at your knees'. Clouds and the light before dawn are the first inscriptions within conscious boundaries, presented as prophetic signs, but in fact also 'loaded' with Australian circumstances. Clouds are a Ruskinesque site open to interpretation (for example, 'On rushing Cloudland's stage above/ Dark hints of what may be', O'Dowd, 'Dawnward'). Or they may be more specific: for instance, federation clouds appear to cloak Australia's shameful convict origins in a necessary decency, in a common trope that has continued: 'the *shadow* of the penal system still *clouded* the eastern colonies' (emphasis added).[4]

Night, like clouds, is an unopened file, which contains the convict past but more particularly subsumes the events of contact with the Aboriginal people. Aborigines are generally absent as an explicit theme from poetic inscriptions of historical or utopian Australia in poetry of the period. The morality and immorality of the processes of dispossession had, however, been constantly disputed in written discourses from the 1820s onwards, so that muted, often elliptical references to that bloodshed can be identified. O'Dowd, in 'The Bush', makes the perennial melancholy that characterises the bush for so many commentators derive from acts of violence, instancing wholesale murder of Aborigines:

> Nardoo with Burke's faint sweat is dank for ever:
> Spectral a tribe round poisoned rations shrieks:
> Till doomsday Leichhardt walks the Never Never...

('The Bush' 1912[5])

The 'official' rhetoric about Aboriginal–European interactions was more like Paterson's summary: 'In sooth there was not much of blood' ('Song of the Future', 1889). Supported by Social Darwinism and imperial discourse such as Kipling's, this verdict demonstrated a desire for closure of an ambiguous moral situation before the blank page, the child-bride, the nation-continent, was defined. In addition, in the hierarchical dualism of colonising Self and inferior Other, the Aborigine needed to be excluded from the rhetoric of the future utopian state, because in it, by definition, no inferior could exist.

The process of exclusion is executed in the common imagery already identified. The past is clothed in night, and night had belonged to the Blacks in poetic discourse. Not only through skin colour, but through European fears of evil, death and chaos, all at their most threatening to settlers at night, poets such as Harpur and Kendall had commonly inscribed Aborigines as night embodied. In poetry of the Nineties, when night is imaged as blank, or is defined as the past, it both names and conceals unavoidable participation by contemporaries in the historical presence of Aboriginal people and of convicts. 'Night' is the condition that has been superseded and transcended.

Light is, by contrast, heavily emphasised, once 'night' is said to be 'past'. Stars, dawn, the sun and the pure white of Woman/Australia are elaborated at length. When 'The wings of dawn / Are beating at the Gates of Day' (Evans, 'Ode for Commonwealth Day', 1901) the Woman arrives; phantasmagoria is solid for long enough to be encoded in visionary rhetoric. She is ascribed a relationship to the men who will her into being. In Stephens' early 'Dominion of Australia', she is rather like a houri making her appearance on stage:

> She is not yet; but he whose sight
> Foreknows the advent of the light,
> Whose soul to morning radiance turns
> Ere night her curtain hath withdrawn,
>
> And in its quivering folds discerns
> The mute monitions of the dawn
> With urgent senses straining onward to descry
> Her distant tokens, starts to find Her nigh.
> Not yet her day. How long 'not yet'? ...
> There comes the flush of violet!
> ('The Dominion of Australia' 1877[6])

The aridity of the land and the guilt and despair provoked by the early history of the colony meant that it was frequently described as of very dubious desirability. Offsetting such ambivalence led to inscriptions of the geopolitical concept of Australia in terms particularly addressed to male sexual desire. For instance, the Australia/Mother of Paterson's 'Song of the Federation' appears in a most unmaternally erotic guise:

> She was as beautiful as morning,
> With the bloom of the roses on her mouth,

> Like a young queen lavishly adorning
> Her charms with the splendours of the South.
>
> ('Song of Federation' 1901[7])

It is highly significant, for nineteenth-century gender relations, that 'she' be asexual herself while being 'object'ified as a masculine ideal of erotic female beauty. Consummation is usually suppressed, which is why mothers and houris—those virgins promised to Muslim men on their entry to heaven—with a sexuality either safely past or permanently postponed, are useful tropes. An identification of the bushland with the idealised woman did not necessarily make her more accessible, despite extensive natural detail:

> From her home beyond the river in the parting of the hills,
> Where the wattle's fleecy blossom surged and scattered in the breeze,
> And the tender creepers twined about the chimneys and the sills,
> and the garden flamed with colour like an Eden through the trees,—
>
> she would come along the gully, where the ferns grew golden fair,
> In the stillness of the morning, like the spirit of the place
> With the sun-shafts caught and woven in the meshes of her hair,
> And the pink and white of heath-bloom sweetly blended in her face.
>
> ('Bashful Gleeson' 1901[8])

Here is Eve in a brand-new Garden-of-Eden continent, a literal emanation of female nature as an ideal, benevolent object of male desire. It is significant that, nonetheless, 'Gleeson' cannot overcome his 'bashfulness' without the mediation of disastrous fire. Fires, especially bushfires, are interchangeable with war and bloodshed in Anglo-Australian male initiation.

In images such as Dyson's, geographical and historical 'Australia' is established as the worshipped woman, to be served by a chivalrous (asexual) band of knights, her admirers and loyal retainers, the bush brotherhood. Jill Roe has demonstrated the pervasiveness of concepts of chivalry across divisions between country and city and classes:

> What began as a ruling class ethic in early Victorian times, by the end of the nineteenth century had been thoroughly democratised, with particular relevance in colonial society where perforce behaviour, not breeding, mattered most.[9]

On the whole, cultural commentators have made little of the debt that the discourses of 'mateship' owed to Scott, Tennyson, and the revived codes of chivalry. Such codes negated 'soft' physical feelings and sexual relations while idealising and negating women. They exclude women, locating masculine pleasure in collective male heroism, sacrifice, endurance and action.

These priorities are elaborated in an inescapable connection between the imaging of the new state and the imaging of the desired relationship of 'her' new citizens to each other and to 'her':

> We have flung the challenge forward: 'Brothers,
>   stand or fall as One!'
> She is coming out to meet us in the splendour of the Sun.
>   From the graves beneath the sky
>   Where Her nameless Heroes lie,
> From the forelands of the Future they are waiting our reply!
>   We can face the roughest weather
>   If we only hold together,
> Marching forward to the Future, marching shoulder-firm together,
>   For the Nation yet to be.
>
> ('A Federal Song' 1903[10])

This is the organisation of O'Dowd's 'mobs' from chaos into a rather ominously military order through relationship to Woman.

Roe emphasises the significance of women citizens' exclusion from the right to bear arms despite having citizenship. Metaphorically, Woman is denied this kind of historical agency almost by definition: 'The female form tends to be perceived as generic and universal, with symbolic overtones; the male as individual, even when it is being used to express a generalised idea'.[11]

In poetry, 'she' is elaborated in terms of the conventions of both classical allegorical female figures and the historical relation of women to men. This generalising tendency suppresses reality, leading to some wonderfully bizarre imaging of female physiognomy. In Stephens' 'Dominion of Australia', for example, his 'spirit-force, transcending sense', the new state, is unequivocally 'woman' but 'she' arrives simultaneously new-born and bride, political state and physical continent. While men await the 'natal hour' to baptise 'her', the poem slips unsignalled into imaging the continent as woman pregnable by the 'divining-rods, men's souls / [which] Bend down to where the unseen river rolls ...'

This is all to do with fertility, first the agricultural fertility that may result from scientific development of artesian water: 'the wisdom of the wise/Conspires with nature to disclose/The blessing prisoned and unseen'. Then an allegorical political pregnancy will result in the emergence from beneath the woman/continent of a 'stream of Common Will'. These metaphors were clearly not meant to be taken literally, but nonetheless reinforce the extent to which Woman was, in poetry by men of the period, there literally to be made into the desired form:

> For She whom all our dreams foreran
> Has leaped to life, a Pallas sprung
>   Consummate from the mind of man,
>   Whom now we hail in mortal guise and gait,
>   Thought clothed with flesh, partaker of our state,
>   Made corporal in us now corporate!
>
> ('Australia Federata' 1902[12])

This allegorical reflection of the legal and social control of women is demonstrated graphically in 'The Bush' (1912), in which O'Dowd distinguishes between the utopian and the paradisal woman (though his female embodiment of the bush is scarcely paradisal). This long poem ends by asking 'Where is Australia, singer, do you know?' and concludes that she, as Woman, is entirely blank, without form except in terms prescribed by male destiny and heterosexual male desire:

> She is the Eldorado of old dreamers,
>   The Sleeping Beauty of the world's desire!
> ... she shall be as we, the Potter, mould:
>   Altar or tomb, as we aspire, despair:
> What wine we bring shall she, the chalice, hold:
>   What word we write shall she, the script, declare:
> Bandage our eyes, she shall be Memphis, Spain:
>   Barter our souls, she shall be Tyre again:
> And if we pour on her the red oblation
>   O'er all the world shall Asshur's buzzards throng:
> Love-lit, her Chaos shall become Creation:
>   And dewed with dream, her silence flower in song.
>
>   ('The Bush'[13])

It is a touching confidence that Woman can become whatever is desired of her beyond the flawed historical world O'Dowd also defines. By contrast, his Bush has a defined personality and physique, though 'she' is in an inert maternal relationship to specifically male colonists:

> The onion-grass upon that dark green slope
> Returns our gaze from eyes of heliotrope:
> But more we seek your undeflowered expanses
>   Of scrub monotonous, or where, O Bush,
> The craters of your fiery noon's romances,
>   Like great firm bosoms, through the bare plains push.
>
> As many, Mother, are your moods and forms
>   As all the sons who love you.
>
>   ('The Bush' 1912)

It is a moot point whether The Mother is so varied that 'she' can accommodate all tastes, or whether it is the Sons' love that causes 'her' to exist at all.

Poems like 'The Bush' make clear how important the imaging of security was in the colonial context, and that part of the significance of inscribing the land and the polis as Woman was because Woman is also the site of Home.

> Thus we have learned to love our country, learned
> To treasure every inch from foam
> To foam; to title her with name of Home;

> To light in her regard a flame that burned
> No land in vain...
>
> ('The Circling Hearths' 1901[14])

The extent to which the credentials of the desired woman are established through 'her' provision of security for men is demonstrated in Evans's paean to Queen Victoria:

> White Star of Womanhood, whose rays
>   Through years of peace and years of stress
> Shed wide o'er all thy people's ways
>   The light of nobleness—
> A memory in their hearts impearled
>   To nerve thy sons where'er they roam—
> Empress and Queen o'er half a World,
>   Yet Angel of the Home.
>
> ('Victoria' 1928[15])

Mother is the only unproblematised female companion, 'her' ministrations the only source of uneqivocal physical pleasure to be recalled when such ministrations are emphatically denied by an ambiguous Nature that is not-home:

> Gaunt arms stretched with a voiceless yearning—
>   That's how the dead men lie!
> Oft in the fragrant hush of nooning
> Hearing again their mother's crooning,
> Wrapt for aye in a dreamful swooning—
>   That's how the dead men lie!
>
> ('Where the Dead Men Lie' 1897[16])

Poems about the geopolitical identity of 'Australia' that do not rely on allegories of sexual relations are rare. Mary Gilmore's 'Australian' has an ungendered speaking subject, and avoids establishing power relations to the point that it is difficult to tell, in the first stanzas, which it is that speaks—land or human:

> Lie close to my heart, little bird, lie close!
> The hawk wheels high in the sky,
> Fierce is his beak and wild his cry—
> Lie close little bird, lie close.
>
> ('Australian' 1918[17])

The relationship is tender and mutually nurturing even in the deliberate ambiguity as to who is nurturing whom, Australia or Australian. The poem uses conventional images of war to elaborate the inseparable co-existence of land and speaker, word and context. Only in the concluding stanza is identity made clear:

> Lie close to my heart, little bird, lie close!
> Blood shall be shed, full tide to its flood,

> Ere ever shall rise to the pitiless skies
> Thy last long cry, land that I love!
> Then wilt thou lie, O, close to my heart,
>   ... Over my heart.

Such imaging of a mutual, ungendered responsibility, rather than creation and conquest, is rare in poetry about either land or state. Usually, the desire to exert power, to control space and (future) time, is implicit in narrow allegorical representations of both state and citizens. Mackellar's 'My Country', at first glance the deeply conventional rhetoric that might be expected of the nineteen-year-old the poet then was, also differs from most other federation poems in accepting and celebrating an existing diversity of land-as-Woman. It endorses self-determination, instead of existence only within limiting terms of desire, and also hints at a female sensuality:

> The stark white ring-barked forests,
> All tragic to the moon,
> The sapphire-misted mountains,
> The hot gold hush of noon.
> Green tangle of the brushes,
> Where lithe lianas coil,
> And orchids deck the tree-tops
> And ferns the warm dark soil.
>
> An opal-hearted country,
> A wilful, lavish land—
> All you who have not loved her,
> You will not understand—
>
> ('My Country' 1904[18])

It is possible that this imaging of acceptance of a multitudinous land expresses a yearning for acceptance of a multitudinous, non-ideal female self.

The drought witch

The image of the carnal woman is frequently used to represent negation of male desire. Sometimes predatory and self-determining, more often in the pay of opposing forces, 'she' is unfailingly negative. The fallen woman was a frequent trope in Australian, as in English culture of the period, and 'she' served a variety of functions. 'She' was in the pay of 'Fatman,' in the anti-Federationist Melbourne journal *Tocsin*:

> We've wan and wasted legions, true,
>   And scourge of 'ring' and 'trust':
> Battalions sad of women who
>   Perform the chores of lust.

> We've lost so much by lure and dole
>   The pick of their brigades
> Were Sons of Labour, sucked of soul
>   By wet-lipped Mammon's maids.
>
> ('Foreboding' 1898[19])

Such imaging invites a militaristic response as a different production of desire; resistance by brothers united in a collective cause. The seductive Woman validates such a response:

> And do they think we sleep, boys,
>   Lulled by their Siren Song;
> And do they think to creep boys,
>   And bind with *parchment* thong.
> But, no, we're wide awake, boys:
> We'll make them fear and quake, boys,
> All for Australia's sake, boys.
>   *Australia.*
>
> ('An Anti-Bilious Ode' 1898[20])

Co-existent with this siren as political agent, and profoundly endorsed by the legend of the Nineties, is the development of the image of the land itself as a destructive, predatory Woman. At times, 'she' came to prove an object of desire after all:

> ... she seemed to be,
> To those first weakling wooers who ventured near,
>   A menacing, barbaric deity;
> Till on a destined day there came a bold
>   Rover who knew no fear;
> Who saw no goddess, but a girl to hold;
>   A maiden eager for the wedding-year.
>
> ('Australia'[21])

European occupation of the dry hinterland in the 1880s and 1890s, and the severe droughts of the period, led to representation of women's sexual agency as devastating to male welfare.[22] These works belong to the 'paradisal' conventions in that they elaborate physical attributes of Australia, rather than the political. Boake created an instance of what became a very influential convention, drawing on classical weather gods as well as sexual Woman:

> Where brown Summer and Death have mated—
>   That's where the dead men lie!
> Loving with fiery lust unsated—
>   That's where the dead men lie!
>
> ('Where the Dead Men Lie' 1897)

The predatory Woman's existence more often draws on a combination of the conventions of the Vice and Death. 'She' provides boundaries for the unbounded coloniser of the written text:

> She sits in the West—Australia!—brooding in proud disdain,
> And her gaze goes out to the burning sky, far over the burning plain;
> Never her word the silence breaks, never she laughs or sighs,
>   And her mouth is set in the fiercest smile; but a man would die for her eyes.
>
> She sits in the west, in the desert West, till her web of fate be spun;
> Her feet are swathed in the sand-wreaths, her head flung free to the sun;
> Ever she beckons and threatens, threatens and beckons the bold,
> And of whitened bone she has built her throne, above a reef of gold.
>
> ('Bailey's Reward' 1911[23])

This figure has been imaged as a combination of tantalising allure and threat of death, and to die is presented as an irresistible temptation. It seems it is only in death that either Australia or Woman can be reached. A.G. Stephens may be addressing the specific allure of the gold strikes in Western Australia, but the terms chosen to image the historical situation suggest a more complex script. Australia remains Woman; 'she' challenges the male libido. The poems examined show that the challenge is articulated in these terms in order to facilitate male bonding both against this predatory female and against the land. By such means the poets of the Nineties propagated relationships which defined national identity, the land and the new state. Their aim was to represent unbounded possibilities of desire in calling the nation-state into being. The effect was the opposite. By encoding all relationships within the existing discourses of patriarchal gender relations, they in fact devised strategies of rigid containment and limitation for men and women. The poetry is a curious comment on the enfranchisement of women in Australia. And now? How different might other representations be?

> *Marking a boundary to define a space. A space to live in. Space for an idea. Marking the boundaries of it. Creating the space, making it empty so something can appear. Squares of blue sky framed by the window. An object moves across it. A clear shape in the blue.*[24]

14 The New Woman and the Coming Man: Gender and genre in the 'lost-race' romance
Robert Dixon

> Abolition of everything is the advanced woman's *raison d'être*, but there is nothing she yearns for the abolition of more than that of her natural rival—man.
> —*Bulletin*, 23 June 1888

In her essay 'The politics of respectability', Marilyn Lake describes 'the contest between men and women at the end of the nineteenth century for the control of the national culture'.[1] In this chapter I want to take up the argument advanced by Fiona Giles and Susan Sheridan, among others, that the genre of romance fiction was one important site of this contest for historical agency.[2]

My particular interest is in the lost-race romance, whose narrative conventions focus on changing definitions of gender and power by bringing into conflict those two characters in my title, the New Woman and the Coming Man. Although the lost-race romance was essentially a masculine and metropolitan form, it also attracted authors from widely differing locations in the broader imperial culture, including a number of Australian men and, surprisingly perhaps, at least one Australian woman author. It is the possibility of comparing these different examples that makes the lost-race romance an ideal site for examining the relationship between gender and genre. Given the social location of the male writer of romance, it is likely that his work will be less ambivalent and more accepting of literary conventions and gender norms than comparable texts by women authors of the same period.[3] Women writers, too, were at times conservative in their handling of romance conventions; but, as Susan Sheridan argues, by 'working within and against the narrative conventions of popular romantic fiction', they did offer a literary challenge to the masculinist definition of Australian culture.[4]

H. Rider Hággard's best-selling novel *She: A History of Adventure* (1887) was the most popular lost-race romance, and provides striking evidence of the social construction of (white, European) masculinity through confrontation with its racial and sexual others. Its combative response to an emergent feminist culture allows, in dominant readings at least, a fictional resolution to the threat posed by the 'New Woman' of the late nineteenth century. George Firth Scott's Australian novel, *The Last Lemurian: A Westralian Romance* (1898), was strongly influenced by *She*. Despite certain nationalist inflections, it substantially reproduces the ideology of its metropolitan model, and suggests that masculine writing not only relies on traditional gender norms, but defends them vigorously when they are most under challenge. Read against the grain, however, *The Last Lemurian* reveals the instability of an apparently unified masculine subjectivity. Rosa Praed's novel, *Fugitive Anne: A Romance of the Unexplored Bush* (1902), was also strongly influenced by Haggard. But Praed's handling of the lost-race romance suggests that women novelists of the period were able to work both 'within and against' its conventions to produce new and alternative meanings.

She was published in 1887, the year of Queen Victoria's Golden Jubilee. Sandra M. Gilbert argues that its appeal lay in the combination of desire and anxiety aroused in male readers by its heroine, Ayesha, who, as the all-powerful ruler of a matriarchal society, was a type of the New Woman.[5] The plot is initiated by Ludwig Holly's discovery that his ward, Leo Vincey, is the descendant of an ancient Egyptian woman whose husband was murdered by Ayesha, Queen of the now ruined city of Kor. Ayesha has discovered the secret of eternal life, and Leo must travel to East Africa to kill her in vengeance. She not only enthralls the two heroes, but threatens to return with them to England and rule as their Queen.

She invites readers to 'view' the body of this beautiful and powerful woman from a masculine point of view. As Holly confesses, 'I am in love with Ayesha myself to this day ... if anybody who doubts this ... could have seen Ayesha draw her veil and flash out in beauty on his gaze, his view would exactly coincide with my own. Of course, I am speaking of any *man*. We never had the advantage of a lady's opinion of Ayesha.'[6] Holly's knowing appeal to the male gaze strongly genders the reading position, and invites comparison with Laura Mulvey's analysis of visual pleasure in narrative cinema. Using Freud's theory of voyeurism, Mulvey argues that the masculine pleasure in looking is bound up with an illusion of power to possess and control, and has become inscribed in the dominant codes of cinematic representation.[7] On several occasions in the novel, Holly's role resembles that of the cinematic hero in Mulvey's analysis. This is the case when Holly climbs through a tunnel to spy on Ayesha in her private rooms through a hole in the wall (figure 14.1): 'For a moment she stood still, her hands raised high above her head, and as she did so the white robe slipped

Fig. 14.1 'For a moment she stood still, her hands raised above her head, and as she did so the white robe slipped from her down to her golden girdle, baring the blinding loveliness of her form'.

from her down to her golden girdle, baring the blinding loveliness of her form' (pp. 178–9).

In Mulvey's Freudian analysis, the image of woman implies the threat of castration, and can disrupt the illusion of masculine control over the narrative process. Masculine dominance, she argues, must be reasserted either through fetishism, or by the male hero taking part in narrative events that reaffirm his dominance. The destabilising effects of the erotic image become rapidly apparent to Holly: 'Suddenly I thought of what would happen if she discovered me ... Supposing she should hear me, or see me through the curtain, supposing I even sneezed, or that her magic told her that she was being watched—swift indeed would be my doom' (p. 179). This episode displays and attempts to conceal both the ambiguity of the masculine response to female power and the possibility of an alternative point of view. It allows the image of woman to be displayed and enjoyed voyeuristically, but Holly's fear demands that she be put back in her proper place under masculine control. It is therefore significant that Holly confesses to being 'a bit of a misogynist' (p. 107).

Even 'locked up in her living tomb' Ayesha is a threat to masculine power, but her goal is to become Queen of England. As Holly realises, that possibility 'would have revolutionised society, and even perchance have changed the destiny of Mankind' (p. 301). It is therefore important that *She* was published in the year of Queen Victoria's Golden Jubilee. Holly explains to Ayesha that Victoria is 'venerated and beloved by all right-thinking people'; but 'real power in our country rested in the hands of the people' (p. 263). The text's political unconscious is clear: Britain's Queen Victoria is loved by her people, but loved precisely because she has no real power, which is vested in Parliament. Victoria signifies the benign values of the domestic sphere, but Ayesha is a female monarch of unbounded ambition. Quite apart from the shame of those who have enjoyed the sight of her body, her political threat to 'Mankind' demands that she be ritually destroyed by the very narrative that has called her into being as spectacle.

The 'pillar' of flame in which Ayesha is incinerated evokes a phallic code that is often instrumental in the closure of adventure tales: 'Ayesha turned towards it, and stretched out her arms to greet it. On it came very slowly, and lapped her round with flame. I saw the fire run up her form. I saw her lift it with both hands as though it were water, and pour it over her head. I even saw her open her mouth and draw it down into her lungs, and it was a dread and wonderful sight' (p. 297). In this literally spectacular conclusion the male characters and—by invitation—the masculine reader, bear witness to Ayesha's subjection to the images of phallic power: 'She, who but two minutes before had gazed upon us the loveliest, noblest, most splendid woman the world has ever seen...lay still before us...no larger than a monkey—and...too hideous for words!'(p. 299). In this way 'She-Who-Must-Be-Obeyed' is controlled by the discourse of social Darwinism; she has become an image of the past rather than the future—a monkey—suggesting an association between feminism and cultural devolution.

Within three months of its publication in 1887, *She* had sold 25000 copies. One reviewer, echoing the culturally dominant reading, complained that it is 'impossible in any house to attempt any conversation which is not interrupted by the abominable introduction of *She*.'[8] But *She* was not only widely read and discussed; it was also widely imitated, often by writers whose nationality or gender might be marginalised by its narrative form. It was here that dominant readings might be negotiated, and new meanings produced through a rewriting of romance conventions. At a time when Australian national identity was increasingly defined through its assertion of difference from the metropolitan culture, it is perhaps surprising that *She* produced a spate of Australian imitations.[9] One reason for this ready assimilation of the lost-race romance may be that its handling of the relationship between masculine and feminine culture corresponds closely to the oppositional relation between mateship and women in the Australian tradition. As Kay Schaffer puts it, 'The exclusion of women ... creates the condition and possibility for mateship.'[10] Thus, in George Firth Scott's romance *The Last Lemurian*, we find evidence of the same 'masculine economy' that Schaffer identifies in the realist texts of the *Bulletin* writers.

THE NEW WOMAN AND THE COMING MAN

Fig. 14.2 *The Last Lemurian: A Westralian Romance*.

As in the Lawson stories she examines, 'The bond between teller and listener, like the bond of mateship between men in the bush, establishes a connection between men which mediates the alien threat [of woman].'[11]

Dick Halwood, the narrator of *The Last Lemurian*, is working on Curriewildie Station in South Australia when he is suddenly dismissed by the absentee owner, an English widow. His colloquial tone and hostility to English capital construct a reading position that is both anti-English and misogynistic. When the overseer announces to Dick that they are all sacked, he refers to 'our late esteemed employeress' as 'that [expletive deleted]'.[12]

The heroes of this Australian romance are not English gentlemen like Haggard's Sir Henry Curtis and Ludwig Holly, but types of the Coming Man—a version of the Anglo-Saxon male that has evolved in the outposts of empire.[13] This important distinction is evident in Dick Halwood's meeting with his mate, the Hatter, which corresponds to the meeting of Allan Quatermain and Sir Henry Curtis in *King Solomon's Mines*. The Hatter is 'a fine-built man, tipping six feet, and with a frame loosely hung and wiry, after the fashion that comes to any one who has spent many years in the hot air of the Australian bush' (p. 7). He tells of rich goldfields beyond a mysterious range in the desert, where a race of pygmies is ruled by the giant yellow woman Tor Ymmothe. Instead of going to the fields at Coolgardie, Dick sets off with his new mate. Their pact positions the reader still further within the discourse of mateship: 'He rose and stretched out his hand, and as I took it his fingers closed round mine and I felt as if I were being filled with some strange, warm fluid, which streamed from his fingers into my hand, up my arm, and through my entire frame ... I heard him say: "It's a bargain. Whether it's death or whether it's wealth, we're mates in it to the end".' (pp. 14–15).

The conventions of the lost-race romance now define mateship by opposition to its racial and sexual others. The goldfields are guarded by the yellow woman who, though of a fictional race, is nonetheless associated with the Australian Aborigines (figure 14.2). To win this wealth, the mates must subdue the Aborigines and overcome the psychic powers of Tor Ymmothe. But the Queen is too strong, and the mates return to Adelaide deeply troubled, their friendship threatened by the Hatter's unmanly desire to become one of her subjects.

While Dick is returning to Adelaide after a holiday in England, he reflects upon this threat to both mateship and the racial supremacy of the Anglo-Saxon male. His anxiety reaches a crisis on the Suez Canal, that boundary line between East and West with which Britain inscribed its regime of difference upon the world: 'As I gazed across the water and over the barren sandy waste [of Asia] beyond, a terror came upon me ... a fear which was part of a horror ... of absolute negation and personal eradication ... A feeling of being and yet not being; a sense of existence without all of those tokens which give security and reality to existence' (pp. 93–94). This suggests Alice Jardine's description of male paranoia as a 'fear of the loss of borders'.[14] Dick's fear is that the boundaries that make up his subjectivity as an Anglo-Saxon male will disappear. The discourses of colonialism and anti-feminism intersect here in the fear of miscegenation. To give himself over to a powerful woman, especially one of another race, would be to risk both sexual and racial degeneration. A series of oppositions arrange themselves in his mind and threaten to collapse: the water of the canal is other than the sand of the desert; the Anglo-Saxon stock is other than the degenerate Arabs through whose lands the canal has been cut; male is other than female. It is the fear that these differences will collapse that gives rise to Dick's feeling of negation and personal eradication. This moment constitutes itself as the central problem of Scott's text: a vortex of terror in which the subjectivity of the male narrator might dissolve. As in Haggard's *She*, the narrative will now work to resolve this threat to the 'tokens' of difference by the actions of its male protagonists, who return to the Australian desert to kill the Lemurian Queen.

Fig. 14.3 *The Last Lemurian: A Westralian Romance*

The climactic chapter, 'The Conquest of the Queen', brings the discourse of phallic power into violent opposition with images of castration (figure 14.3). Dick is carried into the Lemurian palace in a state of 'passive inertia' (p. 198). Before his audience with the Queen, he is forced to put on a Lemurian robe, which makes him look feminine, or like a member of another race (p. 204). As Kay Schaffer argues, the threat posed by the New Woman is that 'men', in their weakness, may become 'women'.[15] Tor Ymmothe 'came towards me and took my hands in hers ... and I felt my strength oozing out of my body. I knew that she was drawing out of me all that made me a sentient, strong, human being' (p. 221). The imagery recalls Dick's first meeting with the Hatter, a mateship that is now threatened by the Hatter's enslavement to Tor Ymmothe. Dick fumbles for his revolver beneath the robe and fires, though 'unable at the moment to know whether the barrel was pointing up or down' (p. 225). His bullet pierces the roof of the underground chamber, and brings down upon the Queen the waters stored in a volcanic lake above their heads.

Overlapping Dick's battle with the Queen is his quest to liberate a young Lemurian woman whom he has loved in a former life. While Tor Ymmothe represents a brand of feminism that threatens traditional gender roles, the girl embodies a culturally acceptable femininity. Having adjusted the aberrant role represented by the Queen, Dick is now able to re-establish normal relations with womankind by marrying the passive and conventionally pretty girl. Without Dick her life has been empty, but with him the conventional woman is complete: 'The medical experts said it was a complete vindication of their theory that my lovely Margaret only needed rousing from her lethargic apathy to become the bright, happy, intelligent woman she now is' (p. 339).

The Last Lemurian not only accepts traditional codes of gender representation, but functions actively to defend them against the threat of change. Such is not the case with Rosa Praed's *Fugitive Anne: A Romance of the Unexplored Bush* (1902). *Fugitive Anne* opens dramatically with a challenge to patriarchal authority when Mrs Anne Bedo goes missing from the steamship *Leichardt* [sic] to escape from her drunken and brutal husband.[16] Anne has hidden away on board with her Aboriginal servant and flees with him into the bush inland from Cooktown when the *Leichardt* next calls into port. In remote country at the base of Cape York Peninsula she meets the Danish explorer Eric Hansen, who is there to confirm his theory that the interior of Australia is inhabited by a lost race.

Praed's use of the lost-race formula from this point strongly suggests the influence of Haggard's *She*. More important than her use of sources, however, are the consequences of her rewriting of masculine romance. Peter Pierce suggests that in Keorah, Praed's version of Ayesha, she was able to envisage the possibility of women's future freedom and to take pleasure in the exercise of power over men, and it is certainly through Keorah that the text makes its most iconoclastic statements: 'The elementary instincts of that sex so long held in unnatural subjection, had arisen triumphantly and were wantoning in their emancipation' (p. 298). But in the end, Pierce argues, Praed is 'mastered' by the conventions she uses: 'Keorah ... is ostentatiously destroyed, as though Praed guessed that her male readers would wish it to be.'[17]

I want to return to this notion of 'mastery'. But what is especially valuable here is the distinction between the process of closure, which fulfils the way 'male readers would wish it to be', and the implication that Praed was able to imagine freedom and the exercise of power only in discrete episodes that must be separated from the narrative as a whole. This is an important distinction because it points away from reading *Fugitive Anne* as if it were masculine romance toward the idea advanced by Susan Sheridan that the achievement of nineteenth-century women writers is not to be found in a 'unified moral vision', but must take account of the ambivalence and fragmentation that characterise so much of their work.[18]

Fugitive Anne is in fact a generically complex and heterogeneous text whose meanings tend to be overdetermined, multiple and even contradictory. One consequence of placing Anne in what is normally a male role is that the encounter between the New Woman and the Coming Man becomes a confrontation between two rival women. This gives the central section of the novel a structure similar to that of a feminine romance like *Jane Eyre*, and causes a de-centring of the female subject like that between Jane and Bertha Mason. At times this de-centring causes tension within the text. This is most dramatically revealed during a rewriting of one of the key episodes of masculine romance. At the crisis in her battle with Keorah for the wavering affections of Eric Hansen, Anne arranges to meet him in her apartment and as they talk quietly Keorah approaches through a tunnel to spy into the room from the darkness behind a tapestry. Praed's text transforms this trace of *She* intertextually by inverting the conventional ways of looking, and the result is something that Haggard would not allow—'a lady's opinion' of the Ayesha figure. In *She* the reader looks with Holly into Ayesha's room, but in *Fugitive Anne* it is Keorah who takes up the position of the masculine spectator, while the reader shares Anne's sense that her privacy has been violated. When Keorah finally declares her presence it is Hansen who describes the conflict: 'He felt himself between two opposing forces, and ... feared that serious damage might result from the clash against each other of these two floods of feminine passion' (p. 380).

Despite these moments of tension, however, the opposition between Anne and Keorah is as enabling as it is disabling. The contrast between two opposing types of women is common in Praed's fiction, and her sympathies are often highly ambivalent. In *The Bond of Wedlock* (1887), for example, she satirises the romantic notions of her married heroine, Ariana, while showing understanding for her unconventional opposite, Babette. Although contrasted, the two women are linked by the metaphor of the theatre, which implies that both act within roles that are constructed for them by the culture they inhabit. Babette, like Keorah, consciously takes on the role of immorality for the sake of her freedom.[19]

The generic diversity and de-centered perspective of *Fugitive Anne* suggest that Praed's rewriting of the masculine lost-race romance may have enabled a break with dominant readings which rely upon uniformity of viewpoint and the *resistible* move toward ideological closure. This has an interesting parallel in recent critiques of Laura Mulvey, whose theory of the male gaze I used earlier to build up masculinist readings of Haggard and Scott. Barbara Creed, for example, argues that Mulvey's male gaze 'invariably relegates the woman in the fiction to the position of a threatening but ultimately powerless figure'.[20] Creed suggests that a way of freeing critical discussion from this tendency is to rethink the concept of spectatorship in terms of phantasmatic identification rather than interpellation. Fantasy, with its stress on the fluidity of identification, opens up the possibility of multiple subject positions for the characters and multiple points of entry for both the male and female spectator.

Praed's heterogeneous rewriting of the lost-race romance—barely controlled as it often is—is like an act of critical intervention: it produces a new 'reading' of this masculine form that breaks its tendency toward closure, superimposing a new economy of multiple viewpoints and contradictory meanings in which alternative definitions of power might emerge. This shift seems confirmed by the flippancy of the conclusion, which is far less effective in sealing up the text's diversity than the closures of *She* and *The Last Lemurian*. Unlike Haggard, Praed does not describe Keorah's death, while Anne's second marriage and accession to title and property are announced briefly and without conviction in an epilogue as the stuff of 'story' and 'romance' (p. 427).

The early sections of the novel quickly establish this pattern of rewriting masculine conventions to produce new meanings and new points of entry for the reader. The motive of Praed's plot is not male vengeance, as in *She*, or male greed, as in *The Last Lemurian*, but Anne's desire for freedom from the tyranny of an uncongenial marriage. Anne's quest, in contrast to Keorah's, begins with a move away from the world of men, from whom she becomes a 'fugitive'. Her flight into the bush releases her from the confinements of both race and gender. In *The Last Lemurian*, Dick's fear that traditional gender roles will be disrupted causes his moment of paranoia on the Suez Canal; but for Anne, disruption of difference is a source of pleasure and a vehicle for freedom from patriarchal authority. In escaping from the *Leichardt* she poses not only as a boy, but also as a Lascar (pp. 28–29).

The theme of flight through transgression is continued when Anne becomes a prisoner of the hostile Maianbar tribe and lives with them as a captive. This long episode has similarities to the narratives of Eliza Fraser's captivity, which Praed would almost certainly have known. In nineteenth-century Australian writing, as in American, captivity narratives were often used to construct masculine concepts of the feminine. John Curtis's *Shipwreck of the Stirling Castle* (1838), for example, offers Mrs Fraser's devotion to her husband as an exemplum of virtuous Christian womanhood.[21] Unlike Eliza, however, Anne is able to modify her captivity by pretending to be a goddess, and comes to enjoy her life in the bush away from 'that hated bondage' to her husband (p. 102).

Anne's strategy of flight is contrasted with Keorah's quest for power, and these alternative roles are examined with considerable ambivalence, marked by a constant flexibility in the narrative point of view. Keorah's very existence seems to push Anne back into a relatively conventional role. Shortly after her arrival in the lost city, Anne undergoes a test to decide whether she will supplant Keorah as High Priestess. The ceremony ends apparently in Anne's favour but the victory is really Keorah's, who gladly escapes the vow of chastity involved in the office. The mark of Anne's defeat is her subjection to the phallic power of the god Aak, a giant prehistoric tortoise: 'the reptile's head, which had been partially indrawn, was protruded ... The thick creases of the throat smoothed as the telescopic neck lengthened itself' (p. 251). Anne's subjection to the tortoise recreates her subjection to Elias Bedo, and suggests that she may remain a fugitive and a victim.

Despite Anne's courageous attempts to become 'master of the situation' (p. 252), the narrative openly requires the more assertive Keorah to set Anne free. When Bedo turns up to reclaim his runaway wife and her inheritance Anne is forced to admit that 'she had never been brave in the presence of this man' (p. 409). It is left for Keorah to seduce and execute Elias Bedo, finally quelling the threat of patriarchal retribution for Anne's flight from the ship, and releasing her from the bond of her first marriage. But despite her usefulness, Keorah's dangerous 'want of self control' is compared unfavourably with Anne's 'quiet dignity' (p. 314) and, like Ayesha, she is rewarded with death.

While Keorah represents one facet of the female subject, she is also instrumental in a critique of masculinity that we would have to read *against* a male-authored romance to produce. Ironically, the very power of her female gaze derives from her origins in masculine discourse. Sandra M. Gilbert recognises Ayesha's origins in male fantasy when she describes her as the embodiment of 'the fears of countless male writers'.[22] She also notes that feminist thinkers have long understood this point, quite consciously using this image of man's own creation against him. Praed's ability to use Keorah for this purpose is nowhere more striking than in Keorah's subjugation of Elias Bedo. It is as if Ayesha's ability to destroy Holly—always held in check by Haggard—were set free of authorial control. In another episode rewritten from *She*, Keorah allows her mantle to fall, baring her throat and breasts to Bedo's gaze: '... she softly pulled him by the hand...[and] he followed stupidly where she led him' (p. 397). Lest there be any doubt, it is stated that 'Keorah felt supreme contempt for Bedo' (p. 390). Even Hansen falls victim to Keorah's 'mesmeric gaze' and Anne is moved to 'defend him against himself' (p. 298). This radical shifting of the conventional ways of looking dramatises a knowledge of female power that the male-authored texts attempt to conceal.

Given Praed's contradictory relation to this figure of male fantasy, it is hardly surprising that the text also expresses reservations about Keorah— and not simply in the final moments, when the closure demands her destruction. In expressing these reservations, Praed may also have felt the need to distance herself from this *masculine* stereotype of the independent woman, disclosing the need for a concept of freedom untainted by masculine models.

As Barbara Creed observes, although the female spectator may be able to identify with a multiplicity of subject positions, she will often still find herself forced to identify with characters that in general 'belong to someone else's fantasy'.[23] Praed's text deals with this problem by making a clear distinction between Anne's unselfish 'yearning for freedom' and Keorah's 'craving ... for pleasure and power' which, in her public seduction of Hansen, is condemned for taking the masculine form of a desire for power over others (p. 387). Praed seems here to recognise the possibility of an ethics that is, in Marilyn French's phrase, 'beyond power', even if, in 1903, she is unable to define precisely what form this might take.[24]

These reservations about Keorah find interesting support in Judith Allen's research on the Edwardian feminist Rose Scott,[25] who believed that women should not accept masculine paradigms of freedom—and this is precisely what Keorah represents. Read in this way, the destruction of Keorah in a volcanic eruption at the end of the novel can be seen to do more than simply reproduce the masculine economy of Haggard's *She*: it would suggest that writers can work against discourses that are not of their own making, even as they use them.

The lost-race romances of Haggard, Scott and Praed suggest that the romance narrative was one important site of the struggle of men and women for historical agency at a time when traditional gender roles were under review. Haggard's *She* offered Australian writers a ready-made structure in which to enact and then resolve the crisis caused by the meeting of the New Woman and the Coming Man. But they did so in different ways. *The Last Lemurian* resolves this crisis by destroying the New Woman and reinstating a passive femininity that does not threaten the basis of mateship. While appearing to do much the same thing, Praed's novel may also go some way toward undoing this masculine opposition by maintaining an internal distance from both Anne and Keorah. In a male-authored text like *The Last Lemurian* the unity of the masculine subject is protected from ambivalence and alternative readings are difficult to produce; Praed's text, on the other hand, creates alternative subject positions and the possibility of a powerful female gaze from within the received conventions. Normally, it would probably be undesirable to frame a novel by Rosa Praed within a masculine tradition in this way. But *Fugitive Anne* seems to represent an active intervention on her part into the lost-race romance that produced a new strategy of reading and a critique of masculinity. Far from being 'mastered' by masculine conventions, Praed's rewriting suggests that a discourse is never simply imposed—it can also be a 'point of resistance and a starting point for an opposing strategy'.[26]

15 Water, gold and honey: A discussion of *Kirkham's Find* Dorothy Jones

> ...but this is fixt
> As are the roots of earth and base of all;
> Man for the field and woman for the hearth
> Man for the sword and for the needle she:
> Man with the head and woman with the heart:
> Man to command and woman to obey;
> All else confusion.
>
> —Tennyson, 'The Princess'

Social changes occurring in the final decades of the nineteenth century, which resulted in many Australian women receiving the vote and entering the paid workforce in increasing numbers, also prompted much rhetoric about separate spheres for men and women both as an argument against female suffrage and in support of measures excluding women from better-paid jobs.[1] Women's literary activity was similarly restricted by the notion of separate spheres. They were expected to write romantic fiction and condemned for literary display if they departed from the genre,[2] but their work could be criticised as lightweight, marginal or even un-Australian if they remained within it. The prominence accorded the *Bulletin* writers of the 1890s, with their masculinist ideals of mateship and noble bushmen, meant that the substantial contribution of nineteenth-century women authors, who did not usually view their art in such nationalistic terms, was largely dismissed. Only very recently has it begun to find a toehold within the Australian literary canon. As Fiona Giles points out, romance 'which traces the heroine's quest for domestic fulfilment, love and a sense of self-determination' gives embarrassing prominence to female subjects within a culture that has been presented as predominantly masculine.[3]

Mary Gaunt's novel *Kirkham's Find*, first published in 1897, is particularly interesting because it alternates the male world of the bush with the female realm of domesticity and romantic love, using each to comment upon the other. It also raises issues of women's economic independence in relation to the institution of marriage which were attracting widespread public attention at the time.[4] Gaunt contrasts the loves and fortunes of two sisters, Phoebe and Nancy Marsden, setting their story against that of two young men, the native-born Allan Morrison and his new-chum cousin, Ned Kirkham. Both begin as rivals for the pretty Nancy and end by falling in love with her plain elder sister, Phoebe. Early in the novel they leave their farm, neighbouring the Marsden property outside Ballarat, to seek their fortunes in the outback where their adventures as boundary riders and gold prospectors alternate with accounts of Phoebe's struggles in rural Victoria. Phoebe, mocked by her family for being plain, and deciding she is unlikely to attract a husband worth loving, scorns to make a mercenary marriage, as Nancy eventually does. She aspires to independence through earning her own living—'I don't care how little I earn at first, if I can go on improving, like a man'[5]—but although penniless young gentlemen may earn their own livelihoods, Phoebe's desire to do so is considered outrageous and unnatural. In the end, however, she achieves financial independence through bee-keeping, first on her father's property and then by establishing a small farm at Warrnambool. Her success is presented as the exact equivalent of Allan and Ned's discovery of a gold-bearing reef in the Kimberleys, although Ned leaves that behind to return and work in Victoria where he meets up again with Phoebe whom he eventually marries, for she, not the gold, represents Kirkham's find.

Gaunt's novel complements the work of Lawson, Furphy and Rudd, adding an extra dimension to traditional literary representations of life on the land by contrasting male and female images of pioneering. But it also draws heavily on English literary tradition where comparison between two sisters, one fair, one dark, one conventionally attractive, the other less so, one frivolous, the other high-minded, is a constantly recurring motif. Given her preoccupation with thwarted female aspiration, Gaunt could well have drawn on George Eliot's Dorothea and Celia Brooke as models. There are echoes of Jane Austen as Phoebe's abortive attempts at match-making for her young sister Lydia recall Emma's attempts to marry off Harriet Smith, and, like Austen in *Pride and Prejudice*, Gaunt also delineates the links between money, marriage and romance for undowered middle-class girls. *Kirkham's Find*, however, offers more detail about the heroine's financial situation than is customary in romantic fiction. We are told exactly what each piece of bee-keeping equipment costs, how much Phoebe pays for a new outfit to impress the storekeepers she hopes will buy her honey, and how she contrives it all out of the monthly dress allowance of £1/13/4 grudgingly bestowed by her father. Profit and loss accounts provided throughout the novel resemble those set down by Defoe's heroine in *Moll*

Flanders and Phoebe herself embraces a slightly more refined version of the same bourgeois pragmatism:

> Lydia, dear, I'm sorry, but if you join me it means hard work. You see, we must always keep ahead of our expenditure and have something to put by, because we don't want to be as poor as this all our lives. (p. 276)

Wealth, its acquisition and its absence appear to have been major preoccupations of colonial life, as Rachel Henning, newly arrived from England, disdainfully notes: '... it is a good thing that the colonial mind should be informed that there are things in earth and heaven besides money-getting and the price of hides and tallow'.[6] But Britain regarded the colonies primarily as sources of potential prosperity, where able young men, like Rachel Henning's own brother, might hope to garner, repair or maintain family fortunes. In *Kirkham's Find*, Ned and Allan, dissatisfied with a meagre living from 'cockatoo farming', can set off in search of greater wealth, simultaneously participating in the Australian legend: 'the next time you see your friends they'll be tramping the country looking for work, with swags on their backs and quart pots in their hands'. (p. 17) But impecunious young women, like the Marsden sisters, can advance their fortunes in a socially approved manner only through matrimony, although Gaunt continually reminds us how vital money is to female happiness and self-respect. Her novel suggests, however, that colonial life offers some slender financial opportunity even for a young middle-class woman, provided she has sufficient determination.

In sending her two young men outback, the author offers an image of the bush both different from and similar to that presented by the *Bulletin* writers, for Gaunt writes not only from a woman's point of view, but reveals a bourgeois rather than a working-class bias. Instead of mocking the freshly arrived English new chum, for example, she presents the rigours of bush life through his eyes, positioning readers to endorse his repugnance and alienation, so that her novel sometimes echoes an earlier, colonialist type of pioneer romance, like Henry Kingsley's *The Adventures of Geoffrey Hamlyn*. Nevertheless, she also draws on attitudes and motifs used by writers like Lawson. Threatened death from an Aboriginal ambush forges bonds of mateship as Ned risks his life to bring Allan to safety: 'They did not speak much, where was the use? The one man had done his best to induce the other to escape, and since he would not, no words of his, he felt, could thank him for so great a sacrifice ...' (p. 81). When Ned, working on a lonely outstation, falls into despair on receiving Nancy's letter breaking her engagement to him, it is Allan's intuitive awareness of his plight which restores his sense of balance, though, significantly, Gaunt insists that closeness between men comes a long way short of female intimacy.

> It is a fact that men don't confide in one another as women do, but these two were alone in the wilderness. It was night in the open air, and their only light

was the moonlight and the glow from the dying fire; their pipes were alight, and one was firmly convinced in his own mind that the other had saved him from taking his own life, and the other, though he said nothing, had more than a suspicion of the truth. The occasion seemed even to demand confidences. (p. 182)

Lonely outback life in a surreal landscape threatens madness as Ned believes himself haunted by a multitude of crows 'who sat on the ground in rings round him' waiting to peck his eyes out (p. 176). And, in a detail reminiscent of 'The Bush Undertaker', the two young men, on discovering their gold-bearing reef, stumble over the skeleton of a prospector long dead from thirst while 'the little lizard that had made his home among the old prospector's bones, crawled out and surveyed them from the top of the whitened skull thoughtfully' (p. 214).

The gold deposits Ned and Allan discover, though rich, do not afford ready wealth, for expensive quartz-crushing machinery is required to extract the metal in viable quantities and an influx of prospectors to the site means miners must pay prohibitive prices for water and provisions. Lawson's comment in 'The Loaded Dog': 'There is always a rich reef supposed to exist in the vicinity', indicates a quality of ironic resignation to fate's harshness which characterises the bush myth of the 1890s, and something of this is reflected in the sense of disappointment and defeated promise associated with prospecting in *Kirkham's Find*. Gaunt also conveys impressions of that rough male camaraderie, with its dismissal of women and domesticity, so traditionally a feature of outback life. Allan and Ned's prospecting companion, Sam McAllister, says mockingly of their bush hut: 'The dust'll get into the drarin'-room an' spile the furniture' (p. 116) and then comforts Ned for Nancy's absence:

> Cheer up, old man; if it isn't her, there'll be another gal waiting for you. After you haven't seen a woman for a year or two you won't care a damn which it is, so long as she wears petticoats and ain't your grandmother (p. 118)

Ned, however, thinks that they are 'just sinking to the level of savages' (p. 111) and both he and Allan long 'for the comforts and luxuries of civilisation' (p. 114). In a contrast customary in the writing of the 1890s, these are associated with an image of rural Arcadia, first on the Marsden property and then on Phoebe's little farm at Warrnambool. Partly because of their association with the world of women's life and work, Gaunt invests these idealised landscapes with an Edenic quality, drawing our attention to this via an epigraph from Kipling.

> Now if we could win to the Eden Tree where the four great rivers flow,
> And the wreath of Eve is red on the turf as she left it long ago,
> And if we could come when the sentry slept, and softly scurry through,
> By the favour of God we might know as much as our father Adam knew.
> (p. 228)

When Phoebe, now well established, extends her farming activities to include poultry and cows as well as her bees, the land, flowing with milk and honey, becomes even more of an earthly paradise in Gaunt's literary version of the domesticated farm idyll so frequently depicted by painters of the Heidelberg school.

> It did not take Lydia long to put on the clean print she always milked in, and then, with her stool and her bucket under her arm, she called on Phoebe to join her. The cow-byre was clean and dry, and Phoebe leaned up against one of the posts and looked over the green grass where the shadows were lengthening in the evening sunlight. So fair and rich the land lay before her, so bright the evening, there was ... a consciousness of all things done well in her heart ...
> (p. 311)

Throughout the novel, images of water signify abundance and fertility, while the delusive search for gold is linked with its loss or absence. Ned and Allan's first attempt at prospecting, in what is now the Northern Territory, is foiled by an attack from hostile blacks who cut off their access to the water hole. (While Gaunt challenges prevalent attitudes to gender, she participates in the racism of the period.) After the Aborigines have been massacred in punishment for their ambush, Ned and Allan return to the same site, but when they finally succeed in digging down to the wash dirt, prolonged drought sets in, the water hole evaporates and they have to dry-blow the dirt. Even though they find traces of gold, lack of water means they can no longer remain to work a claim. There is 'not a drop of water within twenty miles' of the reef Ned later stumbles across in the Kimberleys and the false promise of his discovery is indicated by the mirage of a lovely and extensive lake he must ride through to reach it. Rural landscapes, on the other hand, are associated with abundant water. Sometimes there may be too much moisture, as on the day Phoebe arrives in Warrnambool, with roads ankle-deep in mud and rain washing down the ruts in streams, but this is far preferable to drought with all its associations of personal loss and thwarted hopes. She has dreaded the possibility of a really dry summer with no food for her poor bees (p. 133), while for Ned at the Lone Hand outstation drought comes to represent the destruction of his romantic dreams of Nancy. Phoebe's struggles to achieve autonomy as a bee-keeper are equated with his hardships in seeking gold. The sparsely furnished cottage where she sets herself up corresponds to his bush hut on the outstation, 'a single room built of corrugated iron, about twelve feet by twenty in size with one door and one window' (p. 154). The lake he sees in a mirage by the gold-bearing reef has, as its counterpart, swampy Lake Pertobe which Phoebe passes on the way to her cottage (p. 233). But this lake full of real water and teeming with bird life augurs the success of her farming venture.

This contrast, so important to the narrative structure of *Kirkham's Find*, between the arid male terrain of the outback and a well-watered rural landscape where women characters lead their lives is also a means of constructing gender relations in nineteenth-century Australian nationalist myth. Sue Rowley has shown how in 1890s literature and painting, 'Courtship is associated with natural plenitude, thus drawing on the ancient mythical sympathy between women and water.'[7] In Gaunt's novel, water is linked with another female image, the moon, an association reinforced by the heroine's name, for Phoebe is an alternative title for Artemis, virgin moon-goddess of Greek mythology. The division in national myth between a fertile Arcadia, where sweethearts remain behind, and the inhospitable bush, where men they yearn for ride off adventuring, represents yet another assumption of separate spheres for men and women. As Rowley sums it up: 'A man is out of place at home, and the bush is no place for a woman. Her place is bounded by the sliprails; the nation is formed beyond the spur.'[8]

Gaunt, however, assigns different values to these regions by celebrating the space within the sliprails. Her concern is not national identity but social interaction and civility, which flourish more readily in an Arcadian setting than they ever could in the bush; so her solution to the great gulf of gender division is to move the man out of the bush into the woman's domestic space to assist with the tasks she performs there.

On returning to Victoria, Ned Kirkham takes a job as manager of a butter factory, where he meets Phoebe again by chance. While courting her, he does various carpentry jobs around the house, helps with the milking and suggests ways she might develop her farm.

> Suppose she crossed her fowls with Indian game, as Kirkham had suggested, suppose she went in for growing big table poultry, and bred for export, as he was urging her to do; if she were to take in that other twenty acres from Mrs Mackenzie, would she ever be able to make it pay? Ned Kirkham said she would. (p. 292)

In addition, Ned brings news of the wider world to Phoebe and Lydia, the young sister who now lives with her: 'he broadened the women's lives altogether, as a man is bound to do who takes an intelligent interest in the women he meets and does not regard them as created merely for his amusement' (p. 291). The image of Phoebe in her rural domain contrasts sharply with portrayals of those 'haggard women' struggling to maintain outback holdings in their husbands' absence found in the work of writers like Lawson. As Sue Rowley points out, this image is associated with the idea of loss and represents an underlying anxiety about the threat posed to family and nationhood by the defection of male breadwinners forcing female intrusion into the realm of male labour, with a consequent assumption that they must thereby neglect or abandon their responsibilities as mothers.[9] Although Gaunt challenges the concept of separate spheres through Phoebe's success as a farmer, her heroine remains throughout the entire novel within the domain of the sweetheart, and her farm work of harvesting honey, tending poultry and milking cows is of a kind considered compatible with accepted views of female domesticity. Phoebe's achievement is that she maintains her farm by and for herself rather than as a wife and mother.

In *Kirkham's Find* love and courtship are presented from the sweethearts' point of view rather than the customary bushman's perspective. Neither Nancy, in love with Ned, nor Phoebe, who is initially in love with Allan Morrison (though he has eyes only for her sister), pines away and dies of sorrow as sweethearts characteristically do in stories and ballads of the bush.[10] Both girls take their destinies into their own capable hands—Phoebe by bee-keeping, and Nancy by marrying a wealthy Ballarat lawyer rather than wait interminably for Ned to make an income sufficient to support her. Feminist critics and, no doubt, many women readers have greatly admired the strong feminist discourse which Gaunt constructs: 'It is the sense of immediacy and the intensity of the debate about women's lives which gives this novel much of its fascination.'[11] Sue Martin writes: '*Kirkham's Find* is Mary Gaunt's most outspoken critique of the unequal treatment of the sexes, the absence of work for women, and the viability, indeed attractiveness, of spinsterhood.'[12]

The novel generates great sympathy for Phoebe's frustration and thwarted aspiration while she lives under her father's domination, burdened with domestic labour, derided for being plain, debarred from earning an income and threatened with utter impoverishment when Mr Marsden dies. Although she believes she can manage a property more competently than her father or her neighbour Allan Morrison, no-one will give her the opportunity. She must also endure the taunts of her brother Stanley who regularly fails his exams at Melbourne University while ridiculing the few women studying alongside him. (As one of the first two women who enrolled there, Mary Gaunt herself must have been painfully familiar with such sentiments.)[13]

> Well a girl ought to stick at home. She oughtn't to bother her head about Latin and Greek. Who wants his wife to know anything about mathematics? My wife's going to dance beautifully, and she must play and sing, and she might paint a bit—just enough to decorate the drawing-room. And then if she can cook a bit and sew a little, that's all I want. (p.10)

Phoebe's determination to achieve independence is impressive and her struggles to succeed as an apiarist form the principal focus of narrative interest, but Sue Martin's claim that the novel presents spinsterhood as attractive is open to question. While her two young sisters envy the independent life Phoebe describes in her letters home, she herself experiences a deep sense of lack.

> A woman ought to marry and have children—yes, that was what she was created for, that is her use in life, and Phoebe felt sad, sometimes as she sat over her lonely fire, that such happiness could never come to her. (p. 252)

Although she will not contemplate marriage merely for the sake of a secure income or social position—'to make a sort of business of choosing a husband, like the boys do in choosing a profession' (p. 31)—and considers her chosen occupation as bee-keeper far superior to economic dependency on father or brother, Phoebe believes a woman's ultimate fulfilment lies in marrying a man she truly loves.

The contrast between her burning desire for financial independence and her yearning for personal fulfilment in marriage touches on a significant social issue of the times. Susan Magarey describes how during the last two decades of the century, when extra-domestic employment opportunities opened up for women, the number who married fell dramatically, suggesting that, 'given a choice, a significant proportion of women preferred economic independence to marriage'.[14] Gaunt, however, seeks to reconcile Phoebe's capacity to be self-supporting with her attainment of romantic fulfilment by showing the practical gains which marriage offers her heroine. Sensuous descriptions of Phoebe in the latter part of the novel suggest a woman with a capacity for sensual pleasure, but for a woman of Phoebe's principles and social background sexual expression is impossible outside marriage. Being married is also materially advantageous, since the £2 a week Ned earns at the butter factory will substantially supplement her income, allowing time and scope for the more interesting and cultivated life she desires: 'to be decently dressed ... and be able to travel about a little, and buy books and have money to give away' (p. 100). In devising her conclusion to Phoebe's story, Gaunt may have drawn back from the revolutionary implications of insisting on women's entitlement to economic independence. It is equally possible that she became trapped within the inherently conservative conventions of romantic fiction which encode the dominant gender discourse of a patriarchal society by representing marriage as women's ultimate destiny.[15] In romance, a happy ending equates with the heroine marrying the man of her dreams. But while Phoebe's marriage to Ned provides the conventional closure to a work of romantic fiction, it also represents a reward for both parties, as her integrity and his good judgment in choosing her are simultaneously validated. Once again Arcadia is contrasted against the bush, and wealth is related to the ideal of personal fulfilment through a surprisingly explicit sexual metaphor when the account of Ned's proposal is followed almost immediately by a description of Allan Morrison in the Kimberleys waiting for the first ore-crushing at the claim known now as 'Kirkham's Golden Hole'.

The idea of marriage as a love match where both partners contribute equally to the work of farm and homestead runs counter to the view presented within the Australian bush myth in which 'Men and women are represented as cultural aliens, between whom no understanding can pass'.[16] Despite its 'happy ending', there is considerable debate about marriage in *Kirkham's Find*. Gaunt seems anxious that Phoebe's triumph as an independent woman should not devalue it, while expressing anger at the social and economic constraints forcing women into loveless unions, a view canvassed by a number of nineteenth-century feminists.[17] Two types of femininity are contrasted, the socially approved model embodied in the conventionally pretty, frivolous, self-centred Nancy, and the more unorthodox figure of the independent, serious yet spirited woman into which Phoebe develops. Gaunt suggests, a trifle optimistically, that men of good sense, while attracted initially by the former model, will inevitably come to prefer the latter, for both Ned Kirkham and Allan Morrison shift their allegiance from one sister to the other while even Nancy's husband comes to respect his sister-in-law more than his wife. It is significant that Phoebe's appearance improves markedly through the self-confidence she develops as her farm prospers—'this handsome woman with the true, honest dark eyes, who carried her head as if she had been a princess of the blood royal' (p. 302). The need to look smart so shopkeepers will buy her honey forces her to dress well, which also enhances her attractiveness, so that, by the end of the novel, Phoebe has ceased to be a plain woman, conforming far more to the standard criteria of marriageability than she did at the beginning.

The frivolous Nancy, however, has something to say on her own account, and, although she is a relatively unsympathetic character who is severely judged for breaking her engagement to Ned to marry a wealthy lawyer, her voice contributes to what the narrative reveals about women's choices. She exclaims at the prospect of waiting till Ned can afford to marry her for, if a woman's looks are her only asset, she must invest early before they depreciate:

> For ten years? Till I'm old and faded? He'll more likely think it was because I couldn't get anybody else, and he will bless having to take such an old thing and wish he could have a nice fresh young girl. (p. 148)

While Gaunt acknowledges the force of these sentiments, she counters them by having Ned fall in love with Phoebe at the advanced age of 30. Nancy's married life proves boring, if luxurious, and although her husband's name, Josiah Sampson, together with repeated references to his thinning hair, suggests she might one day prove unfaithful, yearly pregnancies take the shine off her beauty. The burden of frequent pregnancies forms a subtext to the marriage debate in the novel. Mrs Marsden has borne nine children while struggling to maintain genteel standards on an inadequate income. Phoebe comments: 'I often think she grew old much too soon' (p. 148), and her own relatively late marriage will, presumably, place some limit on childbearing. Ironically, however, the mercenary marriage for which Nancy stands condemned enables Phoebe to achieve full independence, for when Mr Marsden orders the hives off his property, it is Josiah Sampson who lends her the 50 pounds which enables her to transfer them to Warrnambool. Nancy too proves generous to her sister with gifts of clothes and furniture which help ease the austerity of her new existence, and the novel suggests that, despite their conflicting philosophies, the sisters remain friends, even though affection is sorely tried with the discovery that Ned is in love with Phoebe.

One reason for dismissing the romantic fiction produced by nineteenth-century Australian women writers is an assumption that it endorses class divisions, in contrast to the egalitarian ideal promoted in Australian nationalist myth. Gaunt, however, shows that, like Phoebe's determination to earn her own living, a demand that marriage be based on mutual love rather than social or economic considerations may lead to an unsettling of class boundaries. Mrs Marsden, a figure of fun as well as a pathetic character, continually urges the correct view of ladylike behaviour, 'A man well sunburnt looks nice, but a woman ... It looks so—so common' (p. 92), and, when Phoebe talks about selling honey, she exclaims, 'A lady loses caste at once if she attempts anything of the sort' (p. 98). She is also full of platitudes like 'Every nice woman loves her husband' (p. 95) and 'a young marrried woman is more attractive and entertaining than a girl' (p. 95). Both Phoebe, whose father is, after all, 'a University man' and Ned, son of an English clergyman, laugh at the apparent 'unsuitability' of their current occupations. He tells her, 'Darling, you're going to marry the manager of a butter factory', to which she replies, 'It's a rise in the world for me ... I'm the woman that supplies the Western Hotel with poultry' (p. 320). Phoebe, however, is less accepting of her young sister Lydia's choice of husband, Jack Fletcher, whose father was a most respectable pork butcher.

> 'Yes, he is a good, honest fellow who will make any woman a good husband. She will be quite safe with him, and if he isn't very polished—'
> Phoebe groaned.
> 'He sucks up his gravy with his knife,' she said.
> Kirkham laughed at her lugubrious face.
> 'His principles are sound. What's the good of bothering about his manners?'
> 'And Lydia is very fond of him, and I've always held it's the best thing in the world to marry for love.' (p. 326)

Gaunt, nevertheless, seems to accept that marrying for love may involve transgressing class boundaries, leaving us with the impression that Lydia's marriage to Jack Fletcher will be happier and more vital than Nancy's to Josiah Sampson.

In *Kirkham's Find* Mary Gaunt takes over the contrast established strongly in Australian nationalist mythology between the man's world of the bush and the fertile Arcadia where sweethearts live, but subverts it by dismissing the male world as sterile and peripheral and giving prominence to the female domain. Separate spheres, she suggests, have little to offer men or women and a man of sound judgment would find more fulfilment in a marriage of shared affections, interests and activities than in adventuring in the wilderness.

16 Things a bushwoman cannot do
Sue Rowley

In the Australian bush mythology of the 1890s, there are unresolved tensions and conflicts in the relations between men and women and in the delineation of public and private domains. These are played out in the context of the imaginary formation of the nation. In the rhetoric, the distinction between the public and private realms seemed definitive and unproblematic. Domesticity and the home were the private realm, and this was seen to be the proper place for women. The rest was the public world of men. This differentiation of gender in terms of a dichotomy between public and private space has been widely referred to as 'separate spheres'. Labour within the home was properly 'women's work', whereas women's work outside the home appeared to breach the natural order of things. In public discourse, this notion of separate spheres of influence was like a vessel which formed and contained the articulations of tensions and conflicts in gender relations. But cracks appearing in the walls of this vessel suggest that the ideological construct was itself under great stress.

This chapter focuses on women's work outside the home in order to sketch the ways in which this stress is written into bush mythology. In particular, it looks at the representation of women's work in terms of two topical and controversial issues of the 1890s.

The first issue is the perceived disordering of the working-class family resulting from the absence of male authority and material support. State and charitable intervention in the affairs of destitute families subjected them to male authority, but where the private and public domains had previously seemed partitioned by impermeable barriers, these barriers now became porous, diffusing the divisions between the two domains.

The second issue is the ideological response to women's perceived incursion into the paid labour force. Other chapters in this book demonstrate that the actual shifts in patterns of paid employment were far more complex than commentators of the 1890s—or, indeed, the 1980s—recognised.[1] Even so, the causes, patterns and consequences of changes in the labour force were, and are, subject to debate. The problem was not that women were engaged in paid employment, for as Paula Hamilton shows, domestic service was a widespread form of female employment. And, though there were tensions related to women's employment in retailing, it was the apparent shifts in female factory employment that precipitated complaints that women were 'out of place' and 'taking men's jobs'.[2]

The ramifications of this belief were felt by men, not only in the work force, but also in their domestic lives. Erosion of male authority over women within the home emerges in the bush literature as a troubling consequence of women's productive labour outside the home. But the anxiety about the erosion of patriarchal authority within the domestic sphere undermines notions of women's 'sovereignty' over their own realm that had been integral to the rhetoric of the separate spheres. Consequently, we perceive again an unsettling of the idea of discrete domains of public and private spheres. The apparent certainty in the rhetoric of 'separate spheres' masked the extent to which the relations between men and women were characterised by uncertainty, anxiety and change. But the rhetoric could no longer account for, nor subsume, lived experience in both the public and the private sphere.[3] As Susan Magarey has argued, the strident invocations of the dichotomy of public and domestic spheres occurred partly because its material existence was under threat.[4]

Significantly, this problematic representation of gender relations is embedded in texts which bear witness to the emergence of Australia-as-nation, and articulate a *national* cultural identity. Because the writers and artists saw themselves as laying the foundations of national art and literature, and because they sought to shape locations, stories and characters which were distinctively Australian, their work has occupied a significant place in our arts and culture. Consequently, their construction of gender has continued to reverberate through Australian culture throughout this century.

In suggesting that bush mythology was nationalist, I do not mean that it was wholly and essentially shaped around questions of nationalism and national culture, any more than it is exhaustively shaped around gender issues. But bush mythology does afford important insights into the evolving relationship between men and women, while at the same time, that relationship has played a significant role in the shaping of national culture. This is in part because, in Australia, the formation of the nation, formally in

Federation, as well as in the imagination, was concurrent with significant changes in the relationships between men and women and the re-ordering of public and private domains.

The construction of the idea of nationalism, as much as the specific character of the 'national identity', is a historical process, and one which is unlikely to be a single, unified and coherent project. Certainly there are tensions, conflicts and unresolved problems in the late nineteenth-century imaginary formation of the nation. Significantly for the positioning of women, two irreconcilable nationalist imperatives are at work in bush mythology. On the one hand, the struggle to tame the land as the territory of the emerging nation draws men away from their families; on the other, the stability of the young nation is seen to rest on the intact family unit. Concurrently, the family unit was being defined to consist of breadwinner husband, dependent wife and children.[5] Masculine independence and the disordering of the family unit emerge as two sides of the same coin. This chapter examines the terms under which women enter these narratives of nation-formation.

'Hardship, loneliness and toil'

'Men's work' almost invariably connotes work on the land. The link between rural labour and the 'making of Australia' underpins much of the painting and literature which takes as its theme the taming and settlement of the land. In the poem 'The Men Who Made Australia' (1901), for example, Henry Lawson contrasts the absent bushmen with the status-conscious and feminised urban elite which gathers to meet royalty.

> Round the camp fire of the fencers by the furthest panel west,
>   In the men's hut by the muddy billabong,
> On the Great North-Western Stock-routes where the drovers never rest,
>   They are sorting out the right things from the wrong.
> In the shearers' huts the slush lamp shows a haggard, stern-faced man
>   Preaching war against the Wool-King to his mates;
> And wherever go the billy, water-bag and frying-pan,
>   They are drafting future histories of states! [6]

This poem is one of the clearest articulations of the centrality of masculine labour to opening up the land in nationalist mythology, but its constituent elements are recurrent ones. It functions like a template, sketching a crude outline from which finely detailed work can be drawn.

A cast of itinerant and semi-nomadic bushmen, consisting primarily of drovers, shearers, timber-getters, carriers, boundary-riders and station hands, was implicit in this celebration of 'strong masculine labour'. In literature and painting, as in life, these occupations were not open to women, and married men travelled 'unencumbered'. Gender differentiation, then, was constructed in terms of labour and place: women were not engaged in what Russel Ward has described as 'the real work of the pastoral world',[7] nor were they to be found in the places where men lived and worked.

There are very few instances of women actually depicted as engaged in labour outside their 'proper' sphere.[8] Women are depicted fighting natural disasters to protect their farms and their homes, but significantly, these actions are more frequently recalled and retold than described. They are depicted scratching out the barest subsistence for their families in the absence of husbands, but rarely are they engaged in agricultural or pastoral farming. Not for women the fertile land and clement weather: women who work 'as men' farm barren, drought-stricken land.

Thus, women are present in 'The Men Who Made Australia', but the terms of their inclusion reveal the ambiguous positioning of women in the concept of the heroic struggle to 'make Australia':

> Call across the scrubby ridges where they clear the barren soil,
>   And the gaunt Bush-women share the work of men—
> Toil and loneliness for ever—hardship, loneliness and toil—

Their labour is differentiated from that of men, and the marks of their toil are registered not on the land but on the women themselves. In 'The Last Review', Lawson sees 'my haggard women plainly as they were in life', and he asks that it be remembered 'That I pitied haggard women—and wrote for them with all my soul.'[9] The labour of bushwomen renders them pitiable. Though they work 'like men', the bushwomen are not the 'true and straight' leaders, 'born to conquer fate'. Rather, they are the subjects of fate which determines that they should be defeated, physically and spiritually, by the struggle. Like madmen, these women are positioned not as the heroes of the battle but as its casualties.

Bushwomen's plight

Deep anxiety about the disordered family is the dark side of the valorisation of mateship and 'unencumbered' masculine labour. The plight of the selector's wife, alone with children and no visible means of support, is a recurring theme in Lawson's writing, and undermines his celebration of masculine bush culture. Lawson does not embrace the ideal of masculine independence without registering concern about the disordering of the family unit that male absence connotes. Consequently, the family without a male breadwinner is represented in terms of plight and disorder.

In the bush stories, physical separation of men and women is the result of the inability, at least initially, of the selection to support the family and the need for an income to bring potentially productive land under cultivation.[10] Permanent separation is consequently associated with the barrenness of the land. The bushwoman's domain does not mark the frontier. Rather, hers is the land that men have left behind, the barren, unproductive scrub. Like the women who inhabit them, these selections are well along the road of decline and disintegration. The labour of such women as the drover's wife and Mrs Spicer ekes only the barest subsistence from the reluctant land. They labour 'as men' only to preserve what they have. The image of women doing farm work is thus one of loss: of their husbands, their identity and the productivity of the land.

It is to the late nineteenth-century city that we must look for the meanings of this ambivalent and anxious response to the disordered family.[11] The representation of the plight of fatherless families in the bush can be read as a metaphorical expression of an urban social problem of great concern to middle-class observers: that of destitution of families seen to be a consequence of desertion by breadwinners. Responses to desertion and pauperisation set the terms within which the bushwoman left alone to fend for herself was represented.

By the 1890s, the belief that desertion was on the increase was entrenched, and 'vicious and immoral' men who left their families were admonished for placing an intolerable burden on charitable and state institutions for the support of destitute wives and children. Public concern was focused on the difficulties of coercing fathers and husbands into supporting their families and of extracting maintenance from deserting fathers.[12]

Nevertheless, as Shirley Fisher argues, the Sydney economy, revolving around pastoral and construction industries and the trading activities associated with Sydney's role as a port, called for a geographically mobile, casually employed labour force. Unemployment and under-employment of working-class men, and their absences from the family as they searched for work or were engaged in casual labour away from home, 'placed extreme stress on the formation and maintenance of families'.[13] The structure of the labour market itself generated recurrent male unemployment, which could be intermittent or chronic, and resulted in men's absence from families who remained economically dependent on their support.[14]

While reformers vilified the deserting husband, they found it difficult to draw clear-cut lines of distinction between the absences of responsible men in search of casual labour and those of deserters. They were compelled to acknowledge that desertion was frequently the outcome of absences necessitated by the search for labour.[15]

Given the reluctance of state and charitable institutions to assume the responsibility for dependent families, many women with small children worked as outworkers, earning insecure and meagre incomes under appalling conditions. Yet this form of employment was itself under notice. Campaigns against sweated labour toward the end of the decade brought outwork into disrepute, and the introduction of payment by time rather than piece virtually eliminated outwork in the early years of this century.[16] Poverty, hard labour and insecurity rendered 'hardship, loneliness and toil' the plight of many urban working-class women.

Lawson was keenly aware of the structural conditions which underpinned men's absence from home. He refutes the prevalent bourgeois view that these men, even those who are 'more or less gone for good', are mean, vicious or immoral. He writes of married men supporting families by sending home their cheques. When illness or misfortune interrupts their employment, their mates send the hat round to take up a collection for the families. Married men who waste their cheques on drinking sprees are frequently represented as weak and irresponsible, if not actually culpable.[17]

Constructing an image of the poor

The way in which middle-class, and generally male, observers could comprehend working-class women's lives was to frame their social and cultural experience in terms of their plight and their poverty. Thus their efforts to protect working-class women from the consequences of poverty were also expressions of their determination to control this class. As Griselda Pollock has commented, the entry of working-class people into art subjects the social group to specifiable forms of scrutiny, and necessitates manufactured and carefully managed forms of visibility.[18]

Leon (Sonny) Poole's painting 'The Village Laundress' (c. early 1890s) is interesting here because it depicts a woman at work (figure 16.1). It is nevertheless a pleasurable image of an attractive woman, conveying none of the ambivalence that attended women's engagment in productive labour. Rather, the image is constructed in such a way as to divert our attention from the heavy, hot work of the laundry and the subsistence income that the woman's labour could earn. The painting depicts a young woman with her two daughters walking along a track through open paddocks, away from a cluster of houses, carrying a basket and a bundle of laundry. From the quiet rectitude of the woman, her plain clothing and the sweet, resigned expressions on the faces of both woman and girls, we may infer her widowhood. This family is set apart from the village community, physically within the picture space itself, narratively through the assumption that their home is at a distance from the cluster of houses they have left behind, and socially by the assumption of the absent husband and father.

In spite of this 'displacement', the representation of the woman stands in significant contrast to that of the isolated bushwomen in Lawson's writing. Where their faces and bodies tell the story of their hardships, this woman's complexion is porcelain-fine, and the play of light emphasises her rounded breasts and hips and her trim waist. The woman's body is open to the gaze of the viewer, who may take pleasure from her modest yet sexually coded form. Her face is turned to the side and her eyes, like those of her daughters, are averted, and do not question the viewer's privileged scrutiny. Her protective gesture towards the younger child shows affection and warmth. The elder child, carrying the other side of the basket, is separated from the mother and young daughter, but she is turned towards them, her posture echoing that of her mother, and her dress is the grey of her mother's dress, while the younger child's dress is pink. The separation

Fig. 16.1 'The Village Laundress'.

between elder daughter and mother suggests not alienation but maturation. Though they walk through the sombre bare grass, little details of unobtrusive plant forms in the foreground suggest a degree of variety and pleasure in their lives. Though the paddock through which they walk is in shadow, their heads reach into the golden sunshine of the distant land and the pale, clear sky.

This representation of a woman out in the open and engaged in paid labour is not an ambivalent or troubled image: it is coloured with optimism and security. The sense of security imparted by the painting lies, of course, less in the projection of the family's future than in the sense that the social order represented here is intact. Though she is out in the open, the labour she undertakes will be done at home, and though she is engaged in paid labour, her work is appropriate to her social position. The woman is in 'her place', both as the object of approving scrutiny and as the representation of a woman whose respectability and mothering have withstood her poverty and her labour. The composition of the work, with its emphasis on the horizontal structure of the land, offset by the verticality of the figures themselves, contributes to the evocation of stability and serenity.

The expression of sympathy for women does not imply that the painters and writers identified with them. While Lawson 'pitied haggard women', he observed them across barriers of class and gender difference that implicitly shaped his representations of isolated bushwomen. The ways of perceiving the domestic lives of working-class people served to reinforce the ideological justification for intervention in, and often punitive restructuring of, the family unit. In distinguishing between blameless hardship and culpable poverty, notions of cleanliness and dirt were invoked to connote moral values. The moral degradation of the 'delinquent' poor could be conveyed by images of dirt and filth. But the interplay of images of cleanliness and dirt in Lawson's story, ' "Water Them Geraniums" ' suggests that the sense of the degradation of poverty was deep-seated. In spite of Mrs Spicer's efforts to maintain the appearances of respectability, the rhythmic reiteration of Joe Wilson's account of the barren desolation and filth of the yards around her hut conveys his disgust: '... the dusty ground round the house was almost entirely covered with cow-dung' (p. 725). His account of the dung, the smell and the dirt of the yard is coloured by his loathing of the dung 'crumpled to dust that rose in the warm, sickly, sunrise wind' and the ankle-deep 'black liquid filth'(pp. 727–8).

Given her circumstances, Mrs Spicer is powerless to withstand the engulfing embrace of poverty. Her attempts to maintain a 'decent' environment come to grief, and, since her story is a foreboding of Mary Wilson's future, Lawson questions whether any woman could face such destitution without finally succumbing to its degradation.

From the 1880s, desertion and the failure of parents to support their children were widely perceived as serious threats to the social order, violating the stability of the nuclear family and breeding crime, vice and immorality.[19] Indeed, Mrs Spicer's daughter, it is hinted, has become a prostitute, and her son is apprehended for stealing a horse. Lawson alludes to the question of moral degradation in bush families in *Crime in the Bush* (1899):

> There are things done in the bush (where large families, and sometimes several large families, pig together in ignorance in badly partitioned huts) known well to neighbours; or to school-teachers ...—or even to the police; things which would make a strong man shudder. Clean-minded people shrink from admitting the existence of such things.[20]

Though he says 'we want light on these places', Lawson was unable to go further towards naming the implied domestic sexual violations. His imagery of darkness and filth contrasted with light and cleanliness traces out the terms of the bourgeois attempt to render comprehensible the lives of working-class families.

Women's productive labour

It was not only men's prolonged absences that threatened the stability of the family. Bush mythology can be seen to articulate profound misgivings that attended women's participation in the paid labour force. Public disquiet about women's employment stressed their perceived undercutting of men's wages and conditions. However, misgivings expressed in the bush mythology appear to have been directed towards the disordering of the family that was seen to result from women's productive labour outside the home. Women working on the land were represented as unable to fulfil their primary responsibility as 'mothers of the yeomanry of our infant nation',[21] and as achieving an authority within the home that undermined the proper order of the patriarchal family.

Women's labour outside the home was seen fittingly to take its toll in the private sphere, for which they were primarily responsible. Their toil and hardship is etched deeply into their faces and bodies, and their lifestyles and child-rearing practices will perpetuate the harsh cycle of poverty and emotional deprivation.

Mrs Grogan, the widow in Steele Rudd's story 'In the Drought Time', provides an interesting example of this interplay between rural labour and domesticity. 'The only female on Sleepy Creek who owned a selection', she also furnishes one of the few examples in the bush mythology of a woman cultivating a crop.[22]

Rudd's youthfully naive narrator informs the reader that, when her husband died, Mrs Grogan 'cheerfully' inherited the selection, ten children, a mortgage and 'a heavy bill to pay, and the fence to mend, and the ploughing to do'.[23] 'For a year she strained and struggled—put on a man's hat and shirt, cleared land, humped water, ploughed through the hottest day, or tramped beside the harrow' (p. 288). The cost of the harvest of 'several bags of wheat' is high. The 'frail, jaded widow with bent back and sunken cheeks', with her 'train of ragged, helpless offspring at her heels, crying and complaining of hunger, and of burr and *bindai* in the shoeless feet' are 'objects of pity'. Her ability to care for her children is undermined by the demands of farm work. The demands of child-rearing are incompatible with her labour, and public concern about the plight of children whose mothers undertook paid employment is echoed by Mrs Grogan herself: 'Oh! it's a worry with so many, so 'tis, an' one can't see to them all as y' would like an' be out workin' in th' paddick' (p. 291). Mrs Grogan is not to succeed in farming her selection, but it is her house, not her crop, that burns, leaving the family homeless and desolate.

The connotation of maternal deprivation is as central to the meaning of this story as is maternal affection and nurturing to that of Poole's painting 'The Village Laundress'. Significantly, the labour of the laundress, implicitly located within the home, is constructed through the image as compatible with mothering, whereas the children of the farming woman are likened to 'motherless little lambs'. The children of both women are engaged in labour, but the laundress's daughters work alongside her, in chores appropriate to their gender and class. Mrs Grogan's eldest children contribute to the family's labour, but are separated from their mother by it, and loaded with too great a responsibility for such young shoulders.

The representation of women such as Mrs Spicer and Mrs Grogan, impoverished mothers with large families forced to work the land in order to survive, struggling against overwhelming odds to keep their families intact and virtuous, articulates the late nineteenth-century discourse of social disorder. In the context of nationalist mythology, underlying the sympathy for the plight of the woman is a deep concern about the ability of such women to nurture and rear the nation's 'human capital', their children.

Women's labour and the authority of the husband

Rather than directing their hostility towards the machinery which degraded their traditional craft skills or against the employers who introduced the machinery, working men and their union representatives tended to focus their grievances on the women who were 'out of their proper sphere'. In the bush mythology, however, women are rarely seen as effectively competing with men. Two bushwomen, Squeaker's Mate and Mary Wilson, undertake work which, if done by a man, could be celebrated as 'strong masculine labour'. But in both 'Squeaker's Mate' and 'A Double-Buggy at Lahey's Creek', it is not the women's competitive labour that is at issue, but the authority relations within the home.

Barbara Baynton's story 'Squeaker's Mate' describes a 'disordered' relationship, in which the woman presides over both the work on the selection and the home.[24] Where she is strong, competent, authoritative, honest, he is morally stunted, lacking in both imagination and empathy, indolent, infantilely opportunistic and dependent to the point of inflicting great pain and bitter grief on his 'mate'. Baynton hints that Squeaker's moral and emotional incapacity is, at least in part, a consequence of the Mate's authority, competence and indulgence. She is alert to his deceitful strategies to avoid hard work, always at her expense, but 'her tolerance was one of the mysteries'.

The other bushmen have great respect for the woman who has laboured alone 'for every acre and hoof on that selection'. They find it incomprehensible that she has taken up the selection in Squeaker's name, even though the money was her own (p. 15). Her labour cuts across conventional notions of women's and men's work, as she fells trees with axe and crosscut saw, sizes them up for fence posts and rails, runs some sheep, and sells the honey she collects, strains and boils. And it is she who lifts the heavy end of logs, and carries the heavy tools, while Squeaker carries the billy and the tucker. Though the women 'pretended to challenge her right to womanly garments' (p. 11), the realisation that she does not wear male clothing for bush work comes as a surprise.

The woman's back is broken when the thick branch of a worm-riddled tree falls on her. She lies unable to move, and the fire-stick that the impatient Squeaker thrusts into her incapacitated hand falls and sets her clothes smouldering, burning her arm. She is brought home and, unable to move, is bed-ridden and totally dependent on the callously indifferent

Squeaker. The strength of her character that held Squeaker to her commitment to acquire the selection and farm it, depended on her ability to provide for him. A stronger but more loathsome Squeaker, no longer dependent on her, sets about realising his assets without the restraint his old mate had exercised over his short-sighted self-indulgence.

In the context of this discussion of the representation of women engaged in 'the work of men', this story picks up themes found in the Lawson and Rudd stories. In spite of Squeaker's 'agency', the woman's injury, her immobilisation and her humiliation are the result of the natural order: the rotten tree; the new, younger and fertile mate. The inversion of the social order that her authority and her labour implied could be righted only by the reinstatement of her extreme physical dependence, her powerlessness and her confinement to the hut.

To be placed in a position of dependency on and subordination to a man such as Squeaker is, nevertheless, the ultimate subjection. Baynton's story is subversive of the ideology of separate spheres because, by reinstating the 'proper relations' of the gender order, she indicates the contemptible inadequacy of Squeaker to occupy a position of such authority and power.

If we read 'Squeaker's Mate' as a metaphorical treatment of the vexed question of women's engagement in paid employment outside the home, then it is significant that the other bushmen accepted this woman as a 'mate': and 'agreed that she was the best long-haired mate that ever stepped in petticoats' (p. 11). As long as she 'hard-grafted with the best of them', and interacted with them through economic exchange, the men perceived her fraternally, not as competition, but as a colleague. It is when she is reduced to a dependent woman that her 'uncompromising independence' is severely punished by ostracism by both women and men, since 'most husbands accept their wives' views of other women' (p. 15). But the confinement, immobilisation and dependency of the woman which result from her inability to work 'as a man' are represented in this story in terms of humiliating powerlessness.

Baynton's story registers a shift in the ideology of separate spheres, away from a notion of complementary partnership between men and women, sovereigns in their own spheres of influence and engaged in productive and interdependent labour, towards the notion of breadwinning husbands supporting dependent wives whose domestic work was no longer thought of as productive labour.[25] Women's participation in the paid labour force was curtailed, and as Desley Deacon has argued,[26] the awareness of their contribution to the nation's prosperity through labour was suppressed. Not only were men to be protected from what they perceived as competition from women workers, but also their authority within the home was to be augmented by wives' economic dependency on their 'natural guardians'.[27]

Nevertheless, the achievement of this shift was neither automatic nor untroubled. In bush mythology, though women's labour outside the home is seen to undermine the proper relations of authority of a man over his wife, women do not readily concede to their husbands authority over domestic matters. Conflict and dissent within the ideology of separate spheres finds expression in matters relating to child-rearing practices and the location of the family home as the division between the public and private spheres becomes permeable and contested. Further, it is possible that the concept of separate spheres itself implicitly assumes the permanent location of the home. The experience of family mobility in bush literature suggests that the husband's decision to move the family may have been an area of unresolved tension. This is a recurring theme in the stories of Joe and Mary Wilson,[28] but also emerges in the *On Our Selection* stories in Mother Rudd's vehement opposition to the shift from Shingle Hut to Saddletop.

The issue of matrimonial authority is a recurring, and never resolved, issue in the Joe Wilson stories. 'A Double-Buggy at Lahey's Creek' combines the negotiation of authority with Mary Wilson's intervention in the cultivation of the land. Mary not only persuades Joe to plant the crop that begins his run of good luck and prosperity, but also manages the preparation of the paddock for planting, in his absence, without his assent and in spite of his initial reluctance:

> And Mary was down on the bank superintending. She'd got James with the trace-chains and the spare horses, and had made him clear off every stick and bush where another furrow might be squeezed in.[29]

Like many such bushwomen, Mary wears her husband's clothes for unwomanly work. Unlike most, she wears his new boots, rather than the clothes they have discarded:

> 'I thought I'd make the boots easy for you, Joe,' said Mary.
> 'It's all right, Mary,' I said, 'I'm not going to growl.' Those boots were a bone of contention between us; but she generally got them off before I got home. (p. 736)

The result is 'the finest potato crop ever seen in the district'. There is a degree of ambiguity in the recounting of this project, which is told by Joe Wilson years later. On the one hand, the competition for the boots suggests that Mary's successful cultivation of the land undermines Joe's authority and achieves a degree of autonomy through her labour and management of production outside the domestic sphere. On the other hand, the cooperation and intimacy suggested by their joint venture as Joe enters 'into the spirit of the thing' is rare in bush mythology.

The eventual outcome of the prosperity, however, reminds us that Mary's labour does not connote authority in decisions about the way in which income is spent. The buggy that she had set her heart on long before they could afford such a luxury is Joe's gift to her. 'The great acts of generosity', says Mauss, 'are not free from self interest': 'to give is to show one's superiority.'[30]

In the emerging construction of modern gender relations, the bond between men and women is redefined away from mutuality in favour of guardianship and dependency. Joe Wilson's gift to Mary reflects his greater earning power and his overall control over the family budget, and as such it celebrates, symbolises and reaffirms the unequal marriage relationship, functioning as a means of social control, analogous to charity or patronage.[31]

If, however, the 'proper' relations of husband and wife are re-established through the gift in 'A Double-Buggy at Lahey's Creek', the stories of Mary and Joe Wilson nevertheless offer a rare glimpse of a mature relationship, characterised not only by loss of romance and conflict, but also by partnership, affection and commitment.

Conclusion

The 1890s witnesssed the production of the modern family unit in which the husband supported his dependent wife and children. The texts of the bush mythology by and large subscribe to this ideal, and represent the bourgeois nuclear family as fundamental to the stability of the emerging nation. But this commitment cuts across another major theme of the nationalist mythology, that of the centrality of rural labour in the formation of the nation. The valorisation of 'strong masculine labour' evokes anxiety for the family as the site of reproduction of future generations of Australians.

The differentiation of men and women in terms of the separate spheres implied that women engaged in productive labour outside the home were 'out of place'. But the spatial metaphor is reinforced by the assumption that such labour was 'men's work'. The continuity of the rhetoric of separate spheres masked both the extent to which the public domain interpenetrated the private realm, and the reorganisation of both the labour market and domestic lives. The ideology itself was also undergoing significant transformation. Notions of sovereignty and complementary labour in the relations between men and women were to be displaced by those of guardianship and dependency.

In the imaginary formation of the nation, women's contribution was to be made through their reproductive, rather than productive, labour. Women's labour outside the home was seen to offer few benefits to the nation, and the cost was measured in the women's distraction from their primary responsibility as mothers of the nation's future generations. As mothers in their 'proper place', women's contribution to the emerging nation could be celebrated unambiguously.

But when all is said and done, we are left with the images of women. Squeaker's mate's fierce independence and her broken back, Mrs Spicer's numbing sense of loss, and Mary Wilson's resistance—such images outdistance the construction of meaning through metaphor in these narratives.

They remind us that, if women could live in 'their proper place' only when their bodies and spirits were broken, this may have been too high a price to pay.

17 Henry Lawson, the drover's wife and the critics
Kay Schaffer

The 1890s. The phrase resonates with meaning for Australians. It conjures up a particular significance for the decade before Federation—a decade when an Australian ethos takes shape in the form of the bushman as hero with his egalitarian values and ideals of mateship; a decade when the Australian legend is immortalised, at least for modern readers. In one of my favourite descriptions of the era, Harry Heseltine writes that the decade presents us with a unique Australian vision of 'a happy band of brothers marching bravely forward to a political and social Utopia, united in their hatred of tyranny, their love of beer, their rugged manliness and independence'.[1] Heseltine's 'over-the-top' description deliberately borders on the parodic. It was written in an important 1960 essay designed to shift readers' perspectives from a patriotic affiliation with a naive democratic nationalism to a modernist New Critical reappraisal of the Australian tradition. There would be many challenges to the myth in the next 30 years but none would blunt its enduring influence on Australian culture.

It was not until the 1920s and 1930s, in fact, that the reputation which attends the 1890s today began to take shape. In the inter-war years writers for the first time began to take seriously the proposition that Australia was an entity worth writing about, with specific cultural attributes and a unique identity. Nettie Palmer's *Modern Australian Literature* (1924), Keith Hancock's *Australia* (1930) and William Moore's *The Story of Australian Art* (1934) attempt to define the nation and its differences from the British parent culture. These studies select certain themes from the *Bulletin* and certain aspects of the 1890s to construct a sense of national identity. This limited and focused construction then comes to stand for the whole. The texts establish a nascent discourse on national identity.

Other studies, like Vance Palmer's *Legend of the Nineties* (1954), A.A. Phillips's *The Australian Tradition* (1958) and Russel Ward's *The Australian Legend* (1958) follow a generation later. A debate about the meaning and significance of the legend arises. Positions are contested as the voices of modernist new critics replace those of their democratic nationalist brothers. In the 1970s, feminist texts like Anne Summers' *Damned Whores and God's Police* (1975) and Miriam Dixson's *The Real Matilda* (1975) appear. They challenge the masculine biases inherent in the culture and its histories and attempt to reinterpret Australia and women's place differently. A number of feminist literary and historical studies follow. But they will have virtually no impact on the debates between men.

The 1980s give rise to new studies which challenge the legend and the whole concept of national identity from a number of dissident perspectives. Studies like Richard White's *Inventing Australia* (1983), John Docker's *In a Critical Condition* (1984) and Graeme Turner's *National Fictions* (1986) call attention to social and ideological issues. They suggest that national identity is an invention, a cultural construction. Our sense of what it means to be an Australian emanates not from actual historical events but from their representations in literature, history, art, film and the like. What we take to be 'reality' emanates from these discursive materials. Whose 'reality' is given credence depends on the shifting power relations and the interests of dominant groups within the society. Yet these studies, despite their attention to power relations and ideologies, do not seriously attend to questions of gender. It is as if the feminist debate had not occurred; or as if the need to maintain a separate sphere for women overrode the challenge to deconstruct the masculine or phallocentric assumptions embedded in the myths of a national culture.

In *Women and the Bush* (1988), I attempt to trace the outlines of this discourse on national identity and the place of women within it.[2] I suggest that although women are largely absent from the debates, the idea of Woman (or the feminine) is everywhere present in metaphors of landscape against which the Australian native son measures his identity. In the book, as in virtually every study of Australian culture, Henry Lawson looms large. In my study the focus is not the man himself but the idea of Lawson which has been enlisted in the cause of nationalism throughout the twentieth century. Nationalist writers identify their vision of the Australian character with reference to Lawson's short stories of the 1890s. According to the tradition, in his writings and those of the *Bulletin* school we find a unique and original Australian creation, 'the voice of the bush', which comes to be equated with the voice of Australia. Here I would like to reiterate and extend some of those arguments with reference to Lawson and his classic short story 'The Drover's Wife', which first appeared in the *Bulletin* in 1892.

The drover's wife is an interesting signifier for Australian culture for several reasons. In the first place, she is a woman in a nationalist tradition in which women rarely appear. Her depiction has been and continues to be viewed as an authentic representation of the pioneering woman's life in the bush. Second, her position as a pioneering hero/victim in the bush reinforces the masculine tradition. That is, she becomes a part of man's battle against the land as a masculine subject. Third, she also maintains and upholds British cultural traditions in the bush in her roles as wife and mother. By studying the critical reputation of the drover's wife as a story, as a female character, and as a representative of the nationalist tradition through the twentieth century, we can trace shifting ideological perspectives on Australian culture and woman's place within them.

In this chapter I propose, first, to outline the varying critical approaches to 'The Drover's Wife' in an argument which largely follows my discussion in *Women and the Bush*. Then I will extend the argument to include consideration of several fascinating variants, three fictional and one filmic, to the text. These include short stories by Murray Bail, Frank Moorhouse and Barbara Jefferis and the film *Serious Undertakings* by Helen Grace. The creative revisions which have emerged since 1975 secure 'The Drover's Wife' as *the* classic story of the 1890s. They also tell us something about debunking as a specifically Australian form of humour/tribute. And they give evidence to the dissident voices of feminist and deconstructive critique emerging in the 1980s. If it is true that in Australia 'parody is the highest form of praise', Lawson and the drover's wife should be feeling mighty chuffed by now.

Henry Lawson holds pride of place in the Australian legend as Australia's authentic native son—the boy from the bush who alerted Australians to what was unique about the life around them. In most of his stories the characters who struggle against the hostile and alien bush are men, but this is not necessarily the case. The position of 'native son' could, in an exceptional circumstance, be filled by a woman. That is, the bushwoman can stand in place of her husband, lover or brother and take on masculine attributes of strength, fortitude, courage and the like in her battle with the environment (as long as she also maintains her disguise of femininity). She could be called and have the status of a pioneering hero. This is the position of the drover's wife.

Ideas about women and femininity circulate in the culture in diverse ways. The representation of women's character, like the character of the drover's wife, is one of them. Metaphors of otherness, employed to signify femininity, are another. The land as an object of representation is virtually always represented as feminine. The land functions as a metaphor for Woman—as in father sky to mother earth, colonial master to the plains of promise, native son to the barren bush, contemporary Australians to the red/dead centre. All of these equations reproduce the 'perfect' couple—masculine activity and feminine passivity. Within Lawson's imaginary representations the land is a harsh, cruel, barren and alien environment against which both men and women struggle. His harsh depictions of the bush have become integral to the Australian legend. The writings of Lawson as they have been taken up in the debates on national identity constitute an important site for the construction of femininity in Australia. When one looks at the Australian legend from the perspective of the 1990s these gender-specific inclusions and exclusions in language become relevant to the debates on culture and woman's place.

The classic woman in the bush is Lawson's drover's wife. Although a character in fiction, it is she whom both W.K. Hancock in his history, *Australia* (1930), and Manning Clark in his six-volume appraisal, *The History of Australia* (1973–1988), cite as an authentic historical embodiment of woman's existence. Anne Summers in *Damned Whores and God's Police* (1975) recognised her as the classic 'coper', idealised by Clark as the 'bush Mum'. All Australians know her. As children they read of her story in school. As adults they encounter it more often than any other story in anthologies of Australian prose. Lawson must have loved her, because she helped to make his reputation in England. Edward Garnett, the British critic, from whom Nettie Palmer took her lead in assessing Lawson as the 'voice of the continent', had this to say about 'The Drover's Wife': 'If this artless sketch be taken as the summary of a woman's life, giving its meaning in ten short pages, Maupassant has never done better.'[3]

One can register the ideological significance of the story by tracing its changing reputation within the dominant discourses on national identity as they emerge throughout the twentieth century. The fortunes of Henry Lawson may have waxed and waned through the years but the reputation of the drover's wife has remained secure—although critics have disagreed as to just what she or the story stands for. In the early decades of the century, when Lawson's prose was deemed 'authentic' by sympathetic reviewers, his 'realistic' short stories were judged to be representative, photographic and sincere. The drover's wife took on the guise of historical truth.[4] In the 1920s, Australia entered a conservative phase. It was an era when the concept of racial purity was enlisted to stand against the Yellow Peril. Lawson-as-cultural-object became the site of an ideological battle among critics intent on bolstering the national image. The bush, through the symbol of the wattle, came to represent the land of joy and wholesomeness. Fred Davison, editor of the monthly journal *Australia*, complained that 'Lawson failed most abjectly to sense that joy and to give it expression'. He 'didn't know Australia—not the real Australia—and couldn't write about it'.[5] But, although critics severely chastise Lawson for his 'woeful' portrayal of bushmen, the drover's wife is spared.

After the First World War the culture enlists Lawson into the cause of mature nationhood. The gold-rush digger, the noble bushman, the Anzac soldier fuse into a single image of manly strength, independence and courage. At the same time critics begin to alter the image of Lawson. His bush becomes the terrain on which national pride is built. The drover's wife becomes a 'large and symbolic figure' who 'opened the eyes of other writers to what is really poignant and dramatic in the life around them'.[6] After both World Wars, the image of manly toughness, 'born of the lean loins of the country itself', would link the academic nationalists to their literary brothers of the 1890s.[7] And the drover's wife, though a woman, is seen to personify these traits.

With a shift of national interests away from the bush and towards the city, away from particular forms of working-class republicanism and towards a so-called universal middle-class culture, Lawson and the literature of the 1890s also experience a reinterpretation. Whereas earlier commentators had described the bush as a physical threat to man's identity, the modernist new critics imagined it as a moral, spiritual and existential threat. When this attitude is explored with reference to 'The Drover's Wife', as in Brian Matthews' *The Receding Wave,* the story is described as one of 'ruthless pessimism' in which the woman confronts the bush as a 'common enemy' to men and women alike. Her life of hardships culminates in a 'sense of spiritual and emotional exhaustion'.[8]

Colin Roderick is one critic whose views on Lawson and 'The Drover's Wife' have changed over time. In the 1960s Roderick described her situation as that of 'the self-sacrificing lonely life of the bushwoman who in those days helped to lay the foundation of our prosperity'.[9] This position aligns the author with the attitudes of the Democratic Nationalists. But in his study, *The Real Henry Lawson*, Roderick shifts ground and incorporates the metaphysical concerns of the modernist new critics into his narrative. He cites 'The Drover's Wife' as Lawson's 'first short story of high quality' and maintains that the dominant note is one of melancholy. 'The bush suffered a change which reflected his own fears and insecurity. Nothing attractive, nothing lovely, nothing of good to report entered his portrait of it: it was all sinister and destructive. It developed from a mere background into an active alien force against which human fortitude spent itself until it was crushed.'[10]

But Manning Clark has another story to tell. For him, 'The Drover's Wife' presents to Australians an awareness of both a surface heroism and a metaphysical terror. He explains that the surface story tells of a wife's heroism and her sacrifice for her children, but underneath it all she confronts and conquers all the fears of despair and defeat which 'touched him [Lawson] deeply'. He proclaims, 'Lawson knew that her heroism, the halo of glory with which he endowed this bush mum, was of a high order.'[11]

'The Drover's Wife', in the hands of the critics, has been a prized commodity for public consumption. The many interpretations this story has received demonstrate both the evocative, symbolic richness of the text and the ways in which the story as a cultural object has been enlisted in the defence of dominant ideological perspectives concerning the nature of Australian culture. The commentators refer to 'The Drover's Wife' as a cultural entity in three ways. As literature, the story has grown from an artless sketch to a work of high quality. As a figure, the wife has been described as a tough dramatic individual symbolising courage and hope and also one of crushed fortitude exhibiting emotional and spiritual exhaustion. As an image of the Australian character, her situation reflects the nation's prosperity and its pessimism. The former depictions belong to writers associated with the Democratic Nationalists who share a view of progress which celebrates the country's prosperity and initiative. In their view, the literature of the 1890s is realistic. The tough stock of transplanted Britons whom the drover's wife personifies produce for them a national type which will lead the country to maturity as an independent, strong and resourceful nation. Women are pioneers. They function as symbols of hope.

The later depictions emerge out of the writings of critics associated with the bourgeois modernists, who would deny a faith in historical progress. Their construction of the literature of the 1890s emphasises the nihilistic, violent and irrational dark side of the Australian tradition. They decry Australia as a static nation, tied to worldwide economic and political realities which limit future growth. Nationalism as a concept has grown both 'sour and barren'.[12] Women personify the national dilemma. They function symbolically as figures of defeat.

Whether referring to Lawson's story, the figure of the drover's wife as an historical entity, or the woman as a dimension of the national character, the two sides of the argument depend on a series of dichotomies within Western thought. The debate contrasts the objective with the subjective; optimism with pessimism; reason with doubt; realism with romanticism. The former qualities are desired, while the latter are feared; the former associated with the masculine, the latter with the feminine within the critical discourses on Lawson and the Australian tradition. Peter Pierce suggests that the whole construction of this 'literary historiographic melodrama apes the conflicts of convicts against their gaolers, bushrangers against squatters'.[13] It is interesting in this context to note that both the Democratic Nationalists and the New Critics embrace 'The Drover's Wife' in their attempts to define and master the national character.

In *Women and the Bush* I attempt to deconstruct this monolithic bush mum. I analyse her place not as an authentic historical entity (which she is not in any sense beyond imaginary representation) but as a cultural construction. I suggest that the drover's wife is interesting as a signifier in that she has been enlisted into the debates which span the spectrum of ideological perspectives and that within them she occupies both masculine and feminine positions. She represents to the Australian tradition both masculine sameness and feminine otherness. Named only as 'the drover's wife', her existence in the family is defined as that of a wife and mother in relation to man. Although a female, wife and mother, and given attributes similar to those of the bush she inhabits, she takes up a masculine position in the story. When she moves to confront the snake, the evil within, with the help of her son, the dog and a stick, she masters the threat of the bush.

She stands in the place of her absent husband. The drover's wife is woman. But heroic status is conferred upon her through her assumption of a masculine identity.

At the same time she acts in the role of God's police within the family, dressing the children for Sunday walks, mending the clothes, and otherwise maintaining a 'proper' respectable life in the bush, without complaint. These feminine attributes link her to a culture and civilisation to be found in the city and, beyond the city, in England. It is a situation from which the bushman seeks escape. In addition she is associated with the landscape and its evil—although she also stands against it. She too is harsh and sunbaked like the land. She too is Eve in a fallen garden, linked to the snake, the black fellow and the evil against which man must struggle. As an object in discourse the drover's wife becomes a pioneering hero. As a hero (and a mother) she is able to mediate the threat of the feminised bush landscape, which is variously represented as wilderness, evil, the snake and the 'original curse' of mankind, in a very specific way.

Through this story Lawson and subsequent critics achieve several contradictory goals. They secure the place of both women and men as masculine subjects within the Australian tradition. They also maintain gender differences between women and men, in which women uphold ties to the father's law and the parent culture, which men resist. In addition, they maintain the category of the feminine as otherness through the sliding signification which links the bush and woman as feminine objects in discourse. 'The Drover's Wife' is a powerful signifier for Australian culture. When we investigate the drover's wife as a cultural construction which comes to be seen as an authentic historical representation of women in the bush we can more fully understand how Manning Clark could maintain that her 'halo of glory ... was of a high order'.[14]

More recently the drover's wife has become something of a national joke. Both Murray Bail and Frank Moorhouse, or his Italian comrade, Franco Casamaggiore, have had a go at her.[15] Not only does Lawson's 1892 story come up for review, but Russell Drysdale's 1945 painting 'The Drover's Wife' gets a bit of a blast as well. What can we make of these changing fortunes for the composite drover's wife? George Bowering, the Canadian critic, has recently written that the tendency to debunk national myths, evident in both Canada and Australia, is a deconstructive instance of postmodernist irony.[16] His essay concerns Murray Bail's 1975 story 'The Drover's Wife' but could be applied to Frank Moorhouse's 1980 story as well. His argument is that the grandsons of the pioneers have begun, once again, to call the legend into doubt by attempting to topple the monument/the authoritative text/the work of art through their anti-authoritarian gestures of comedy. The effect, he suggests, is to deconstruct the ethos of nationalism to which the originating story gave rise and to presage a new cultural history appropriate to our postmodern era.

This is an interesting argument and one which might carry more conviction if it weren't for the fact that Australian humour has always characteristically debunked cultural heroes and icons from an anti-authoritarian stance. Bowering's conclusions may be a bit premature. In Bail's story the narrator is a dullard of a dentist from Adelaide (where Drysdale's painting 'The Drover's Wife' is housed in the South Australian Art Gallery). He spies the painting and its title and declares that the woman is not the drover's wife—'She is my wife', who left him and the kids for a drover. The dentist apparently knows nothing of the Drysdale painting nor the Lawson short story which precedes it. He's a city lad for whom the bush is a nuisance (and not a symbol of the Australian ethos). His former wife Hazel's love of it was always a bit of an embarrassment to him. She enjoyed chopping wood at the beach shack where she also killed a snake. These actions made her less attractive to the dentist. He wanted a proper postwar city wife, not a bush-girl 'drover's wife'.

In addition, Bail's dullard of a dentist views art only in concrete referential terms. He chastises Drysdale for leaving out the flies in his painting. Lawson left out the flies as well. Battling flies in the bush somehow cannot equate with the heroism involved in the struggle against floods and bush fires, snakes and loneliness. Bowering sees the narrator's naivety as a ploy on Bail's part through which he creates a postcolonial citizen free from a British colonial history and the icons of Australian cultural identity. He suggests, as well, that the story encourages us to view the Australian legend as the creator as well as the expression of a national ethos—one which it deconstructs through its irony. 'Hazel—it is Hazel and the rotten landscape that dominate everything', the dentist concludes—a statement which can be variously read as referring (in its 'everything') to the Drysdale painting, the dentist's sad life and/or the Australian tradition.

With a differing emphasis Dorothy Jones and Barry Andrews place the story, and that of Frank Moorhouse, squarely within a tradition of national humour.[17] For them the special characteristics which mark Australian humour are a tendency to self-parody, an ironic tone, and an attitude of individuals manipulated by circumstances they are powerless to control. Jones and Andrews also characterise Australian humour as 'heavily male-oriented'. All of this applies, of course, to the humour in both the Bail and Moorhouse narratives. When women appear at all they are 'perceived as at best outsiders, and at worst the enemy' (somewhat like the metaphorical bush-as-enemy, I would add).[18] One might say that this tendency itself is being parodied in both the Bail and Moorhouse stories.

Frank Moorhouse's story 'The Drover's "Wife" ' is ostensibly a transcription of a paper given by an Italian student of Australian literature (Franco Casamaggiore, no doubt an intimate friend of the author) at a conference on Commonwealth Writing in Milan. The graduate student, through a careful process of literary detection, has discovered an 'insider's' joke underlying Lawson's short story, Drysdale's painting and Bail's narrative. The joke is that since it is an 'historical fact' that there were no women in Australia for a century or more of its pioneering history, the Drover's 'Wife' is not a wife at all, but rather a sheep. The story derives its considerable humour from having a go at literary critics and conventions via sexuality (and its absence from the Australian ethos). Jones and Andrews conclude that 'Moorhouse mocks at academic pretensions along with narrowly defined notions of Australian literary culture, while showing how intangible in essence that culture may prove for an outsider'.[19] For them the story both dissolves and augments the literary myth of the bush legend.

Jones and Andrews suggest, however, that the literary myth 'is further deconstructed' by Barbara Jefferis in her story 'The Drover's Wife'. This comment calls for further consideration. Is a feminist version necessarily deconstructive or can it also be seen as constitutive of the myth and the masculinist culture out of which it arises? How can one read 'The Drover's Wife' from a deconstructive position?

Catherine Belsey, in her study *Critical Practice*, describes the deconstructive process in the following way:

> The object of deconstructing the text is to examine the *process of its production*—not the private experience of the individual author, but the mode of production, the materials and their arrangement in the work. The aim is to locate the point of contradiction within the text, the point at which it transgresses the limits within which it is constructed, breaks free of the constraints imposed by its own realist form. Composed of contradictions, the text is no longer restricted to a single, harmonious and authoritative reading. Instead it becomes *plural*, open to re-reading, no longer an object for passive consumption but an object of work by the reader to produce meaning. [emphasis in original].[20]

If the terms of an emerging postmodernist debate are deconstruction versus reconstruction of the myth, there are a number of reasons why Jefferis's story, although told from a woman's perspective, might be aligned more closely to a reconstructive defence rather than a deconstruction of the bush legend. In the first place, her narrator is the composite drover's wife of the masculine imagination—the woman or women who are the subjects of the stories of Lawson, Bail and Moorhouse. She attends not to the ways in which the previous stories have been produced but to the absence from them of a woman's perspective. She supplies the missing content. The account is ironic, given woman's relative absence from the tradition, but not parodic of the legend itself. Second, the story conforms to the traditions of realism. Jefferis's version sets the record straight by providing what might be seen (in the terms of narrative realism) as a serious view of the drover's wife as a complex and misunderstood woman. In this the attempt is not unlike that of Kate Grenville in *Joan Makes History* (1988). In both of these texts, pioneering bush wives speak through the narrative space opened for them by their male creators at the end of the nineteenth century. The drover's wife, 'knows' Lawson as her 1890s counterpart in Grenville's text, the forlorn wife of Frederick McCubbin's triptych painting 'The Pioneers', 'knows' McCubbin. The references to originating authors serve to validate origins of the myth of the 1890s and to authenticate them through the presence of the woman's voice: 'I was there. I know.'

In these 'realistic' accounts of Jefferis's and Grenville's women the horrors of the bush life for men, as represented in the masculine tradition, are nothing when compared to the fears and sufferings of bush women, particularly in childbirth. Jefferis's drover's wife gently rebukes men for their ignorance of women's lives—they just don't know ... 'they don't understand the strength women have got—won't see it, because they think it takes away from them'.[21] Later in the piece, Jefferis's heroine slides into the late twentieth century and justifies leaving the Adelaide dentist of Bail's story (they were his kids, not hers. And he was a city wimp, not a real man—a bushman). The voice, emphasis and perspective of the narrative are female but the reading effect reinforces the masculine nationalist tradition all the same—co-opting women into its ethos and the prescribed places for men and women within it. Although it challenges male biases in the Australian bush tradition, the story naturalises rather than problematises the myth as construction. In addition, it is necessary for the reader to know the previous versions of the story to appreciate the wit, the nuances, and the multiple voices it contains. An unproblematic reading of Jefferis's story positions the reader inside the myth, giving it the substance of the woman's point of view, the woman who is, ironically, the product of her masculine histories.

This is not the case in the stories of Bail and Moorhouse, each of which, metaphorically speaking, cuts a new path through the scrub, whereas Jefferis's drover's wife takes another Sunday walk through it. She waves her hands in the air, demanding that we see, hear and recognise her as a significant presence. At the same time the story is indebted to and dependent upon the three preceding male versions of Lawson, Bail and Moorhouse. This feminist version, therefore, clears a space for women within the ongoing bush legend, while it also preserves the male versions and revitalises the masculine tradition.

Helen Grace's film *Serious Undertakings* attempts to deconstruct the Australian tradition from a feminist position different from that of Jefferis. The film attempts to challenge the nationalist ideology of the bush. It shifts viewers' interest away from the possibility of women making new or supplementing old meanings. Rather it focuses on the role of the spectator in producing and maintaining pre-existing meanings and ideologies. In this way, the film challenges ideologies of the past, while it demands critical attention on the part of the viewer to such issues as viewer position, masculine gaze, narrative form and non-narrative techniques. It opens with a voice-over reading of 'The Drover's Wife' ('Bush all around—bush with no horizon, for the country is flat. No ranges in the distance'), while viewers watch rush-hour traffic on modern inner-city freeways heading for the Sydney Harbour Bridge. The film is different in kind not only from Jefferis's story but from all earlier versions of 'The Drover's Wife'. This is so not only because of its medium but also because of the questions it takes up. For Grace the question 'What is woman's place?' might be variously answered as: an empty space, a void of meaning, a space of absence not previously theorised.

The title, 'Serious Undertakings', refers to a statement made by Julia Kristeva, a French feminist theorist, referring to the cultural perception that the work and roles of women (as mothers) are trivial undertakings while the work and roles of non-mothers (that is, men) are perceived as serious undertakings.[22] The film plays with these positions and the 'natural' gender divisions which support them. There is an ironic juxtaposition of male and female roles, of the public and the private sphere, of innocence and violence, of the maternal and the political. The film does not attempt to flesh out the Australian tradition, giving it substance by the inclusion of women in the place of their prior apparent absence. Instead, the boundaries of national identity and gender identity are abolished as fictions. The Australian tradition is seen as a masculine tradition in which the feminine, as distinct from the ways women have been defined by men and male culture, is wholly absent. So, as a voice-over reads again from 'The Drover's Wife', we watch as the pioneering woman depicted in McCubbin's triptych 'The Pioneers' disappears—she is air-brushed out of existence and all that is left in the place of her absence is the bush. In another place in the film the drover's wife's pram, with which she takes the children for Sunday walks, becomes the pram used as a radical political weapon of terrorism by the Baader-Meinhoff gang. We are reminded here and elsewhere of an early sequence in which a new mother in a maternity hospital (a site where innocence is manufactured) speaks of terrorism.

Throughout the film the whole idea of a national history or an 'authentic' Australian culture is questioned and dismantled. The film refuses narrative closure or interpretation in the conventional sense. Its message is playful and open-ended. It takes up a feminist deconstructive position, one which employs different strategies for approaching the culturally constructed category of the feminine beyond previously established masculine positions for Woman or women. A deconstructive position, like Grace's or my own, not only parodies or debunks the tradition; it also attempts to challenge previously received notions of identity, voice and presence. Does this approach presage a new cultural history for the next 100 years? Can it interrupt the power relations and vested economic interests of the dominant interest groups which have been well served by outmoded but prevalent notions of national identity? Only to a minor degree, perhaps, given our history as a colonial nation still searching for national identity in a postmodernist and post-colonial age. The drover's wife in her many disguises may be with us for a few years yet. Desire, which motivates the debate, continues to urge the settling rather than the deconstruction of questions of national identity—even though we know that this desire can never be satisfied; even though we know that the tradition acts as a supplement to absence. Still, it fills the void. If the past is prologue, the present is plural and the future open and yet to be explored. The drover's wife may have a few lessons to teach us yet. I never despair of the twists and turns of old wives' tales.

Notes

Chapter 1: The politics of respectability: identifying the masculinist context

We thank Marilyn Lake and *Historical Studies* for permission to reprint this paper. (M. Lake, 'The politics of respectability: Identifying the masculinist context', *Historical Studies*, vol. 22, no. 86, 1986, pp. 116–131.)

1 Notable exceptions in Australian history are D. Walker, 'The getting of manhood', and R. White, 'The importance of being *Man*', in P. Spearritt and D. Walker (eds), *Australian Popular Culture*, Allen & Unwin, Sydney, 1979. In American history there is B. Ehrenreich's innovative *The Hearts of Men: American Dreams and the flight from Commitment*, Pluto, New York, 1983; in New Zealand, J. Phillips, 'Mummy's boys: Pakeha men and male culture in New Zealand', contained in a collection ed. P. Bunkle and B. Hughes, ironically entitled *Women in New Zealand Society*, Allen & Unwin, Auckland & Boston, 1980.
2 'Contribution history' is Gerda Lerner's phrase, describing history which looks at women's contribution to 'recognised social and political movements and categories'; G. Lerner, 'Placing women in history: A 1975 perspective', in B.A. Carroll (ed.), *Liberating Women's History*, University of Illinois Press, Urbana, Ill., 1976.
3 G. Davison, 'Sydney and the bush: An urban context for the Australian Legend', *Historical Studies*, vol. 18, no. 71, 1978.
4 R. White, *Inventing Australia: Images and Identity, 1688–1980*, Allen & Unwin, Sydney, 1981, p. 100.
5 A.W. Jose, *The Romantic Nineties*, Angus & Robertson, Sydney, 1933, p. 34; see also George Taylor's portrayal of the 'Bohemian boys' in *'Those Were the Days': being reminiscences of Australian artists and writers*, Tyrells, Sydney, 1918.
6 F. Adams, *The Australians*, T. Fisher Unwin, London, 1893, p. 144.

7 C. Hall, 'The early formation of Victorian domestic ideology', in S. Burmann (ed.), *Fit Work for Women*, (1979) Croom Helm in assoc. with Oxford University Women's Committee and ANU Press, London, 1982.
8 *ibid.*, p. 23.
9 M. Grellier, 'The family: Some aspects of its demography and ideology in mid-nineteenth century Western Australia', in C.T. Stannage (ed.), *A New History of Western Australia*, University of Western Australia Press, Nedlands, 1981, pp. 498–9.
10 YMCA, First Annual Report; contained in *100th Annual Report*, McLaren Collection, Baillieu Library, University of Melbourne.
11 *Bulletin*, 3 November 1888.
12 R. Bedford, *Naught to Thirty-Three*, new edn, Melbourne University Press, Carlton, 1976, p. 73, (first pub. 1944).
13 Adams, *The Australians*, p. 86.
14 S. Stephen, 'Marriage and the family in bohemian Melbourne 1890–1914', *Australia 1888 Bulletin* no. 9, 1983, p. 22.
15 *ibid.*, p. 23.
16 *ibid.*
17 S. Lawson, *The Archibald Paradox: A strange case of authorship*, Allen Lane, Melbourne, 1983, p. 160; *Bulletin*, 12 May 1888.
18 Cartoon, 'Above Suspicion', *Bulletin*, 2 May 1885.
19 *Bull-Ant*, 2 April 1891.
20 *Bulletin*, 12 February 1886.
21 See, for example, the cartoon entitled 'Relief', *ibid.*, 28 March 1885.
22 R. Ward, *The Australian Legend*, Oxford University Press, Melbourne, 1958, pp. 97–100.
23 H. Reynolds, *The Other Side of the Frontier: an interpretation of the Aboriginal response to the invasion and settlement of Australia*, History Department, James Cook University, Townsville, 1981, p. 58. It is clear that some European men established long-lasting relationships with Aboriginal women, but I think it is safe to assume that most frontiersmen abandoned the women and their 'half-caste' children.
24 H. Lawson, 'The sliprails and the spur', in *Winnowed Verses*, Angus & Robertson, Sydney, new edn, 1944.
25 Archibald, quoted in S. Lawson, *The Archibald Paradox*, p. 24.
26 Taylor, *Those Were the Days*, p. 29.
27 *Bulletin*, 10 April 1886.
28 Quoted in S. Lawson, *Archibald Paradox*, p. 152.
29 Ward, *Australian Legend*, p. 199.
30 H. Lawson, 'The Vagabond', in *Winnowed Verses*.
31 F. Adams, 'The Men of the Nation', in *Songs of the Army of the Night*, Federal Steam Printing & Binding Works, Sydney, 1888.
32 W.G. Spence, *Australia's Awakening: Thirty years in the life of an Australian agitator*, Worker Trustees, Sydney, 1890 and *Hummer*, 16 January 1892, quoted in N. Ebbels (ed.), *The Australian Labor Movement 1850-1907*, Hale & Iremonger, Sydney, 1983, pp. 121, 166.

33 S. Lawson, *op. cit.*, p. 197.
34 P. McDonald, *Marriage in Australia*, ANU Press, Canberra, 1975, pp. 113, 135.
35 Introduction to K. Daniels *et al.* (eds), *Women in Australia. An Annotated Guide to the Records*, AGPS, Canberra, 1977, p. xiii.
36 A.E. Dingle, "'The truly magnificent thirst'': An historical survey of Australian drinking habits', *Historical Studies*, vol. 19, no. 75, 1980, p. 236.
37 J. McCalman, *Struggletown. Public and Private Life in Richmond 1900–1965*, Melbourne University Press, Carlton, 1984, p. 27.
38 K. Saunders, 'The study of domestic violence in colonial Queensland: Sources and problems', *Historical Studies*, vol. 21, no. 82, 1984, p. 77.
39 'Document: The tale of an errant life', *Push from the Bush*, no. 16, October 1983, p. 71.
40 F. Murray-Greenwood (ed.), *Land of a Thousand Sorrows. The Australian Prison Journal 1840–42 of the Exiled Canadian Patriote, Francois-Maurice Lepaillieur*, Melbourne University Press, Carlton, 1980, p. 94.
41 Quoted in L. Frost (ed.), *No Place for a Nervous Lady: Voices from the Australian bush*, McPhee Gribble/Penguin, Melbourne, 1984, p. 181.
42 McCalman, *Struggletown*, p. 26.
43 *Bulletin*, 5 June 1886.
44 Saunders, 'Study of domestic violence', p. 78.
45 S. Tiffin, 'In pursuit of reluctant parents. Desertion and non-support legislation in Australia and the United States 1890–1920', in Sydney Labour History Group, *What Rough Beast?: the State and social order in Australian history*, Allen & Unwin, Sydney, 1982, pp. 139–40.
46 Quoted in *Bulletin*, 28 March 1885.
47 McCalman, *Struggletown*, p. 24.
48 'Mitchell on Matrimony' in *On the Track*, [1900] Eagle Press, Sydney, 1923–1925, p. 77.
49 Quoted in Stephen, 'Marriage and the Family', p. 24.
50 *Bulletin*, 5 May 1888.
51 *Bull-Ant*, 5 March 1891.
52 *Bulletin*, 21 May 1888.
53 McDonald, *Marriage in Australia*, pp. 110–11.
54 W. Leach, *True Love and Perfect Union: The Feminist Reform of Sex and Society*, Routledge & Kegan Paul, London, 1981; P. Bunkle, 'The origins of the women's movement in New Zealand: The Women's Christian Temperance Union 1885–1895', in Bunkle and Hughes (eds), *Women in New Zealand Society*, Allen & Unwin, Auckland & Boston, 1980, pp. 52–76.
55 See, for example, the cartoon reprinted in J. Mackinolty and H. Radi (eds), *In Pursuit of Justice: Australian women and the Law, 1788–1979*, Hale & Iremonger, Sydney, 1979, p. 106.
56 J.D. Bollen, *Protestantism and Social Reform in New South Wales 1890-1910*, Melbourne University Press, Clayton 1972, p. 51.
57 *Bull-Ant*, 19 March 1891.
58 *ibid.*, 26 February 1891.

59 *Bulletin*, 23 June 1888.
60 Quoted in P. Grimshaw, 'Bessie Harrison Lee and the fight for voluntary motherhood' in M. Lake and F. Kelly (eds), *Double Time, Women in Victoria, 150 Years*, Penguin, Ringwood, 1985, p. 143.
61 *Herald*, 8 October 1888.
62 *Bulletin*, 20 October 1888.
63 *ibid.*, 3 November 1888.
64 See M. Lake, 'The limits of hope: Soldier settlement in Victoria 1915–1938', Ph.D. thesis, Monash University, Melbourne, 1984, pp. 66–7.
65 W Lane, *The Workingman's Paradise*, Brisbane, 1892, p. 45; advertisement from first paperbound edition, 1893.
66 Report of the Royal Commission on the Basic Wage, *Commonwealth Parliamentary Papers*, 1920–21. vol. 4., AGPS, Canberra.
67 Lake, 'Limits of hope', p. 264.

Chapter 2: The Feminist Legend: A new historicism?

1 cf. René Wellek, *Confrontations* (Princeton University Press, New Jersey, 1966), chapter on 'Carlyle and the philosophy of history'; John Docker, *In a Critical Condition*, Penguin, Ringwood, 1984, pp. 16–22, 37–8, 120.
2 *Historical Studies*, vol. 22, no. 86, 1986. See also Lake's 'Socialism and manhood: The case of William Lane', *Labour History* 50, 1986; Susan Sheridan, '"Temper, romantic; bias, offensively feminine": Australian women writers and literary nationalism', in Kirsten Holst Petersen and Anna Rutherford, eds. *A Double Colonization. Colonial and Post-Colonial Women's Writing* (Dangaroo, Denmark, 1986); Judith Allen, '"Mundane" men: Historians, masculinity and masculinism', *Historical Studies*, vol. 22, no. 89, 1987; also the essays on feminism and the Nineties by Susan Sheridan, Kerry M. White, and Judith Allen in *Australian Feminist Studies* 7 and 8, 1988.
3 Russel Ward, *The Australian Legend* (1958); O.U.P., Melbourne, 1966, pp. 1–2.
4 Graeme Davison, 'Sydney and the Bush: An urban context for the Australian legend', *Historical Studies*, vol. 18, no. 71, October 1978.
5 Frank Lentricchia, 'Foucault's legacy: A new historicism?', in H. Aram Veeser, ed. *The New Historicism*, Routledge, New York, 1989, p. 235.
6 Judith Lowder Newton, 'History as usual? Feminism and the "new historicism"', in *The New Historicism*, p. 166.
7 cf. *In a Critical Condition*, pp. 120, 122, and my 'Manning Clark's Henry Lawson', *Labour History* 37, 1979.
8 See Bruce Nesbitt, 'Literary nationalism and the 1890s', *Australian Literary Studies* (1971), and the note on the *Bulletin* Debate in *The Oxford Campanion to Australian Literature*.
9 *Bookfellow*, 25 March 1899, p. 38.
10 Sylvia Lawson, *The Archibald Paradox*, Allen Lane/Penguin, Ringwood, 1983, pp. 3, 158, 216.
11 cf. A. Grove Day, *Louis Becke*, Hill of Content, Melbourne, 1967, p. 40.
12 A point made by Chris McConville, 'Rough women, respectable men and social reform: A response to Lake's "Masculinism"', *Historical Studies*, vol. 22, no. 88, 1987.
13 See, for example, *Bulletin*, 4 January 1896, p. 6.

14 See, for example, *Bulletin*, 22 December 1894, p. 7, and 7 March 1896, p. 11.
15 *Bulletin*, 23 March 1895, p. 14.
16 See John Docker, *The Nervous Nineties*, O.U.P., Melbourne, 1991, ch. 6.
17 See Peter F. McDonald, *Marriage in Australia*, Australian Family Formation Project, Monograph no. 2, ANU, 1975, pp. 144–5.
18 Miles Franklin, *Laughter, Not for a Cage*, Angus & Robertson, Sydney, 1956, pp. 79–83, quoted in Susan Sheridan, 'Ada Cambridge and the female literary tradition', in Susan Dermody, John Docker, Drusilla Modjeska, eds. *Nellie Melba, Ginger Meggs, and Friends. Essays in Australian Cultural History* (Kibble, Malmsbury, 1982), p. 173.
19 J.S. Bratton, *The Victorian Popular Ballad*, Macmillan, London, 1975, pp. 184–5.
20 See John Docker, 'Popular culture and bourgeois values', in Verity Burgmann and Jenny Lee, eds. *Constructing a Culture*, McPhee Gribble/Penguin, Melbourne, 1988, pp. 253–4.
21 Natalie Davis, *Society and Culture in Early Modern France*, Stanford University Press, Stanford, 1975, ch. 5.
22 John Docker, 'Postmodernism, cultural history, and the feminist legend of the Nineties: *Robbery Under Arms*, the novel, the play', in Ken Stewart, ed. *Behind the Nineties*, University of Queensland Press, St. Lucia, forthcoming.
23 See Dominick LaCapra, *Rethinking Intellectual History: Texts, Context, Language*, Cornell University Press, Ithaca, 1983; *History and Criticism*, Cornell University Press, Ithaca, 1985; *Soundings in Critical Theory*, Cornell University Press, Ithaca, 1989.

Chapter 3: A redivision of labour: Women and wage regulation in Victoria 1896–1903

Material presented in this chapter was first published in Jenny Lee, 'A redivision of labour: Victoria's Wages Boards in action, 1896–1903', *Historical Studies*, vol. 22, no. 88, 1987, pp. 352–72.

1 Calculated from CIFS (Chief Inspector of Factories and Shops) Reports, 1890, 1895 and 1900 (1890 figures for adult males derived using proportions from 1891 census).
2 *Australasian Typographical Journal*, April 1888.
3 *Age*, 15 February 1898; *Argus*, 15 February 1898.
4 For a set of unemployment estimates see P. Macarthy, 'Wages in Australia 1891–1914', Australian Economic History Review, vol. 10, 1970, pp. 20, 24. The desertion of families is discussed in VPRS 5690, nos. 2ff, and in C. Strong's evidence to the Royal Commission on Old Age Pensions, *VPP*, 1898, vol. 3, no. 28, q.444.
5 See CIFS, 1891 and 1901.
6 Assuming the man was earning the old unskilled standard of around 36s, and that a woman and three juveniles aged 19, 16 and 14 would earn around 15s, 12s, 8s and 2s 6d respectively. This is a rough estimate only. Much would depend on whether the juveniles were boys or girls, and whether the woman was able to take factory work.

7 See eg. RCFS, *VPP*, 1902-3, vol. 2, no. 31, evidence of C. Anderson, qq.12529, 12533; also Wages Board History files, Public Record Office of Victoria, VPRS 5466, 37 (Cigar Makers) and 98 (Ham and Bacon).
8 Report of the Secretary, Department of Neglected Children and Reformatory Schools, VPRS 5690 no.2, 1893, p.3.
9 On rising prices, see P. Macarthy, 'Wages in Australia', pp. 66–7.
10 See Victorian Trades Hall Council Minutes, 1897–98, Victorian Trades Hall Collection, Melbourne University Archives.
11 As Macarthy has pointed out, the minimum wages specified for men were highly variable, and only skilled tradesmen approached the 42s per week benchmark established as a living wage by the Harvester judgement in 1907. P. Macarthy, 'Victorian Wages Boards', *Journal of Industrial Relations*, vol. 10, 1968, pp. 124–5.
12 Most tradesmen's wage levels ranged between 45s and 50s, with the bootmakers going as low as 36s. For 'general' hands, or men without a trade, rates were lower on the whole. Although in a few industries labourers were awarded wages of between 36s and 40s, in other cases general hands' wages ranged as low as 25s or 30s. These and later citations of Wages Board minima are taken from the compilations of Wages Board determinations included as appendices to the Reports of the Chief Inspector of Factories and Shops (CIFS) 1901–1903, *Victorian Parliamentary Papers* (*VPP*) 1901, 2, 28; 1902, 2, 16 and 1903, 3, 14.
13 See eg. evidence to the Royal Commission appointed to Inquire in the Factories and Shops Act (RCFS), *VPP*, 1902-3, 2, 31, qq.6048, 6715, 7710, 8040, 8101, 8550, 11773.
14 RCFS, evidence of W. Cabena, q. 7556.
15 Jam manufacturers' statement, 3 April 1902 in VPRS 5466, 193.
16 RCFS, evidence of P. Ploog, q. 9202.
17 See VPRS 5466, 135; also RCFS, qq. 8715, 11745, 11762, 11769.
18 Correspondence on the controversy is included in VPRS 5466, 193.
19 See VPRS 5466, 37.
20 VPRS 5466, 19.
21 RCFS, qq. 7861, 7922, 7951, 7954, 8001–3.
22 See appendices to CIFS reports 1895–1900 for ruling wage rates.
23 These and subsequent comments are based on the summaries of Wages Board determinations in CIFS, 1900–02 and the files at VPRS 5466.
24 On the first set of allies see e.g. R.T. Fitzgerald, *The Printers of Melbourne: the History of a Union*, Melbourne, 1967, pp. 84–5; on the master craftsmen in various trades see Ord's trade summaries and comments on Wages Board applications in VPRS 5466, 19, 37, 193; employers' correspondence at *ibid.*, 8; RCFS, qq. 7586, 8006, 8143, 8193, 8551, 11926.
25 See for example T. Bride to RCFS, qq. 12567ff.; A. Edgar to Royal Commission into Old Age Pensions, *op.cit.*, q.321.
26 Ord to T.F. Bride, 10 September 1902, in VPRS 5466, 193; Ord to Peacock, 30 July 1902, in VPRS 5466, 19.
27 H. Hartmann, 'The unhappy marriage of Marxism and feminism: towards a more progressive union', in L. Sargent, ed., *Women and Revolution: a discussion of the unhappy marriage of Marxism and feminism*, South End Press, Boston, 1981, esp. pp. 20–2.

NOTES 217

28 RCFS, qq. 13947ff. For examples of women's protests see VPRS 5466, 19, 193; the trimmers' petition is in the Federated Felt Hatters' Union Collection, Melbourne University Archives.
29 See determinations at CIFS, 1900; the female rate in the boot trade was set on the chairman's casting vote.
30 Figures from CIFS, 1900.
31 RCFS, qq. 7700, 1954, 8001, 8158.
32 Blencowe's evidence to RCFS, q. 7729. The restrictions on learners had a similar effect (Barrett to RCFS, q. 7954).
33 CIFS, 1901.
34 *ibid.*.
35 See T.B. Guest letterbooks, 1888ff., Melbourne University Archives, especially correspondence with F.T. Derham.
36 RCFS, evidence of S. Barker, q.8207.
37 On the task system see for example RCFS, qq. 7606, 7866–7, 8231, 9646.
38 *ibid.*, q. 8254.
39 *ibid.*, qq. 8207, 10295, 10416, 12513; VPRS 5466, 193, J. Keleher to Ord, 18 November 1903.

Chapter 4: Knocking out a living: Survival strategies and popular protest in the 1890s depression

I am indebted to Rae Frances for comment and child-care and Josie Underhill and Patrice Hicks for typing and technical assistance. I also thank the editors for their invaluable assistance.

1 On the need to expand labour history beyond its institutional basis see Jonathon Zeitland, 'Rank and filism and labour history: A rejoinder to Price and Cronin', *International Review of Social History*, vol. 34, no. 89, p. 102. Marilyn Lake, 'The politics of respectability: Identifying the masculinist context', *Historical Studies*, vol. 22, no. 86, April 1986, p. 117–19.
2 Bruce Scates, 'A struggle for survival: Unemployment and the unemployed agitation in late nineteenth-century Melbourne', *Australian Historical Studies*, vol. 23, no. 94, April 1990, pp. 42–48.
3 Cases of Mesdames Morgarain and Abrams, 24 January 1893, 24 February 1891, Benevolent Society of New South Wales (BSNSW) House Committee Minutes, Mitchell Library (ML); see complaints of a deputation re relief works, 21 April 1896.
4 Charity Organisation Society, *Annual Report ... for the Year Ending 30 June 1891*, Melbourne, p. 34.
5 Case of Mrs Laird, 26 March 1895 BSNSW House Committee Minutes; Shirley Fisher, 'The family and the Sydney economy in the late nineteenth century' in Patricia Grimshaw *et al* (eds), *Families in Colonial Australia*, Allen & Unwin, Sydney, 1985, pp. 157–8.
6 Cases of Mesdames Philpott, Patsies and White (all with eight children) 23 February 1897, 16 April 1896, 3 December 1895, BSNSW House Committee Minutes; case of Mrs Sheehy, 29 March 1896; Society of St Vincent de Paul (St V de P) Ashfield Branch Minutes, ML ms 2984 20(20); case of Mrs Meehan, 12 March 1894, St V de P, St Bedes (Pyrmont) Branch, ML ms 2984

kIS516. For the continuity of this experience see Susan Tiffin, 'In pursuit of reluctant parents: Desertion and non-support legislation in Australia and the United States 1890–1920,' Sydney Labour History Group (ed), *What Rough Beast? The State and Social Order in Australian History*, Allen & Unwin, Sydney, 1982, pp. 130–150.

7 Case of Mrs Nienua, 12 July 1892, MLBS Minutes; case of Mrs Williams, 15 July 1890, BSNSW House Committee Minutes; case of Mrs Lindsay, 28 June, 6 September 1896, 31 January, 14 February 1897; 3, 10 January, 23 May 1897, St V de P (Ashfield) Minutes.

8 Tamara Hareven, *Family Time and Industrial Time. The Relationship between the Family and Work in a New England Industrial Community*, Cambridge University Press, Cambridge, 1982, p. 208; Anne P. O'Brien, 'The poor in New South Wales, 1880-1918', PhD thesis, University of Sydney 1982, p. 50.

9 For representative case histories see Mrs Levers, 24 November 1892, Melbourne City Mission Minutes, University of Melbourne Archives; Mrs Sanders, 24 March 1892, MLBS Minutes; Mrs Morrison, 25 June 1894, St V de P (St Bedes) Minutes.

10 Case of Mrs Wilcox 29 July 1894, St V de P (St Bedes) Minutes; case of Mrs Murray, 18 October 1896, *ibid*, (Ashfield) Minutes.

11 Charity Organisation Society, *Annual Report for the Year Ended 30 June 1897*, Melbourne, pp. 9, 20; case of Mrs Kelly, 5 June 1895, St V de P (St Bedes) Minutes.

12 Jane Lewis (ed.), *Woman's Welfare, Women's Rights*, Croom Helm, London, 1983, p. 8.

13 William Lane, *The Workingman's Paradise: an Australian labour novel*, Edwards Dunlop, Sydney, 1892, p. 9.

14 Case of Ernst Henry Edwards, 13 December 1893, Nautical Ship Vernon, Admission Book, New South Wales State Archives (NSWSA), 8/1744.

15 Charity Organisation Society, *Annual Report ... for the Year Ended 30 June 1897*, Melbourne, 1897, p. 20.

16 Rae Frances & Bruce Scates, *Lives of Labour: Women at Work in Australia's Cities and Towns*, Cambridge University Press (forthcoming), Cambridge, Chapter 2.

17 'Skill' itself is an ideological term and one which devalues women's work. For the complexities surrounding its use see Richard Price, 'Conflict and co-operation. A reply to Patrick Joyce', *Social History*, vol. 9, no. 2, May 1984, pp. 217–224.

18 Frances and Scates, *Lives of Labour*, introduction; for the problems surrounding women's industrial organisation see W. Nicol, 'Women and the trade union movement in New South Wales, 1880–1900', *Labour History*, No. 36, May 1979, pp. 18–30.

19 Letter: Mary Graham to the office of Public Instruction, Redfern, October 1898, in Redfern School File, Department of Education, NSWSA 5/174/50.

20 Case of Joseph Michael Holland, 21 January 1891, Vernon Admission Book; case of Mrs Kelly, 10 August 1895, St V de P (St Bedes) Minutes.

21 Case of Mrs Wilcox, 29 July 1894, St V de P (St Bedes) Minutes.

22 R.F. Davidson (Frances), 'Prostitution in Perth and Fremantle and on the Eastern Goldfields 1895–September 1939', MA thesis, University of Western

Australia, 1980, ch. 5. Frances' observations are equally germane to the Eastern colonies, see Hilary Golder & Judith Allen, 'Prostitution in New South Wales 1870–1930: Restructuring an industry', *Refractory Girl*, December 1979, pp. 17–24; for case studies see minutes of the Female Refuge Society, Sydney, ML; case of James Cronan, 9 February 1891, Vernon Admission Book.
23 Case of Mrs Kelly, 23 June 1895, St. V de P (St. Bedes) Minutes; case of Mrs Pinto, 12 July 1892, MLBS Minutes.
24 Scates, 'A Struggle for Survival', p. 48; Charity Organisation Society, *Annual Report ... for the Year Ended 30 June 1897*, Melbourne, 1897, p. 20.
25 I owe this observation to Anne O'Brien, *Poverty's Prison: The Poor in New South Wales 1880–1918*, Melbourne University Press, Melbourne, 1988, pp. 98–9; for operation of these laundries see case of Mrs Fosters, 5 November 1889, BSNSW House Committee Minutes.
26 Case of Mrs Roberts, 7, 14, April 1895, St V de P (St Bedes) Minutes; for similar cases see Minutes of the Charity Organisation Society, 8 September 1896, U.M.A.
27 Jenny Lee, 'A redivision of labour: Victoria's Wages Board in action 1896–1903', *Historical Studies*, vol. 22, no. 88, 1987, p. 357.
28 Rae Frances, 'The politics of work: Case studies of three Victorian industries, 1880–1939', PhD Thesis, Monash University, 1988, pp. 39-40.
29 'Testimony of John Wing', Chief Inspector of Factories Reports, 1892, VPP, 1983, vol. 2, no. 28.
30 Cases of Mrs Chisholm and Mrs Holder, 20 May, 22 July 1894, St V de P (St. Bedes) Minutes; *Argus* July 1893; Case of Mrs Broadfall, 13 October 1891, NSWBS Minutes, Case of Mrs Shelds, 22 March 1892, MLBS Minutes.
31 Charity Organisation Society, *Annual Report ... for the Year Ended 30 June 1894, Melbourne, 1894*, p. 39. Cases of Mesdames Dobson and McBride, 24, 9 August 1892, MLBS Minutes.
32 Olwen Hufton, 'Women in Revolution', *Past and Present*, 53, November 1971, p. 92. J.W. Scott & L.A. Tilley, 'Women's work and the family in nineteenth century Europe', in Alice H. Amsden (ed), *The Economics of Women and Work*, Penguin, Harmondsworth, 1980, p. 103.
33 Case of 'a poor woman, living in Foster Street, Leichhardt', 9 May 1892, St V de P (St Aloysius Boys Home), Minutes MLMS 2984 19(20); case of Mrs Stirling and Mr Coles, 2 September 1896, 4 October 1892, BSNSW House Committee Minutes; cases of Mesdames Fitzpatrick and Deny, 20 September 1896, 16 June 1895, St V de P (Ashfield) (St Bedes) Minutes. Much of this analysis was suggested by Ellen Ross's work 'Survival Networks', *History Workshop Journal*, 15, Spring 1983, pp. 4–27.
34 See for example the case of Ellen Hobson who owed the baker £7 and the landlord 'a large amount of arrears'. She had seven children all 'in absolute want of food'. Her husband was 'unemployed and afflicted', 27 June 1893, BSNSW House Committee Minutes.
35 Case of Mrs Stirling, 2 September 1896, BSNSW House Committee Minutes, Case of Mrs Walsh, 11 August 1891, MLBS Minutes; *Brunswick Reformer*, 13 February 1892.
36 Case of William John Bingham, Application for Exemption, 30 September 1898, Redfern School File; see also the case of Mrs Holmes, 10 September 1891, MLBS Minutes.

37 Case of Mrs Ross, 23 May 1893, BSNSW House Committee Minutes; Charity Organisation Society, *Annual Report...for the Year Ended 30 June 1898*, p. 50.
38 See index entry for 'Smith', St V de P (St Bridgets) Minutes. Case of Annie Moffat, 27 February 1897, BSNSW House Committee Minutes. See also the COS's description of 'tent colonies', *Report on the Unemployed*, pp. 73–4.
39 Case of Mrs Lewis, 21 March 1893, BSNSW House Committee Minutes, also the case of Louisa Ryan found in a paddock by police, 19 December 1892, BSNSW, Inmates Journal.
40 Harevan, *Family Time, Industrial Time*, p. 209.
41 Pat Grimshaw, 'Women and the family in Australian history—A reply to *The Real Matilda*', *Historical Studies*, vol. 18, no. 72, April 1979, p. 415. The tenacity of the family unit is illustrated by the case of Anne McFadyen, 'unemployed, living with an unemployed sister and aged mother' 2 May 1893, BSNSW House Committee Minutes.
42 Annie Fraser is a typical example; 'in receipt of rations, in arrears for rent' she accepts the committee's advice to 'come into the Asylum with her family'. Her husband was 'away', 10 November 1891, BSNSW House Committee Minutes; Entry for Agnes Jane Duncan, 25 May 1893, BSNSW Inmates Journal, Charity Organisation Society, *Annual Report...for the Year Ended 30 June 1898*, Melbourne, 1898, pp. 50–51; Entry for Joanna, Alfred, Margaret and Elsie Waters, 27 October 1892, BSNSW Inmates Journal.
43 See foundling entries for 18 November 1892, 9 June, 31 January 1893, BSNSW Inmates Journal.
44 *New South Wales Police Gazette*, 6 January, 9 March 1892; see also Judith Allen's study, 'Octavius Beale reconsidered', in Sydney Labour History Group (ed), *What Rough Beast*, p. 120.
45 Frances and Scates, 'Lives of Labour', Ch. 5; Kathy Lester, 'Frances Knorr: She killed babies didn't she', in Marilyn Lake and Farley Kelly, *Doubletime: Women in Victoria. 150 Years*, Penguin, Ringwood, 1985, pp. 148–157.
46 Scates, 'Struggle for Survival', pp. 52–53; Brian Dickey, *No Charity There: A Short History of Social Welfare in Australia*, Nelson, West Melbourne, 1980, pp. xx–xvi.
47 Judith Godden, '"The Work for Them and the Glory for Us!" Sydney Women's Philanthropy 1870–1900' in Richard Kennedy (ed), *Australian Welfare History: Critical Essays*, Macmillan, Melbourne, 1982, pp. 90–93. Anne Summers, 'A Home from Home—Women's Philanthropic Work in the Nineteenth Century' in Sandra Burman (ed), *Fit Work for Women*, Croom Helm, London, New York, 1979, pp. 64–97.
48 Charity Organisation Society, *Annual Report...for the Year Ended 30 June 1893*, Melbourne, 1893, pp. 10–11. COS Minutes, 18 June 1895.
49 Cases of Mesdames Rumieson and Norton, BSNSW House Committee Minutes, 13 May, 16 September 1890.
50 Richard Kennedy, *Charity Warfare: the Charity Organisation Society in Colonial Melbourne*, Hyland House, Melbourne, 1985, p. 150.
51 Scates, 'A Struggle for Survival', pp. 60–61; Case of Mrs Roberts, 2 June 1895, St V de P (St Bedes) Minutes; *Brunswick Reformer*, 3 July 1892.
52 MLBS Minutes, 6, 20 September 1890.

NOTES 221

53 BSNSW House Committee Minutes, 8 June 1896, 7 March 1897; 22 March 1892; 13 July 1897.
54 See eg. John Hirst, 'Historical Reconsiderations 1: Keeping colonial history colonial: The Hartz thesis revisited', *Historical Studies*, vol. 21, no. 82, April 1984, pp. 85–104; Lake, 'Politics of Respectability', pp. 117–118.
55 *Australian Workman*, 17 April 1897; Charity Organisation Society, *Annual Report...for the Year Ended June 1892*, Melbourne 1892.
56 *ibid*; Petition by village settlers, Kooweerup, Report of the Printing Committee, *V.P.P.*, 1896, vol. 1, no. 1.
57 Report by Constable Wardley, 16, 23 June 1892, Victoria Police Records (VPR), Victorian Public Records Office, X936, *Age* 26 May 1892; S.A. Rosa, *The Truth about the Unemployed Agitation*, Melbourne 1891, pp. 11–30.
58 Cases of Mrs Corsett and Mary Ellis, 27, 10 November 1891, BSNSW House Committee Minutes; Charity Organisation Society, *Report on the Unemployed*, p. 76.
59 Cases of Mesdames Ressimusson, and Gallagher, 15 September 1891, 24 April 1894, BSNSW House Committee Minutes; case of Mrs Deny, 13 October 1891, St V de P (St Bedes) Minutes; see the case of Mary Ellis whose 'manner became so objectionable that it was decided not to be of assistance and she was requested to leave the room', 13 October 1891, BSNSW House Committee Minutes.
60 Case of Mary Kelly, 13 August 1889, BSNSW House Committee Minutes; Charity Organisation Society, *Report...for the Year Ended 30 June 1889*, Melbourne, 1889, pp. 14–15.
61 Report by Constable Geelan, 4 September 1892; Speech by William Maloney, Victorian Parliamentary Debates (VPD), Legislative Assembly (LA) 31 May 1892, p. 230.
62 Barbara Taylor, 'The men are as bad as their masters... 'Socialism, feminism and sexual antagonism in the London tailoring trade in the 1830s', in J.L. Newton *et al* (eds) *Sex and Class in Women's History*, Routledge & Kegan Paul, London & Boston, 1983, p. 200; Report by Constable Wardley, 16 June 1892, VPR.
63 E.P. Thompson, 'The moral economy of the English crowd in the nineteenth century', *Past and Present*, 50, February 1971, p. 79.
64 Jane Rendall, *The Origins of Modern Feminism*: *Women in three Western Societies, Britain, France and the United States. 1780–1860*, Schoken Books, New York, 1984, pp. 90-91.
65 Reports by Constables Wardley, Geelan and Wardley, 1 June; 4 September 1892, VPR.
66 Ann Curthoys, Review of Judith A. Allen, *Sex and Secrets: Crimes Involving Australian Women Since 1880*, Melbourne 1990, in *Australian Historical Studies*, No 95, October 1990, p. 306. John Bohstedt, 'Gender, household and community politics: Women in English riots 1790–1810', *Past and Present*, no. 120, 1988, p. 95; Judith Smart, 'Feminism, food and the fair price, *Labour History*, 50, May 1986, pp. 13–31.

67 Report by Constable Wardley, 4 September 1892 VPR; note also advertisements in the Melbourne *Age* soliciting women's support, 4 September, 1890.
68 Bruce Scates, 'Faddists and Extremists', PhD thesis, Monash University, 1987, vol. 2, pp. 643–687; Charity Organisation Society, *Report on the Unemployed*, p. 44.
69 *Commonweal*, 16 July 1892; *Truth*, 30 August 1891; also 'Women and Co-operation', *Australian Workman*, 19 September 1891.
70 *Carlton Gazette* and *Argus* 17 June 1892.
71 *Justice* 10 February 1894; 31 March 1895 Australian Order of Industry 'Handbills etc', ML; Active Service Brigade, *Social Co-operative Congress*, Sydney, 1895.
72 Bruce Scates, 'Socialism and feminism: The case of William Lane', *Labour History*, no. 59, November 1990; 'The home front: Gender, household and community politics in the maritime strike of 1890', AHA Paper, Brisbane, 1990.

Chapter 5: Reorganising the masculinist context: Conflicting masculinisms in the New South Wales Public Service Bill debates of 1895

1 Nancy Cott, *The Grounding of Modern Feminism*, Yale University Press, New Haven, 1987 discusses these differences and conflicts in early twentieth-century US feminism. The classic contemporary example of conflict within feminism is the Sears case, analysed by Joan Wallach Scott, 'The Sears Case', in *Gender and Politics of History*, Columbia University Press, New York, 1988, pp. 167–177. For class, gender and state in nineteenth and early twentieth century Australia see Desley Deacon, *Managing Gender: The State, the New Middle Class and Women Workers 1830–1930*, Oxford University Press, Melbourne, 1989. For favourable conditions for a cross-gender alliance see Kathryn Kish Sklar, 'Hull House in the 1890s: A community of women reformers', *Signs* vol. 10, no. 4, Summer 1985, pp. 658–77.
2 Marilyn Lake, 'The politics of respectability: Identifying the masculinist context', *Historical Studies*, vol. 22, no. 86, 1986, pp. 116–131; Chris McConville, 'Rough women, respectable men and social reform: A response to Lake's "masculinism" ', *Historical Studies*, vol. 22, no. 86, 1987, pp. 432–40, 'Mundane men: Historians, masculinity and masculinism', *Historical Studies*, vol. 22, no. 89, 1987, pp. 617–28.
3 New South Wales Parliamentary Debates 1895 (PD), pp. 1642–3, 1650, 1821–9, 1877–88.
4 See Deacon, *Managing Gender*, chapters 1 and 2 for equality by default, chapters 3 and 4 for the movement for public service reform.
5 The following account of debate on the Bill draws on PD, pp. 1642–3, 1650, 1821–9, 1877–88. A more extended discussion of the debate and the issue of married women's work is found in Deacon, *Managing Gender*, chapter 5.
6 See Graeme Davison, 'Sydney and the Bush: An urban context for the Australian legend', *Historical Studies*, vol. 18, no. 71, 1978; Lake, 'Politics of respectability'.

NOTES 223

7 For the decline of the rural economy and public service retrenchment see Deacon, chapters 3–6.
8 For family patronage and women in the post and telegraph offices see Deacon, chapters 1–3. For the different history of women in the post and telegraph offices in Victoria see Claire McCuskey, 'Women in the Victorian Post Office', in Margaret Bevage, Margaret James and Carmel Shute (eds), *Worth Her Salt: Women at Work in Australia*, Hale & Iremonger, Sydney, 1982, pp. 49–61.
9 Deacon, pp. 153–8; Brian Matthews, *Louisa*, McPhee-Gribble, Melbourne, 1987.
10 Deacon, pp. 70–7, 178–9.
11 For Coghlan and Barling see Deacon, ch. 4–6.
12 7 May 1902, Coghlan papers, ANL MS 6335; see Deacon, p. 170.
13 For an extended discussion of single women in the public service see Deacon, ch. 6–7.
14 59 Vic. no. 25, s. 36.
15 See Deacon, pp. 149–50.
16 See Deacon, ch. 7.
17 NSW Arbitration Reports, vol. 4, pp. 309–10, quoted D.T. Sawkins, *The Living Wage in Australia*, Melbourne University Press, Melbourne, 1933, p. 12.
18 See Deacon, ch. 8.
19 Lake, Politics of respectability, pp. 130–31.

Chapter 6: The sexual politics of selling and shopping

1 Memoranda of Agreement between David Jones and Company and Santa Maria Baker, 30 October 1891, and Caroline Suttle, 21 March 1892; letters to Edward Lloyd Jones from John Pomeroy, 29 February 1892, 1 August 1892; letters to Edward Lloyd Jones from William Newman, 23-5 April 1892, 8 August 1892. (David Jones Archives, hereafter DJA, BRG 1/8 and 1/24).
2 Jennifer MacCulloch, '"This Store is Our World": Female shop assistants in Sydney to 1930' in *Twentieth Century Sydney. Studies in Urban and Social History*, ed. Jill Roe, Hale & Iremonger, Sydney, 1980.
3 *A Bunyip Close Behind Me. Recollections of the Nineties*. Retold by her daughter Eugenie Crawford, Hawthorn Press, Melbourne, 1972, p. 69.
4 Susan Porter Benson, *Counter Cultures. Saleswomen, Managers and Customers in American Department Stores 1890–1940*, University of Illinois Press, Urbana, 1987.
5 Marilyn Lake, 'The politics of respectability: Identifying the masculinist context', *Historical Studies*, vol. 22, no. 86, 1986, pp. 116–131.
6 Judith Allen, 'Mundane Men: Historians, Masculinity and Masculinism', *Historical Studies*, vol. 22, no. 89, 1987, pp. 624–5.
7 *Australian Storekeepers' Journal*, March 1895, p. 9; July 1895, p. 92; Aug. 1900, pp. 24, 28.
8 David Jones and Company, *Souvenir*, 1887, (DJA BRG 1/69).
9 *Australian Town and Country Journal*, 8 Oct. 1887, p. 758; *Australian Storekeepers' Journal*, Aug. 1898, p. 7.

10 Letter to Edward Lloyd Jones from John Pomeroy 13 July 1891 (DJA BRG 1/24).
11 Letter to David Jones & Co from Harry Clemson 10 Feb 1893 (DJA BRG 1/13); letter to Edward Lloyd Jones from John Pomeroy 1 Aug 1892 (DJA BRG 1/24).
12 *Australian Storekeepers' Journal*, May 1896, p. 128; Letter to Edward Lloyd Jones from William Newman 4 July 1892 (DJA BRG 1/24).
13 Letter to David Jones & Co from Edward Wilcox 6 Nov. 1891 (DJA BRG 1/13).
14 Letter to Edward Lloyd Jones from John Pomeroy 7 Nov. 1892 (DJA BRG 1/24); *Australian Storekeepers' Journal*, Oct. 1895 p. 176.
15 Nov. 1892, editorial.
16 *Australian Storekeepers' Journal* Apr 1898, p. 107; *Draper of Australasia* (hereafter *Draper*) Aug 1901, p. 11.
17 See, for example, David Jones staff agreements 1873–1906 in DJA BRG 1/8.
18 See, for example, transcript of evidence heard before the NSW Arbitration Court 1907 in Archives Office of NSW 2/95–98, vol. 45, p. 1781.
19 David Jones agreement with Elizabeth Spear 11 July 1892 (DJA BRG 1/8); letter to David Jones & Co from Edward Wilcox 29 July 1887 (DJA BRG 1/13); letter to Edward Lloyd Jones from William Newman 23–25 Apr 1892 (DJA BRG 1/24); letter to David Jones & Co from Edward Wilcox 22 Aug 1889 (DJA BRG 1/13).
20 Letter to Edward Lloyd Jones from John Woodward 12 Aug 1889 (DJA BRG 1/13).
21 Letter to David Jones & Co from Edward Wilcox 29 July 1887 (DJA BRG 1/13); Letter to David Jones & Co from Edward Wilcox 8 July 1892 (DJA BRG 1/13); letter to David Jones & Co from John Woodward 18 Feb 1887 (DJA BRG 1/13); letter to David Jones & Co from Edward Wilcox 15 Aug 1889 (DJA BRG 1/13); David Jones staff agreement with Annie Banks 10 July 1884 (DJA BRG 1/8).
22 Letter to David Jones & Co from Edward Wilcox 22 July 1892 (DJA BRG 1/13).
23 Letter to Edward Lloyd Jones from William Newman 5 Sept 1892 (DJA BRG 1/24).
24 Series of letters to Edward Lloyd Jones from various members of the London office 13 July 1891 to 18 Nov 1892 (DJA BRG 1/24).
25 Nov. 1894, p. 8.
26 *Draper*, Aug. 1901, p. 15; *Australian Storekeepers'* Journal, Jan. 1899, p. 3.
27 *Draper and Warehouseman*, May 1894, p. 3; *Australian Storekeepers' Journal*, Apr. 1899, p. 93.
28 *Draper*, Aug. 1901, p. 6.
29 Letter to Edward Lloyd Jones from William Newman 13 July 1891 (DJA BRG 1/24).
30 Letter to Edward Lloyd Jones from [?] 8 June 1891 (DJA BRG 1/24); *Draper and Warehouseman* Aug 1893, pp. 5–6.

NOTES 225

31 Series of letters to Edward Lloyd Jones from William Newman 19 Oct 1891 to 18 Jan 1892 (DJA BRG 1/24).
32 New South Wales Government Printer, *Report of the Royal Commission on Strikes*, 1891, pp. 395–8.
33 Sydney Labour Council General Meeting minutes 28 Nov 1901–9 Jan 1902 (Mitchell Library microfilm 4/1128).
34 Gail Reekie, 'The Shop Assistants Case of 1907 and labour relations in the Sydney retail industry' in *Foundations of Arbitration. The Establishment of the Compulsory Arbitration System, 1890–1914*, eds Stuart Macintyre and Richard Mitchell, Oxford University Press, Melbourne, 1989. See also Edna Ryan, *Two-Thirds of a Man. Women and Arbitration in New South Wales 1902–1908*, Hale & Iremonger, Sydney, 1984.
35 No investigations of shops appear to have been carried out by the adult male inspector, indicating that male shop assistants were not considered to be at risk in the same way as women.
36 *Report of the Operations of the Factories and Shops Act 1896*, p. 1394; 1899, p. 15.
37 *ibid.*, 1897, p. 1395.
38 *ibid.*, p. 1395; 1900, p. 5.
39 *ibid.*, p. 1374.
40 *ibid.*, p. 1395.
41 *ibid.*, p. 1395.
42 For a general account of the Early Closing Movement see Denise Roberts, 'The movement for the early closing of shops in New South Wales 1890–1899', B.A. Hons. thesis, University of New South Wales, 1981. For biographical information on some of the women involved, see entries on Eliza Pottie (by Judith Godden) and Rose Scott (by Judith Allen) in *200 Australian Women. A Redress Press Anthology*, ed. Heather Radi, Redress Press, Sydney, 1988.
43 Letter from Senior Showroom Employees, Grace Brothers, to Rose Scott, 1897, in Rose Scott correspondence vol. 20, pp. 243–4 (MLMSS 38).
44 *Sydney Morning Herald*, 13 Oct. 1898, clipping in collection of documents relating to the Early Closing Assocation of New South Wales (Mitchell Library Q331.11/E); *Report of the Operations of the Factories and Shops Act 1900*, p. 9; paper on Early Closing read by Rose Scott at meeting of the National Council of Women, reported in *Evening News*, 19 Nov. 1898 (Scott papers, MLMSS 38/50).
45 See, for example, Raelene Davidson, 'Dealing with the "social evil": Prostitution and the police in Perth and on the Eastern Goldfields, 1895–1924' in *So Much Hard Work. Women and Prostitution in Australian History*, ed. Kay Daniels, Fontana, Sydney, 1984, pp. 167–8.
46 *Woman's Voice*, 9 Feb., 1895, pp. 170–1.
47 Great Britain and Ireland Home Office. *Report on the Acts for the Regulation of the Hours of Employment in Shops in Australia and New Zealand*, 1908, p. 17.
48 *Daily Telegraph* 8 Dec. 1898, clipping in Rose Scott papers (MLMSS 38/50).

49 Speech on Early Closing in Rose Scott papers (MLMSS 38/28), pp. 267-9.
50 'Speech on Early Closing', p. 269.
51 *Worker*, 6 June, 1907, p. 15.
52 *Evening News*, 19 Nov. 1898.
53 *Australian Economist*, 24 Nov. 1898, p. 86.
54 July 1897, p. 222.
55 *Happy Homes*, Oct. 1891 and Dec. 1891, n.p.
56 *Woman's Voice*, Oct. 19, 1895, p. 371.
57 *Woman*, Feb. 1892, p. 3; Mar. 1892, p. 6.
58 Speech on Dress and Character, n.d. (Rose Scott papers, MLMSS 38/29), pp. 339–351.
59 Feb. 9, 1895, p. 174.
60 *Woman's Voice*, 6 Apr. 1895, p. 211.
61 Excerpts from the *Dawn* July 1891 and Sept. 1893 reproduced in Olive Lawson, *The First Voice of Australian Feminism. Excerpts from Louisa Lawson's The Dawn, 1888–1895*, Simon & Schuster, Brookvale, N.S.W., 1990, pp. 237–40.
62 *Dawn*, Apr. 1904, p. 6.
63 *Woman's Voice*, 27 July, 1895, p. 307.
64 *ibid.*, 23 Mar. 1895, p. 197.
65 'Dress and Character', p. 347.
66 *Woman's Voice*, 18 May 1895, p. 244.
67 Unmarked newspaper clipping (Rose Scott papers MLMSS 38/50). This lecture, presented to the National Council of Women by Mr F. Rotheray of the Society for the Prevention of Cruelty to Animals, and ensuing lively discussion probably took place on 29 Oct 1908 [thanks to Jennifer MacCulloch for helping me date this reference]. It seems plausible that the sentiments expressed by women like Mrs Molyneux Parkes and Rose Scott were held by them and other women in the 1890s.

Chapter 7: Domestic dilemmas: Representations of servants and employers in the popular press

My thanks to Ann Curthoys, John Docker and Gunther Kress, who made helpful suggestions along the way, and a special acknowledgment to Sue Rowley for her patient assistance with ideas and drafting.

1 Dana Polan, *Power and Paranoia*, Columbia University Press, New York, 1986, p. 10.
2 Here I have relied on the historical methodology used to great effect by cultural historians such as Robert Darnton, *The Great Cat Massacre and Other Episodes in French Cultural History*, Vintage, New York, 1985. See also the Introduction by Chandra Mukerji & Michael Schudson (eds) in *Rethinking Popular Culture. Contemporary Perspectives in Cultural Studies*, University of California Press, Berkeley, 1991, and Kaplan, C. '"Like a housemaid's fancies": The representation of working-class women in nineteenth-century writing' in Susan Sheridan (ed.), *Grafts. Feminist Cultural Criticism*, Verso, London, 1988.

3 Michael Bommes & Patrick Wright, ' "Charms of residence": The public and the past', in CCCS: *Making Histories, Studies in history-writing and politics*, Hutchinson & Co, London, 1982, p. 259.
4 Christina Walkley, *The Way to Wear 'Em. 150 Years of Punch Cartoons*. See also Mary Douglas, 'Jokes', in *Implicit Meanings*, Routledge & Kegan Paul, London, 1975.
5 Livingston Hopkins, for example, had a great many problems with servants. See Letter from Bayview Asylum (Hattie Hopkins Papers MLMSS, 1944) and a description of the case involving his daughter in Stephen Garton's *Medicine and Madness: a social history of insanity in New South Wales 1880–1940*, New South Wales University Press, Kensington, (1987). I am grateful to Stephen Garton for this reference.
6 Russell, P., 'Mrs Cole's servants: A study in domestic politics. *Lilith: a feminist history journal*, no. 4, Summer 1988, pp. 49–50.
7 Kingston, B. *The Oxford History of Australia, Vol. 3, 1860–1900: Glad Confident Morning*, OUP, Melbourne, 1988, p. 280.
8 For more detail, see Paula Hamilton, 'No Irish Need Apply: Aspects of the employer–employee relationship in Australian domestic service, 1860–1900', *Working Papers in Australian Studies*, Institute of Comonwealth Studies, University of London, no. 1, October, 1985. Overseas studies include Sutherland, D.E., *Americans and their Servants: Domestic Service in the US from 1800–1920* (1981); Hansen, K.T., *Distant Companions. Servants and Employers in Zambia, 1900–1985* (1989); Katzman, D., *Seven Days a Week. Women and Domestic Service in Industrializing America* (1978).
9 Rowe, C.J., 'Household troubles in the Australian colonies', *Westminster Review*, vol. 134, July–December 1890, p. 514.
10 I am grateful to Kimberly Webber, Social History Curator at the Powerhouse Museum, for this suggestion.
11 Sinclair, W.A., 'Women and economic change in Melbourne 1871–1921', *Historical Studies*, vol. 20, no. 79, 1982; Dyster, B. & Meredith, D., *Australia in the International Economy in the Twentieth Century*, Cambridge University Press, Sydney, 1990, Chapter 1. See also Paula Hamilton, 'The "servant class": Poor female migration to Australia in the nineteenth century' in Eric Richards (ed), *Poor Australian Immigrants in the nineteenth century. Visible Immigrants: Two*, RSSS, Canberra, 1991.
12 Dudden, Faye, 'Experts and servants: The National Council on Household Employment and the decline of domestic service in the twentieth century', *Journal of Social History*, vol. 20, no. 2, Winter 1986, p. 175.
13 Hamilton, Paula, 'The "servant class"' in *Poor Australian Immigrants*.
14 *Melbourne Punch*, 15 April 1880, p. 152.
15 Kunzle, D., 'World upside down: The iconography of a European broadsheet type', in Barbara A. Babcock, *The Reversible World. Symbolic Inversion in Art and Society*, Cornell University Press, Ithaca, 1978; Davis, N. Zemon, Women

on top in *Society and Culture in Early Modern France. Eight Essays*, Stanford University Press, Stanford, California, 1975.
16 Susan Yates has explored this in more depth. see Yates, S.,'The enemy within: the maid in the nineteenth-century French novel', in Robert Aldrich (ed), *France: Politics, Society, Culture and International Relations*, Papers from the Seventh George Rude Seminar in French History and Civilisation, the University of Sydney, 21–23 July 1990, Occasional Publication, Department of Economic History, University of Sydney, 1990.
17 Marsh, M., 'Suburban men and masculine domesticity 1870–1915', *American Quarterly*, vol. 40, no. 2, June 1988; Marsh, M., From separation to togetherness: The social construction of domestic space in American suburbs, 1840–1915, *Journal of American History*, 1989; Magarey, S., Notes towards a discussion of sexual labour: Australia 1880–1910', *Lilith. A Feminist History Journal*, no. 6, Spring, 1989, pp.10–32.

Chapter 8: Sexual labour: Australia 1880–1910

An earlier version of this article was published under the title 'Notes Toward a Discussion of Sexual Labour: Australia 1880–1910' in *Lilith: A Feminist History Journal*, no. 6, Spring 1989. A re-worked version was presented at the Eighth Berkshire Conference on the History of Women, Douglass College, Rutgers University, June 1990.

1 Marilyn Lake, 'The politics of respectability: Identifying the masculinist context', *Historical Studies*, vol. 22, no. 86, 1986; Judith Allen, '"Mundane" men: Historians, masculinity and masculinism', *Historical Studies*, vol. 22, no. 89, 1987; see also Chris McConville, 'Rough women, respectable men and social reform: A response to Lake's "masculinism"', *Historical Studies*, vol. 22, no. 88, 1987.
2 Susan Sheridan: 'Ada Cambridge and the Female Literary Tradition' in Susan Dermody, John Docker & Drusilla Modjeska (eds) *Nellie Melba, Ginger Meggs and Friends: Essays in Australian Cultural History*, Kibble Books, Malmsbury, 1982; '"Temper, romantic; bias, offensively feminine": Australian women writers and literary nationalism' in Kirsten Holst-Peterson, Anna Rutherford (eds), *A Double Colonization: Colonial and Post-Colonial Women's Writing*, Dangaroo Press, Aarhus, 1986; 'Louisa Lawson, Miles Franklin and feminist writing, 1888–1901', *Australian Feminist Studies*, nos 7&8, 1988; Sue Rowley, 'Sliprails and spur: Courting bush sweethearts in Australian nationalist mythology', *Span*, 26, 1988; Kay Schaffer, *Women and the Bush: Forces of Desire in the Australian Cultural Tradition*, Cambridge University Press, Cambridge & Melbourne, 1988.
3 Jenny Lee, 'A redivision of labour: Victoria's Wages Boards in action, 1896–1903', *Historical Studies*, vol. 22, no. 88, 1987, p. 357; Ray Markey,'Women and Labour 1880–1900' in Elizabeth Windschuttle (ed.), *Women, Class and History: Feminist Perspectives on Australia 1788–1978*, Melbourne, 1980, pp. 91–92.

4 J.C. Caldwell & L.T. Ruzicka, 'The Australian fertility transition: An analysis', *Population and Development Review*, vol. 14, no. 1, 1978, p. 87.
5 Peter F. McDonald, *Marriage in Australia: Age at first Marriage and Proportions Marrying, 1860–1971*, ANU Press, Canberra, 1974, p. 134. Gordon A. Carmichael, *With This Ring: First Marriage Patterns, Trends and Prospects in Australia*, ANU Press, Canberra, 1988, simply summarises McDonald on this period.
6 See the classic J.A. & Olive Banks, *Feminism and Family Planning in Victorian England*, Liverpool University Press, Liverpool, 1965; and, for example, Jane Lewis, *Women in England 1870–1950: Sexual Divisions and Social Change*, Wheatsheaf Books, Sussex, and Indiana University Press, Bloomington, 1984, ch. 1; Martha Vicinus, *Independent Women: Work and Community for Single Women 1850–1920*, Virago, London, 1985, Table 1; and, *contra*, Richard J. Evans, *The Feminists: Women's Emancipation Movements in Europe, America and Australasia 1840–1920*, Croom Helm, London and New York, 1977, pp. 26–29.
7 Royal Commission on the Decline of the Birth-Rate and on the Mortality of Infants in New South Wales, vol. 1, *Report*, Sydney, 1904, p. 9; W. Balls-Headley, *The Evolution of the Diseases of Women*, Smith, Elder & Co., London, 1894, p. 9.
8 McDonald, *Marriage in Australia*, pp. 148, 149, 134.
9 Pat Quiggin, *No Rising Generation: Women and Fertility in Late Nineteenth-Century Australia*, Department of Demography, ANU, Canberra, 1988, p. 77.
10 Ada Cambridge, *Unspoken Thoughts*, London, 1887, p. 94.
11 Olive Schreiner, *The Story of an African Farm*, Penguin, Harmondsworth, 1939, p. 155. I am grateful to Susan Sheridan for this reference.
12 Rose Scott, undated notebook entry, Rose Scott Papers, Mitchell Library MSS 38/22/9.
13 Charlotte Perkins Gilman, *Women and Economics: A Study of the Economic Relation Between Men and Women as a Factor in Social Evolution*, first pub. 1898, ed. Charles Degler, Harper & Row, New York 1966, p. 97; Emma Goldman, 'The Traffic in Women', first pub. 1910, in Emma Goldman, *Anarchism and Other Essays*, with a new introduction by Richard Drinnon, Dover Publications, New York, 1969; Cicely Hamilton, *Marriage as a Trade*, first pub. 1909, Women's Press, London, 1981, p. 11.
14 C.H. Spence, *Some Social Aspects of South Australian Life: by a colonist of 1839*, R. Kyttin Thomas, Adelaide, 1878.
15 Annie Golding, 'The industrial and social condition of women in the Australian Commonwealth', *Proceedings of the Third Australasian Catholic Congress*, 1910, quoted in Kay Daniels & Mary Murnane (comps), *Uphill all the Way: A Documentary History of Women in Australia*, University of Queensland Press, St Lucia, 1980, p. 187.
16 Lee, 'A redivision of labour', pp. 360–2.

17 Ruth Teale (ed), *Colonial Eve: Sources on Women in Australia 1788–1914*, Oxford University Press, Melbourne 1978, pp. 204–211; Desley Deacon, *Managing Gender: The State, the New Middle Class and Women Workers 1830–1930*, Oxford University Press, Melbourne, 1989, pp. 70–77; Helen Jones, *In Her Own Name: Women in South Australia*, Wakefield Press, Adelaide, 1986, p. 73.

18 *Herald*, 8 October 1888, quoted in Patricia Grimshaw, 'Bessie Harrison Lee and the fight for voluntary motherhood', in Marilyn Lake and Farley Kelly (eds), *Double Time: Women in Victoria—150 Years*, Penguin, Ringwood, 1985, p. 143.

19 Cambridge, 'A Wife's Protest', *Unspoken Thoughts*, pp. 95–103.

20 Ada Cambridge, Sisters, first pub. 1904, Penguin, Ringwood, 1989, p. 227.

21 Circular letter from James Coulter to Northern Superintendents of Police, 22 October 1886, Archives Office of Tasmania, CSD 13/69/1261, quoted in Kay Daniels, 'Prostitution in Tasmania during the transition from penal settlement to "civilised" society', in Kay Daniels (ed), *So Much Hard Work: Women and Prostitution in Australian History*, Fontana/Collins, Sydney, 1984, p. 64.

22 A. Jefferis Turner, MD, 'The State and venereal diseases', reprint from the *Australasian Medical Gazette*, 20 November 1911, quoted in Raymond Evans, '"Soiled doves": Prostitution in colonial Queensland', in Daniels (ed), *So Much Hard Work*, p. 144.

23 Rose Scott, 'The Social Problem', undated lecture, Rose Scott Papers, Mitchell Library, MSS 38/23.

24 Brettena Smyth, *The Social Evil*, Rae Bros, North Melbourne, 1894, pp. x, xi.

25 Clara Weekes, *Woman's Sphere*, 10 June 1903, quoted in Daniels & Murnane (comps), *Uphill all the way*, p. 132.

26 Bessie Harrison Lee, *Marriage and Heredity*, Melbourne, 1893, p. 15, quoted in Grimshaw, 'Bessie Harrison Lee and the fight for voluntary motherhood', p. 143.

27 Royal Commission on the Decline of the Birth-Rate, vol. 1, *Report*, p. 22.

28 Ailsa Burns, 'Population structure and the family', in Ailsa Burns, Gill Bottomley and Penny Jools (eds), *The Family in the Modern World: Australian Perspectives*, Allen & Unwin, Sydney, 1983, p. 41.

29 Evidence of doctors performing ovariotomies is to be found in the *Australian Medical Journal*; the quotation comes from Alexander Paterson, *Physical Health of Woman, Useful Knowledge for Maiden, Wife and Mother*, Edwards Dunlop, Sydney, 1890, pp. 57, 59.

30 e.g. Rose Scott, untitled lecture on contagious diseases acts, [1903]; undated lecture, 'The Social Problem', Rose Scott papers, Mitchell Library MSS 38/23; undated, untitled lecture on the need to purify social life, Rose Scott papers, Mitchell Library MSS 38/30. See also Judith Allen, '"Our deeply degraded sex" and "The animal in man": Rose Scott, feminism and sexuality 1890–1925', *Australian Feminist Studies*, nos. 7 & 8, 1988.

NOTES 231

31 Scott papers, as in footnote 30; *Fifth Annual Records and Methods of Work done by the Women's Christian Temperance Union of Victoria during the Year 1892*, pp. 33–4.
32 e.g. Brettena Smyth, *Limitation of Offspring*, 8th edn, Rae Bros, Melbourne, 1893; see also Farley Kelly, 'Feminism and the family: Brettena Smyth', in Eric Fry (ed), *Rebels and Radicals*, Allen & Unwin, Sydney, 1983; Golding, 'Industrial and social condition of women in the Australian Commonwealth'.
33 *Herald*, 8 October 1888, quoted in Grimshaw, 'Bessie Harrison Lee and the fight for voluntary motherhood', p. 143.
34 Rose Scott, Undated, untitled narrative on 'what men are!', Rose Scott papers, Mitchell Library MSS 38/22/11.
35 Scott, herself, was one; others include Catherine Spence, Vida Goldstein, Alice Henry, and Miles Franklin.
36 See Sheridan, this volume.
37 Lee, 'A redivision of labour', p. 361.
38 *Tocsin*, 18 November 1897; *Age*, 15 February 1898; *Argus*, 15 February 1898: all quoted in Lee, 'A redivision of labour', p. 357.
39 Desley Deacon, 'The naturalisation of dependence: the state, the new middle class and women workers 1830–1930', PhD thesis, Australian National University, 1985, pp. 198–204; Ken Buckley & Ted Wheelwright, *No Paradise for Workers: Capitalism and the Common People in Australia 1788–1914*, Oxford University Press, Melbourne, 1988, p. 147.
40 Edna Ryan & Anne Conlon, *Gentle Invaders: Australian Women at Work*, first pub. 1975, Penguin, Ringwood, 1989, pp. 56–61, 63, 74; Lee, 'A redivision of labour', pp. 361–2, 367–8; Raelene Francis, '"No more Amazons": Gender and work process in the Victorian clothing trades, 1890–1939', *Labour History*, no. 50, 1986, p. 105; Deacon, 'Naturalisation of dependence', pp. 199–204.
41 McDonald, *Marriage in Australia*, p. 134.
42 Royal Commission on the Decline of the Birth-Rate, vol. 1, *Report*, p. 17, and, especially, pp. 52–4.
43 Judith A. Allen, *Sex and Secrets: Crimes Involving Australian Women Since 1880*, Oxford University Press, Melbourne, 1990, pp. 67–8.
44 Both quoted in Carole Pateman, *The Sexual Contract*, Polity, Cambridge, 1988, ch. 6, to which this paragraph owes a great deal.
45 See, e.g., John Mackinolty, 'The Married Women's Property Acts', in Judy Mackinolty and Heather Radi (eds), *In Pursuit of Justice: Australian Women and the Law 1788–1979*, Hale & Iremonger, Sydney, 1979; Hilary Golder, *Divorce in 19th Century New South Wales*, New South Wales University Press, Kensington, 1985; and, e.g., Anne Summers, *Damned Whores and God's Police: The Colonization of Women in Australia*, Penguin, Ringwood, 1975, ch. 11.

Chapter 9: The 'equals and comrades of men'?: *Toscin* and 'the woman question'

I am grateful to Penny Russell for her assistance in research for this chapter, which focuses on part of the broader study I am undertaking of working-class women and families and the state in late nineteenth-century Australia. The work of Penny Russell was supported by an ARC grant.

1. M. Lake, 'The politics of respectability: Identifying the masculinist context', *Historical Studies*, vol. 22, no. 86, 1986, pp. 116–131.
2. See H. Anderson (ed), *Tocsin: Radical Arguments Against Federation, 1897–1900*, Drummond, Richmond, Vic, 1977.
3. See M. Lake, 'Socialism and manhood: The case of William Lane', *Labour History*, no. 50, May 1986, pp. 54–62.
4. B. Taylor, *Eve and the New Jerusalem: Socialism and Feminism in the Nineteenth Century*, Virago, London, 1983. For a discussion of feminism and Marxism see: L. Sargent (ed), *Women and Revolution: A Discussion of the Unhappy Marriage of Marxism and Feminism*, South End Press, Boston, 1981; M. Barrett, *Women's Oppression Today: Problems in Marxist Feminist Analysis*, Verso, London, 1980.
5. *Tocsin*, 12 October 1899, p. 3.
6. ibid., 22 September 1898, p. 7.
7. ibid., 24 November 1898, p. 5.
8. ibid., 14 September 1899, p. 3.
9. ibid., 16 August 1900, p. 7.
10. ibid., 9 August 1900, p. 5.
11. ibid., 31 August 1899, p. 2.
12. ibid., 16 October 1897, p. 4.
13. ibid., 30 November 1899, p. 6.
14. ibid., 6 April 1899, p. 6.
15. ibid., 5 January 1899, p. 6.
16. ibid., 15 March 1900, p. 5.
17. ibid., 26 April 1900, p. 6.
18. ibid., 9 November 1899, p. 5.
19. ibid., 10 May 1900, p. 5.
20. ibid., 7 July 1898, p. 4.
21. ibid., 28 July 1898, p. 5.
22. ibid., 1 September 1898, p. 4.
23. ibid., 23 August 1900, p. 4.
24. ibid., 31 May 1900, p. 5.
25. ibid., 9 August 1900, p. 5.
26. ibid., 5 April 1900, p. 5.
27. ibid., 4 January 1900, p. 5.
28. ibid., 13 September 1900, p. 4.
29. ibid., 23 August 1900, p. 4.
30. ibid., 13 September 1900, p. 4.
31. ibid., 9 October 1897, p. 4.
32. ibid., 21 October 1897, p. 4.

33 *ibid.*, 2 March 1899, p. 5.
34 *ibid.*, 30 November 1899, p. 2.
35 *ibid.*, 13 April 1899, p. 6.
36 *ibid.*, 28 April 1898, p. 8.
37 *ibid.*, 28 October 1897, p. 6.
38 *ibid.*, 28 October 1897, p. 4.
39 *ibid.*, 18 November 1897, p. 4.
40 *ibid.*, 18 November 1897, p. 4.
41 *ibid.*, 2 March 1899, p. 5.
42 *ibid.*, 10 May 1900, p. 5.
43 *ibid.*, 17 August 1899, p. 4.
44 *ibid.*, 16 August 1900, p. 7.
45 *ibid.*, 2 October 1897, p. 4.
46 *ibid.*, 26 January 1899, p. 7.
47 *ibid.*, 1 September 1898, p. 6.
48 *ibid.*, 21 July 1898, p. 4.
49 *ibid.*, 15 March 1900, p. 5.
50 *ibid.*, 28 December 1899, p. 5.
51 *ibid.*, 22 December 1898, p. 2; 12 October 1899, p. 3.
52 *ibid.*, 7 December 1899, p. 5.
53 *ibid.*, 14 December 1899, p. 4.
54 *ibid.*, 29 December 1898, p. 2.
55 *ibid.*, 14 December 1899, p. 1.
56 *ibid.*, 18 August 1898, p. 4.
57 *ibid.*, 6 October 1898, p. 3.
58 *ibid.*, 13 October, 1898, p. 4.
59 *ibid.*, 14 December 1899, p. 5.

Chapter 10: The *Woman's Voice* on sexuality

1 For instance, a few poems on marriage by Ada Cambridge, the metaphorical import of Barbara Baynton's stories about abused women, and Rose Scott's unpublished notes on questions of sexuality. On Scott, see Judith Allen, '"Our Deeply Degraded Sex" and "The Animal in Man": Rose Scott, feminism and sexuality 1890–1925', *Australian Feminist Studies* 8 & 9, 1988.
2 See Patricia Grimshaw on *Tocsin*, Chapter 9 of this volume, and Elaine Zinkhan, 'Louisa Albury Lawson: Feminist and Patriot' in D. Adelaide (ed.) *A Bright and Fiery Troop*, Penguin, Ringwood, 1988; also Susan Sheridan, 'Women and the *Worker* in NSW' in Ken Stewart (ed), *Behind the Nineties*, University of Queensland Press, St Lucia, forthcoming, and 'Louisa Lawson, Miles Franklin and Feminist Writing', *Australian Feminist Studies* 8 & 9, 1988.
3 For example Judith Allen, '"Our Deeply Degraded Sex" ... ' and also 'Feminism and masculinity' in Barbara Caine *et al* (eds), *Crossing Boundaries*, Allen & Unwin, Sydney, 1988; Sheila Jeffreys, *The Spinster and Her Enemies*, Pandora, London, 1985; Susan K. Kent, *Sex and Suffrage in Britain*, Princeton

University Press, 1987; Ellen DuBois & Linda Gordon, 'Seeking ecstasy on the Battlefield: Danger and pleasure in nineteenth-century feminist sexual thought' in Carole Vance (ed), *Pleasure and Danger*, Routledge & Kegan Paul, Boston, 1984.

4 Both analogies were in common feminist use at the turn of the century: see for example Cicely Hamilton, *Marriage as a Trade*, Chapman & Hall, London, 1909, and Olive Schreiner's much-quoted passage on marriage as a form of prostitution in *The Story of an African Farm* ('by Ralph Iron'), Chapman & Hall, London, 1883.

5 Marilyn Lake, 'The politics of respectability: Identifying the masculinist context', *Historical Studies*, vol. 22, no. 86, 1986, was the first to construe this feminist challenge as an attack on masculinism.

5a *Woman's Voice*, vol. 3, no. 10 (December 21, 1895), p. 419. Further page references to *Woman's Voice* are included in the text, using the journal's sequential pagination.

6 Editorial, *Woman's Voice*, vol. 1, no. 1 (August 9, 1894), p. 1, and Editor's Note, which appeared on the front page of every issue. It is hard to know what role this radicalism played in the fate of the journal. The reason she gave in the final issue for closing it after eighteen months was financial: insufficient subscriptions and advertisements. But other interests, and grief over the accidental death of her son some months earlier, may have contributed to her decision.

7 Leila Thomas, 'The Woman's Voice', *Australian Highway*, vol. 1, no. 6, August 1919, pp. 11–13.

8 Champion was an English socialist journalist who migrated to Melbourne in 1890; a supporter of feminist causes, he married Vida Goldstein's sister, Elsie.

9 On the 'new man' of the period see Lake, 'The Politics of respectability'; also Jock Collins, 'Mummy's boys: Pakeha men and male culture in New Zealand' in P. Bunkle and B. Hughes (eds), *Women in New Zealand Society*, Allen & Unwin, Auckland, 1980.

10 See Thomas, 'The Woman's Voice', p. 13.

11 'Seeking ecstasy on the battlefield', p. 37; see also Lake, 'The politics of respectability', pp. 129–31; Phillida Bunkle, 'The origins of the women's movement in New Zealand: The Women's Christian Temperance Union 1885–1895' in P. Bunkle and B. Hughes (eds), *Women in New Zealand Society*, Allen & Unwin, Auckland, 1980.

12 In answer to the irate 'John Strong', who waited in vain for someone to defend the 'holy estate of matrimony', Wolstonehome maintains that 'every letter on the marriage question sent to us for publication has been printed' (p. 152)—though the wording here would allow her to withold those she considered not intended for publication.

13 Henrietta Dugdale (1826–1918) was a prominent Melbourne suffragist.

14 DuBois and Gordon, 'Seeking ecstasy on the battlefield', p. 34.

15 Sarah Grand, *The Heavenly Twins*, Heinemann's Colonial Library, London, 1894, 2 vols.

16 DuBois and Gordon, 'Seeking ecstasy on the battlefield', p. 35, note 10.
17 Kent, *Sex and Suffrage*, pp. 92–4.
18 Linda Gordon, 'Why nineteenth-century feminists did not support "birth control" and twentieth-century feminists do', in B. Thorne and M. Yalom (eds), *Rethinking the Family*, Longman, New York, 1982, p. 45.
19 Besant had earlier been notorious for her public advocacy of contraception; she visited Australia in 1894.
20 Quoted from the Washington Woman's Club moral education journal, Alpha, June 1, 1879, by William Leach, *True Love and Perfect Union: The Feminist Reform of Sex and Society*, Routledge & Kegan Paul, London, 1981, p. 93.
21 Maybanke [Wolstoneholme] Anderson, *Mother Lore*, Angus & Robertson, Sydney, 1919, p. 15.
22 DuBois and Gordon, 'Seeking ecstasy on the battlefield', p. 40. See also Alison Mackinnon & Carol Bacchi, 'Sex, resistance and power: Sex reform in South Australia, c.1905', *Australian Historical Studies*, vol. 22, no. 90, 1988, p. 64; this article discusses the work of two Adelaide women who promulgated views similar to those in the *Voice*: Rosamond Benham (*Sense about Sex by a Woman Doctor*, with supplement, *Circumvention*, 1905) and her mother, Agnes Nesbit Benham (*Love's Way to Perfect Humanhood*, 1904).
23 Kent, *Sex and Suffrage*, pp. 93–4.
24 *Arena*, 13 (1895), pp. 59–73.
25 Michel Foucault, *The History of Sexuality*, vol. 1, Penguin, Harmondsworth, 1979.
26 See Nancy Cott, *The Bonds of Womanhood*, Yale University Press, New Haven, 1977.
27 *Arena*, 13 (1895), p. 63.
28 In the original, this passage is attributed to Gerald Massey (*Arena*, 13 (1895), p. 68).
29 That 'the race' referred to the white race was rarely made explicit in such contexts, but see Knapman, Chapter 11 in this volume. The racist nature of the discourse was recognised and strenuously opposed by black women activists in the US; see Angela Davis, *Women, Race and Class*, Random House, New York, 1982; Hazel Carby, '"On the threshold of Woman's era": Lynching, Empire and sexuality in feminist theory', *Critical Inquiry*, vol. 12, no. 1 (Autumn, 1985), pp. 262–77.
30 Balls-Headley, W., *The Evolution of the Diseases of Women*, Smith, Elder, London, 1894).
31 As even such a scholarly feminist text as Susan Kent's *Sex and Suffrage* (1987) does.
32 Kerreen Reiger makes this point, but says their goals were different, in *The Disenchantment of the Home*, Oxford University Press, Melbourne, 1985, pp. 178–82. Wolstoneholme's commitment to social as well as personal reform brings her into line with what Reiger has called the 'new class' of the Australian bourgeoisie which began in this period to promote state intervention to regulate social life, especially in areas of health and education. Her response to the

Contagious Diseases legislation, for example (*Voice*, pp. 300, 312) places her on the side of state intervention.

Chapter 11: Reproducing Empire: Exploring ideologies of gender and race on Australia's Pacific frontier

1 Charles Stember, *Sexual Racism: The Emotional Barrier to an Integrated Society*, Harper and Row, New York, 1978; Michael Banton, 'Gender roles and ethnic relations', Fawcett Memorial Lecture for 1978–79 in *New Community*, vol. 7, no. 3, 1979, pp. 323–32; Doris Lessing, *The Grass is Singing*, Plume, New York, 1976; Nadine Gordimer, *Occasion for Loving*, Jonathan Cape, London, 1978.
2 Marie de Lepervanche, 'Breeders for Australia: A national identity for women?', *Australian Journal of Social Issues*, vol. 24, no. 3, 1989, p. 163.
3 Jan Pettman, 'Australia's Future in the Global Context', *Social Alternatives*, vol. 9, no. 2, 1990, p. 33.
4 de Lepervanche, 'Breeders for Australia', p. 163.
5 Marilyn Lake, 'Women, gender and history', *Australian Feminist Studies*, vols. 7 & 8, 1988, p. 6.
6 Donald Denoon,'The Isolation of Australian History', *Historical Studies*, vol. 22, no. 87, 1986, p. 252, his emphasis.
7 *ibid.*
8 John Young, *Adventurous Spirits: Australian Migrant Society in Pre-Cession Fiji*, University of Queensland Press, St Lucia, 1984.
9 *Fiji Census Report*, 1901, Colony of Fiji.
10 Claudia Knapman, *White Women in Fiji 1835–1930: The Ruin of Empire?*, Allen & Unwin, Sydney, 1986.
11 Kerreen Reiger, *The Disenchantment of the Home: Modernizing the Australian Family 1880–1940*, Oxford University Press, Melbourne, 1985, p. 380.
12 See, for example, Carol Christ, 'Victorian masculinity and the angel in the house' in *A Widening Sphere: Changing Roles of Victorian Women* Martha Vicinus (ed.), Indiana University Press, Bloomington, 1977, p. 146.
13 Anne Summers, *Damned Whores and God's Police: The Colonization of Women in Australia*, Penguin, Melbourne, 1975.
14 Anna Davin, 'Imperialism and Motherhood', *History Workshop*, no. 5, 1978, pp. 9–65.
15 Reiger, *Disenchantment of the Home*, p. 39.
16 *ibid.*
17 Desley Deacon, *Managing Gender: The State, the New Middle Class and Women Workers 1830–1930*, Oxford University Press, Melbourne, 1989, p. 131.
18 Judith Walkowitz, *Prostitution and Victorian Society: Women, Class and the State*, Cambridge University Press, Cambridge, 1980.

19 Summers, *Damned Whores and God's Police*.
20 Knapman, *White Women in Fiji*.
21 Ann McGrath, '"Spinifex Fairies": Aboriginal Workers in the Northern Territory, 1911–39' in *Women, Class and History: Feminist Perspectives on Australia 1788–1978*, ed. Elizabeth Windschuttle, Fontana/Collins, Melbourne, 1980.
22 Brij Lal, *Girmitiyas: The Origins of the Fiji Indians*, The Journal of Pacific History, Canberra, 1983, p. 98.
23 Ahmed Ali, *Girmit: The Indenture Experience in Fiji*, Fiji Museum Bulletin 5, 1979.
24 Davin, 'Imperialism and Motherhood'.
25 Deacon, *Managing Gender*, p. 211.
26 Bryan Gandevia, *Tears Often Shed: Child Health and Welfare in Australia from 1788*, Pergamon Press, Sydney, 1978; Karen O'Connor, *Our Babies the State's Best Asset: A History of 75 Years of Baby Health Services in New South Wales*, New South Wales Department of Health, Sydney, 1989.
27 'Royal Commission on the Decline of the Birth-Rate, 1904', cited in *Colonial Eve: Sources on Women in Australia 1788–1914*, ed. Ruth Teale, Oxford University Press, Melbourne, 1978, p. 133.
28 Knapman, *White Women in Fiji*.
29 William Boyd, *School Ties*, Hamish Hamilton, London, 1985, p. 28.
30 Richard Meckel, 'Childhood and the historians: A review essay', *Journal of Family History*, vol. 9, no. 4, 1984, pp. 415–24.
31 Denoon, 'The Isolation of Australian History', p. 258 and this chapter, paragraph 4.
32 Rose Heighway, 'Diary Jan. 1 1906–May 7, 1907', unpublished manuscript in private possession.
33 Claudia Knapman, 'The White Child in Colonial Fiji, 1895–1930', *The Journal of Pacific History*, vol. 23, no. 2, 1988, pp. 206–13.
34 Jan Morris, *Pax Britannica: The Climax of an Empire*, Penguin, Harmondsworth, 1981, p. 220.
35 Charles Allen, *A Scrapbook of British India 1877–1947*, Penguin, Harmondsworth, 1979, p. 16.
36 John McClure, *Kipling and Conrad: The Colonial Fiction*, Harvard University Press, Cambridge, Mass., 1981, p. 107.
37 Ann McGrath, *'Born in the Cattle': Aborigines in Cattle Country*, Allen & Unwin, Sydney, 1987.
38 Knapman, *White Women in Fiji*.

Chapter 12: Sovereignty and sexual identity in political cartoons

We would like to thank Rob Hood and Henry Lee for finding cartoons for us. Sue Rowley was both perceptive and encouraging at a crucial stage. We are also indebted, for comments on earlier drafts of this chapter, to the editors and to the

History and Politics Postgraduate Seminar at the University of Wollongong in September 1990. Marguerite Mahood, *The Loaded Line. Australian Political Caricature 1788–1901*, Melbourne University Press, Melbourne, 1973 was a valuable source of illustrative material.

1 The iconographical contours of this tradition are mapped out in Marina Warner, *Monuments and Maidens: The Allegory of the Female Form*, Picador, London, 1987; Maurice Agulhon, *Marianne into Battle*, Cambridge University Press, Cambridge, 1981; and *idem*, 'Esquisse pour une archéologie de la République: L'allégorie civique féminine', *Annales*, vol. xviii, no. 1, janvier-février 1973, pp. 5–34.

2 cf. on the uses of sexual disguise, Sandra Gilbert & Susan Gubar, *No Man's Land: The Place of the Woman Writer in the Twentieth Century*, vol. 2, *Sexchanges*, Yale University Press, New Haven, 1989, esp. pp. 333–334; Rudolf M. Dekker & Lotte C. Van de Pol, *The Tradition of Female Transvestism in Early Modern Europe*, Macmillan, London, 1990; and Annette Kuhn, Sexual Disguise and Cinema, in *The Power of the Image*, Routledge & Kegan Paul, London, 1985.

3 Coghlan was the NSW Government Statistician, while Beale was a member of the Royal Commission into the decline of the birthrate in 1903.

4 The tale, at least its general outline, is probably fairly familiar from any *Classics Illustrated* version—or even from Freud's wilful interpretation of its meaning (see for example *The Interpretation of Dreams*). Its sources in classical drama are Sophocles' Theban plays, especially *Oidpíous Túrannos (Oedipus Rex)*, Euripides' *Phoenissae (Phoenician Maidens)*, and Seneca's *Oedipus*, which in turn are based on older Theban legends. For pictorial sources, see Martin Robertson, *Greek Painting*, Skira, London, 1959, pp. 52–53, 68. On versions of the story in other cultures, see Apollodorus, *Library*, Appendix viii, 'The Legend of Oedipus', and Eva Baer, *Sphinxes and Harpies in Medieval Islam: An Iconographical Study*, Israel Oriental Society, Jerusalem, 1965.

5 Panofsky calls this type of mutation 'pseudomorphosis': the way in which figures become invested with a meaning not present in their classical prototypes, something not necessarily due to ignorance but to a realignment of the figure in relation to a different set of images or concerns. See Erwin Panofsky, 'Father Time', in *Studies in Iconology: Humanistic Themes in the Art of the Renaissance*, Harper & Row, New York, 1962, pp. 70-71. See also Claude Lévi-Strauss, *The Origin of Table Manners: Introduction to a Science of Mythology 3*, trans. John and Doris Weightman, Harper & Row, New York, 1978, pp. 129–31.

6 We are not of course suggesting that Gibbs was familiar with all the classical antecedents or textual variants of the sphinx or of Oedipus: the version of the sphinx story that came down to him probably did so willy nilly, through tradition rather than direct from the sources.

7 See for example Franz von Stuck's 'Kiss of the Sphinx' (c.1895), or Fernand Khnopff's 'L'Art des Caresses' (1896), printed in Edward Lucie-Smith, *Sym-*

NOTES 239

bolist Art, Thames & Hudson, London, 1972, fig. 135, p. 155, and fig. 96, p. 123. See also the versions of the story in the work of Moreau in Pierre-Louis Mathieu, *Gustave Moreau: Complete Edition of the Finished Paintings, Watercolours and Drawings*, trans. James Emmons, Phaidon, Oxford, 1977, especially cat. nos. 64, 65, 66 and 285. Generally, see Bram Dijkstra, *Idols of Perversity: Fantasies of Feminine Evil in Fin-de-Siècle Culture*, Oxford University Press, New York, pp. 325–330.

8 See, variously, Eric Hobsbawm, 'Man and Woman in Socialist Iconography', *History Workshop*, no. 6, Autumn 1978, pp. 121–138; Tim Mason, 'The Domestication of Female Socialist Icons: A Note in Reply to Eric Hobsbawm', *History Workshop*, no. 7, Spring 1979, pp. 170–175; Maurice Agulhon, 'On Political Allegory: A Reply to Eric Hobsbawm', *History Workshop*, no. 8, Autumn 1979, pp. 167–173; Sally Alexander, Anna Davin, Eve Hostettler, 'Labouring Women: A Reply to Eric Hobsbawm', *History Workshop*, no. 9, Autumn 1979, pp. 174–182; and Londa Schiebinger, 'Feminine Icons: The Face of Early Modern Science', *Critical Inquiry*, vol. xiv, no. 4, Summer 1988, pp. 661–691.

9 Neil Hertz, 'Medusa's Head: Male Hysteria under Political Pressure', *Representations*, no. 4, Fall 1983, p. 38.

10 'Hop, His Confessions: Chapters from the Autobiography of Livingston Hopkins', *Lone Hand*, 1 June 1914, pp. 18–19.

11 See for example *ibid.* pp. 50, 69, 161.

12 See Marian Sawer & Marian Simms, *A Woman's Place: Women and Politics in Australia*, Allen & Unwin, Sydney, 1984, Table 1.1.

13 *ibid.* p. 168.

Chapter 13: 'Woman' in federation poetry

The date cited after each quotation refers to earliest publication records. References in the Notes are to currently accessible sources.

1 S. Bennett, *Federation, Sources 1897–1901*, Cassell, Sydney, 1975, p. 5.

2 M. Wilding (ed.), *Portable Marcus Clarke*, University of Queensland Press, St. Lucia, 1976, p. 643.

3 Bernard O'Dowd, *The Poems of Bernard O'Dowd*, Lothian, Melbourne and Sydney, 1944, p. 35.

4 Vance Palmer, *The Legend of the Nineties*, Melbourne University Press, Melbourne, paperback edn, 1966, p. 15.

5 *The Poems of Bernard O'Dowd*, p. 193.

6 Brunton Stephens, *The Poetical Works of Brunton Stephens*, Angus & Robertson, Sydney & Melbourne, 1902, p. 5.

7 A.B. Paterson, *The Collected Verse of A.B. Paterson*, Angus & Robertson, Sydney, 1923. This poem was printed in 1901 and sold as a NSW Bookstall souvenir.

8 W. Dyson, *The Bulletin Reciter 1880–1902*, *Bulletin*, 1901, reprinted Lansdowne Press, Melbourne, 1975, p. 142.

9. Jill Roe, 'Chivalry and social policy in the Antipodes', *Historical Studies*, vol. 22, no. 88, April 1987, p. 401. I am indebted to Susan Sheridan for drawing this article to my attention.
10. George Essex Evans, *The Collected Verse of G. Essex Evans*, Angus & Robertson, Sydney and Melbourne, 1928, p. 7.
11. Marina Warner, *Monuments and Maidens*, Picador, London, 1985, p. 11.
12. L. Cantrell (ed.), *The 1890s: Stories, Verse and Essays*, University of Queensland Press, St Lucia, 1977, p. 132.
13. Bernard O'Dowd, *The Poems*, pp. 208–9 and 194–5.
14. Roderic Quinn 'The Circling Hearths', Cantrell (ed.) *The 1890s*, p. 120.
15. G. Evans, *Collected Verse*, 1928, p. 27. I have not found a prior publishing date for this poem, but it was presumably written well before Victoria's demise in 1905.
16. Barcroft Boake, 'Where the Dead Men Lie', T. Inglis Moore *From the Ballads to Brennan*, Angus & Robertson, Sydney, 1964, p. 115.
17. Mary Gilmore, *Selected Verse*, Angus & Robertson, Sydney, 1948, p. 16.
18. T. Inglis Moore, *From the Ballads to Brennan*, Angus & Robertson, Sydney, 1964, pp. 251–2.
19. 'Danton,' probably O'Dowd, in Hugh Anderson, *Radical Arguments Against Federation 1897–1900*, Drummond, Victoria, 1977, p. 140.
20. *Tocsin*, 'An Anti-Bilious Ode', Anderson, p. 137.
21. Adamson, in Mary Wilkinson *Poems of Manhood*, Whitcombe and Tombs, Melbourne, p. 192.
22. Not only in literature. Streeton for example painted 'The Spirit of the Drought' (1895), a seductive nude in a red veil poised beside the skeleton of a bullock. (Australian National Gallery, Canberra)
23. A.G. Stephens, in Wilkinson, *Poems of Manhood*, p. 122.
24. Anna Couani & Peter Lyssiotis, *The Harbour Breathes*, Masterthief/Seacruise, Melbourne, 1989, unnumbered.

Chapter 14: The New Woman and the Coming Man: Gender and genre in the 'lost-race' romance

This paper was read at ASAL 89, Monash University, July 1989. I am grateful to Kay Ferres, Betty Holt, Sylvia Kelso, Elizabeth Perkins, Graeme Turner and Elizabeth Webby for their comments.

1. Marilyn Lake, 'The politics of respectability: Identifying the masculinist context', *Historical Studies*, vol. 22, no. 86 (April 1986), p. 116.
2. See Susan Sheridan, '"Temper, romantic; bias, offensively feminine": Australian women writers and literary nationalism', *Kunapipi*, 7, 2 and 3 (1985), pp. 49–58; and Fiona Giles, 'Romance: An embarrassing subject', in L. Hergenhan (ed.) *The Penguin New Literary History of Australia*, Penguin, Ringwood, 1988, ch. 14.
3. cf. Chris Weedon, *Feminist Practice and Poststructuralist Theory*, Blackwell, Oxford, 1987, p. 168.

NOTES 241

4. Sheridan, loc. cit. p. 57.
5. Sandra M. Gilbert, 'Rider Haggard's Heart of Darkness', *Partisan Review*, vol. 50, no. 3 (1983), p. 444.
6. H. Rider Haggard, *She: A History of Adventure*, 1887, Macdonald, London, 1963, p. 252. All subsequent references are to this edition and appear in parentheses in the text.
7. Laura Mulvey, 'Visual pleasure and narrative cinema', *Screen*, vol. 16, no. 3, 1975; reprinted in Tony Bennett *et al* (eds), *Popular Television and Film*, BFI, London, 1981, pp. 206–215.
8. Cited in Morton Cohen, *Rider Haggard: His Life and Works*, Hutchinson, London, 1960, p. 100.
9. See J.J. Healy, 'The Lemurian Nineties', *Australian Literary Studies*, vol. 8, no. 3, 1978, pp. 303–316; and Van Ikin, 'Dreams, visions, utopias', in L. Hergenhan (ed.) *The Penguin New Literary History of Australia*, Penguin, Ringwood, 1988, ch. 16.
10. Kay Schaffer, *Women and the Bush: Forces of Desire in the Australian Cultural Tradition*, Cambridge University Press, Cambridge, 1988, p. 101.
11. *ibid.*, pp. 122–3.
12. G. Firth Scott, *The Last Lemurian: A Westralian Romance*, James Bowden, London, 1898, p. 3. All subsequent references are to this edition and appear in parentheses in the text.
13. cf. Richard White, *Inventing Australia: Images and Identity 1688–1980*, Allen & Unwin, Sydney, 1981, ch. 5.
14. Alice Jardine, *Gynesis: Configurations of Woman and Modernity*, Cornell University Press, Ithaca, 1985, ch. 4.
15. Schaffer, *Women and the Bush*, p.127.
16. Rosa Praed, *Fugitive Anne: A Romance of the Unexplored Bush*, John Long, London, 1902, p. 7. All subsequent references are to this edition and appear in parentheses in the text.
17. Peter Pierce, '"Weary with travelling through realms of air ...": Romance fiction of "Boldrewood", Haggard, Wells and Praed', *Westerly*, vol. 32, no. 2 (June 1987), p. 87.
18. Susan Sheridan, 'Gender and genre in Barbara Baynton's *Human Toll*', *Australian Literary Studies*, vol. 14, no. 1, 1989, p. 73.
19. Rosa Praed, *The Bond of Wedlock*, 1887, Pandora Press, London, 1987, p. 45.
20. Barbara Creed, 'A journey through *Blue Velvet*: Film, fantasy and the female spectator', *New Formations*, no. 6 (Winter 1988), p. 115.
21. See Robert Dixon, 'Public and Private Voices', in L. Hergenhan (ed.) *The Penguin New Literary History of Australia*, Penguin, Ringwood, 1988, p. 133.
22. Gilbert, 'Rider Haggard's Heart of Darkness', p. 444.
23. Creed, 'A journey through *Blue Velvet*', p. 116.
24. cf. Marilyn French, *Beyond Power: On Women, Men and Morals*, Jonathan Cape, London, 1986.

25 Judith Allen, 'Rose Scott's vision: Feminism and masculinity 1880–1925', in Barbara Caine (*et al*) (eds), *Crossing Boundaries: Feminisms and the Critique of Knowledge*, Allen & Unwin, Sydney, 1988.
26 Michel Foucault, *The History of Sexuality*, Penguin, Harmondsworth, 1981, vol. 1, p. 101.

Chapter 15: Water, gold and honey: A discussion of *Kirkham's Find*

1 See Susan Magarey, 'An insurrection of subjugated knowledges: Feminism in Australia in the 1890s', Conference Paper, *Seventh Berkshire Conference on the History of Women*, Wellesley College, Wellesley, Mass., 19–21 June, 1987.
2 Debra Adelaide, 'Introduction: A tradition of women' in *A Bright and Fiery Troop, Australian Women Writers of the Nineteenth Century*, Debra Adelaide (ed.), Penguin Books, Ringwood, 1988, p. 6.
3 Fiona Giles, 'Romance, an Embarrassing Subject', in *The Penguin New Literary History of Australia*, Laurie Hergenhan (ed.), Penguin, Ringwood, 1988, p. 227.
4 See Susan Magarey, 'Sexual labour: Australia 1880–1910', Chapter 8 in this volume.
5 Mary Gaunt, *Kirkham's Find*, Penguin, Ringwood, 1988, p. 100. Further references to this edition are given in brackets in the text.
6 David Adams, ed., *The Letters of Rachel Henning*, Penguin, Harmondsworth, 1979, p. 76.
7 Sue Rowley, 'Sliprails and spur: Courting bush sweethearts in Australian nationalist mythology', *Span*, no. 26, April, 1988, p. 18.
8 *ibid*, p. 20.
9 See Sue Rowley, 'Things a bushwoman cannot do', Chapter 16 in this volume.
10 Sue Rowley, 'Sliprails and spur', p. 15.
11 Dale Spender, 'Afterword' in Mary Gaunt, *Kirkham's Find*, p. 335.
12 Sue Martin, '"Sad sometimes, lonely often...dull never": Mary Gaunt, traveller and novelist' in *A Bright and Fiery Troop*, ed. *Adelaide*, p. 188.
13 *ibid*, p. 184.
14 Magarey, 'Sexual labour: Australia 1880–1910'.
15 For a detailed discussion of how generic conventions frequently impede writers' attempts to adopt an oppositional stance see Anne Cranny-Francis, *Feminist Fiction: Feminist Uses of Generic Fiction*, Polity Press, Cambridge, 1990, pp. 15–22.
16 Rowley, 'Sliprails and spur', p. 31.
17 See Magarey, 'Sexual labour'.

Chapter 16: Things a bushwoman cannot do

My thanks to Jim Falk, Paula Hamilton, Susan Magarey and Susan Sheridan for their assistance.

1 See chapters in this volume by Jenny Lee, Bruce Scates, Desley Deacon, Gail Reekie, Paula Hamilton.

2 Note, however, the debate in this book between Jenny Lee and Bruce Scates on the nature of the changes in female factory employment.
3 American historian Margaret Marsh distinguishes between 'separate spheres' ideology that could extend to legitimising women's engagement in political campaigns to make the world 'homelike', and 'domestic' ideology that confined the location of women's activities to the home itself. Margaret Marsh, 'From separation to togetherness: The social construction of domestic space in American suburbs, 1840–1915,' *Journal of American History*, 1989.
4 Susan Magarey, 'An insurrection of subjugated knowledges: Feminism in Australia in the 1890s', Conference Paper, *Seventh Berkshire Conference on the History of Women*, Wellesley College, Wellesley, Mass., 19–21 June, 1987, p. 7.
5 Desley Deacon, 'Political arithmetic: The Nineteenth-century Australian Census and the construction of the dependent woman', *Signs*, vol. 11, no. 1, 1985, pp. 27–47.
6 Henry Lawson, 'The men who made Australia' (1901) in *A Fantasy of Man*, Lansdowne, Sydney, 1988, p. 117.
7 Russel Ward, *The Australian Legend*, Oxford University Press, Melbourne, 1978, p. 219.
8 Marilyn Lake, 'Helpmeet, slave, housewife: Women in rural families, 1870–1930', in P. Grimshaw, C. McConville, E. McEwan (eds), *Families in Colonial Australia*, Allen & Unwin, Sydney, 1985, p. 179. Note, however, that the notion of 'women's work' could be extended to include house-paddock activities, such as milking and poultry-raising. The pictorial conventions for representing bushwomen engaged in *appropriate* rural labour suggest a romantic contemplation of women at work, which, I have argued elsewhere, is associated with masculine leisure. S. Rowley, 'Sliprails and spur: Courting bush sweethearts in Australian nationalist mythology', *Span*, no. 26, 1988, pp. 29–31.
9 Henry Lawson, 'The last review', in *A Fantasy of Man*, p. 194.
10 See Henry Lawson, '"Water them geraniums"', in *A Camp-Fire Yarn*, Lansdowne, Sydney, 1988, pp. 719–32; Steele Rudd, 'Before We Got the Deeds', *On Our Selection*, University of Queensland Press, St Lucia, 1987, p. 14.
11 Graeme Davison, 'Sydney and the Bush: An urban context for the Australian legend,' in J. Carroll (ed.), *Intruders in the Bush: The Australian Quest for Identity*, Oxford University Press, Melbourne, p. 111.
12 See Susan Tiffin, 'In pursuit of reluctant parents: Desertion and non-support legislation in Australia and the United States, 1890–1920', in Sydney Labour History Group (ed.) *What Rough Beast? The State and Social Order in Australian History*, Allen & Unwin, Sydney, 1982, pp. 130–150; Anne O'Brien, *Poverty's Prison: The Poor in New South Wales 1880–1918*, Oxford University Press, Carlton, 1988, pp. 102–6.
13 Shirley Fisher, 'The family and the Sydney economy in the late nineteenth century', in P. Grimshaw, *et al.*, *Families in Colonial Australia*, p. 154.
14 Anne O'Brien, *Poverty's Prison*, p. 65.

15 K. Daniels & M. Murnane, *Uphill All the Way: A Documentary History of Women in Australia*, University of Queensland Press, St Lucia, 1980, p. 52.
16 S. Magarey, *An Insurrection*, p. 19.
17 See, for example, Henry Lawson, 'His Brother's Keeper', in *A Fantasy of Man*, pp. 26–34.
18 G. Pollock, 'Bourgeois men and working women: Sexuality and surveillance in Victorian social realism', Power Foundation Lecture, Sydney University, Sydney, 1989.
19 Susan Tiffin, 'In pursuit of reluctant parents', p. 131.
20 Henry Lawson, 'Crime in the Bush', in *A Camp-Fire Yarn*, p. 572.
21 Steele Rudd, dedication, 'Our New Selection' in *On Our Selection*, 1987, p. 117.
22 Steele Rudd, 'In the Drought Time', *On Our Selection, Sandy's Selection*, pp. 287–94.
23 *Ibid.*, p. 288.
24 Barbara Baynton, 'Squeaker's Mate', in *Barbara Baynton*, ed. S. Krimmer & A. Lawson, Portable Australian Authors series, University of Queensland Press, St Lucia, 1980, pp. 11–26.
25 See M. Lake, 'Helpmeet, Slave, Housewife', p. 184.
26 D. Deacon, 'Political arithmetic', pp. 27–47.
27 T.A. Coghlan, *General Report on the Eleventh Census of New South Wales*, Sydney, 1894, pp. 270–75, cited in Deacon, D., 'Political arithmetic', p. 45.
28 See, for example, '"Water them geraniums"', 'A double-buggy at Lahey's Creek'.
29 H. Lawson, 'A Double-Buggy at Lahey's Creek', in *A Camp-Fire Yarn*, p. 736.
30 M. Mauss, *The Gift*, Cohen and West, 1970, p. 72, cited in C. Bell & H. Newby, 'Husbands and wives: The dynamics of the deferential dialectic', in D.L. Barker & S. Allen (eds), *Dependence and Exploitation in Work and Marriage*, Longman, London and New York, 1976, p. 162.
31 *ibid.*, p. 157.

Chapter 17: Henry Lawson, the drover's wife and the critics

1 H.P. Heseltine, 'St Henry—our apostle of mateship,' *Quadrant*, 17 (Summer, 1960–61), p. 5.
2 Kay Schaffer, *Women and the Bush: Forces of Desire in the Australian Cultural Tradition*, Cambridge University Press, Melbourne, 1988.
3 Edward Garnett, 'Academy and literature', London, March 8, 1902, in Colin Roderick (ed.), *Henry Lawson Criticism, 1894–1971*, Angus & Robertson, Sydney, 1972, p. 124.
4 For a discussion see Brian Kiernan, 'From Mudgee hills to London town: A critical biography of Henry Lawson', in *The Essential Henry Lawson: The Best Works of Australia's Greatest Writer*, Currey O'Neil, South Yarra, 1982, p. 12.

NOTES   245

5 Fred Davison (1924), quoted in John Barnes, '"What has he done for our national spirit?"'—A note on Lawson criticism', *Australian Literary Studies*, vol. 8, no. 4, 1978, p. 486.
6 Nettie Palmer, *Modern Australian Literature* (1924) excerpt in Roderick (ed)., *Henry Lawson Criticism*, p. 235.
7 Vance Palmer (1942), quoted in Richard White, *Inventing Australia: Images and Identity, 1688–1980,* Allen & Unwin, Sydney, 1983, p. 153.
8 Brian Matthews, *The Receding Wave: Henry Lawson's Prose*, Melbourne University Press, Melbourne, 1972, pp. iii, 12.
9 Colin Roderick, quoted in Matthews, p. 15.
10 Colin Roderick, *The Real Henry Lawson*, Rigby, Adelaide, 1982, p. 33.
11 Clark, *In Search of Henry Lawson*, Macmillan, Melbourne, 1978, p. 52. Compare these remarks with those made concerning the 'bush mum' in C.M. Clark, *A History of Australia*, vol. 3, Melbourne University Press, Melbourne, 1973, pp. 272–3.
12 Michael Roe, 'Challenges to Australian identity and esteem in recent historical writing', *Tasmanian Historical Association: Papers and Proceedings*, vol. 25, no. 1, 1978, p. 5.
13 Peter Pierce, 'Forms of literary history' in *The Penguin New Literary History of Australia*. ed. Laurie Hergenhan, Penguin, Ringwood, 1988, p. 85.
14 Clark, *In Search*, p.2.
15 See Murray Bail, 'The Drover's Wife' in *The Drover's Wife and Other Stories*, University of Queensland Press, St Lucia, 1984, pp. 5–10, first published in 1975, and Frank Moorhouse, 'The Drover's "Wife"', *Bulletin*, Centenary Issue, Jan. 29 1980), pp. 160–162.
16 George Bowering, 'Wiebe and Bail: Making the story', in *The Imaginary Hand* NeWest Press, Edmonton, 1988, pp. 53–60.
17 Dorothy Jones & Barry Andrews, 'Australian humour', in *The Penguin New Literary History of Australia*. ed. Laurie Hergenhan, Penguin, Ringwood, 1988, pp. 60–76.
18 *ibid.*, p. 69. See also my discussion in 'The Bush and women' in *Women and the Bush*, pp. 52–76.
19 *ibid.*, p. 62.
20 Catherine Belsey, *Critical Practice*, Methuen, London, 1980, p. 104.
21 Barbara Jefferis, 'The Drover's Wife', *Bulletin* (Dec. 23–30, 1980), p. 157.
22 The following section is indebted to discussions with Karen Jennings and Jude Adams, lecturers and former colleagues at the University of South Australia.

Bibliography

Adams, David, ed., *The Letters of Rachel Henning*, Penguin, Harmondsworth, 1979.
Adams, F., *The Australians*, T. Fisher, London, 1893.
Adams, F., *Songs of the Army of the Night*, Federal Steam Printing & Binding Works, Sydney, 1888.
Adelaide, Debra, ed., *A Bright and Fiery Troop, Australian Women Writers of the Nineteenth Century*, Penguin, Ringwood, 1988.
Agulhon, Maurice, *Marianne into Battle*, Cambridge University Press, Cambridge, 1981.
------ On political allegory: A reply to Eric Hobsbawm, *History Workshop*, no. 8, 1979.
Alexander, S., Davin, A., & Hostettler, E., 'Labouring women: A reply to Eric Hobsbawm', *History Workshop*, no. 9, 1979.
Ali, Ahmed, 'Gimit: The indenture experience in Fiji', *Fiji Museum Bulletin*, no. 5, 1979.
Allen, Charles, *A Scrapbook of British India 1877–1947*, Penguin, Harmondsworth, 1979.
Allen, Judith, '"Mundane" men: historians, masculinity and masculinism', *Historical Studies*, vol. 22, no. 89, 1987.
------ 'Our deeply degraded sex', *Australian Feminist Studies*, nos. 7 & 8, 1988.
------ 'Rose Scott's vision: feminism and masculinity 1880–1925', in Caine, B., et al, eds, *Crossing Boundaries: Feminisms and the Critique of Knowledge*, Allen & Unwin, Sydney, 1988.
------ *Sex & Secrets: Crimes Involving Australian Women Since 1880*, Oxford University Press, Melbourne, 1990.
Anderson, Hugh, *Radical Arguments Against Federation 1897-1900*, Drummond, Victoria, 1977.
Anderson, Maybanke [Wolstoneholme], *Mother Lore*, Angus & Robertson, Sydney, 1919.

BIBLIOGRAPHY

Bail, Murray, *The Drover's Wife and Other Stories*, University of Queensland Press, St Lucia, 1984.

Balls-Headley, W., *The Evolution of the Diseases of Women*, Smith Elder, London, 1894.

Banks, J. A., & Banks, Olive, *Feminism and Family Planning in Victorian England*, Liverpool University Press, Liverpool, 1965.

Banton, Michael, 'Gender roles and ethnic relations', Fawcett Memorial Lecture for 1978–79 in *New Community*, vol. 7, no. 3, 1979.

Barnes, John, '"What has he done for our national spirit?"—A note on Lawson criticism', *Australian Literary Studies*, vol. 8, no. 4, 1978.

Baynton, Barbara, *Barbara Baynton*, Krimmer, S., & Lawson, A., eds, Portable Australian Authors Series, University of Queensland Press, St.Lucia, 1980.

Bedford, R., *Nought to Thirty-Three*, Melbourne University Press, Melbourne, 1944.

Belsey, Catherine, *Critical Practice*, Methuen, London, 1980.

Bennett, S., *Federation, Sources 1897–1901*, Cassell, Sydney, 1975.

Bohstedt, John, 'Gender, household and community politics: Women in English riots 1790–1810', *Past and Present*, no. 20, 1988.

Bollen, J. D., *Protestantism and Social Reform in New South Wales 1890–1910*, Melbourne University Press, Melbourne, 1972.

Bommes, Michael, & Wright, Patrick, 'Charms of residence: The public and the past', in *Making Histories: Studies in History Writing and Politics*, Hutchinson, London, 1982.

Bowering, George, *The Imaginary Hand*, NeWest Press, Edmonton, 1988.

Boyd, William, *School Ties*, Hamish Hamilton, London, 1985.

Bratton, J. S., *The Victorian Popular Ballad*, Macmillan, London, 1975.

Buckley, Ken, & Wheelwright, Ted, *No Paradise for Workers: Capitalism and the Common People in Australia 1788–1914*, Oxford University Press, Melbourne, 1988.

Bunkle, P. & Hughes, B., eds, *Women in New Zealand Society*, Allen & Unwin, Auckland, 1980.

Burgmann, Verity, and Lee, Jenny, eds, *Constructing a Culture*, McPhee Gribble/Penguin, Melbourne, 1988.

Burmann, S., ed., *Fit Work for Women*, London, 1982.

Burns, Ailsa, 'Population structure and the family', in Burns, A., Bottomley, G., & Jools, P., eds, *The Family in the Modern World: Australian Perspectives*, Allen & Unwin, Sydney, 1983.

Caldwell, J. C., & Ruzicka, L. T., 'The Australian fertility transition: An analysis', *Population and Development Review*, vol. 14, no. 1, 1978.

Cantrell, L., ed., *The 1890s: Stories, Verse and Essays*, University of Queensland Press, St Lucia, 1977.

Carby, Hazel, '"On the threshold of Woman's era": Lynching, Empire and sexuality in feminist theory', *Critical Inquiry*, vol. 12, no. 1, 1985.

Carmichael, Gordon A., *With This Ring: First Marriage Patterns, Trends and Prospects in Australia*, Australian National University, Canberra, 1988.

Carroll, B.A., ed., *Liberating Women's History*, University of Illinois Press, Urbana Ill., 1976.
Christ, Carol, 'Victorian masculinity and the angel in the house' in Vicinus, M., ed., *A Widening Sphere: Changing Roles of Victorian Women*, Indiana University Press, Bloomington, 1977.
Clark, C. M., *A History of Australia*, Vol. III, Melbourne University Press, Melbourne, 1973.
—— *In Search of Henry Lawson*, Macmillan, Melbourne, 1978.
Cohen, Morton, *Rider Haggard: His Life and Works*, Hutchinson, London, 1960.
Cott, Nancy, *The Bonds of Womanhood*, Yale University Press, New Haven, 1977.
—— *The Grounding of Modern Feminism*, Yale University Press, New Haven, 1987.
Couani, Anna, & Lyssiotis, Peter, *The Harbour Breathes*, Masterthief/Seacruise, Melbourne 1989.
Cranny-Francis, Anne, *Feminist Fiction : Feminist Uses of Generic Fiction*, Polity Press, Cambridge,1990.
Crawford, Eugenie, *A Bunyip Close Behind Me: Recollections of the Nineties*, Retold by her daughter Eugenie Crawford, Hawthorn Press, Melbourne, 1972.
Creed, Barbara, 'A journey through *Blue Velvet*: Film, fantasy and the female spectator', *New Formations*, no. 6, 1988.
Daniels, Kay, ed., *So Much Hard Work: Women and Prostitution in Australian History*, Fontana/Collins, Sydney, 1984.
Daniels, Kay, *et al.*, eds, *Women in Australia: An Annotated Guide to the Records*, AGPS, Canberra, 1977.
Daniels, Kay, & Murnane, Mary, *Uphill All the Way: A Documentary History of Women in Australia*, University of Queensland Press, St Lucia, 1980.
Darnton, Robert, *The Great Cat Massacre and Other Episodes in French Cultural History*, Vintage, New York, 1985.
Davidson, R.F. (Frances), *Prostitution in Perth and Fremantle and on the Eastern Goldfields 1895–September, 1939*, MA Thesis, University of Western Australia, 1980.
Davidson, Raelene, 'Dealing with the "social evil": Prostitution and the police in Perth and on the Eastern Goldfields, 1895–1924' in Daniels, K., ed., *So Much Hard Work: Women and Prostitution in Australian History*, Fontana, Sydney, 1984.
Davin, Anna, 'Imperialism and motherhood', *History Workshop*, no. 5, 1978.
Davis, Angela, *Women, Race and Class*, Random House, New York, 1982.
Davison, Graeme, 'Sydney and the bush: An urban context for the Australian legend,' in Carroll, J., ed., *Intruders in the Bush: The Australian Quest for Identity*, Oxford University Press, Melbourne.
Deacon, Desley, *Managing Gender: The State, the New Middle Class and Women Workers 1830-1930*, Oxford University Press, Melbourne, 1989.
—— 'The naturalisation of dependence: the state, the new middle class and women workers 1830–1930', Ph.D. thesis, Australian National University, Canberra, 1985.
—— 'Political arithmetic: The nineteenth-century Australian Census and the construction of the dependent woman', *Signs*, vol. 11, no. 1, 1985.

BIBLIOGRAPHY

Dekker, Rudolf M., & Van de Pol, Lotte C., *The Tradition of Female Transvestism in Early Modern Europe*, Macmillan, London, 1990.

de Lepervanche, Marie, 'Breeders for Australia: A national identity for women?', *Australian Journal of Social Issues*, vol. 24, no. 3, 1989.

Denoon, Donald, 'The isolation of Australian history', *Historical Studies*, vol. 22, no. 87, 1986.

Dickey, Brian, *No Charity There: A Short History of Social Welfare in Australia*, Nelson, Melbourne, 1980.

Dingle, A. E., '"The truly magnificent thirst": An historical survey of Australian drinking habits', *Historical Studies*, vol. 19, no. 75, 1980.

Dixon, Robert, 'Public and private voices', in Hergenhan, L., ed., *The Penguin New Literary History of Australia*, Penguin, Ringwood, 1988.

Docker, John, *In a Critical Condition*, Penguin, Ringwood, 1984.

_____ *The Nervous Nineties*, Oxford University Press, Melbourne, 1991.

_____ 'Postmodernism, cultural history, and the feminist legend of the nineties: *Robbery Under Arms*, the novel, the play', in Stewart, Ken ed., *Behind the Nineties*, University of Queensland Press, St.Lucia, forthcoming.

Douglas, Mary, 'Jokes', in *Implicit Meanings*, Routledge & Kegan Paul, London, 1975.

DuBois, Ellen, & Gordon, Linda, 'Seeking ecstasy on the battlefield: Danger and pleasure in nineteenth-century feminist sexual thought' in Vance, C., ed., *Pleasure and Danger*, Routledge & Kegan Paul, Boston, 1984.

Dudden, Faye 'Experts and servants: The National Council on Household Employment and the decline of domestic service in the twentieth century', *Journal of Social History*, vol. 20, no. 2, 1986.

Dyson, W., *The Bulletin Reciter 1880–1902*, Bulletin, 1901, reprinted Lansdowne Press, Melbourne, 1975.

Dyster, B. & Meredith, D., *Australia in the International Economy in the Twentieth Century*, Cambridge University Press, Sydney, 1990.

Ebbels, N., ed., *The Australian Labor Movement 1850–1907*, Hale & Iremonger, Sydney, 1983.

The Essential Henry Lawson: The Best Works of Australia's Greatest Writer, Currey ONeil, South Yarra, 1982.

Essex Evans, George, *The Collected Verse of G. Essex Evans*, Angus & Robertson, Sydney, 1928.

Evans, Raymond, '"Soiled doves": Prostitution in colonial Queensland', in Daniels, K., ed., *So Much Hard Work: Women and Prostitution in Australian History*, Fontana/Collins, Sydney, 1984.

Evans, Richard J., *The Feminists: Women's Emancipation Movements in Europe, America and Australasia 1840–1920*, Croom Helm, London, 1977.

Firth Scott, G., *The Last Lemurian: A Westralian Romance*, James Bowden, London, 1898.

Fisher, Shirley, 'The family and the Sydney economy in the late nineteenth century', in Grimshaw, P., et al., eds., *Families in Colonial Australia* Allen & Unwin, Sydney, 1985.

Foucault, Michel, *The History of Sexuality*, Penguin, Harmondsworth, 1981.

Frances, Rae, '"No more Amazons": Gender and work process in the Victorian clothing trades, 1890–1939', *Labour History*, no. 50, 1986.

_____ *The Politics of work: Case studies of three Victorian industries, 1880–1939*, PhD Thesis, Monash University, Melbourne, 1988.
Frances, Rae, & Scates, Bruce, *Lives of Labour: Women at Work in Australia's Cities and Towns*, Cambridge University Press, Cambridge, forthcoming.
French, Marilyn, *Beyond Power: On Women, Men and Morals*, Jonathan Cape, London, 1986.
Frost, L., ed., *No Place for a Nervous Lady: Voices from the Australian Bush*, McPhee Gribble/Penguin, Melbourne, 1984.
Gandevia, Bryan, *Tears Often Shed: Child Health and Welfare in Australia from 1788*, Pergamon Press, Sydney, 1978.
Garnett, Edward, 'Academy and literature', in Roderick, C., ed., *Henry Lawson Criticism, 1894–1971*, Angus & Robertson, Sydney, 1972.
Gilbert, Sandra, 'Rider Haggard's Heart of Darkness', *Partisan Review*, vol. 50, no. 3, 1983.
Gilbert, Sandra, & Gubar, Susan, *No Man's Land: The Place of the Woman Writer in the Twentieth Century*, vol. 2, *Sexchanges*, Yale University Press, New Haven, 1989.
Giles, Fiona, 'Romance: An embarassing subject', in Hergenhan, L., ed., *The Penguin New Literary History of Australia*, Penguin, Ringwood, 1988.
Gilmore, Mary, *Selected Verse*, Angus & Robertson, Sydney, 1948.
Godden, Judith, '"The work for them and the glory for us!" Sydney women's philanthropy 1870–1900' in Kennedy, R. ed., *Australian Welfare History: Critical Essays*, Macmillan, Melbourne, 1982.
Golder, Hilary, *Divorce in 19th Century New South Wales*, NSW University Press, Kensington, 1985.
Golder, Hilary & Allen, Judith, 'Prostitution in New South Wales 1870–1930: Restructuring an industry', *Refractory Girl*, December, 1979.
Goldman, Emma, 'The Traffic in Women' first pub. 1910, in Emma Goldman, *Anarchism and other essays*, Dover, New York, 1969.
Gordimer, Nadine, *Occasion for Loving*, Jonathan Cape, London, 1978.
Gordon, Linda, 'Why nineteenth-century feminists did not support "birth control" and twentieth-century feminists do', in Thorne, B., and Yalom, M., eds, *Rethinking the Family*, Longman, New York, 1982.
Grand, Sarah, *The Heavenly Twins*, Heinemann's Colonial Library, London, 1894.
Grimshaw, Patricia, 'Bessie Harrison Lee and the fight for voluntary motherhood', in Lake, M., & Kelly, F., eds, *Double Time: Women in Victoria—150 Years*, Penguin, Ringwood, 1985.
_____ 'Women and the family in Australian history: A reply to, *The Real Matilda*', *Historical Studies*, vol. 18, no. 72, April, 1979.
Grimshaw, Patricia *et al*, eds, *Families in Colonial Australia*, Allen & Unwin, Sydney, 1985.
Hamilton, Cicely, *Marriage as a Trade*, Chapman & Hall, London, 1909.
Hamilton, Paula, 'No Irish need apply: Aspects of the employer–employee relationship in Australian domestic service, 1860–1900', *Working Papers in Australian Studies*, Institute of Commonwealth Studies, University of London, no. 1, October, 1985.
_____ 'The "servant class": Poor female migration to Australia in the nineteenth century' in Richards, E., ed., *Poor Australian Immigrants in the Nineteenth Century. Visible Immigrants: Two*, RSSS, Canberra, 1991.

Hareven, Tamara, *Family Time and Industrial Time: The Relationship Between the Family and Work in a New England Industrial Community*, Cambridge University Press, Cambridge, 1982.
Harrison Lee, Bessie, *Marriage and Heredity*, Melbourne, 1893.
Hartmann, H., 'The unhappy marriage of Marxism and feminism: towards a more progressive union', in Sargent, L. ed., *Women and Revolution: a Discussion of the Unhappy Marriage of Marxism and Feminism*, South End Press, Boston, 1981.
Healy, J. J., 'The Lemurian Nineties', *Australian Literary Studies*, vol. 8, no. 3, 1978.
Hertz, Neil, 'Medusa's head: Male hysteria under political pressure', *Representations*, no. 4, 1983.
Heseltine, H. P., 'St. Henry—our apostle of mateship,' *Quadrant*, no. 17, Summer, 1960–61.
Hirst, John, 'Historical reconsiderations 1: Keeping colonial history colonial, the Hartz thesis revisited', *Historical Studies*, vol. 21, no. 82, April, 1984 .
Hobsbawm, Eric, 'Man and woman in socialist iconography', *History Workshop*, no. 6, 1978.
'Hop, his confessions: Chapters from the autobiography of Livingston Hopkins', *Lone Hand*, 1 June 1914.
Hufton, Olwen, 'Women in revolution', *Past and Present*, no. 53, November, 1971.
Inglis Moore, T., *From the Ballads to Brennan*, Angus & Robertson, Sydney, 1964.
Jardine, Alice, *Gynesis: Configurations of Woman and Modernity*, Cornell University Press, Ithaca, 1985.
Jefferis, Barbara, 'The Drover's Wife', *Bulletin*, Dec. 23–30, 1980.
Jefferis Turner, A., M.D., 'The State and venereal diseases' reprint from the *Australasian Medical Gazette*, no. 20, November, 1911.
Jeffreys, Sheila, *The Spinster and Her Enemies*, Pandora, London, 1985.
Jones, Dorothy, & Andrews, Barry, 'Australian humour', in Hergenhan, L., ed., *The Penguin New Literary History of Australia*, Penguin, Ringwood, 1988.
Jones, Helen, *In Her Own Name: Women in South Australia*, Wakefield Press, Adelaide, 1986.
Jose, A.W., *The Romantic Nineties*, Angus & Robertson, Sydney, 1933.
Kaplan, C, '"Like a housemaids fancies": The representation of working-class women in nineteenth century writing' in Sheridan, S., ed., *Grafts: Feminist Cultural Criticism*, Verso, London, 1988.
Kelly, Farley, 'Feminism and the family: Brettena Smyth', in Fry, E., ed., *Rebels and Radicals*, Allen & Unwin, Sydney, 1983.
Kent, Susan K., *Sex and Suffrage in Britain*, Princeton University Press, Princeton, 1987.
Kingston, B., *The Oxford History of Australia, vol. 3, 1860–1900: Glad Confident Morning*, Oxford University Press, Melbourne, 1988.
Knapman, Claudia, 'The white child in colonial Fiji, 1895–1930', *The Journal of Pacific History*, vol. 23, no. 2, 1988.
―――― *White Women in Fiji 1835–1930: The Ruin of Empire?*, Allen & Unwin, Sydney, 1986.

Kunzle, D., 'World upside down: The iconography of a European broadsheet type', in Babcock, B.A., *The Reversible World: Symbolic Inversion in Art and Society*, Cornell University Press, Ithaca, 1978.

Lake, Marilyn, 'Helpmeet, slave, housewife: Women in rural families, 1870–1930', in Grimshaw, P., McConville, C., & McEwan, E., eds, *Families in Colonial Australia*, Allen & Unwin, Sydney, 1985.

—— 'The limits of hope: Soldier settlement in Victoria 1915–1938', PhD thesis, Monash University, Melbourne, 1984.

—— 'The Politics of respectability: Identifying the masculinist context', *Historical Studies*, vol. 22, no. 86, 1986.

—— 'Women, gender and history', *Australian Feminist Studies*, vols. 7 & 8, 1988.

Lake, Marilyn, and Kelly, F., eds, *Double Time, Women in Victoria 150 Years*, Penguin, Ringwood, 1985.

Lal, Brij, 'Girmitiyas: The origins of the Fiji Indians', *The Journal of Pacific History*, Canberra, 1983.

Lane, William, *The Workingman's Paradise: an Australian Labour Novel*, Edwards Dunlop, Sydney, 1892.

Lawson, Henry, *A Camp-Fire Yarn*, Lansdowne, Sydney, 1988.

—— *A Fantasy of Man*, Lansdowne, Sydney, 1988.

—— *Winnowed Verse*, new edn, Angus & Robertson, Sydney, 1944.

Lawson, Olive, *The First Voice of Australian Feminism: Excerpts from Louisa Lawson's The Dawn 1888–1895*, Simon & Schuster, Brookvale, 1990.

Lawson, S., *The Archibald Paradox: A Strange Case of Authorship*, Allen Lane, Melbourne, 1983.

Leach, William, *True Love and Perfect Union: The Feminist Reform of Sex and Society*, Routledge & Kegan Paul, London, 1981.

Lee, Jenny, 'A redivision of labour: Victoria's Wages Boards in action, 1896–1903', *Historical Studies*, vol. 22, no. 88, 1987.

Lentricchia, Frank, 'Foucault's legacy: A new historicism?', in Veeser, H. Aram, ed., *The New Historicism*, Routledge, New York, 1989.

Lessing, Doris, *The Grass is Singing*, Plume, New York, 1976.

Lewis, Jane, ed., *Woman's Welfare, Women's Rights*, Croom Helm, London, 1983.

Lewis, Jane, *Women in England 1870–1950: Sexual Divisions and Social Change*, Indiana University Press, Bloomington, 1984.

Lowder Newton, Judith, 'History as usual? Feminism and the "new historicism"', in Veeser, H. Aram, ed., *The New Historicism*, Routledge, New York, 1989.

McCalman, J., *Struggletown: Public and Private Life in Richmond 1900–1965*, Melbourne University Press, Melbourne, 1984.

Macarthy, P., 'Victorian Wages Boards', *Journal of Industrial Relations*, vol. 10, 1968.

—— 'Wages in Australia 1891–1914', *Australian Economic History Review*, vol. 10, 1970.

McClure, John, *Kipling and Conrad: The Colonial Fiction*, Harvard University Press, Cambridge, Mass., 1981.

McConville, Chris, 'Rough women, respectable men and social reform: A response to Lake's "masculinism" ', *Historical Studies*, vol. 22, no. 88, 1987.

MacCulloch, Jennifer, ' "This store is our world": Female shop assistants in Sydney to 1930' in Roe, Jill, ed., *Twentieth Century Sydney: Studies in Urban and Social History*, Hale & Iremonger, Sydney, 1980.

McCuskey, Claire, Women in the Victorian Post Office, in Bevege, M., James, M., & Shute, C., eds, *Worth Her Salt: Women at Work in Australia*, Hale & Iremonger, Sydney, 1982.

McDonald, Peter F., *Marriage in Australia* Australian Family Formation Project, Monograph no. 2, Australian National University, 1975.

—— *Marriage in Australia: Age at first Marriage and Proportions Marrying, 1860–1971*, Australian National University, Canberra, 1974.

McGrath, Ann, *'Born in the Cattle': Aborigines in Cattle Country*, Allen & Unwin, Sydney, 1987.

—— ' "Spinifex fairies": Aboriginal workers in the Northern Territory, 1911–39' in E. Windschuttle, ed., *Women, Class and History: Feminist Perspectives on Australia 1788–1978*, Fontana/Collins, Melbourne, 1980.

Mackinnon, Alison, & Bacchi, Carol, 'Sex, resistance and power: Sex reform in South Australia, c.1905', *Australian Historical Studies*, vol. 22, no. 90, 1988.

Mackinolty, Judy, & Radi, Heather, eds, *In Pursuit of Justice: Australian Women and the Law 1788–1979*, Hale & Iremonger, Sydney, 1979.

Magarey, Susan, 'An insurrection of subjugated knowledges: Feminism in Australia in the 1890s', Conference Paper, *Seventh Berkshire Conference on the History of Women*, Wellesley College, Wellesley, Mass., 1987.

—— Notes towards a discussion of sexual labour: Australia 1880–1910', *Lilith. A Feminist History Journal*, no. 6, 1989.

Markey, Ray, 'Women and Labour 1880–1900' in Windschuttle, E., ed., *Women, Class and History: Feminist Perspectives on Australia 1788–1978*, Melbourne, 1980.

Marsh, Margaret, 'From Separation to togetherness: The social construction of domestic space in American suburbs, 1840–1915,' *Journal of American History*, 1989.

—— 'Suburban men and masculine domesticity 1870–1915', *American Quarterly*, vol. 40, no. 2, June 1988.

Martin, Sue, ' "Sad sometimes, lonely often . . . dull never": Mary Gaunt, traveller and novelist' in Adelaide, D., ed., *A Bright and Fiery Troop: Australian Women Writers of the Nineteenth Century*, Penguin, Ringwood, 1988.

Mason, Tim, 'The domestication of female socialist icons: A note in reply to Eric Hobsbawm', *History Workshop*, no. 7, 1979.

Matthews, Brian, *Louisa*, McPhee Gribble, Melbourne, 1987.

—— *The Receding Wave: Henry Lawson's Prose*, Melbourne University Press, Melbourne, 1972.

Meckel, Richard, 'Childhood and the historians: a review essay', *Journal of Family History*, vol. 9, no. 4, 1984.

Moorhouse, Frank, 'The Drover's "Wife" ', *Bulletin*, Centenary Issue Jan. 29, 1980.

Morris, Jan, *Pax Britannica: The Climax of an Empire*, Penguin, Harmondsworth, 1981.

Mukerji, Chandra, & Schudson, Michael, eds, in *Rethinking Popular Culture: Contemporary Perspectives in Cultural Studies*, University of California Press, Berkeley, 1991.

Mulvey, Laura, 'Visual pleasure and narrative cinema', *Screen*, vol. 16, no. 3, 1975.

Murray-Greenwood, F., ed., *Land of a Thousand Sorrows: The Australian Prison Journal 1840-1842 of the Exiled Canadian Patriote, Francois-Maurice Lepaillieur*, Melbourne University Press, Melbourne, 1980.

Nesbitt, Bruce, 'Literary nationalism and the 1890s', *Australian Literary Studies*, 1971.

O'Brien, Anne, *Poverty's Prison: The Poor in New South Wales 1880–1918*, Melbourne University Press, Melbourne, 1988.

O'Connor Karen, *Our Babies the State's Best Asset: A History of 75 Years of Baby Health Services in New South Wales*, New South Wales Department of Health, Sydney, 1989.

O'Dowd, Bernard, *The Poems of Bernard O'Dowd*, Lothian, Melbourne & Sydney, 1944.

Palmer, Nettie, *Modern Australian Literature*, 1924.

Palmer, Vance, *The Legend of the Nineties*, Melbourne University Press, Melbourne, 1966.

Paterson, A. B., *The Collected Verse of A. B. Paterson*, Angus & Robertson, Sydney, 1923.

Perkins Gilman, Charlotte, *Women and Economics: A Study of the Economic Relation Between Men and Women as a Factor in Social Evolution*, Harper & Row, New York, 1898.

Pettman, Jan, 'Australia's future in the global context', *Social Alternatives*, vol. 9, no. 2, 1990.

Pierce, Peter, 'Forms of literary history' in Hergenhan, L., ed., *The Penguin New Literary History of Australia*, Penguin, Ringwood, 1988.

―――― '"Weary with travelling through realms of air..."': Romance fiction of "Boldrewood", Haggard, Wells and Praed', *Westerly*, vol. 32, no. 2, 1987.

Polan, Dana, *Power and Paranoia*, Columbia University Press, New York, 1986.

Pollock, Griselda, 'Bourgeois men and working women: Sexuality and surveillance in Victorian social realism', *Power Foundation Lecture*, Sydney University, Sydney, 1989.

Porter Benson, Susan, *Counter Cultures: Saleswomen, Managers and Customers in American Department Stores 1890–1940*, University of Illinois Press, Urbana, 1987.

Praed, Rosa, *The Bond of Wedlock*, 1887, Pandora Press, London, 1987.

―――― *Fugitive Anne: A Romance of the Unexplored Bush*, John Long, London, 1903.

Quiggin, Pat, *No Rising Generation: Women & Fertility in Late Nineteenth Century Australia*, Department of Demography, Australian National University, Canberra, 1988.

Radi, Heather, ed., *200 Australian Women: A Redress Press Anthology*, Redress Press, Sydney, 1988.

BIBLIOGRAPHY

Reekie, Gail, 'The Shop Assistants Case of 1907 and labour relations in the Sydney retail industry' in Macintyre, S., & Mitchell, R., eds, *Foundations of Arbitration: The Establishment of the Compulsory Arbitration System, 1890–1914*, Oxford University Press, Melbourne, 1989.

Reiger, Kerreen, *The Disenchantment of the Home: Modernizing the Australian Family 1880–1940*, Oxford University Press, Melbourne, 1985.

Rendall, Jane, *The Origins of Modern Feminism: Women in Three Western Societies, Britain, France and the United States, 1780–1860*, Schocken Books, New York, 1984.

Report of the Royal Commission on the Basic Wage, *Commonwealth Parliamentary Papers*, 1920–21, vol. 4.

Reynolds, H., *The Other Side of the Frontier: an Interpretation of the Aboriginal Response to the Invasion and Settlement of Australia*, James Cook University, Townsville, 1981.

Rider Haggard, H., *She: A History of Adventure*, 1887, Macdonald, London, 1963.

Roderick, Colin, *The Real Henry Lawson*, Rigby, Adelaide, 1982.

Roe, Jill, 'Chivalry and social policy in the Antipodes', *Historical Studies*, vol. 22, no. 88, 1987.

Roe, Michael, 'Challenges to Australian identity and esteem in recent historical writing', *Tasmanian Historical Association: Papers and Proceedings*, vol. 25, no. 1, 1978.

Rosa, S.A., *The Truth about the Unemployed Agitation*, Melbourne 1891.

Rowe, C. J., 'Household troubles in the Australian colonies', *Westminster Review*, vol. 134, July–December, 1890.

Rowley, Sue, 'Sliprails and spur: Courting bush sweethearts in Australian nationalist mythology', *Span*, no. 26, 1988.

Rudd, Steele, *On Our Selection*, University of Queensland Press, St. Lucia, 1987.

Russell, P., 'Mrs Coles servants: A study in domestic politics', *Lilith: a Feminist History Journal*, no. 4, 1988.

Ryan, Edna, *Two-Thirds of a Man: Women and Arbitration in New South Wales 1902-1908*, Hale & Iremonger, Sydney, 1984.

Ryan, Edna, & Conlon, Anne, *Gentle Invaders: Australian Women at Work*, Penguin, Ringwood, 1989.

Saunders, K., 'The study of domestic violence in colonial Queensland: sources and problems', *Historical Studies*, vol. 21, no. 82, 1984.

Sawer, Marian & Simms, Marian, *A Woman's Place: Women and Politics in Australia*, Allen & Unwin, Sydney, 1984.

Sawkins, D. T., *The Living Wage in Australia*, Melbourne University Press, Melbourne, 1933.

Scates, Bruce, 'A struggle for survival: unemployment and the unemployed agitation in late nineteenth century Melbourne', *Australian Historical Studies*, vol. 23, no. 94, April, 1990.

—— *Faddists and Extremists*, PhD Thesis, Monash University, Melbourne, 1987.

Schaffer, Kay, *Women and the Bush: Forces of Desire in the Australian Cultural Tradition*, Cambridge University Press, Melbourne, 1988.

Schiebinger, Londa, L., 'Feminine icons: The face of early modern science', *Critical Inquiry*, vol. xiv, no. 4, 1988.

Schreiner, Olive, *The Story of an African Farm*, first pub. 1883, Penguin, Harmondsworth, 1939.
Scott, J. W. & Tilley, L. A., 'Women's work and the family in nineteenth century Europe', in Amsden, A. H. ed, *The Economics of Women and Work*, Penguin, Harmondsworth, 1980.
Sheridan, Susan, 'Ada Cambridge and the female literary tradition' in Dermody, S., Docker, J., & Modjeska, D., eds, *Nellie Melba, Ginger Meggs and Friends: Essays in Australian Cultural History*, Kibble Books, Malmsbury, 1982.
―――― 'Louisa Lawson, Miles Franklin and Feminist Writing', *Australian Feminist Studies*, nos. 8 & 9, 1988.
―――― 'Gender and genre in Barbara Baynton's *Human Toll*, *Australian Literary Studies*, vol. 14, no. 1, 1989.
―――― '"Temper, romantic; bias, offensively feminine": Australian women writers and literary nationalism', in Petersen, K. H., & Rutherford, Anna, eds, *A Double Colonization: Colonial and Post-Colonial Women's Writing*, Dangaroo, Denmark, 1986.
―――― 'Women and the worker in NSW' in Stewart, K., ed, *Behind the Nineties*, University of Queensland Press, St.Lucia, forthcoming.
Sinclair, W. A., 'Women and economic change in Melbourne 1871–1921', *Historical Studies*, vol. 20, no. 79, 1982.
Smart, Judith, 'Feminism, food and the fair price, *Labour History*, no. 50, May, 1986.
Smyth, Brettena, *Limitation of Offspring*, 8th ed., Rae Bros., Melbourne, 1893.
―――― *The Social Evil*, Rae Bros., North Melbourne, 1894.
Spearritt, P & Walker, D., eds, *Australian Popular Culture*, Allen & Unwin, Sydney, 1979.
Spence, C. H., *Some Social Aspects of South Australian Life: By a Colonist of 1839*. R. Kyffin Thomas, Adelaide, 1878.
Stannage, C.T., ed., *A New History of Western Australia*, University of Western Australia Press, Nedlands, 1981.
Stember, Charles, *Sexual Racism: The Emotional Barrier to an Integrated Society*, Harper & Row, New York, 1978.
Stephens, Brunton, *The Poetical Works of Brunton Stephens*, Angus & Robertson, Sydney & Melbourne, 1902.
Summers, Anne, 'A home from home: women's philanthropic work in the nineteenth century' in Burman, S. ed., *Fit Work for Women*, Croom Helm, London, 1979.
Summers, Anne, *Damned Whores and God's Police: The Colonization of Women in Australia*, Penguin, Ringwood, 1975.
Sydney Labour History Group, ed., *What Rough Beast? The State and Social Order in Australian History*, Allen & Unwin, Sydney, 1982.
Taylor, Barbara, '"The men are as bad as their masters ..." Socialism, feminism and sexual antagonism in the London tailoring trade in the 1830s', in Newton, J. L., *et al*, eds, *Sex and Class in Women's History*, Routledge & Kegan Paul, London, 1983.
Taylor, George, *Those Were the Days*, Unwin, Sydney, 1918.
Teale, Ruth, ed., *Colonial Eve: Sources on Women in Australia 1788–1914*, Oxford University Press, Melbourne, 1978.

Thomas, Leila, 'The Woman's Voice', *Australian Highway*, vol. 1, no. 6, 1919.
Thompson, E. P., 'The moral economy of the English crowd in the nineteenth century', *Past and Present*, 50, February, 1971.
Tiffin, Susan, 'In pursuit of reluctant parents: Desertion and non-support legislation in Australia and the United States, 1890–1920', in Sydney Labour History Group, ed., *What Rough Beast? The State and Social Order in Australian History*, Allen & Unwin, Sydney, 1982.
Van Ikin, 'Dreams, visions, utopias', in Hergenhan, L., ed., *The Penguin New Literary History of Australia*, Penguin, Ringwood, 1988.
Vicinus, Martha, *Independent Women: Work and Community for Single Women 1850–1920*, Virago, London, 1985.
Walkley, Christina, *The Way to Wear Em: 150 Years of Punch Cartoons*.
Walkowitz, Judith, *Prostitution and Victorian Society: Women, Class and the State*, Cambridge University Press, Cambridge, 1980.
Ward, R., *The Australian Legend*, Oxford University Press, Melbourne, 1958.
Warner, Marina, *Monuments and Maidens: The Allegory of the Female Form*, Picador, London, 1987.
Weedon, Chris, *Feminist Practice and Poststructuralist Theory*, Blackwell, Oxford, 1987.
White, R., *Inventing Australia: Images and Identity 1688–1980*, Allen & Unwin, Sydney, 1981.
Wilding, M., ed., *Portable Marcus Clarke*, University of Queensland Press, St Lucia, 1976.
Wilkinson, Mary, *Poems of Manhood*, Whitcombe & Tombs., Melbourne.
Yates, S., 'The enemy within: the maid in the nineteenth century French novel', in Aldrich, R., ed., *France: Politics, Society, Culture and International Relations*, Papers from the Seventh George Rude Seminar in French History and Civilisation, the University of Sydney, 21–23 July 1990, Occasional Publication, Department of Economic History, University of Sydney, Sydney, 1990.
Young, John, *Adventurous Spirits: Australian Migrant Society in Pre-Cession Fiji*, University of Queensland Press, St Lucia, 1984.

Index

Aborigines, bicentenary and, xv; cartoons, 76; literature, in, 154–5, 168, 170, 177, 179; servants, as, 134; women, 5, 129
Active Service Brigade, 48
Adams, Francis, 3, 4, 6
Age, 103, 112
Allen, Judith, xvii, xviii, 50, 61, 91, 98, 174
Andrews, Barry, 206, 207
Anthony Hordern and Sons, 61, 62, 64
Anti-Sweating League, 29
Archibald, J.F., xviii, 3, 4, 5, 22–3, 24
Arena (USA), 120
art, *see also* cartoons; cultural history; writers; feminist xvi, xix; national identity and, xix, xxiii, 187, 200, 205, 206, 209; women represented in, xxiii, 190–1, 193; working class, 190
Austen, Jane, 176
Australia, 202
Australian Storekeepers' Journal, 62, 67
Australian Tit-Bits, 142

Bail, Murray, 201, 205, 206, 207, 208
Baker, Santa Maria, 59–60, 62, 63

Bakhtin, M., (theorist), xix
Balls-Headley, Dr W., 123
Barling, Joseph, 56
Barton, Edmund, 136, 137, 145–7, 148
Bavister, Tom, 51
Baynton, Barbara, 22, 194–5, 197
Beale, Octavius, 137
Bebel, August, 101, 111
Becke, Louis, 23
Bedford, Randolph, 3, 4, 7
Bellamy, Edward, 101, 119
Belsey, Catherine, 207
Benevolent Asylum, 39, 43, 44
Benevolent Society, 43, 45
Benson, Susan Porter, 60, 64
Besant, Annie, 120
Binns (cartoonist), 86
Boake, Barcroft, 20, 161–2
Bohemians, 3–5, 10, 14, 18, 22, 50, 60
Bohstedt, John, 48
Boldrewood, Rolf, 26
Bollen, J.D., 12
Bommes, Michael, 73
Bowering, George, 205, 206
Boyd, William, 131
Brady, E.J., 4, 5
Bratton, J.S., 25
Brazil, Angela, 48
Brazilian League, 48

INDEX

Brown-Rrap, Julie, xix
Brushmakers' Board, 31, 32
Buckley, Vincent, 16
Bull-Ant, 3, 4, 10–11, 12, 13
Bulletin, xviii, 3, 4–5, 6, 11, 12–14, 16, 18, 19, 20, 22, 23, 24–5, 50, 54, 55, 56, Chapter 7 *passim,* 100, 103, 140, 141, 142, 144, 163, 166, 175, 177, 199, 200
Bulletin Reciter, 152
Bunkle, Phillida, 11
bushman legend, xix, 2–7 *passim; see also* rural life; *Bulletin* and, 3, 4–5, 14, 20, 21–2, 175; Drover's wife and, xxiii, Chapter 17; feminist criticism and, xv, xvii, xix, xx, Chapter 1, Chapter 2; Lone Hand, 2, 5, 7, 54, 58; national identity and, xvii, xix, xxiii, Chapter 1, 17, 186, 187, Chapter 17; urban sources of, 2, 17–18, 54; writers and, xix, 6, 10, 17–18, 20–2, 150, 151, 152, 154, 156, 158, 168, 175, 178, 180, 184, 187, 188, 191, 192, 194–5, Chapter 17

Cambridge, Ada, 93–4, 95
Carr, Archbishop, 112
cartoons, domestic servants, xxii, Chapter 7; federation, xxiii, Chapter 12; political, xxiii, Chapter 12
Castien, John Buckley, 100
Castle, Josie, xxiii, Chapter 12
Catholic Congress, 3rd Australian, 94
Champion, H.H., 116
Charitable Institutions, 53
charity, xxi, 38–9, 42, 43, 44–5, 46–7, 185, 189
Charity Organisation Society, 42, 45
Chevalier, Nicholas, 141–2
childbirth, *see* children
children, abandoned, 44; baby farming, 10, 44, 117; Benevolent Asylum, 44; child and juvenile labour, 28, 30, 31, 32, 39, 193; childbirth issues, xxii, 9, 10, 53, 96, 110, 112, 115, 118, 120, 121, 122–3, 130, 183; childcare, 9, 40, 48, 110; colonial childrearing, xxii, 129–35;

259

custody of, 102, 112; depression, in, 39, 40, 42, 43–4, 46, 48, 192; domestic violence and, 7; education of, 122, 132–4; given to relatives, 43, 44; health, 43, 44, 46, 107, 118, 121, 123, 130; illegitimate, 107–8, 110, 111; infant mortality, 44, 130; infanticide, 44; large families, 9, 43, 112, 130, 193, 194; rural children, 5, 193–4; women sole support for, 39, 40, 46, 96, 104, 107–8, 110, 192, 193, 194
Christesen, Clem, 16
churches, missionaries, 132; temperance movement, 12, 18
Cigar Board, 31
Cigar Makers' Society, 31
Civil Service Stores, 60
Claflin, Tennessee, 116
Clark, Manning, 20, 202, 203, 205
Clarke, Marcus, 152, 153
class analysis, domestic servants, xxi, xxii, 74–5, 77, 78–9, 83–4, 86, 87–9, 128, 132, 133–4; gender and, xviii, xxii, 1, 6, 47, 50, 58, 60, 69, 97, 98, Chapter 9, 128, 129, 130; growth of middle class, 56, 57, 77, 128; industrialisation, 91; national identity and, xvii; race and, 129, 130; representations of working class, 190, 192; romantic fiction and, 184; *Tocsin* and, Chapter 9; worker/employer struggle, xix, xxii, 29–30, 58
Clipper, 150
Clothing Board, 31, 33, 34
Coghlan, Timothy, 56, 57, 58, 137
Colonial Sugar Refining Company (CSR), 126
colonialism, xv, xix, Chapter 11, 168, 177
Confectioners' Board, 31, 35
Connell, Bob, xvii
Cotton, Frank, 52, 53
Cowper, W., 3
Creed, Barbara, 171, 174
Cronan, James, 41
Cronan, Mrs, 41
Cross, Ellen, 53, 54

Crothy, Miss, 63
cultural history, Chapter 1, Chapter 2, Chapter 17; *see also* art; class analysis; national identity; race; women's movement; writers; anti-historicist, 23; class analysis, xvii, xviii, xix, xxii, 1; constructions of, Introduction, Chapter 1, Chapter 2; 'contribution', 1; deconstructionist, xix, xxi, 18, 205, 207, 209; feminist, Introduction, Chapter 2, 41–2, 48–9, 60–1, 70, 91, 95, 181, 200, 209; formulism, 18; historicist, xx, 16–17, 18–19, 20; Leavisites, 16–17, 20; masculinist, Introduction *passim*, Chapter 1, 17, 18, Chapter 5, 60–1, 70, 91, 95, 100, 175; modernist, xx, 16; national identity and, Introduction *passim*, Chapter 1, Chapter 2, 70, 91, 125–6, 138, 163, Chapter 13, 179–80, 184, 185, 187, 197, 198, Chapter 17; New Critics, 16–17, 18, 20, 197, 198, 203; New Historicists, 18–19; postmodernist, xix, 19, 205, 207, 209–10; poststructuralism, xviii, 18, 23; radical nationalists, xx, 16–17, 20; structuralism, 19
Curthoys, Ann, xviii, 47
Curtis, John, 172

Daily Telegraph, 74
Daley, Victor, 22
Daly, Eliza, 54
Dampier, Alfred, 26
Daniels, Kay, 7
Dauncey (cartoonist), 148
David Jones and Company, xxii, 59–60, 61–4
Davis, Natalie Zemon, 25–6, 83
Davison, Fred, 202
Davison, Graeme, 2, 17, 21
Dawn, 25, 55, 68, 74, 114; *see also* Lawson, Louisa
Deacon, Desley, xxi, Chapter 5, 128, 195
Defoe, Daniel, 176
Denoon, Donald, 126, 127, 131
department stores, Chapter 6

depression, charity, xxi, 38–9, 42, 43, 44–5, 46–7, 189; children, 39, 40, 42, 43–4, 46, 48, 192; family survival, Chapter 4 *passim*; health, 42–3, 46; housing, 43, 48; Labor party, 38; male mobility, xxi, 38, 39; relief projects, 38–9, 44, 48; retailing industry, 61–2; starvation. 42–3; trade unions, 38, 40, 44, 94, 97; unemployment, xxi, 38, 39, 41, 42, 43, 94; women, xxi, Chapter 4 *passim*, 138; work, 39–42, 94
Derrida, Jaques, 26
Dialectical Society, 119
Dingle, Tony, 7, 8
Dixon, Ella, 117
Dixon, Robert, xxiii, Chapter 14
Dixson, Miriam, 200
Docker, John, xviii, xx, 16, Chapter 2, 200
domestic servants, 40, 44, 45, 64, Chapter 7, 94, 107, 128, 132, 133, 134, 186; cartoons of, xxi, xxii, Chapter 6, 141; race and, 71, 77, 84–5, 127, 128, 132, 133–4; unionisation, 80–2
Draper and Warehouseman, 62, 63
drapery stores, Chapter 6
Drysdale, Russell, 205, 206, 207
Du Bois, Ellen, 117, 120
Dudden, Faye, 78
Dugdale, Henrietta, 118
Duncan, Annie, 64–5, 66
Dyson, Edward, 156

Early Closing Movement, xxii, 65, 67
Edwards, Lucy, 40
Eliot, George, 176
Elliot, Mrs, 40
Elmy, Elizabeth Wolstoneholme, 119
employment, *see* work
Engels, Friedrich, 101
Esson, Louis, 4
Evangelicalism, 2–3, 4
Evans, George Essex, 152, 155, 159
Evans, M. Sanger, 119
Everylady's Journal, 14

factory workers, *see* work

INDEX

family, *see* marriage and family
Farmers, 60, 61
farming, *see* rural life
Federation, xx, 185, 186–7, 197, 199; cartoons, xxiii, Chapter 12; poetry, xxiii, Chapter 13
Federation Convention, 145
femininity, *see* women and femininity
feminism, *see also* women's movement; 1970s, xv, xviii; contesting masculine culture, xvi, xvii–xviii, 11–12, 14, 25, 92; fashion and, 68–9; 'feminist legend', xx, Chapter 2; first wave, xvi, xviii, 25, 151; history and criticism of, Introduction, Chapter 2, 48–9, 60–1, 70, 91–2, 95, 124, 181, 200, 209; male responses to, 12–14, 24–5, 92, Chapter 9, 121–2; rural feminism, 54–5, 57; sex and marriage, 94, 96–7, 98, Chapter 9; socialist, 101, 109; work and, 66–7, 69
Ferris, Lizzie, 53, 54
Fisher, Shirley, 189
Fleming, 'Chummy', 28
Flower, B.O., 120–1, 122–3
Foucault, Michel, 18, 19, 121
Frances, Rae, 42
Franklin, Miles, 25
Fraser, Eliza, 172
French, Marilyn, 174
Freud, Sigmund, 164
Furphy, Joseph, 176

Garnett, Edward, 202
Garrard, Jacob, 52, 53
Gaunt, Mary, xxiii, Chapter 15
gender, *see also* men and masculinity; women and femininity; cartoons, in, Chapter 7, Chapter 12; child education and, 131–5; class analysis and, xviii, xxii, 1, 6, 47, 50, 58, 60, 69, 97, 98; federation poetry, in, Chapter 13; fiction, in, Chapter 14, Chapter 15; history and criticism, in, Introduction, Chapter 1, 17–18, 46, 181, 209; home, in, *see* marriage and family; national identity and,

xv, xvi–xvii, xix, xx, Chapter 1 *passim*, 18, 70, Chapter 13, 179–80, 186–7, Chapter 17; political cartoons, in, Chapter 12; race and, 15, 47, 50, Chapter 11; rural life/bushman legend, Chapter 1, Chapter 2, Chapter 16, Chapter 17; sex and, Chapter 8, 110–11, 112, Chapter 10, Chapter 13 *passim;* socialist writers and, Chapter 9; work and, xxi–xxii, Chapter 3, Chapter 4, Chapter 5, Chapter 6, 106–9, Chapter 16
Gibbs, Herbert C., 137, 138, 139, 142, 143, 145, 147, 148
Gilbert, Sandra M., 164, 173
Giles, Fiona, 163, 175
Gilman, Charlotte Perkins, 94, 110
Gilmore, Mary, xxiii, 159–60
Golding, Annie, 94, 97
Goldman, Emma, 94
Gordon, Adam Lindsay, 152
Gordon, Linda, 117, 120
Grace, Helen, xvi–xvii, 201, 208–9
Grace Brothers, 61, 65
Graham, Mary, 40
Grand, Sarah, 118
Greig, Edward Jukes, 142
Grellier, Margaret, 8
Grenville, Kate, 207–8
Grimshaw, Patricia, xxii, Chapter 9

Habermas, Jurgen, 73
Haggard, H. Rider, xxiii, 164–6, 167, 168, 170, 171, 172, 173, 174
Hall, Catherine, 2
Hamilton, Cicely, 94
Hamilton, Paula, xxi, Chapter 7, 186
Hancock, Keith, 199, 202
Happy Homes, 67
Hardy, Thomas, 117
Harpur, Charles, 155
Hartmann, Heidi, 32
health, depression, 42–3, 46; sex and, 7, 95–6, 110–11, 112, 121, 122, 123; *see also* sex; workplace, 64–5, 66, 67, 107, 108
Hegel, Georg, 17
Henning, Rachel, 177
Herald, 13

Herald, Melbourne, 95
Hertz, Neil, 139
Heseltine, Harry, 16, 199
Heydon, Judge, 15
Higgins, Justice, 14–15
Hill, Benny, 138
history, *see* cultural history
Hoadley's jam factory, 107
Holloway, Barbara, xxiii, Chapter 13
Hopkins, Livingston, 71–3, 77, 78, 140–1, 142, 143, 144–6
housework, *see* work
housing, depression, 43, 48; rented, 110
Hughes, William, 53

immigration, 2, 77; *see also* race
Industrial Court (NSW), 58
International Council of Women, 119
Irving, Terry, xvii
Irwin, Margaret, 66

Jacobs, Hart and Co., 31
Jam Board, 31, 35
Jardine, Alice, 168
Jefferis, Barbara, 201, 207–8, 209
Jephson, Lady, 68
Jones, Dorothy, xxiii, Chapter 15, 206, 207
Jones, Edward Lloyd, 59
Jubelin, Narelle, xix, xxv

Kelly, Kate, 26
Kelly, Mary, 46
Kelly, Mrs, 40
Kendall, Henry, 155
Kingsley, Henry, 177
Kingston, Beverley, 75
Kipling, Rudyard, 155, 178
Knapman, Claudia, xxii, Chapter 11
Kramer, Leonie, 16
Kristeva, Julia, 209

Labor party, 38
labour movement, *see* trade unions and the labour movement; wages; work
LaCapra, Dominick, 26
Laird, Mrs, 39

Lake, Marilyn, xvii–xviii, xx, xxi, Chapter 1, Chapter 2 *passim*, 25, 26, 38, 46, 50, 58, 60, 70, 91, 95, 100, 163
land, *see* bushman legend; rural life; selection life
Lane, William, 6, 14, 19–20, 24
Lawson, Bertha, 10
Lawson, Henry, xxiii, 6, 10, 16, 18, 20–2, 55, 167, 176, 177, 178, 180, 187, 188, 189–90, 191–2, 195, 196–7, Chapter 17
Lawson, Louisa, 24, 25, 54, 55, 56, 68, 114, 116; *see also Dawn*
Lawson, Sylvia, xviii, 23, 24
Leach, William, 11
Leavisites, *see* cultural history
Lee, Bessie Harrison, 13, 95, 96, 97
Lee, Jenny, xx, xxi, Chapter 3, 41–2
Leist, Fred, 142
Lentricchia, Frank, 18
Lepailleur, François-Maurice, 8
Lepervanche, Marie de, 125
Levy, Frances, 69
Lewis, Annie, 43
Lewis, Jane, 40
Lindsay, Mr, 39
Lindsay, Mrs, 39
literary criticism, *see* cultural history; writers
Lone Hand, 74
Lyne, William, 52, 54, 55, 56, 143

Mackellar, Dorothea, xxiii, 160
Magarey, Susan, Introduction, Chapter 8, 114, 182, 186
Marcus Clark, 61
Mark Foys, 61
marriage and family, abortion, 10, 110, 111, 117; alcohol, 7–8, 9, 10, 111, 190; baby farmers, 10, 44, 117; birth control, *see* sex; *Bulletin* on, 3–4, 9, 12–13, 72; children and childbirth, *see* children; de facto relationships, 110, 111, 112, 117; depression, Chapter 4; desertion, male, xxi, 3, 7, 9, 10, 38–9, 45, 96, 110, 180, 185, 189, 190, 192; division of labour in, xxi, 28, 36–7, 39–40, 41, 46, 52, 53,

INDEX

56, 67, 94, 96, 97, 98, 104, 106–7, 109–10, 111, 112, 127, 128, 185, 186, 187, 196, 197, 205, 209; divorce, xvii, 4, 9, 10, 92, 96, 112, 117; domestic servants, Chapter 7, 128, 132, 133–4; domestic violence, 7, 8–9, 50, 110, 115, 118, 119, 122; infanticide, 44; maintenance payments, 10, 189; marriage, xxii, 6, 11, 86–9, Chapter 8, 110, 111, 112, Chapter 10 *passim*, 172, 173, 174, 175, 181, 182, 183, 184; married women's property, 102; money, 10, 39–43; sex, *see* sex; single men, 3, 15, 18; single women, xxii, 4, 11, 93, 97, 117, 123, 181; statistics, 7, 11, 92–3, 96; work, *see* work
Martin, Sue, 181
masculinity, *see* men and masculinity
Matthews, Brian, 203
Maupassant, Guy de, 202
Mauss, M., 196
Maxted, Sophia, 53
Maxted, Sydney, 53
Maybanke College, 115
McCalman, Janet, 8
McConville, Chris, xvii, xviii, 50
McCubbin, Frederick, xix, 208, 209
McDonald, Peter, 97
McElhone, John, 53, 54
McGrath, Ann, 134
McKenny, Miss, 67
McMillan, William, 52
McNeill, Eugenie, 60, 66
Meeham, Mrs, 39
Melbourne Ladies Benevolent Society, 45
Melbourne Punch, 72, 80, 81–2, 84, 141–2
men and masculinity, Chapter 1; *see also* gender; marriage and family; women and femininity; Anzacs and, 15, 202; bush ethos, *see* bushman legend; cartoons and, Chapter 12 *passim*; Coming Man, xxiii, 1, 163, 171, 174; constructions of, xv, xvii, xix, xxiii, Chapter 1, Chapter 2, 46, 50, 56, 58, 60–1, 67, 70, 92, 95, 98, 99, 150, 153, 156, Chapter 14, 185,

186, 187, 188; Domestic Man, 2–3, 4, 18; domestic servants and, 83, 86, 87, 89, 90; drinking, smoking and gambling, 3, 7, 8, 10–11, 12, 13, 18, 190; marriage, *see* marriage and family; mateship, xix, 3, 6, 14, 17, 18, 46, 150, 156, 166, 167, 168, 174, 175, 177, 188; rural, 54, 55, 58, 187–8, 192, 194–7; *see also* bushman legend; sex, *see* sex; work, *see* work
Mill, John Stuart, 98
Moore, William, 199
Moorhouse, Frank, 201, 205, 206–7, 208
Mulvey, Laura, 164, 165, 171
Murray-Smith, Stephen, 16

National Council of Women, NSW, 65, 66, 69
national identity, Introduction *passim*, Chapter 1, Chapter 2, 70, 91, 125–6, 138, 163, Chapter 13, 179–80, 184, 185, 187, 197, 198, Chapter 17; *see also* bushman legend; cultural history; Federation
New Australia Cooperative Settlement Association, 14, 19
Newman, William, 59
Newton, Judith Lowder, 18–19
Norton, Jane, 45

O'Dowd, Bernard, 4, 100, 154, 157, 158–9
O'Dowd, Rudel, 4
O'Sullivan, E.W., 51–2, 54, 55, 56
Ord, Harrison, 32
outback, *see* bush legend

Palmer, Nettie, 16, 199, 202
Palmer, Vance, xix, 16, 20
Parkes, Henry, 145
Parkes, Mrs Molyneux, 69
Pastrycooks' Union, 31
Pateman, Carole, 98
Paterson, Banjo, 21, 22, 23, 154, 155–6
Paterson, Alexander, 96
philanthropy, *see* charity

Phillips, A.A., 16, 200
Piddington, A.B., 52
Pierce, Peter, 170, 204
poetry, *see* writers
Polan, Dana, 71
politics, *see* class analysis; colonialism; cultural history; Federation; race; socialism; trade unions and the labour movement; women's movement
Pollock, Griselda, 190
Pomeroy, John, 59
Poole, Leon, 190–1, 193
Post and Telegraph Offices, 55
Post Office, 54
Pottie, Eliza, 65
Power, Michael, 8
Praed, Rosa, 22, 164, 170–4
Prevention of Cruelty to Animals, Society for, 69
Pringle, Helen, xxiii, Chapter 12
prostitution, *see* work
Public Instruction, Dept of (NSW), 57
Public Service Board (NSW), 51, 56, 57, 58
Public Works (NSW), 56
Punch Annual, 148

Quinn, Roderic, 22

race, Aborigines, 5, 76, 129, 134, 154–5, 179; *Bulletin* and, *see Bulletin*; children and, xxii, 131–5; Chinese labour, 6, 47, 56, 202; colonialism, xv, xix, Chapter 11, 168; fiction and, 168, 179; gender and, 1, 5, 50, Chapter 11; humour, 71, 76; immigration debates, 125; Irish domestic servants, 71, 77, 84–5; Kanaka labour, 146; labour movement and, 6, 108; Pacific islanders, xxii, 5, Chapter 11; sexual relations, 5, 98, 129; unemployment and, 47; white Australia, 6, 128, 138, 202
Reekie, Gail, xxi, xxii, Chapter 6
Reid, George Houston, 51, 53, 55, 56
Reiger, Kerreen, 127
religion, *see* churches

Rendell, Jane, 47
Republican, 55
Reynolds, Henry, 5
Roberts, Mrs, 41
Roberts, Tom, xix
Roderick, Colin, 203
Roe, Jill, 156, 157
Rowley, Sue, Introduction, 180, Chapter 16
Royal Commissions, birthrate, 1903–04, NSW, 98, 130; Civil Service, 1895, NSW, 55; strikes, 1891, NSW, 64; wages, 1901, Vic., 30, 32, 33
Rudd, Steele, 6, 176, 193, 194, 195, 196
Rumison, Mrs, 45
rural life, xxiii, 5–6, 54–5, 57, 58, 109, 152, 176, 178–9, 180, 181, 182, Chapter 16; *see also* bushman legend
Russell, Penny, 74

Said, Edward, xviii
Saunders, Kay, 8, 9
Scates, Bruce, xx, xxi, Chapter 4
Schaffer, Kay, xvii, xix, xxi, xxiii, 166, 169, Chapter 17
Schreiner, Olive, 93–4, 117
Scott, George Firth, 164, 166–70, 171, 172, 174
Scott, Rose, 57, 65, 66, 67, 68, 69, 70, 94, 96, 97, 174
Scott, Thomas, 156
Selby, Penelope, 8
servants, *see* work
sex, *see also* marriage and family; men and masculinity; women and femininity; age of consent, xvii, 92, 103; birth control, 11, 13, 14, 96, 97, 98, 111–12, 115; birthrate, 92, 98, 111–12, 130; *Bulletin* and, 12–13, 14, 18, 24; church and, 121; domestic servants, 86, 87, 89; education, 116, 118, 122; marriage, in, xxii, 7, 12–13, 89, Chapter 8, 110, 112, Chapter 10, 192; men and, 5, 86, 92, 96–7, 98, 102, Chapter 10 *passim*; prostitution, 40, 41, 65–6,

91, 93, 94, 96, 99, 110, Chapter 10 *passim*, 129, 192; race and, 5, 98, 129; rape, 24, 50, 111, 115, 118, 119, 122; sexual harassment, 66, 67, 86, 102; sexually transmitted disease, 7, 95–6, 114, 115, 116, 118, 122; *Woman's Voice* and, xxii, Chapter 10; women and, Chapter 8, Chapter 10, 153, 156, 159, 160, 161, 173, 182; women's movement and, xvii, xxii, 12–13, 65, 66, 67, 92, 93, 96–7, 111, Chapter 10
Sharpe, Lucinda, *see* Lane, William
Sheridan, Susan, Introduction, Chapter 10, 163, 170–1
Shirt Board, 33
Shop Assistants' Union, 64
shopping, xxi, Chapter 6
Sketch, 117
Smart, Judith, 48
Smyth, Brettena, 96
socialism, 19, 60, 70, 137; *see also* trade unions and the labour movement; *Tocsin* and, Chapter 9
Spence, Catherine Helen, 24, 94
Spence, W.G., 6
Stanton, Elizabeth Cady, 119
State Children's Department (NSW), 44
State Children's Relief (NSW), 53
Stead, W.T., 65
Stephen, Sarah, 3
Stephens, A.G., 22, 23, 155, 157, 162
Storey, David, 52
Strong, Peter, 64
suffrage, *see* women's movement
Summers, Anne, 127, 200, 202
Suttle, Caroline, 59, 63
Swallow and Ariel, 103
Sydney Labour Council, 64
Sydney Morning Herald, 55, 74

Tailoresses Union, 42, 64
Taylor, Barbara, 101
Taylor, George, 5
Taylor, Harriet, 98
Taylor, Lucy, 119
Telegraph Department, 54
Telegraph Office, 55

Tennyson, Alfred Lord, 156, 175
Thompson, E.P., 47
Thompson, William, 98
Tiffin, Susan, 9
Tinsmiths' Board, 30, 31, 32, 35
Tocsin, xxii, 27, Chapter 9, 160–1
trade unions and the labour movement, *see also* wages; work; unemployment; depression, in, 38, 40, 44, 46, 48–9, 62, 94, 97; division of labour and, xxi, 36; domestic servants, 80–2; equal pay and, 30–1; leadership, 19; mateship and, 6, 46; outworkers, 33–4; race and, 6; strikes, 64, 69; wages, 28, 29, 30, 33, 34, 106, 109; women and, xxi, 6, 27, 33–5, 36, 40, 44, 48–9, 56, 57, 58, 64, 69, 97, Chapter 9, 194
Trades and Labour Council, 69
Trades Hall, 29
Trades Hall Council, 105
Tunnecliffe, Tom, 100, 104
Turnbull, Ada, 105
Turner, George, 141, 142
Turner, Graeme, 200

Underclothing Board, 33
unemployment, depression, xxi, Chapter 4 *passim*, 57; drapery employees, 62; manufacturing industry, 28; men, xxi, 27, 28, 94, 189; political protest, xxi, 45–6, 47–8; race, 47, 108; relief, 45; relief work, 38–9, 44, 48; women blamed for, xxi, 27, 194
unions, *see* trade unions and the labour movement
universities, women in, 102, 137, 181
University of Melbourne, 102
utopians, 6, 19, 24, 101, 151, 199

'Vernon', 40, 41
Victoria, Queen, 159, 166
Victorian Employers' Federation, 35
Vincent, 141, 142
vote, *see* women's movement

W.A. Bulletin, 136

wages, *see also* work; cuts, 28, 62–3; domestic servants, 81; equal pay campaign, 30–2, 108; family wage, xxi, 32–3, 50, 56, 57, 58; juvenile, 28, 31, 32, 39; men, 28, 29, 30, 35, 36, 56, 57, 58, 193; minimum, 14, 106; outworkers, 33–4, 189; regulation of, 29, 30–4, 35, 36; trade unions and, *see* trade unions; Wages Boards (Victoria), xxi, 29, 30–4, 35, 36, 42; women, 27, 30–2, 33, 34, 35, 39, 40–1, 42, 54, 57, 62, 64, 65–6, 102, 106, 107, 108–9
Wages Boards (Victoria), xxi, 29, 30–4, 35, 36, 42
Walch, Garnet, 26
Walker, David, xviii
Ward, Russel, xix, 2, 5, 6, 10, 16, 17, 18, 187–8, 200
Waters, 60
Weekes, Clara, 96
Whiddon, Samuel, 52
White, Richard, 2, 200
White Australia policy, *see* race
Wilcox, Mr, 63
Wilcox, Mrs, 41
Wilkes, G.A., 16
Windeyer, Justice, 9
Wing, John, 42
Wolstoneholme, Maybanke, 114, 115–18, 120, 122
Woman, 14, 68
Womanhood Suffrage League of NSW, 115
Woman's Sphere, 96
Woman's Voice, xxii, 66, 67, 68, 69, Chapter 10; *see also* Wolstoneholme, Maybanke
women and femininity, *see also* feminism; gender; marriage and family; men and masculinity; women's movement; alcohol and addiction, 8, 41, 50; cartoons of, xxii, xxiii, Chapter 7, Chapter 12 *passim*; constructions of, xv, xvii, xxiii, 1, 38, 51–2, 53, 56, 57, 58, 60, 66, 67, 70, 75, 92, 95, 98, Chapters 9–13, 170, 174, 182, 183, Chapter 16, Chapter 17; depression, in, xxi, Chapter 4 *passim*; financial dependence, 6, 7, 9, 52, 56, 58, 94, 97, 115, 181, 182, 183, 184, 187, 189, 195, 197; politics, in, *see* women's movement; race, *see* race; rural, xxiii, 5, 6, 54–5, 57, 109, Chapter 16, Chapter 17; sex, *see* sex; shopping, xxi, Chapter 6; symbolism and, xxiii, Chapter 13, 180, 200, 201, 204, 205; trade unions and, *see* trade unions and the labour movement; work, *see* work
Women's Christian Temperance Union, xvii, 103, 115
women's movement, *see also* feminism; depression, 47–9; divorce, xvii, 92; emergence of, xvi, xviii, 11–12, 14, 25, 92, 98–9, 151; industrialisation and, 14; male responses to, xvii, xix, 11, 12–14, 19, 24–5, 92, 98, 99, Chapter 9, 116, 121–2, 168, 170; marriage, xxii, 93–4, 96–7, 98, 104, Chapter 10, 182; middle class and, xviii, xxii; New Woman, xiv, xxiii, 25–6, 163, 171, 174; Rational Dress, 24, 68, 69; rural women and, 54–5, 57; sex and, *see* sex; shop workers, xxii, 61, 64–5, 66–7, 69, 70; smoking, 12; socialist feminism, Chapter 9; suffrage, xiv, 12, 92, 94, 98–9, 102, 103, 106, 111, 115, 137, 143, 175; temperance movement, xvii, 11, 12, 13, 14, 18, 19, 103; *Tocsin* and, xxii, Chapter 9; work and, xxii, 64–6, 67, 69, 92, Chapter 9 *passim*
Women's Political and Social Crusade, 105–6
Women's Progressive Association NSW, 94
Women's World, 14
Woodward, John, 63
Woollen Board, 31
work, *see also* trade unions and the labour movement; unemployment; wages; begging, 42; boarders, 40, 41, 45; businesses, 54, 55; charity, 44–5, 53; charring, 40, 41, 128; childcare, 40, 48, 107–8, 132;

INDEX

clerical, 95, 97, 99; clothing trades, 28, 33–4, 35, 39, 40, 42, 55, Chapter 6; conditions, xxii, 64–5, 69, 80, 81, 92, 107; depression, in, xxi, 39–42; domestic service, xxii, 40, 44, 45, 64, Chapter 7, 94, 107, 127, 128, 132, 133, 134, 141, 186; equal opportunity, 52–3, 57, 58, 109; factories, Chapter 3, 41, 42, 45, 94, 99, 107, 108, 186; food trades, 31, 34–5, 42, 107; gender segregation, xxi, 6–7, 30, 31, 32, 33, 34, 36–7, 45, 62, 91, 106, 128; hawking, 41; health and, 64–5, 66, 67, 107, 108; hours, 30, 35, 64, 65, 66–7, 69; housework, 40, 48, 101, 109–10; Industrial Appeals Court (Victoria), 29; industrialisation, 6, 14, 35, 36, 41–2, 91, 94–5; juvenile employment, 28, 30, 39; married women, xxi, 28, 35–6, Chapter 5, 97, 106; mateship and, 6, 14, 46; men and, 6–7, 27, 28, 29, 30, 38, 39, 41, 46, 52, 56, 57, 69, 91, 103–4, 106, 108, 135, 195, 197; outwork, 28, 29, 33–4, 35, 189; part-time, 42; post and telegraph, 53, 54, 55, 95; prostitution, 40, 41, 65–6, 91, 93, 94, 96, 99, 110, Chapter 10, 129, 192; public service (NSW), xxi, Chapter 5; race and, *see* race; retailing, xxi, xxii, Chapter 6, 99; rural, 5–6, 54–5, 109, 128, 176, 178–9, 180, 181, 182, Chapter 16; sexual harassment, 66, 67, 86; single women, 51, 55, 56, 57, 58, 86, 97, 106; teachers, 52–3, 54, 57, 95; washing, 39, 40, 41, 48, 190–1; women and, xxi–xxii, xxiii, 6–7, 9, Chapter 3, 39–42, Chapter 5, Chapter 6, Chapter 7, Chapter 8, 101, 103, 106–7, 128–9, 175, 176, 180, 181, 185, 186, 191, 192–3, 195–6, 197
Worker, 114
Worker (Brisbane), 19
Wright, Patrick, 73
writers, *see also* cultural history; national identity; bush and, *see* bush legend; 'lost race' fiction, xxiii, Chapter 14; magazine, Chapter 1, Chapter 2, Chapter 9, Chapter 10; poets, xxiii, Chapter 13; romance fiction, xvi, xxiii, Chapter 15; socialist, 60
Wyse, Mary, 35

Young Men's Christian Association (YMCA), 3

Zahalka, Anne, xix, xxv